John Feinstein

THE BACK ROADS TO MARCH

John Feinstein is the #1 *New York Times* bestselling author of the classic sports books *A Season on the Brink* and *A Good Walk Spoiled*, along with many other bestsellers including *Quarterback, The Legends Club, Where Nobody Knows Your Name*, and *The First Major*. He currently writes for *The Washington Post, Golf Digest*, and *Golf World* and does commentary on the CBS Sports Radio Network.

www.jfeinsteinbooks.com

Also by John Feinstein

THE BACK ROADS TO
MARCH

THE BACK ROADS TO

MARCH

THE UNSUNG, UNHERALDED, AND UNKNOWN
HEROES OF A COLLEGE BASKETBALL SEASON

John Feinstein

ANCHOR BOOKS
A Division of Penguin Random House LLC
New York

FIRST ANCHOR BOOKS EDITION, MARCH 2021

Copyright © 2020 by John Feinstein

All rights reserved. Published in the United States by Anchor Books, a division of Penguin Random House LLC, New York, and distributed in Canada by Penguin Random House Canada Limited, Toronto. Originally published in the United States by Doubleday, a division of Penguin Random House LLC, New York, in 2020.

Anchor Books and colophon are registered trademarks of Penguin Random House LLC.

The Library of Congress has cataloged the Doubleday edition as follows:
Name: Feinstein, John, author.
Title: The back roads to March : the unsung, unheralded, and unknown heroes of a college basketball season / by John Feinstein.
Description: First edition. | New York : Doubleday, 2020. | Includes index.
Subjects: LCSH: NCAA Basketball Tournament. | Basketball teams—United States—History—21st century. | College sports—United States—History—21st century.
Classification: LCC GV885.49.N37 F43 2020 | DDC 796.323/640973—dc23
LC record available at https://lccn.loc.gov/2019047926

Anchor Books Trade Paperback ISBN: 978-0-525-56475-1
eBook ISBN: 978-0-385-54449-8

Author photograph © Christine Bauch Feinstein
Book design by Michael Collica

www.anchorbooks.com

Printed in the United States of America
10 9 8 7 6 5 4 3 2

This is for Jack Scheuer and Dick (Hoops) Weiss . . .
Mentors. Friends. Companions. I cherish every minute
we spend together—especially in the Palestra.

To win the game is great . . .
To play the game is greater . . .
But to love the game is the greatest of all.

CONTENTS

THE BACK ROADS TO
MARCH

INTRODUCTION
WHY THE BACK ROADS

As soon as the buzzer sounded, I closed my computer. Ever helpful, the NCAA had put out its one millionth printed statement of Final Four weekend prior to the start of the game, warning all of us in the media that confetti would come pouring out of U.S. Bank Stadium's ceiling as soon as the national championship game ended.

Sure enough here it came, and I quickly closed the computer so as not to have to spend several minutes picking confetti from the keys. Not my first rodeo. It was 10:40 central time in Minneapolis—11:40 in the east—and, as was always the case on Monday night, time was precious.

For a moment, while waiting to be able to safely open the computer and resume writing, I flashed back nine years to another Monday night. There were thirty-one seconds left in the NCAA championship game between Duke and Butler, and the Bulldogs had the ball and had just called a time-out, trailing 60–59.

Ohio State athletic director Gene Smith, who was that year's chairman of the NCAA basketball committee, was sitting to my left. As the buzzer sounded to end the time-out, Smith leaned over to me and said, "Okay, you're the ultimate defender of the little guy. But you're also a Duke graduate. What do you want to see happen here?"

I looked at my watch. It was 11:37 p.m. in Indianapolis. Prior to the game, my editor at the *Washington Post* had told me that if I wanted my column to make the home edition of the newspaper, he needed it in the office by midnight.

I had spent most of the last thirty minutes writing and rewriting as the game swung back and forth. The first ten paragraphs were unwritten, pending the outcome.

"Gene, it's 11:37 p.m.," I said. "I have to hit the send button by midnight or my column won't make most of the morning's papers. The only thing I don't want to see is f—— overtime."

Smith laughed. I could not have been more serious. The late, great Dave Anderson, the Pulitzer Prize–winning *New York Times* columnist, had explained to me early in my career that "the first rule of sportswriting is simple: it's always okay to root for yourself."

On that crisp April evening in 2010, I wasn't rooting for Butler—the David of college basketball—a team that had pulled one upset after another to reach the final game and now had close to seventy thousand fans screaming for one last shocker to finish the Disney movie.

I wasn't rooting for Duke—my alma mater—coached by Mike Krzyzewski, someone I had known well, liked, and admired for more than thirty years. In the minds of most college basketball fans, Duke wasn't just Goliath; it was Darth Vader. The evil empire in shorts.

I wasn't rooting for either team. I was rooting, at that moment, for me. I knew I had a great story—regardless of the outcome. I just needed to have time to write it so that the *Post*'s readers would get a chance to read it.

Nine years later, I had felt much the same way as the Virginia–Texas Tech national championship game wound down. Like Duke-Butler, it was riveting, the teams taking turns appearing to gain control.

Virginia had led by ten late in the second half, but Texas Tech had rallied to take a 68–65 lead with under twenty seconds to play. Somehow, the Red Raiders, a superb defensive team, lost track of UVA's De'Andre Hunter, leaving him wide-open in the corner.

As soon as I saw Hunter catch the ball, I knew his three-point shot was going in and the game was going to overtime. Texas Tech lost in overtime; I lost in regulation.

But even as the clock ticked toward midnight on the East Coast and I waited impatiently for it to be safe to reopen my laptop, I was smiling while Virginia celebrated.

I was happy for Coach Tony Bennett, who had been brutally

maligned a year earlier after the Cavaliers had become the first No. 1 seed in NCAA Tournament history to lose to a No. 16 seed. Prior to UVA's game in Charlotte against the University of Maryland–Baltimore County, No. 1 seeds had been 135-0 against No. 16 seeds.

Just before midnight on the eve of St. Patrick's Day, that record had become 135-1. UMBC-74, Virginia-54. That score hangs from a banner inside UMBC's Retriever Events Center and will be there for as long as they continue to play basketball.

That loss hung around Bennett's neck for more than a year. He answered every question, never snapped when it came up, and didn't bother to mention that Hunter, arguably his best player, had been injured that night and watched the game from the bench.

Bennett never fell back on the clichés of jock-world losers: "That's in the past, we've moved on"; "I only want to talk about the present"; or the catchall "That was a different team. I'm focused on this team."

In a twist, the coach who most wanted to put UMBC-74, Virginia-54, behind him was UMBC coach Ryan Odom. His slogan for his 2018–19 team was "no looking in the rearview mirror."

Odom's Retrievers were a different team: K. J. Maura and Jairus Lyles, the senior guards who had keyed the upset, were both gone. UMBC wasn't just a different team; it had a different *place* in the college basketball pantheon. No longer did basketball people wonder what the letters *UMBC* meant when spelled out.

Everyone knew what they meant: UMBC-74, Virginia-54. Or, if you preferred, 1-135.

"It's an amazing story, isn't it?" Bennett said to me about an hour after the nets came down in Minneapolis, referencing where his team had been that night in Charlotte and where it was now, walking away with the championship plaque.

Of course, the NCAA had carefully choreographed every moment of the postgame celebration. First the confetti; then the players and coaches being herded onto a platform where NCAA president Mark Emmert would grab the microphone for a few unneeded words; followed by basketball committee chairman Bernard Muir, the athletic director at Stanford, presenting the plaque to Bennett.

Then the nets were cut down, not like in the old days when players hoisted one another and then the coaches up to the rim to get their cuts of the net, but on something called "the official ladder of the NCAA."

Finally came the playing of the impossibly hokey and corny "One Shining Moment," during which the players and coaches were required to stand on the podium looking teary-eyed and the media was required to clear the area around the podium.

Nothing interferes with "One Shining Moment." It is, after all, a tribute to the purity of the great moments that make up the NCAA Tournament. Forget the FBI corruption investigations, the coaches with multimillion-dollar salaries; this is all about the "student-athletes."

Virginia was a worthy and eminently likable champion. And, within three weeks of the playing of "One Shining Moment," four of their starters—all underclassmen—had declared for the NBA draft.

From "One Shining Moment" to "Show Me the Money."

I didn't blame any of them even a little bit.

As I watched the Virginia players cut down that final net, my mind raced sixty-one miles down the road from Charlottesville, Virginia, to Farmville, Virginia.

Yes, Farmville, Virginia, is a real place—although my wife was very skeptical about that fact on the night of January 24, 2019, when I had traveled there to watch Longwood University host High Point in a Big South Conference game.

"Classic coaching matchup," Longwood coach Griff Aldrich had said that afternoon. "Me, with twelve career coaching wins, taking on Tubby Smith with six hundred and six—and a national championship."

Griff smiled. "My players better be a *lot* better than his players, because I'm sure as heck not going to outcoach him."

Aldrich's players were good enough that night for a 55–51 victory, cutting the gap between Aldrich and Smith in wins from 594 to 593.

During the game, my wife, Christine, sent me a text. Christine is not exactly a jock. She got her undergraduate degree from Vassar in English literature. She then got a master's from Boston University in English and Irish poetry and worked for five years for Robert Pinsky when he was the U.S. poet laureate. She was later a literary agent and an editor at Random House. She could undoubtedly have written a poem—or perhaps a sonnet—about the matchup between Aldrich and Smith. But she had no idea who they were, where they coached, or why I might be watching their teams play on a cold night in January.

Her in-game text was short and to the point: "I forget where you are tonight," it said. "What time will you be home?"

"I'm in Farmville, Virginia," I wrote back. "Home about midnight."

The response came flying back almost as soon as I'd hit the send button: "You are having an affair," it said. "There is no such place as Farmville, Virginia."

Yes, Christine, there is a Farmville. And there is no question that Willett Hall, with 1,481 in attendance, was *the* place to be that night in Farmville.

The real question, then, was this: Why was I in a not-mythical place called Farmville that night?

The answer to the question really goes back to the night of the national championship game. My first Final Four was in 1978, in what was then called the St. Louis Checkerdome. The first game on semifinal Saturday, between Duke and Notre Dame, began at 12:30 central time. The second game—Kentucky and Arkansas—started just before 3 p.m. local time.

I was the night police reporter for the *Washington Post*, but had convinced sports editor George Solomon to let me fly out there since Duke was playing. I had graduated from Duke the previous May. In my four years as an undergraduate, Duke finished last, tied for last, last, and tied for last in the ACC. In those days, when we talked about making the Final Four it was a reference to the semifinals of the ACC Tournament. It never happened while I was in school; the Blue Devils lost their opening game in the conference tournament every March.

Which is why the notion of being in the real Final Four seemed impossible. My deal with George was—as I would learn in later years—classic George. I paid my own way to St. Louis, shared a hotel room with columnist Ken Denlinger, and wrote a sidebar each day.

All George had to do was come up with a credential for me—sort of. He had sent one of the paper's columnists, Dave Kindred, to cover the women's Final Four, since the Maryland women were playing there. I had Kindred's credential for Saturday's semifinals. For the championship game Monday night, I was on my own.

This was years before media credentials had photos on them or there were security checks to get into a basketball game. After Duke beat Notre Dame on Saturday, Duke sports information director Tom Mickle found Skeeter Francis, the ACC's media director.

"Need a credential for John for Monday," Mickle said.

Skeeter reached into the pocket of his blindingly loud jacket, pulled out a credential, and handed it to me. Simple as that. On Saturday, I sat in Kindred's courtside seat. On Monday night I sat in the seat assigned to the Notre Dame SID. He had gone home.

Those were the days.

They are, of course, long gone. The Final Four hasn't been played in a basketball arena since 1996. Now it's played in seventy-thousand-plus-seat football stadiums, with the court smack in the middle of the football field in order to maximize the number of seats that can be sold.

The benches are below floor level, as are the media seats, and most of the sight lines—even if you aren't sitting upstairs five miles from courtside—aren't very good.

But the Final Four sells out every year and has become one of those mega TV events that are part of the culture, like the Super Bowl, the World Series, and the Masters. People just want to say they were *there*. Corporations pay big bucks to gain all the perks that come with being NCAA "corporate champions."

I still go because I'm fortunate enough that the *Washington Post* still wants me to go—at least nowadays, unlike 1978, the paper pays my way—and because I enjoy seeing friends I've made in both media and coaching through the years. The Final Four is an annual convention of the college basketball world as much as it is a basketball tournament.

But it is no longer the joyride for me that it was in those innocent years when Skeeter Francis could pull a credential out of his pocket and hand it to me.

The first game on Saturday no longer starts at 1:30 eastern time; it starts at 6:10. In 1978, there were six scheduled TV time-outs per game that lasted ninety seconds each. Now there are *ten,* each lasting three minutes. Halftime, once fifteen minutes, is now closer to twenty-two minutes. They put twenty minutes on the clock, but the clock doesn't start until one coach does one of those mind-numbing halftime TV interviews and exits the court.

That means games that once took about an hour and forty-five minutes to play take closer to two hours and fifteen minutes—or more.

On that first Final Four Saturday of my life in St. Louis in 1978, I finished my second game story not long after six o'clock local time and had plenty of time to go out and have dinner. So did most fans, who exited the building after Kentucky's win over Arkansas, soon after five o'clock.

In Minneapolis last year, 2019, the Texas Tech–Michigan State game ended at about 10:15 central time. I finished writing my column a few minutes before midnight. And two nights later, the confetti began falling at 10:40 p.m. in Minneapolis—11:40 on the East Coast.

I was just happy the game didn't go double overtime.

As I walked back to my hotel that night, I was thinking about why I had wanted to do this book so much.

I was trying to find my way back to St. Louis, 1978—or at least to the way I felt about college basketball on that long-ago weekend. I'm not saying the big-time game was pure back then; I'm pretty sure a player was probably paid off fifteen minutes after Dr. James Naismith put up the first peach basket in Springfield 130 years ago. But the stories back then—about players, coaches, schools—*felt* more intimate. There were no interview rooms during the regular season; there were no closed practices; and there were certainly no games with more than fifty minutes of scheduled dead time.

That intimacy still exists—just not at the elite levels of college basketball. Now it's all about interview rooms where players inform the media they just wanted to give "a hundred and ten percent" (which, for the record, is impossible to give) and "step up" for their teammates. But on the back roads, you can still get to know—really *know*—players and coaches who often have stories to tell that are far more fascinating than which sneaker company Zion Williamson will sign with or which one-and-dones Kentucky, Duke, or Kansas have signed for next season.

I wanted to go back to my reporting roots as a young *Post* reporter—finding stories that no one else had noticed. I had grown up in New York City loving college basketball. As soon as I was old enough, I began riding the subway to the Columbia campus to watch the Lions play in old University Gym. I also went to college doubleheaders in Madison Square Garden. Most of the time Manhattan played the first game, NYU the second. Each game took about ninety minutes to play. Every Christmas, I went to the old Holiday Festival when it was still an eight-team event. One of my favorite nights of the year was the triple-header that climaxed the event: fifth-place game at five; third-place game at seven; championship game at nine. My only disappointment was that there was no seventh-place game that tipped at three. I would have been there.

During those early days at the *Post,* I often went to George Washington games in what was then the almost-new Smith Center. I also went often to American University's home games played in the not-at-all-new gym at Fort Myer. In those days, you drove up to the guard gate, said, "Going to the basketball game," and got waved through. Not so much anymore.

The coach at American in those days was Gary Williams, young and intense and very happy that *anyone* in the media was paying attention to his team, even a twenty-one-year-old kid whose real job was to cover cops and courts on the Metro staff.

We became friends—and stayed friends throughout his Hall of Fame career. When Maryland won the national championship in 2002 and I walked onto the court during the postgame celebration, I put out my hand and congratulated Gary. He pulled me in close and said quietly, "We've come a long way from Fort Myer, haven't we?"

We certainly had. By then, American had built an on-campus gym—Bender Arena—and to this day, it is one of my favorite places to go to for a game. But I miss those days in "The Fort," as everyone called it.

Years ago, as media seating in the big-time arenas was moved farther and farther from the court, as the NCAA Tournament became more and more about football stadiums and NBA arenas, I found myself drawn more and more often to games that weren't on national TV; to games where you could walk around a building without encountering security every ten steps; where you could stand on the court prior to a game and talk to coaches and players.

One night about a dozen years ago, I was at a game between what was then a very bad Towson team and a middling UNC Wilmington team. The game was tight, and during a late TV time-out, I realized I was absolutely riveted. There was no one on the court who would play in the NBA, but there were a number of very good players. And all were playing just as hard as the players in a Duke–North Carolina game or an Indiana-Purdue game.

I'm not knocking the rivalry games involving glamour teams; I've written about them on countless occasions. But there is a TV-promoted notion that the players and the multimillionaire coaches somehow *care* more than the players in that Towson–UNC Wilmington game.

They don't. In fact, I can make the case that those who play knowing they aren't going to make a living playing basketball care *more*. And, in many cases, have more interesting stories to tell.

The star in college basketball in 2018–19 was Duke's Zion Williamson. Every time he dunked a basketball, television and the Internet went crazy. Here's a fact: the only reason Williamson was playing at Duke was because the rules required him to play one year of college basketball. The same is true of all the one-and-done stars who do a walk-through in the college game because they have to play *someplace* until they can walk onstage to accept an NBA-logo cap from Commissioner Adam Silver.

Most college basketball players know that basketball ends for them when they play their last game at the college level. Which is why they pour their hearts into playing the game—even when they know there's no pot-of-NBA-gold at the end of the college rainbow.

In many ways, this book is about Bjorn Broman. Unless you are an ardent fan of Winthrop University or follow the Big South Conference on a regular basis, my guess is you've never heard of him.

He was a four-year starter at Winthrop—actually starting 111 of 125 games. As a sophomore, he was part of a team that went 26-7, won the Big South, and played—and lost to—Butler in the first round of the NCAA Tournament.

His final college game was in the quarterfinals of the Big South Tournament last March. The Eagles were decisively outplayed all afternoon and lost to Charleston Southern, 77–63. Broman did everything in his power to keep his team in the game. He scored 18 points—12 on three-point shots—the last two on a backdoor cut for a layup.

Those 2 points gave him exactly 1,000 points for his career. Someday, he'll tell his kids and grandkids that he was a Division 1 basketball player, played in the NCAA Tournament, and scored 1,000 career points.

He was still diving for loose balls in the final minute with the game decided.

"I just didn't want it to end," he said after it ended. "Basketball's been such a big part of my life for so long, I wanted to play as long as I could and as hard as I could."

As long as I could and as hard as I could sums up what most of the players who travel the back roads to March each winter give to and take from basketball. They know the only way they'll be on big-time TV—CBS, TBS/TNT, ESPN, Fox—is if they play a "guarantee" game at a big-time school in November that's on air so people can watch the big-time school play, or if they get that one shining moment (sorry) in the NCAA Tournament in March.

To me, they're what makes college basketball special. Not the pros-in-training; not the money schools with the moneyed fans who think of winning as a birthright. Part of my job is to write about the money schools and the pros-in-training. I get that.

But to me, the real joys of college basketball come on those winter nights when two teams with players like Bjorn Broman face off against each other. I'll take the back roads and the small, off-the-beaten-path gyms any day—or night.

Which is why the old cliché about life being about the journey applied to me last winter as I was researching this book. There were places and stories I came back to repeatedly: the ups and downs of a gray West Point winter, largely seen through the eyes of two remarkable young men, Army guards Tommy Funk and Jordan Fox; how Loyola Chicago and UMBC dealt with "the year after," their moments of March glory; the unique story of Harvard coach Tommy Amaker and his injured star, Seth Towns; life in the MEAC—one of two Division 1 leagues made up of historically black universities and colleges; the first season of a young coach's career: La Salle's Ashley Howard; the last season of an iconic old coach's career: Temple's Fran Dunphy; how a coach—Old Dominion's Jeff Jones—dealt with a cancer scare while never backing off from leading his team.

There were plenty of other people and stories I wanted to get to as the season wore on: Chris Clemons, the five-nine Campbell guard who went largely unrecruited yet ended up as the third-leading scorer in Division 1 basketball *history* when he graduated (yes, Zion and all one-and-dones, he graduated); Justin Wright-Foreman, Hofstra's star who claimed to be six-two but is no taller than me (six feet) and went from overlooked in high school to an NBA draft pick; and Clayton Custer, who had to lead a Loyola team that felt pressure no one could possibly have prepared anyone for.

I went back to see two of my all-time favorite coaches: Lefty Driesell, who *finally* was inducted into the Hall of Fame, and Jim Phelan, who should have been inducted years ago. I went to the Palestra in Philly every chance I got, because if you love basketball you can't see enough games in the Cathedral.

And I went to Farmville to hang out with a man who gave up an $800,000-a-year job as a lawyer and CEO to become an assistant basketball coach for $32,000 a year—and couldn't be happier.

My only regret is I didn't have more time to go to more places and see more games and talk to more players and coaches. I could easily write *another* book on another season like this one and never run out of stories to tell. I have more memories than I can possibly count, and I've included as many as could fit into my trips along the back roads.

Ultimately, this book is about competing and about camaraderie and about being as good as you can possibly be. Is that corny? Absolutely.

I make no apologies for that. In fact, I revel in it. And in this: the roads I traveled last winter are all about the small plaque that hangs on the concourse inside Philadelphia's historic Palestra, a few steps to the right of the main entrance. It says very simply:

"To win the game is great . . . To play the game is greater . . . But to love the game is the greatest of all."

This was a winter I loved. From start to finish.

A NEW BEGINNING ... AND THE
BEGINNING OF THE END

November 6, 2018, Philadelphia, Pennsylvania

Opening night in college basketball hasn't really been formalized in any way since the days many years ago when everyone began the season on December 1.

That was back when the regular season consisted of twenty-six games and the Final Four was played in March. The term "March Madness"—now trademarked by the NCAA—was first uttered when the season ended in March. Now it stretches into April.

What's more, most teams play thirty-one or thirty-two regular-season games and everyone has a conference tournament. Back in the December 1 launch era, the only conference that had a postseason tournament was the ACC.

Once conference commissioners and athletic directors began to figure out that there was money to be made on conference tournaments, they flourished. Then, "exempt" events began to sprout up on Thanksgiving weekend.

The first exempt event was the Rainbow Classic, which was launched by the University of Hawaii in 1964. In order to get big-name teams from the mainland to make the long trip to Honolulu, Hawaii was able to convince the NCAA to make its eight-team tournament "exempt" from the twenty-six-game regular-season limit, meaning that the three games played in Hawaii didn't count toward the twenty-six-game limit.

Given the chance to play three extra games and to tell recruits they would get a Christmas-time trip to Hawaii, coaches jumped at the chance to play.

The Great Alaska Shootout—initially known as the Sea Wolf Classic—was started in 1978 and, because of the travel, also received an NCAA exemption.

Through the years, more and more exempt events were sanctioned—many of them around the Thanksgiving holidays. I covered the Great Alaska Shootout on Thanksgiving weekend in 1984 when I was the Maryland beat writer for the *Washington Post*.

I was on the same flight to Anchorage with Maryland, and during a stopover in Seattle the players and coaches from Kansas boarded the flight. Kansas's coach at the time was Larry Brown, and he and his wife stopped to say hello to Maryland coach Lefty Driesell.

"Where's Joyce?" Brown's wife (at the time), Barbara, asked Driesell.

"Home," Lefty said. "She didn't want to go to Alaska for Thanksgiving. Only person willing to go with me to Alaska for Thanksgiving is Faahnsteen" (he said, gesturing to me).

I was thrilled to be in Alaska with Lefty. My most vivid memory of the trip was waking up in the pitch dark on Thanksgiving morning to turn on the football game from Detroit—which started at 8:30 a.m. local time. Two hours later the sun came up. By 3:30 it had set.

Nowadays, almost everyone plays in some kind of exempt event. Years ago, the NCAA had a rule that teams could play in an exempt event only once every four years to try to see to it that non–power teams would get invited. Now there are so many tournaments that just about everyone plays in them, and power schools pick and choose where they want to play each year.

The start of the season has gotten earlier and earlier. By December 1—the date that used to start the season—most teams have played at least half a dozen games and many have played in an early-season tournament.

Opening night for the 2018 season was November 6, with almost all the 353 teams in Division 1 men's basketball playing.

The most glamorous place to be that night was in Indianapolis, for an insurance-company-sponsored/TV-created annual doubleheader involving Duke, Kentucky, Michigan State, and Kansas, four of *the* blueblood programs in college basketball.

All four coaches—Mike Krzyzewski, John Calipari, Tom Izzo, and

Bill Self—are already in the Hall of Fame. The teams were ranked No. 1 (Kansas); No. 2 (Kentucky); No. 4 (Duke); and No. 10 (Michigan State) in preseason polls. In the eight years that the doubleheader had been played, only one team (Michigan State in 2011) had not been ranked when the event was held.

Last season, the only one of the four to make it to Minneapolis was the lowest ranked and least feted: Michigan State.

This was the first time the "Champions Classic" (insert the corporate name in front of "Champions") had been held on opening night. The coaches usually liked to get a game or two under their belts before playing another top team.

The rotation called for Kansas to play Michigan State and for Duke to play Kentucky.

I decided to leave the glamour and the hype of the evening to television; basketball's media royalty, and others. Instead, I headed up I-95 to north Philadelphia to see Temple and La Salle open against each other.

I am an unabashed fan of the Big Five—Temple, La Salle, Villanova, St. Joseph's, and Pennsylvania. Once upon a time, whenever teams in the Big Five played one another, the games were played in the Palestra, which is located on Penn's campus in west Philadelphia.

There is no basketball venue like the Palestra, which opened on New Year's Day in 1927. It is *not* the oldest on-campus gym in the country—Northeastern's Matthews Arena opened in 1910 but has been primarily a hockey arena for most of its existence. It first hosted a college basketball game in 1936 but didn't become the regular home of a college basketball team until 1981, when Northeastern began playing home games there.

Fordham's Rose Hill Gym opened in 1925 and Harvard's Lavietes Pavilion a year later and have hosted college basketball games since day one. But neither has the tradition of the Palestra, if only because no place has the tradition of the Palestra.

The Palestra has been called "The Cathedral of College Basketball" because it has hosted so many great players, coaches, and teams through the years. It isn't just a great basketball arena—it seats 8,722 and there isn't a bad seat in the place—it is also a museum.

If you walk around the concourse level of the rectangular building, you are in a museum that chronicles the history of the Big Five,

Philadelphia basketball (the Philadelphia Warriors played in the Palestra when Wilt Chamberlain was their center), and college basketball.

A few years back, Tom Izzo scheduled a game against Penn State in the Palestra. It was a Big Ten conference game, but Penn State coach Patrick Chambers, a Philadelphia native, was more than willing to move the game to Philadelphia from the often mausoleum-like Bryce Jordan Center on the Penn State campus.

Izzo, a Midwesterner, wanted to see the place and wanted to say he'd coached in the Palestra.

"This is going to be a new experience for you guys," he told his players before they left their hotel for the game. "This is old-time college basketball. The locker room we'll be in won't be half the size of what you guys are used to. You're going to have to hang your clothes on hooks. It'll be good for you."

As it turned out, Izzo had one thing wrong. "No hooks," he said. "Just benches to put their clothes on. Cracked me up."

Once upon a time, La Salle's 1954 national championship banner and Villanova's 1985 title banner hung in the Palestra. They were symbolic of the unique bond among the Big Five and the fact that all five teams played one another and, frequently, national powers, in the Palestra.

That changed not long after Villanova stunned Georgetown to win that 1985 national championship. Villanova coach Rollie Massimino decided that the school no longer needed to play four emotional Big Five games in addition to its difficult Big East schedule.

At the same time, Temple president Peter Liacouras, whose stated athletic ambition for his school was for the football team to "play in the Sugar Bowl," also decided that the Big Five was no longer a priority.

As a result, the Big Five almost died in the 1990s. With Villanova and Temple balking at committing to four games a season, Dan Baker, then the executive director, worked out a compromise: the schools would play two Big Five games a year and have the option to play their home games on campus—something Temple and Villanova insisted on.

From 1991 until 1999, the Big Five was on life support. But with Massimino gone and Liacouras about to retire, the schools decided in 1999 to return to playing four games a year. Phil Martelli, who became the coach at St. Joseph's in 1995, agreed to play his Big Five home games in the Palestra. La Salle also played home games in the Palestra.

Only Villanova and Temple categorically refused to play home games away from campus.

In 1997, Temple had moved from its longtime home, McGonigle Hall, into a new building that was called "The Temple of Apollo."

The reason for the new building was simple: John Chaney had rebuilt Temple into a national power. The Owls spent much of 1988 ranked No. 1 in the country, and although he never reached the Final Four, Chaney took Temple to the elite eight five times.

But nationally ranked teams weren't that eager to play at McGonigle, which seated 3,900. The Temple of Apollo had 10,200 seats—often too many for Temple, but enough to attract top teams to play there.

Sadly, in 2000, as part of a going-away present for Liacouras, who was retiring after nineteen years as Temple's president, the building was renamed the Liacouras Center. Thus, one of the coolest names for a sports arena went away.

Chaney's teams slipped in his final years as coach, and he and the school agreed that he should retire after the 2006 season. The team had reached the elite eight again in 2001, but the next five seasons produced five straight trips to the NIT—which is known in the lexicon of college basketball's elite schools as the "Not Invited Tournament."

It is not unusual at conference tournaments involving the sport's power schools to hear mediocre teams serenaded with chants of "NIT, NIT," to remind them that they are having a down season that will end in the tournament for those not invited to the Dance (aka the NCAA Tournament, or nowadays "March Madness," as the NCAA marketing people refer to it nonstop).

Temple fans were spoiled by Chaney's success, and when his teams slipped, it was decided it was time for him to step down at the age of seventy-four.

It didn't take Temple athletic director Bill Bradshaw very long to figure out whom he wanted to succeed Chaney: Fran Dunphy. And why not?

Dunphy had been part of the Big Five for most of his life: as a fan growing up in Drexel Hill—about a thirty-minute drive from the Palestra—then at La Salle as a player, where he and Bradshaw had been teammates on the 1969 team that went 23-1, coached by La Salle icon Tom Gola, for whom the school's arena is now named.

Dunphy went into the Army after graduating in 1970 and played on the All-Army team. One of his teammates was an Army lieutenant named Mike Krzyzewski.

"I think he was a year older than I was," Dunphy remembered years later. "But his basketball knowledge was light-years ahead of all of us. It wasn't just his ability to x-and-o or coach a game, it was his understanding of each player.

"I would come out of a game, and before I'd been sitting down for a full minute, he'd be next to me telling me a half-dozen things I needed to think about before I went back in. He was a player-coach without having a formal title. Playing with him and listening to him was like getting a PhD in basketball."

The two men remained friends long after each left Army. Dunphy served as an assistant coach at West Point for two years under Dan Dougherty before leaving to become the coach at Malvern Prep—his high school alma mater.

Dougherty, who had coached Dunphy at Malvern, didn't have much success at Army after succeeding Bob Knight when Knight left in 1971 to coach Indiana. He had a four-year record of 31-66 and was replaced in 1975 by Krzyzewski. He returned to high school coaching at Episcopal Academy outside Philadelphia and was hugely successful there until retiring in 2010.

Years after leaving Army, Dougherty liked to tell people that he was the answer to a great basketball trivia question: "Who coached Army in between the two Hall of Famers?"

He had, in fact, succeeded Knight and preceded Krzyzewski.

Dunphy moved from his high school alma mater to his college alma mater—La Salle—as an assistant coach in 1979. By then he had a master's degree from Villanova.

He kept moving up in the college ranks until he became Jack Schneider's number one assistant at Pennsylvania in 1988. A year later, Schneider left Penn to become the coach at Loyola of Baltimore, and Dunphy succeeded him.

That began a remarkable seventeen-year run during which Dunphy went 310-163 and won ten Ivy League titles. The Quakers and Princeton dominated the league during that period. One or the other represented the Ivies in the NCAA Tournament in every one of those seasons.

When Bradshaw called, Dunphy was willing to listen. Temple could and would pay him a lot more money than Penn was paying, and, at fifty-seven, Dunphy knew this was probably his last/best chance to make a salary north of $500,000 a year.

Plus, migrating from Penn in west Philadelphia to Temple in north Philadelphia meant he didn't have to move his family or leave his house. And he believed that being part of the Atlantic 10, which annually received more than one NCAA Tournament bid, would give him more chances to play in the tournament. Chaney had reached the tournament seventeen times in his first nineteen seasons before the fade to NIT status in his final five years.

Almost all of that had worked out just as Dunphy and Temple had hoped. Temple made it back to the NCAAs in Dunphy's second season (2007–08) and then made the tournament for six straight seasons.

Twice, the Owls won first-round games, but they were never able to reach the second weekend, which caused some grumbling from the Temple faithful, who had been spoiled by Chaney's postseason success.

Then the school made a huge mistake, choosing to leave the Atlantic 10, which was the perfect basketball conference in terms of both competition and logistics, to join the Big East—a move made strictly for football, with no thought given to how it would affect basketball.

The school's leadership was still fantasizing about playing in the Sugar Bowl.

Temple never competed in the Big East in basketball. The Big East was collapsing: seven of the basketball-only schools left to form a new conference, and a number of the football-basketball schools bolted for the ACC. The basketball schools retained the Big East name, and Temple was left with a conglomerate of schools to become part of the new American Athletic Conference in 2013.

That meant road trips to SMU, Memphis, Houston, South Florida, and Central Florida instead of crosstown trips to La Salle and St. Joseph's and relatively easy trips to Rhode Island, Massachusetts, George Washington, and Duquesne.

Dunphy never complained. Even though the makeup of the new league was bound to hurt recruiting and made each season far more difficult logistically, he just kept coaching.

After a down year in 2014, the Owls bounced back to win twenty-six games the following season and were the highest-rated team left out of the NCAA field. A year later, they were back in the NCAAs, but two mediocre seasons left many alums and donors clamoring for a coaching change.

By then, Dunphy was an icon in Philadelphia basketball circles and had become known as "Mr. Big Five." He'd played and coached at La Salle and had been successful leading the teams at Penn and Temple for twenty-nine years.

And so, the powers that be at Temple decided to use a backdoor cut to change coaches. Without telling Dunphy their plans, they announced he had decided to coach one more season—2018–19—and then retire at the age of seventy.

Dunphy was out of town when the announcement was made and was caught off guard. He never said a word publicly about the way his "retirement" was handled.

Plenty of others did. "It's awful," said Dick (Hoops) Weiss, a Temple grad who has covered basketball in Philadelphia and nationally for fifty years. "You don't do that to Fran Dunphy. You treat him with the dignity and respect he deserves."

And so, on opening night of the thirtieth and final season of his career as a head coach, Dunphy sat in his office inside the Liacouras Center a few yards down the hallway from his team's locker room and insisted all was well in his world.

The season opener against La Salle was an hour away.

"Honestly, I don't feel any different tonight than the first twenty-nine opening games I've coached," he said. "I feel like I'm going to be sick—which is the norm. I feel nervous, but excited. I think this team has a chance to be good, but I really want to see how we handle a real game in front of a real crowd."

He knew everything about La Salle was new—new coach, lots of new players. As Dunphy began his final season as a head coach, Ashley Howard was beginning his first. Dunphy had turned seventy a month earlier; Howard was thirty-eight.

Both were born-and-raised Philly basketball guys: Howard was the son of Maurice Howard, who had grown up in Philadelphia before starring at Maryland under Lefty Driesell in the 1970s. He had played in the NBA briefly before returning home to Philadelphia.

John Chaney had been a close friend of his grandfather's, and Ashley had been a ball boy for the Owls for four years as a kid, starting as an eight-year-old in 1988 for the Temple team that spent much of the season ranked No. 1.

He had hoped to play in the Big Five but ended up at Drexel, recruited first by Bill Herrion and then coached for two seasons by Steve Seymour after Herrion left to become the coach at East Carolina.

Herrion had been hugely successful at Drexel, winning three America East titles in a row and had even won an NCAA Tournament game for the first (and only) time in school history in 1996. Seymour was his top assistant and had played an important role in recruiting Howard, so he was comfortable honoring his commitment to Drexel when Seymour took over for Herrion.

Seymour went 28-29 during Howard's first two seasons, and with Drexel getting ready to move from the America East to the more competitive CAA, the school fired him and hired James (Bruiser) Flint, who had just been fired at Massachusetts after taking on the impossible job there of trying to succeed John Calipari.

College coaching is filled with men who scream intensity whenever they walk into a room. Even in that group, Flint stood out. He'd been nicknamed "Bruiser" as a toddler by his grandfather because he was so rambunctious even then.

That never really changed. He'd grown up in Philadelphia and starred at St. Joseph's in the 1980s. After hooking on as an assistant to Calipari at UMass, he took over in 1996 when Calipari fled to the NBA after building a team that reached the Final Four and also caught the attention of the NCAA police.

Flint lasted five seasons at UMass—making the NCAA Tournament twice—but never was able to shake Calipari's shadow. When he got the chance to return home to Philadelphia and coach Drexel, he jumped at it.

He had one starter returning for the 2001–02 season: Ashley Howard. "It had been four seniors and me starting," Howard said. "They were all graduating. It was my turn. I was going to be the team's leader."

Except that he never played another college basketball game. During an individual workout that spring, Howard felt nauseous, light-headed, and dizzy. He thought perhaps he just hadn't had enough to eat that day. But when the feeling persisted, Flint insisted he go to the hospital for tests.

The tests showed that he had cardiomyopathy, a thickening of the heart that can cause the heart to become enlarged or the heart muscle to become rigid. The doctors were never certain what caused it in Howard—they speculated it could have come from a virus—and they prescribed various medications to control it.

"At one point they wanted to put a defibrillator in," he said. "They said that would make it less likely to happen again. They also said I couldn't play with it. I turned it down. I still wanted to play."

It was Flint who told him he couldn't play anymore. "The doctors couldn't guarantee that I'd be okay if I played," Howard said. "He said to me, 'If there's *any* chance something serious could happen to you, I'm not letting you play.' You know that wasn't easy. He was a first-year coach and I was his one returning starter."

Howard understood that Flint was protecting him, but he was devastated. His junior year was supposed to be his time to shine. He was excited about playing for the mega-intense Flint. And then, just like that, it was over.

"I was like a lot of young guys," he said. "Basketball was my identity, it was who I was. It was what I thought about first every single day waking up. My mom always told me she worried about me because the only thing I really cared about was basketball."

He left school for a while, but in the back of his mind was Flint's offer to keep him on scholarship and make him a student coach. He went back and spent the next two years learning how to teach. He found that he enjoyed learning the details of the game that had never seemed important when he had been playing.

He graduated and, on Flint's recommendation, was hired at La Salle by John Giannini. Four years later, Flint brought him back. Then he spent one year at Xavier—"Bru told me I had to get out of Philly at *some* point in my life," he said, laughing, and then came back to Philly to work for Jay Wright at Villanova.

The next five years were a joyride. The Wildcats' *worst* record was 29-5, and they won two national championships. During the second title run in March 2018, Giannini, Howard's first boss, was fired by La Salle after fourteen seasons.

The Explorers had reached the sweet sixteen of the NCAAs in 2013 but hadn't been close to returning to the tournament in the next five seasons. Giannini was one of the game's good guys—a Chicagoan who seemed to understand the Big Five better than any one of the coaches who came from Philadelphia did.

"Maybe it took an outsider to understand how special what they had was," he said. "They tended to take it for granted, I think, as a given. If you're from anyplace else, you understand it's only a given in Philly—not anyplace else."

Sitting in a restaurant relaxing over lunch, Giannini is about as engaging as anyone you are likely to meet. But, by his own admission, his intensity hurt him in those last years at La Salle. "I got to a point where I was paranoid," he said. "I stopped being comfortable with the media, felt like people were out to get me. I know now, they weren't. But back then, it didn't feel that way."

By the time Giannini was fired, Bill Bradshaw, the same man who had hired Dunphy to coach at Temple, had returned to his alma mater as athletic director. Just as he hadn't looked far when he'd brought Dunphy to north Philadelphia in 2006, he didn't look far when looking for a successor to Giannini.

He wanted young, and he preferred someone with a Philadelphia pedigree—although that wasn't required. He wanted someone from a winning program, and given that La Salle had never had an African American coach, that would be a bonus.

As it turned out, Howard met all the criteria: young, a Philly guy who had been part of a program that had just won two national championships, and African American.

He was named the new La Salle coach a week after helping cut down the nets in San Antonio.

He knew he'd gone from college basketball's penthouse to, if not an outhouse, at least a place in need of a major rebuild.

"I get it," he said. "But I've followed La Salle all my life. I've worked at La Salle. I know the potential's there."

And then he said what all coaches say at the start of a rebuild: "We've just got to get some pieces here."

"Pieces" is the twenty-first-century word for players.

Temple won on opening night, but it wasn't easy. La Salle, led by sixth-year player Pookie Powell (he had been granted a second medical redshirt year by the NCAA) and some of those new "pieces" Howard had talked about, stayed in the game until the very end before Temple finally prevailed, 75–67, in front of a crowd of 6,011.

One couldn't help but think that if the game had been played in the Palestra, it would have been a sellout. Temple fans might be willing to make the trip to North Broad Street for a home game, but La Salle fans and neutral Philly hoops fans, not so much.

Dunphy's pregame talk wasn't much different from any of the 872 he had delivered in the past twenty-nine years. After Aaron McKie—already designated as his successor—had gone through the scouting report, Dunphy reminded his players that La Salle had a new coach and a lot of new players and would be extremely motivated to send a message to the rest of the Big Five on the first night of a new season—and a new era.

The last thing he said to his players before sending them to the court was simple: "Protect the *T*." He pointed at the players' uniforms as he said it, a reminder they were representing Temple.

Standing in the corner of the room, I couldn't help but think it was a shame that Temple hadn't protected Dunphy the way I knew he would always protect the school.

As Hoops Weiss had said, Dunphy deserved better. Most longtime coaches deserve better than what they get in the end. Dave Odom, who had been the head coach at East Carolina, Wake Forest, and South Carolina, often said, "If you stay too long, the ending is rarely a happy one."

Fran Dunphy was still hoping for a happy ending. He was 1-0 to start his final season.

2

AND THE CADETS CAME
MARCHING IN

As I walked out of the Liacouras Center after Temple's opening-night victory over La Salle, I glanced at a television set. Even though it was shortly after ten o'clock, the Duke-Kentucky game had just started and Duke led 14–8.

It wasn't until I reached the Washington Beltway about two hours later that I heard the final score: Duke-118, Kentucky-84. I literally thought I'd heard the score wrong, so I double-checked my computer when I got home.

I'd heard right.

As usual, Duke and Kentucky had the two most heralded freshman classes in the country, filled with one-and-done players who would pass through college basketball for a year and then become NBA multimillionaires.

Because it had a little more experience than Duke, Kentucky had actually been ranked No. 2 (behind Kansas) going into the season, with the Blue Devils No. 4.

The lopsided victory over Kentucky would set off a "Duke is the greatest team ever" frenzy. Not only were people conceding the national championship to Duke; some were claiming they could beat NBA teams.

This sort of thing is the product of today's Internet clicks; Twitter; Facebook; blogs; Snapchat; podcasts; and sports-talk-radio-driven media. I won't go so far as to say that serious reporting has ceased to exist, but it does feel as if far fewer people are practicing it and only a handful of people in their right minds are paying attention to it.

Amid all the screeching, I was reminded of the reaction in 2013 to the same doubleheader. On that night in Chicago, No. 2 Michigan State had beaten No. 1 Kentucky, and No. 5 Kansas had beaten No. 4 Duke.

But that wasn't what had the media in heat that night. It was the presence of three hyped one-and-dones: Kansas's Andrew Wiggins, Duke's Jabari Parker, and Kentucky's Julius Randle. Most thought they would be the top three picks in the NBA draft the following June. Beyond that, they were lock future stars—unless they were (more likely) superstars.

ESPN's Michael Wilbon called the doubleheader "the most exciting night in the history of regular season college basketball."

Maybe I'm just old—I'm two years older than Wilbon—but I remembered the night in the Houston Astrodome when Houston and Elvin Hayes beat UCLA and Lew Alcindor—the first time in Alcindor's two seasons UCLA had lost a game. That was the first regular-season college game televised nationally. There was also Notre Dame's victory over the Bruins six years later that ended UCLA's eighty-eight-game winning streak.

I could also argue that the 1974 ACC championship game between North Carolina State and Maryland, a 103–100 overtime classic with an NCAA Tournament bid on the line, might have been just a little bit more dramatic.

There were others, but that's not the point. Wilbon and his colleagues were going nuts over three freshmen who had just played their second game in college.

How did their college careers turn out? Wiggins averaged 17 points a game, but his Kansas career ended with a thud when he shot 1-for-6 in a second-round NCAA Tournament game against Stanford and the Jayhawks were upset, 60–57.

Jabari Parker's Duke team didn't make the second round, losing in the first round to Mercer, a 14th-seed. Parker became the first freshman in school history to lead the team in both scoring (19 points per game) and rebounding (8 per game). But in the Mercer game, he was completely outplayed by Jakob Gollon, a sixth-year player who had come back from two knee surgeries and two missed years. Gollon had 20 points and 5 rebounds in the game. Parker had 14 points on 4-of-14 shooting.

Randle's Kentucky team didn't flame out early in March. After a mediocre regular season made them an eighth seed going into the tournament, they got on a run, pulling out one buzzer-beater after another to reach the championship game, before losing to Connecticut.

Randle played decently in the championship game—10 points and 6 rebounds—but, like Wiggins and Parker in their teams' earlier losses, he was far from dominant.

Wiggins was still the No. 1 pick in that June's NBA draft; Parker was No. 2 and Randle No. 7. All have had solid, though hardly spectacular, NBA careers—Wiggins the best, with an average of 19 points per game.

All have been traded—Parker twice—and Parker and Randle have lost considerable playing time with injuries. Five years into their NBA careers, they have combined for *zero* all-star appearances.

Which leads me back to my point: November basketball is fun, but it rarely tells us much about what will happen in March, no matter how loudly the TV pundits scream about the greatness of the latest group of one-and-dones.

Army's opening-night win, a 73–69 escape from Marist, wasn't quite as impressive as Duke's rout of Kentucky. Nevertheless, the Black Knights headed to Durham that Saturday to prepare for a Sunday afternoon game in Cameron Indoor Stadium against the newly anointed greatest team in the history of college basketball.

In my mind, Cameron is one of college basketball's great venues—behind the Palestra, but right up there with Kansas's Allen Fieldhouse for a spot in the top three. Kentucky and UCLA fans will no doubt argue that Rupp Arena and Pauley Pavilion have more championship banners—and they do—but neither can match the atmosphere of a sold-out Palestra or Cameron or Allen Fieldhouse.

For the Army players, the chance to play in Cameron was a big deal. They were all keenly aware of how loud it would be; that the students ringing the court created a unique atmosphere; and that Duke's coach was about as famous an Army graduate as there was this side of Ulysses S. Grant or Dwight D. Eisenhower.

There's a poster that one can find in almost every building on post at West Point. It says, "Much of the history we teach was made by the men we taught." It is illustrated with pictures of Grant, Eisenhower, and Robert E. Lee. Mike Krzyzewski doesn't appear on the poster, but within the context of basketball history, he would appear on any poster: five national titles, twelve Final Fours, and three Olympic gold medals—for starters.

Krzyzewski was the major reason why Army was playing at Duke. He had even brought Duke to play *at* Army in 1997 as a favor to Pat Harris, who had played for him at Army and had just become the school's coach.

The teams didn't play annually, but they played often. The other reason for Army making the trip was more practical: a $70,000 guarantee.

"Guarantee games" are a big part of November and December basketball. Teams like Duke, who can sell out every home game, will schedule lower-level Division 1 teams in order to make an easy profit on a game they should be "guaranteed" to win.

Every year, a few of the guarantee games backfire on the home team. In December 2018, UCLA lost back-to-back guarantee games to Belmont and Liberty. As it turned out, both schools made the NCAA Tournament, but their *names* were so unacceptable to UCLA fans and alumni that Coach Steve Alford was forced to resign after his team lost to Liberty by fifteen in Pauley Pavilion.

North Carolina State didn't lose any guarantee games; it just scheduled too many of them—nine. Even though the Wolfpack had a nonconference win against Auburn and twenty-two wins overall, the committee left them out of the sixty-eight-team NCAA field, largely because it had more or less ignored the fact that for about ten years now, the committee has put an emphasis on nonconference strength of schedule.

Duke had six guarantee games—Army being the first of them. Army would play one more guarantee game on the road—at Miami of Ohio. It didn't need to play as many guarantee games as other schools in the Patriot League because (like Navy) it plays at the top level of college football—the Football Bowl Subdivision (FBS).

Most of the 131 schools that play in the FBS make money playing football. The rest of the 353 schools that play Division 1 basketball play at lower levels that don't make money—or don't play football at all.

Some do fine financially without football—Gonzaga is the best example—but there are others. Many, however, are dependent on playing guarantee games on the road to make their budget work: some do it in football; some in basketball; some in both.

In 2015–16, Texas Southern played its first sixteen games on the road—almost all guarantee games. In 2017–18, Grambling State played twelve of its first thirteen games on the road, but managed to make all the travel worthwhile when it stunned Georgia Tech, 64–63, in Atlanta.

Coaches who schedule guarantee games at home live in fear of playing someone good enough to come into their gym and beat them. The attitude power coaches take toward guarantee games was best summed up by then–Villanova coach Steve Lappas years ago when he shook hands with Lafayette's Fran O'Hanlon after barely beating O'Hanlon's team.

"You seem to have forgotten what a guarantee game is," he told O'Hanlon. "We guarantee you money, you guarantee us a win."

Krzyzewski had lost a guarantee game to Wagner early in his third season at Duke, thirty-six years ago. He had never forgotten it. Years later, when Neil Kennett, Wagner's coach in that game, introduced himself to Krzyzewski, he said, "Coach, I don't know if you remember me—"

Krzyzewski cut him off. "You bet I remember you. You're the reason I *never* take any team for granted."

Even after beating the second-ranked team in the country by thirty-six points, Krzyzewski wasn't likely to take a game against his alma mater for granted. He knew it wasn't likely that Army would be intimidated by the noise in Cameron.

"They face a lot more adversity in their daily lives than loud fans," he said.

Jimmy Allen knew what he and his players would be up against going into Cameron. He had been coaching military academy kids for fifteen years—six as an assistant at Navy under Don DeVoe (who had been an assistant at Army when Krzyzewski played there) and nine at Army—the first six as Zach Spiker's top assistant, the next three as head coach after Spiker left for Drexel. In between his stints at Navy and Army he coached at Division 3 Averett, taking over a team that had just gone 0-25 and building it into a program that went to four NCAA Division 3 tournaments in six years.

Spiker always said the smartest thing he had done as Army's coach was to hire Allen. Together, the two had changed Army's approach to basketball 180 degrees. Under previous coaches, Army had always looked to slow the game down. That made sense: when the other team has better athletes, the fewer possessions in a game, the better.

Spiker and Allen threw that notion away and coached up-tempo basketball, for a couple of reasons: first, it was a more appealing way to play for potential recruits; and second, the more often they could beat the other team downcourt and not face a half-court defense, the better Army's chances to score.

The counterintuitive change worked. Army began to recruit better athletes and became a hard team to guard. The lack of size was always going to be an issue, and February remained a tough month because of class schedules and the brutal weather everyone on post woke up to most mornings, but the Black Knights became far more competitive.

I had known Allen since his days at Navy. He has the kind of self-deprecating sense of humor good coaches tend to have: they take winning and losing seriously, but not themselves.

When I called to tell him I was planning to come to Duke and wanted to spend the day hanging out with his team, he laughed.

"I've seen their exhibition games on tape," he said. "Far as I'm concerned, you can give the pregame talk. I've got nothing."

Kidding aside, Allen liked his team. He had an experienced back-court in junior point guard Tommy Funk, who had started every single game since arriving at Army, and shooting guard Jordan Fox, who had initially planned to enlist in the Army after graduating from high school in Jackson County, Kentucky.

"That's what you did most of the time if you came out of my hometown," he said. "Not too many people went to college. I wanted to serve. I thought the best way was to enlist."

After seeing him play in a summer camp between his junior and senior years, Allen had a different idea. He suggested to Fox that he should consider playing basketball for four years at Army and then serve after graduation—as an officer.

Fox was an excellent student, the valedictorian in his class, and he loved basketball. So, he agreed to go to the Army prep school to shore up his academics—his school district was not highly rated academically—and to see if he liked Army life. Four years later, he was Army's second-leading scorer as a junior, behind only center Matt Wilson.

Allen wasn't going to change his team's approach against Duke. He wanted his players to attack on offense every chance they got; he wanted an up-tempo game for forty minutes, even though he knew that was risky given Duke's talent.

"We're not going to do anything different today than any other game," he told his players on Sunday morning. "What we have to do is make them uncomfortable. I think we can do that."

Months later, the scouting report put together by Allen and his assistants after watching three games—two exhibitions and the Kentucky game—resonates with remarkable clarity, given the way Duke's season ended in March.

"They don't like to be crowded," Allen said, showing his team a couple of plays where Duke players didn't handle double-teams very well.

"[R. J.] Barrett still wants to prove he's the number one player, not [Zion] Williamson," he added, showing Barrett trying to make one-on-one plays without thinking to look for a teammate.

Barrett had been rated the top high school player in the class of 2018, but Williamson, his Duke teammate, had become an Internet sensation that summer with a number of spectacular dunks and plays during Duke's exhibition swing in Canada. More and more people were now talking about Williamson as the lock No. 1 pick the next spring after he had played exactly one college game.

"Close the gaps on them, don't let them in the lane," Allen added. "If we make them take a lot of threes, that's a win for us."

In March, those three things—double-teams, Barrett trying to do too much, and inconsistent outside shooting—would ultimately prove Duke's undoing. Allen and his coaches had diagnosed the Blue Devils accurately in November, even while the TV pundits were declaring them unbeatable.

There are few basketball traditions more cherished by coaches than the game-day walk-through. Some teams will go to the arena early and give the players a chance to shoot, in addition to walking through the other team's offense and defense. Visiting teams are especially keen to do this in order to get a feel for the shooting background—although what the players see in an empty arena is entirely different from what they see when the building is full.

Army had practiced in Cameron on Saturday, so, with a one o'clock start, Allen had passed on an early wake-up and decided to skip a morning walk-through in Cameron.

"Sleep is more important for these guys," he said. "Being on the road is a rare chance for them to get some sleep. Back home, they're up at dawn, or earlier. Here, I can let them sleep for a while. That'll help them today and, more important, get them off to a good start for the week when we get back."

And so, the walk-through was literally that: the players finishing breakfast, then looking at tape of Duke before walking through what they'd seen on tape. In the background came the sounds of the members of the Faith Assembly Christian Center singing gospel music across the hall as part of their Sunday morning service.

In the relatively small space, there was no need—or room—to throw a basketball around, so the offense used a one-serving box of Special K as the ball.

"Oh Lord, let us communicate!" Allen yelled at one point as the music continued across the hall.

He then reminded the players of their slogan: BFAST . . . Not short for breakfast but a reminder to Be Fast . . . Accountable . . . Selfless . . . Tough.

He knew his players were likely to be all those things. And he knew, given the athletic ability of the opponent, that probably wouldn't be enough.

It was a beautiful late fall afternoon at Duke.

I always have mixed emotions when I return to my alma mater. Basketball played a major role in my decision to go to Duke. As a high school senior, I attended a Duke-Maryland game on my visit to campus.

Maryland was ranked No. 2 in the country and had players like John Lucas, Tom McMillen, Len Elmore, and Mo Howard. Duke wasn't very good—it would finish 12-14 for the season—but it had a senior guard named Gary Melchionni, who scored 39 points that afternoon.

Cameron jumped with noise all day, and when it became apparent that Duke was going to win, the students began singing the "Amen chorus," which had become Maryland's unofficial victory song under Lefty Driesell. As we walked into a January afternoon with the temperature in the sixties, I turned to my father—who desperately wanted me to go to Yale, where he was teaching a graduate school class at the time—and said, "Dad, if I get in here, this is where I'm going."

I'm not sure my father ever completely got over that moment.

Duke was pretty awful during my four years in school. The overall record was 50-56, and the ACC record was 10-42, including four straight first-round losses in the ACC Tournament. Nowadays, when I quote those numbers to younger people, they sometimes refuse to believe me. They also find it hard to believe that anyone other than Mike Krzyzewski has ever been the basketball coach at Duke.

There were three basketball coaches during my undergraduate years: the first was Bucky Waters, who resigned on September 10 of my freshman year to take a job as a fund-raiser in the Duke hospital. Waters had one year left on his five-year contract and had been told he wouldn't be renewed at the end of the 1973–74 season, so when the hospital job was offered, he took it.

Five weeks later—three days after practice officially began—Neill McGeachy, Waters's top assistant—was given a one-year contract. This came after athletic director Carl James had attempted to hire seventy-two-year-old Adolph Rupp, who had been forced to retire by Kentucky two years earlier when he turned seventy.

McGeachy's team went 10-16, the worst record in Duke history. James then hired Bill Foster, who had successfully built programs at Rutgers and Utah and who did the same at Duke—one year too late for me, at least as a student.

The year after I graduated, Duke went 27-7, won the ACC title, and lost to Kentucky in the national championship game. That group—led by Jim Spanarkel, Mike Gminski, Gene Banks, and Kenny Dennard—never made it back to the Final Four but won seventy-three games in three seasons.

Foster, feeling underappreciated after his remarkable rebuild, fled to

South Carolina in 1980. That was when athletic director Tom Butters shocked the basketball world by hiring the thirty-three-year-old Army coach with the impossible-to-pronounce name. At his first press conference, Krzyzewski explained that one of his goals when he recruited a player was that he be able to pronounce his name correctly by the time he graduated.

I was covering the ACC for the *Washington Post* when Krzyzewski arrived and liked him right away. I felt like he knew what he was doing, even when he went 38-47 his first three seasons.

I was thrilled when he turned things around, beginning with his fourth season, when Duke went 24-10. Two years later, the record was 37-3 and—like Foster's 1978 team—the Blue Devils came up one win short of the national title, losing a taut championship game to Louisville, 72–69.

Unlike Foster, Krzyzewski was able to build on that team's success. Duke went to seven Final Fours in nine years, finally winning the national championship in 1991 and then backing it up by winning again a year later.

My relationship with Duke, however, isn't nearly as warm as my relationship with Krzyzewski. I have been publicly critical of both Nan Keohane and Richard Broadhead—who preceded current president Vincent Price—for reasons too boring to go into now. Heck, Stephen Miller, the insane policy adviser to President Donald Trump, graduated from Duke. That doesn't exactly fill me with pride.

And so, as I crossed the campus on Sunday, November 11, I was filled with warm memories of the place and the cold reality that, because I've publicly criticized the school often, I wasn't exactly welcome here.

But I was there to spend the day with Army. I walked into the locker room with the team and Jimmy Allen handed me a bench pass, meaning I'd be able to sit directly behind the Army bench. I'd asked the Duke people to seat me near the Army bench and had been told that was completely impossible.

This was Duke's first home game of the season, the first look in a real game for the students at the new corps of one-and-done stars Krzyzewski had recruited, led by four freshmen starters: Williamson, Barrett, Cam Reddish, and the point guard, Tre Jones. The latter would return for his sophomore season. The first three were en route to the NBA about fifteen minutes after Duke's season ended.

The game began with Tommy Funk rebounding a Reddish miss and pushing the ball up the floor ("Attack, attack!"). He found Josh Caldwell on the baseline and Caldwell drilled a fifteen-footer.

Thirty-four seconds in, Army led 2–0.

As he glanced at the scoreboard, the thought crossed Allen's mind to call time-out. "I really wanted to freeze the scoreboard long enough to get a picture of that score—us in the lead," he said later. "I mean, I seriously thought it. But then I looked down at Krzyzewski and thought, 'Better not piss him off.'"

Krzyzewski was plenty pissed off by halftime. With a little more than eight minutes left, Duke had opened a 36–25 lead and the students were starting to sense a blowout.

Then Funk—and Army's scouting report—put a stop to that.

First, Williamson tried to split a double-team at the top of the key. Funk stripped him, took off, and found Tucker Blackwell on the right wing. Blackwell drained a three to make it 36–28.

Then it was Barrett's turn. Starting on the right wing, he went left—as always—and tried to go between Funk and Jordan Fox. They combined to knock the ball loose. Funk picked it up in full flight and went in for a layup to make it 36–30.

Furious, Krzyzewski called time with 8:01 to play.

"What were the chances," Army assistant coach Zak Boisvert would say later, "that the first coach to need a time-out today would be Krzyzewski?"

Boisvert has an English degree from Fordham and a dry sense of humor. "I have this English degree and my job is to coach a bunch of future Army officers to box out. My mom asks me all the time when I'm going to get a real job."

At that moment, no one in the Army huddle was thinking about any job other than trying to beat Duke. "They don't want to pass to one another," Allen said—the last two plays being graphic examples.

It was 50–42 at halftime, the Black Knights refusing to let Duke get on any sort of blowout run. Allen's only regret at halftime was not calling the time-out at 2–0.

He pointed out to his players that the supposedly unbeatable team was clearly beatable. "This is a great atmosphere for basketball," he said. "Enjoy it. You've earned it."

Army plays its home games in Christl Arena, which is directly across the street from Michie Stadium. Typically, except when the corps of cadets is required to show up for the annual home game against Navy, attendance is about one thousand. This was very different.

And fun.

"I grew up a Kentucky fan, so you can imagine how I feel about Duke," said Jordan Fox. "But to walk in there and see all the banners and feel all the tradition in the place was amazing. I think for all of us it was a dream come true to play in there. But we wanted to show all those people we could play, not just show up with Army on our uniforms."

It was Fox who began the second half with a three-pointer to cut the margin to 50–45. Then a Matt Wilson follow cut it to 50–47. There was a buzz inside Cameron, a "What the hell is going on here?" buzz.

Duke had last lost in Cameron to a nonconference opponent in 2000–139 straight victories, many of them against ranked teams.

Duke promptly went on an 11–2 run to stretch the lead to 60–49, and Allen called time to settle his team—and, he hoped, the crowd—down. The Blue Devil mascot did his surfing routine—placing a surfboard on the back of the cheerleaders—during the time-out and the roof almost came off.

But Army hung in, cutting the margin back to 67–61 on a Funk jumper just before the under-twelve-minute TV time-out.

The buzz was still there as Allen's players formed their tight huddle so Allen could be heard. "Win these next four minutes and it's an eight-minute game," Allen told them. "Trust me when I tell you they don't want that."

In today's college basketball world, when there is a TV time-out (they are euphemistically called "media time-outs" by TV people even though they exist strictly for TV), coaches tell their players to play and think in four-minute bursts. Army had now gotten through seven of the game's ten four-minute segments. Allen believed if they could get through the next one, there was a chance to steal the game.

Krzyzewski agreed. "We were in a position where we could lose the game," he said later. "That was very real. I was proud of the way my guys responded."

They responded with a lethal, lightning-quick 14–2 run: Reddish hit a jumper and a three; then Barrett hit a three and Allen had to call time-out. But Duke had finally gotten the momentum it had been searching for all afternoon, and the Black Knights suddenly looked gassed. Duke controlled the rest of the game, and the final was 94–72.

"That game was a lot closer than that final score," Krzyzewski said. "This was a good game for us because we found out the Kentucky game was just one game and we've still got a lot of work to do."

When Krzyzewski shook Allen's hand, he pulled him in close and said, "Keep playing like that and you'll have a great season."

He told each player he was proud to have them represent his alma mater, singling out Funk and Fox for an extra moment. Funk had been superb: 12 points, 10 assists, and just 2 turnovers against Duke's pressure. Fox had finished with 10 points, center Matt Wilson with 15. Someone took a photo of Krzyzewski with his arm around Fox. The lifelong Kentucky fan proudly showed it to people whenever he got the chance.

Krzyzewski said he wasn't surprised that Army had played as well as it did or that his team hadn't been as dominant as it had looked against Kentucky.

"They dealt with a lot of noise after the Kentucky game," he said. "That's not easy."

Luke DeCock, the outstanding *Raleigh News and Observer* columnist, asked Krzyzewski a question that made sense: "Mike, you've been dealing with noise around here for more than thirty years—why was this different?"

Kryzewski smiled. "*I've* been dealing with noise for more than thirty years, Luke," he said. "These guys have never dealt with noise before. And it was *loud.*"

The Army locker room was quiet. The players changed into their dress grays for the plane trip home—which they had already been told would be delayed by at least two hours.

"We'll keep checking with the airline for updates," Allen told them, because that's what he'd been told was happening.

Duke's players don't have to worry about checking with airlines. It has been *years* since anyone from Duke—or most of the big-time schools—flew commercial. Twenty years earlier, angered by a lack of enthusiasm during a practice the day before a game at Clemson, Krzyzewski stopped practice and called his players to midcourt.

"I'm telling you right now, if I don't see a *lot* more intensity here in the next ten minutes, we'll fly to Clemson tomorrow commercial," he said. "If you think I'm kidding, try me."

The players responded. Krzyzewski had played his trump card. Jimmy Allen would never have that card available to him.

3

BREAKFAST AND BASKETBALL

In one way or another—for one reason or another—I have been a morning person most of my life. I love the idea of getting a head start on the day, of getting things done in the morning.

No doubt this dates to winter mornings when I was up before the sun to get to swimming practice and summer mornings when I was up with the sun to get to the golf course to work.

I've always said that my favorite sports events begin at noon. I had that conversation with Dean Smith once. He was bemoaning the long hours spent waiting for a nine o'clock tipoff.

"The worst thing about coaching is the waiting," he said. "Especially on game day. I know a lot of coaches who try to kill the time with a long walk-through or shootaround or looking at tape one more time to find a hidden secret.

"I've never been one for any of that. I just want the game to start."

As always, Dean also had a practical reason for abhorring the late starts: "We talk all the time about wanting to do everything we can for the players. [I knew Dean for more than thirty years and never *once* heard him say "student-athletes."] How can it possibly be good for the players to start games after nine o'clock and get home, if you're on the road, at two or three in the morning if not later?"

Dean and I knew why games start at nine o'clock—and in the NCAA Tournament sometimes after ten o'clock—TV. He understood it, but that didn't mean he liked it. Dean was never one to go along with convention without at least protesting. When the North Carolina board of trustees voted to name their $38 million basketball palace the Dean E. Smith Center, Dean objected when the name was presented to him: "You should name it for the players," he said.

The trustees pointed out that would be a bit unwieldy. Dean acquiesced, but he loved pointing out to people the writing at the base of the bronze statue of him that sat in the lobby.

"Dean E. Smith, February 28, 1931— . . . ," he'd say, laughing. "They're just waiting to fill in the blank."

Dean and I always agreed that noon was the best time to start a basketball game. One day when I said the only thing better than a noon start would be an 11 a.m. start, Dean shook his head. "That's *too* early," he said. "I'm not much of a morning person. Noon is fine."

Remarkably, the first college basketball game I ever attended started at 11 a.m. It was the consolation game of the 1965 NIT. My parents had said I could go because the championship game was at one o'clock. When I found out there was a third-place game that started at eleven, I insisted we get there for tipoff. After all, there was a game to be seen, so why not get there when it started?

My mom wasn't thrilled, but she understood. This was at the old Madison Square Garden on Fiftieth Street. If there were a thousand people in the building when the game began, that was a lot. I didn't care.

The championship game was between St. John's and Villanova. It was to be Joe Lapchick's last game as St. John's coach. I had no idea at the time what a big deal that was. All I knew was that St. John's was from New York and Villanova was from Philadelphia, so I was rooting for St. John's.

The consolation game was between two New York–area teams: NYU and Army. Back then, Army's nickname was the Cadets. At the turn of the twenty-first century, for marketing purposes, they became strictly the "Black Knights," as in "Black Knights of the Hudson." Back then, Black Knights was the backup nickname.

Army's coach was Tates Locke. He was also coaching his last game at the school: he was leaving to become the coach at Miami of Ohio.

Locke had one assistant: he was twenty-four years old, and his name was Robert Montgomery Knight. Yup, the first college basketball game I ever saw in person, Bob Knight was involved.

Little did I know. Little did he know.

Army and St. John's both won that day. I loved the atmosphere and the competitiveness of the two games. From that day forward, I was hooked on college hoops. Back then, the Garden frequently hosted regular-season doubleheaders. Most involved Manhattan playing the first game and NYU the second. I could get in with my GO card for two dollars, and it was fairly easy to sneak into the lower bowl since the building was rarely full.

In those days, when the schedule said the games would start at seven and nine, they started at seven and nine. Most college basketball games were played in about ninety minutes. No TV time-outs intervening every four minutes. No twenty-minute halftimes.

I know, I sound old.

When I began going through schedules in late summer to prepare for researching this book, one seemingly innocuous game jumped out at me: November 14—St. Francis (Brooklyn) at Richmond. Tip: 11 a.m.

There was no way I wasn't going. The starting time was both appealing and intriguing. When I called the Richmond people to ask about an 11 a.m. weekday (Wednesday) nonholiday game, I was told it was an annual event: "Education Day." The school invited five thousand students from area elementary, middle, and high schools to come to the game to expose them to college basketball.

A great idea.

If two teams I had little interest in were playing, I'd have gone to the game. But that wasn't the case. My very first story for *Sports Illustrated* in November 1988 had been on Richmond. Dick Tarrant—for whom the court in Robins Center is now named—was the coach. The Spiders had reached the sweet sixteen the previous March by beating Indiana and Georgia Tech. Tarrant had been a high school coach for years before being hired by Lou Goetz, one of his former players, at Richmond in 1979. When Goetz left, Tarrant got the job and turned Richmond into a mid-major power.

Three years after the sweet sixteen run, Richmond had become the first No. 15 seed to win an NCAA Tournament game, upsetting No. 2 Syracuse—with Derrick Coleman and Billy Owens.

I was working for the short-lived *National Sports Daily* at the time. My editor, the great Frank Deford, asked me to write a piece the day before the tournament began listing the eight *best* bench coaches in the tournament and the eight worst. Naturally, I picked Knight to top the best list. Second was Tarrant. I led off the worst list with Jim Boeheim—which I can say with confidence now was one of the dumbest things I've ever written.

Boeheim was an easy target because his teams played free-flowing, often mistake-laden basketball and he had no rules about when to shoot or who could shoot. This was before he'd become the Lord of the 2-3 zone defense. Like I said, easy target. And I couldn't have been more wrong.

On the day the stories came out, Boeheim came after me when his team took the court at Cole Field House to practice.

"You don't know a damn thing about basketball if you don't think I'm a good bench coach!" he yelled.

Naturally, I defended myself. It wasn't until years later that I apologized—both publicly and privately—to Boeheim.

The next night, Richmond stunned Syracuse. As soon as Boeheim walked into the interview room—it was well after midnight—he searched me out.

"You know what *really* pisses me off about this?" he said. "There are now going to be people who think you know something about basketball!"

He was actually smiling—a little—when he said it. To his everlasting credit, he forgave me for being an idiot.

Richmond's coach was now Chris Mooney, who was in his fourteenth season. A lot was expected of Mooney—or any Richmond coach. Tarrant was the benchmark, but Mooney had also followed John Beilein—who had gone on to take Michigan to two national title games before leaving in the spring of 2019 to coach the Cleveland Cavaliers—and Jerry Wainwright, who had also had a winning record before leaving for DePaul.

Mooney had plenty of success. After two losing seasons, he'd had ten straight years without a losing record, including five twenty-win seasons and a sweet sixteen trip in 2011, when the Spiders finished 29-8.

But Mooney had a problem that wasn't really his fault: Virginia Commonwealth. The two schools were six miles apart, and both now played in the Atlantic 10 Conference. VCU was a classic city campus; Richmond, even just a few miles from downtown, was one of the most beautiful campuses in the country. People joked that it should be renamed Richmond Country Club.

VCU's success had been toxic to Mooney. Even during the 2011 run, the Spiders played second fiddle in their hometown to VCU, because that was the year the Rams went to the Final Four. Richmond boosters couldn't understand why VCU could go to seven straight NCAAs, while Mooney had only two trips to the tournament.

When Richmond *did* have a losing season in 2017–18, going 12-20, many boosters were screaming, "Off with his head!" Or at least his clipboard. Richmond had been decimated by injuries the previous season but had rebounded from a 3-10 start to finish a respectable 9-9 in conference play.

The Spiders had lost two key players to transfer during the off-season. Point guard Khwan Fore had joined the legion of graduate transfers—going to Louisville for his fifth year. De'Monte Buckingham, a sophomore who had averaged 12.2 points and 7 rebounds a game, was thrown off the team for what was publicly described as the catchall "violation of team rules." For Mooney to toss a key player like that, Buckingham had to have been a real problem.

And so, Richmond was again very young. None of the three seniors—Julius Johnson, Noah Yates, and Keith Oddo—were starters, and they *combined* to average 7.5 of the team's 70.1 points per game.

St. Francis interested me for an entirely different reason. The Terriers were one of four teams that had played Division 1 basketball since the formation of D-1 in 1947 and had never once reached the NCAA Tournament.

Three years earlier, I had done a series of stories for the *Washington Post* on the five teams that had never gotten to the Dance: Northwestern, St. Francis, the Citadel, William & Mary, and Army. Northwestern has since qualified, making the tournament in 2017.

Each of the schools had a unique story—many involving near misses. Army had employed two Hall of Fame coaches—Bob Knight and Mike Krzyzewski—but had been only to the NIT. In 1968, a 20-4 Army team had been invited to the NCAAs, but Knight had turned down the bid. In those days, the NIT was almost as prestigious as the NCAAs, and Knight thought his team could win the NIT. He *knew* the Cadets couldn't beat UCLA and Lew Alcindor. Nobody could.

St. Francis was located in downtown Brooklyn. I went to a Saturday afternoon game there, parking in a garage two blocks from the school. The problem was, I couldn't find the gym. I stood in front of one building that said "St. Francis College" and asked a passerby where the gym was.

"You're looking at it," he said. "Inside, straight ahead."

I was confused. The guy understood. "The entire college is in this building," he said.

Glenn Braica was the coach. He had grown up in Brooklyn, gone to Queens College, and coached in the New York area his entire career. He'd been Ron Ganulin's assistant at St. Francis for fourteen years, before working as an assistant at St. John's for six years. He was hired as the head coach in 2010, and after two difficult years he talked Ganulin into coming out of retirement to be his top assistant.

Ganulin had come close to scaling the NCAA mountain at St. Francis—twice winning the regular-season title in the Northeast Conference and twice losing the championship game in the tournament. Braica had done the same thing in 2015.

Once I had figured out where the building was, I sat with Braica and Ganulin for nearly two hours prior to their game against Fairleigh Dickinson. I felt completely at home—it was more three New Yorkers swapping stories than me interviewing the two of them. St. Francis had won the NEC regular-season title the previous season and hosted the tournament championship game, only to lose to archrival LIU Brooklyn.

"Couple plays away from the promised land," Braica said. "It was right there for us, and we couldn't quite get over that last hump." He paused. "Someday."

Someday hadn't come yet. St. Francis was consistently competitive in the NEC but hadn't yet won the tournament.

The Terriers had opened the season with an easy win over a Division 3 school and then had lost at Boston College by five—a more-than-respectable loss. Richmond had opened with a disappointing loss to Longwood, making the morning an important one.

I wasn't the only one who thought an eleven o'clock game was a good idea. Two of the three officials—Les Jones and Roger Ayers—were ACC veterans who had worked Final Fours. They had been happy to pick up an extra game, especially one that would be over in time for a late lunch. Brian Kersey, the ACC supervisor of officials—who also assigned Atlantic 10 officials—was there, and so was Bernadette

McGlade, the commissioner of the A-10 and a member of the NCAA basketball committee.

Heck, if they'd started at ten, NCAA president Mark Emmert might have showed up.

I had hoped for a tight game. I didn't get one.

St. Francis's last lead came off a Glenn Sanabria steal and layup that made it 17–16 with 13:16 left in the half. Richmond promptly went on a 9–0 run to lead 25–17 and never really looked back. A jumper by Nick Sherod, who would lead all scorers with 22 points, gave the Spiders a 48–35 halftime lead. The lead grew to 60–42 with 14:15 to go, and St. Francis never got the margin into single digits. The final was 88–66.

The Robins Center's capacity is 7,201—down from a little more than 9,000 when the building first opened in 1972. The lower figure came about when it was renovated in 2016, the multimillion-dollar redo designed to make the seating more comfortable and more fitting with Richmond's needs.

Six miles away, VCU's Siegel Center seats almost the identical number: 7,617. VCU's last nonsellout was in 2011, 134 games ago. On "Education Day," at Richmond the attendance was 6,851.

"I thought it was cool," said Richmond sophomore center Grant Golden, who had 20 points on the day and would go on to make second team all-conference in the A-10. "The kids kept the place loud all morning." He smiled. "Of course, a lot of the time they were cheering at the wrong time, but that was okay too. We appreciated the effort."

It was an impressive win for Richmond because, after losing to Longwood, there was no way to know how the Spiders might play.

"Maybe we should schedule more games for eleven," Golden said. "Although I have to say, a six-forty-five wake-up for pregame meal and shootaround isn't something I'd necessarily look forward to on a regular basis."

"If we play like that, I might get 'em up at six forty-five regardless of when tipoff is," said Mooney, laughing.

At the far end of the hall from the Richmond locker room, the St. Francis players showered and dressed quickly for the six-hour (they hoped) bus ride back to Brooklyn.

"The good news is we should be home at a reasonable hour," Braica said. "Traffic permitting. This is part of playing at a mid-major that people don't see. We played at Boston College Sunday, bused home, had one day at home, and then got on the bus to come here Tuesday. Hey, that's just the way it is."

If Braica had one consistent bright spot—including that morning—it was his point guard, five-foot-eleven-inch Glenn Sanabria, who was a grad student working toward an MBA, studying organizational management.

Sanabria wasn't like a lot of grad students playing college ball, in that he hadn't used his fifth year to transfer to a bigger school with the chance to play under brighter lights.

"Never occurred to me," he said. "I was either going to graduate and move on with my life or go to grad school here [St. Francis] and play one more year. I decided I wanted to play basketball for one last year."

Like a lot of players under six feet, Sanabria was largely overlooked by D-1 schools when he came out of high school on Staten Island. His first exposure to St. Francis was when the coaches at New Jersey Tech invited him to come see them play—at St. Francis.

He'd been a solid player as a freshman, then got hurt and missed his sophomore season. As a fourth-year junior he had averaged 12.2 points, 4.3 assists, and 2.7 rebounds. He was the team's leader—with the ball and without it.

He was hoping for a special final season. "We were picked last in the league last year and finished tied for second," he said. "I think we're good enough to compete in the NEC even if we didn't look that way today."

Walking in the direction of the bus, Braica admitted the day had been disappointing. "I didn't realize how good Golden was," he said. "Sometimes you can't really tell just looking at film. We got caught off guard a little bit. I told the kids not to pay any attention to the Longwood score, but hey, they're kids."

He smiled. "Live and learn I guess. I'm fifty-four and still learning."

It was 1:45 when I walked out of the Robins Center. The temperature was in the mid-fifties and, even though the game hadn't been as close as I'd hoped, it had been a fun day. The kind of hoops day I still love.

And I'd be home in plenty of time for dinner.

FROM 0-135 TO 1-135...
AND BEYOND

It might have been the greatest upset in the history of college basketball.

Late on the night of March 16, 2018, Virginia, the top-ranked team in the NCAA Tournament—the top seeded of the four No. 1 seeds—took the court in Charlotte, North Carolina, to play the University of Maryland–Baltimore County, which is known to most as UMBC.

When the game tipped off that night, shortly before ten o'clock, there had already been 135 games played in tournament history involving No. 1 seeds and No. 16 seeds. Every single one of those games, dating to 1985, had been won by the No. 1 seed. A handful had been close, but most had been—predictably—one-sided.

There was no real reason to think UVA-UMBC would be any different. The Cavaliers were 33-2. They had won the regular-season title in the ACC with a 17-1 record and then swept through the ACC Tournament. While some of their games stayed close for a while, there always seemed to be a burst coming from the Cavaliers that would put the game away.

UMBC was playing in the NCAA Tournament for only the second time and was thrilled to be there. Two years earlier, the Retrievers had won seven games, leading to the firing of Coach Aki Thomas and the hiring of Ryan Odom.

The name Odom was familiar to college basketball fans. Ryan's father, Dave Odom, had been a college head coach for twenty-two years—at East Carolina, Wake Forest, and South Carolina. At Wake Forest, he had recruited Tim Duncan, won two ACC titles, gone to eight NCAA Tournaments, and reached the elite eight in 1996. He had also won an NIT at Wake Forest and then won it twice more while at South Carolina.

"I'm not sure that's a star or a black mark on my résumé," he liked to joke.

A large chunk of Ryan Odom's childhood had been spent in Charlottesville. The Odoms had moved there in 1982 when Ryan was eight and his father had become Terry Holland's top assistant. The Odoms' house was a short bike ride away from University Hall, which was then Virginia's basketball arena.

"If I was a fan of any team growing up, it was probably Virginia," he said. "Those seven years were really my formative years as a basketball fan."

Ryan had played Division 3 basketball at Hampden-Sydney and then followed his father into the coaching business. The road hadn't always been smooth. He had moved up the ladder, starting as a graduate assistant at the University of South Florida and then moving to Furman, UNC Asheville, American, Virginia Tech, and UNC Charlotte.

In 2015, health issues had intervened in his life: one professionally, one personally. His son Connor, who was thirteen, had been diagnosed with obsessive-compulsive disorder and had to drop out of school for a while to deal with the disease.

Alan Major, the coach who had brought Odom to Charlotte and made him his top assistant, had taken a medical leave of absence in the summer of 2014 to deal with surgeries he needed involving his heart and his eyes. Odom had run the program—recruiting, off-season workouts—in his absence. Major had returned for the start of the season but had apparently come back too soon.

On January 6, with the team 6-7, Major announced he was taking another leave of absence. This time, Odom was in charge midseason. The 49ers went 8-11 the rest of the way. A week after the season ended, Major was fired—the official announcement, naturally, said that he and the school had mutually agreed to "part ways."

Odom and the other assistant coaches were also fired. Or mutually parted. It was a low moment for Odom and for his family. At forty, for the first time in his life, he was jobless.

Fortunately, his unemployment didn't last long. Less than a week after the Charlotte staff was formally let go, Odom was hired as the head coach at Division 2 Lenoir-Rhyne. The athletic director was Neill McGeachy—the same Neill McGeachy who had coached Duke in 1974 for one season while Dave Odom was the coach at Durham High School. Ryan had been born in Durham that year. Dave Odom's friendship with McGeachy dated to those days.

The hiring made sense: a young coach who had extensive Division 1 experience as an assistant and had stepped into a difficult breach the previous winter in Charlotte.

The move paid off for McGeachy. Odom's team won twenty-one games and reached the quarterfinals of the NCAA Division 2 tournament. That performance got the attention of—among others—UMBC athletic director Tim Hall.

Hall had been at UMBC for three years. He had arrived with the basketball program in a downward spiral. Aki Thomas had taken over as coach on the eve of the 2012–13 season, and the Retrievers had gone 8-23.

Hall felt Thomas deserved time to try to turn things around. Three years later, after UMBC had gone 7-25, making Thomas's four-year record 28-95, Hall had to make a change. A new $90 million state-funded arena was due to open in the winter of 2017, and UMBC needed to make some progress on its old court before it moved to its new one.

Hall hired Odom as his new coach.

Every coach hired to take over a losing program talks about "changing the culture." Odom knew he had to change the culture radically. Thomas had left behind some talented players, but they knew very little about winning—because they had grown so accustomed to losing.

There was no better example of that than Jairus Lyles. He had come out of one of the great high school basketball programs in history, DeMatha Catholic, which was thirty miles from UMBC's campus, in Hyattsville, Maryland.

Lyles had been heavily recruited coming out of high school and had landed at VCU—at the height of "Shaka-mania" in Richmond. The Rams had gone to the Final Four in 2011, and Coach Shaka Smart was attracting a lot of talent.

Lyles found himself lost on a team with great depth at the guard position. He played exactly forty-four minutes all season—most during garbage time at the end of games—and scored a total of 13 points. Like a lot of young players who want to play more—and shoot more—he opted to transfer, moving to Robert Morris in the fall of 2014. Even before the season started, Lyles decided he'd made a mistake, so he transferred again, this time close to home—UMBC.

He knew the Retrievers needed talent and that he would get plenty of opportunity to play and to shoot once he was eligible.

He did. Lyles averaged 23 points per game in 2016, given the green light to shoot pretty much anytime he touched the ball. One of Odom's first jobs was to convince him to score *less* because he had teammates around him whom he could make better by creating space for them.

Additionally, Odom had recruited a point guard to take some pressure off Lyles and let him play off the ball more. K. J. Maura was from Puerto Rico and had been playing at a junior college in Florida. He had been overlooked by all the major programs and most of the mid-majors because he was tiny. UMBC listed him as five-eight and 140 pounds. He was no more than five-six, and if he weighed 140 pounds, it was with a weight belt on.

But Odom saw something in him other coaches didn't: a knack for the game, a kind of intangible feel for how to play that isn't easy to see.

"Ryan saw what the rest of us missed," said John Gallagher, the coach at the University of Hartford. "We looked at his size and said, 'He won't be able to guard anyone.' Ryan looked at him and said, 'He'll make other point guards crazy.'"

When Odom looked at Maura, he harkened back to his boyhood, when five-foot-three-inch Tyrone (Muggsy) Bogues had terrorized the entire ACC. Bogues was shorter than Maura, but he was built like a fire hydrant. He was quick enough to go *under* people to take the ball from them; strong enough to drive past them and get into the lane.

Maura had Bogues's quickness, but not his strength. But he had that special knack—especially at crucial moments. In his two years at UMBC, no one could remember him missing a free throw in the final minutes of a close game.

In Odom's first season, the Retrievers went from seven wins to twenty-one wins. They went from the bottom of the America East to a tie for fourth place. When they were bounced from the America East Tournament in overtime by New Hampshire, Hall was willing to invest in playing extra games by accepting a bid to the College Insider Tournament—the CIT.

For years, college basketball had two postseason tournaments: the NCAAs and the NIT. For a long time, the NIT was considered almost as important as the NCAAs. Until 1975, only twenty-five teams made the NCAAs, meaning some very good teams played in the NIT every year.

When the NCAA expanded—first to thirty-two teams, then to forty-eight, fifty-three, and in 1985 to sixty-four—the NIT was watered down considerably.

As more and more teams moved into Division 1 in search of TV and postseason gold (dollars), promoters saw an opportunity. Even after the NCAA expanded to sixty-eight teams in 2011 and the NIT, which had briefly been at forty teams, settled back to thirty-two, that meant "only" a hundred teams were reaching the postseason.

That left almost 250 teams (at the time) without a place to play, some with impressive records. Thus, in 2008, the sixteen-team College Basketball Invitational (CBI) was launched and, a year later, the College Insider Tournament began with a twenty-six-team field.

The two were different. The CBI was more about bigger-name teams willing to pay a $50,000 entry fee to participate and was willing to take anyone, regardless of record. The CIT focused more on mid-majors, and a team had to have at least a .500 record to participate. If you wanted a home game, you paid for it. If you were willing to play on the road, there was no fee, but you paid your own expenses.

In short, forty-two teams paid to play postseason. To some degree it was a promoter's scam, preying on teams and coaches that needed to claim "postseason" on their résumé. But it did give some good mid-major teams snubbed by the NIT the chance to keep playing.

Hall and Odom agreed that UMBC, with only one senior—Will Darley—graduating, could use the extra experience and it was worth paying for—literally. And so Hall put up the $30,000 so the Retrievers could host their first-round game against Fairfield. UMBC won. Then, still paying to play at home, the Retrievers beat St. Francis of Pennsylvania and then Liberty, before losing to Texas A&M Corpus Christi in the semifinals.

The four extra games were valuable, and the three wins pushed their record from 18-12 to 21-13. A twenty-win season doesn't mean as much in college basketball as it once did, but it still has meaning. Only UMBC's 2008 team, which won twenty-four games and had been the first in school history to reach the Division 1 NCAA Tournament, had won more often.

Odom recruited a number of new players for the 2017–18 season, but his key recruit was already on campus: Jairus Lyles.

Even though he'd gone to three schools, Lyles was on schedule to graduate in four years. That meant he could opt to transfer to another school to play his fifth year (since he'd sat one out as a transfer) someplace with a higher basketball pedigree than UMBC's.

This is known as the graduate-transfer rule. As with many NCAA rules, it was well intended when it first began. The notion was that if a player in any sport had earned his or her undergraduate degree, had eligibility left, and wanted to play as a graduate student but their school didn't offer a postgraduate program in which they had interest, they could transfer to a school that did offer such a program.

In the simplest terms, if you want to study law and you're at a school with no law school, you can transfer someplace that has a law school. Or a medical school or an MBA program.

Naturally, the rule has been completely abused. Every Division 1 basketball staff in the country has a list of potential graduate transfers. Whether a school has an academic program that makes it more suitable for a player is completely irrelevant. Even the NCAA website mentions the fact that most players make very little progress in the direction of a postgraduate degree.

A top mid-major player like Lyles will be avidly pursued by nationally ranked teams looking to add depth and experience to their teams. The temptation is understandable—players who have played in relative obscurity are suddenly being offered the spotlight.

Lyles certainly could have gone to a big-name program. But he had become close to UMBC president Freeman A. Hrabowski III, a self-described "math nerd" who often informally counsels the school's athletes academically.

Hrabowski is not your typical college president by any stretch. Most are glorified fund-raisers who wield PhDs as if they are absolute proof that they are always the smartest person in the room.

Hrabowski grew up in Birmingham, Alabama, and at the age of twelve took part in a civil rights march led by Dr. Martin Luther King. He was among those arrested and spent several days in jail.

"Arguably the most important moment of my childhood," he said. "It shaped a lot of my views about the world."

Hrabowski—who has a PhD but, unlike so many of his fellow presidents, never introduces himself as "Dr. Hrabowski"—came to UMBC in 1992 and has transformed the school, notably in terms of minority students. In 2009, *Time* magazine named Hrabowski one of the ten best college presidents in the United States and three years later selected him as one of the one hundred most influential people in the world. That same year he was named by President Barack Obama to chair the White House Initiative on Educational Excellence for African Americans.

Hrabowski hardly comes across as the academic that he is. His humor is frequently self-deprecating, and he has a laugh that takes over a room.

Getting to know Hrabowski was an unexpected bonus for me after Odom asked me if I would be willing to do color on UMBC's home telecasts during his first season at the school.

I had known Odom since he was a boy, having first met his father while I was in college and he was the coach at Durham High School. So, when Ryan and his boss, Tim Hall, asked if I could work on some of their games as part of a new TV package put together by the America East Conference, I said yes—in part because I've had the chance to do a number of mid-major games on TV in recent years and enjoyed it greatly, and also because of my longtime friendship with the Odom family.

I never dreamed Odom would be able to transform the Retrievers into a competitive team so quickly or how entertaining the games might be. Or that I would get to know Hrabowski and come to understand what a remarkable life he's led.

Odom and Hrabowski had about as close to a perfect coach–president relationship as you could hope to have: Hrabowski deferred to Odom in all matters basketball, and Odom deferred to Hrabowski in everything else.

"When he comes in to talk to the team [which Odom asks him to do on occasion], he has their complete attention," Odom said. "He doesn't talk to them in clichés, he talks in specifics—what's right, what's wrong, what's important. He never goes on too long. You never see eyes glazing over when he's speaking."

With Lyles being recruited by big-time programs, Odom made no attempt to convince him to stay at UMBC. He explained the options he had and then suggested he talk to Hrabowski before he made a decision.

"More than anything, it was talking to him that helped me decide to stay," Lyles said, almost a year later, while carrying a 4.0 GPA in a graduate-level computer science major. "He said to me, 'I don't really know much about basketball, but I do know about the importance of legacy.' He said if I went somewhere else, no doubt I'd be a good player and contribute to a team that had good players before me and would have good players after me. But if I stayed at UMBC, I had a chance to have a real legacy—one that might last forever. That resonated."

With Lyles and Maura back, and some of the team's young front-court players a year older and better, UMBC established itself as a solid America East contender in Odom's second year. They went from being a nearly automatic win for conference opponents to an extremely tough out.

Except for Vermont. For years, the Catamounts had been the team everyone in the America East aspired to be. Will Brown had put together a very good program at Albany, and Stony Brook had its moments too. But most years, the road to the NCAA Tournament went through Vermont's Patrick Gym.

Beginning in 2003, under Tom Brennan and then under Mike Lonergan and John Becker, Vermont was an America East contender every year. The Catamounts had played postseason ten times—six NCAAs and four NITs—and had been the regular-season champions eight times, including 2018.

They had beaten UMBC twenty-one times in a row coming into the 2017–18 season, although the games the previous season had at least been competitive.

Unfortunately for UMBC, the new basketball arena was ready to be opened in February—just in time for Vermont's trip to Catonsville, the town where UMBC is located.

UMBC was 7-2 in conference play on the afternoon of February 3—its two losses coming at Vermont and at Albany. Vermont was 9-0 in the America East.

If Odom had had his druthers, the new building—the Retriever Events Center (REC)—would not have been opened until the following season. His team had grown very comfortable in the old place—the 2,100-seat Retriever Athletic Center (RAC)—which was old and rickety but felt like *home*.

"It almost has to take away some of your home-court advantage, especially moving in midseason," Odom said. "You haven't practiced there every day, it's about as new to you as it is to a visiting team. But we have to do what the state tells us to do."

Since the sparkling-new arena had been built with state funds—$90 million worth—it had to be used as soon as building inspectors gave it a certificate of occupancy.

And so the opener, with a near-sellout crowd of 4,721 present, was against Vermont. For twenty-five minutes, the game was close, Vermont leading 46–40. And then the Catamounts stopped missing shots and the Retrievers stopped making them. Vermont outscored UMBC 35–13 over the final thirteen minutes, and the final was an embarrassing 81–53.

"That team is good enough to win a game or two in the NCAA Tournament," Dave Odom said when it was over. "You make them a twelve or thirteen seed, and whoever they play is going to have their hands full."

Odom and his wife, Lynn, had traveled north from their home in Winston-Salem to be there for the grand opening of the new building. Like almost everyone else who was there, they assumed Vermont would be the America East's representative in the NCAA Tournament.

There was little doubt that for everyone in the conference, the road to an NCAA bid would have to go through Patrick Gym—again.

Which is exactly where UMBC found itself on the morning of March 10. The America East championship game always begins at 11 a.m. on ESPN on selection weekend Saturday, in order to clear the stage for the glamour teams that will play conference semifinals and finals in the afternoon and evening.

The Retrievers had finished second in the America East and had beaten UMass Lowell (after trailing by eleven at halftime) and Hartford to reach the conference final for the first time in ten years. Vermont, the top seed, had easily defeated Maine and Stony Brook to put itself back in the championship game.

Odom knew if his team could keep the game close and weather the runs, that would inevitably get the crowd in the packed gym going, and the pressure would be on Vermont in the final minutes.

After all, the Catamounts' win streak against UMBC was now at twenty-three and, because they had been so good all year, anything less than an NCAA trip was going to be a letdown.

This is one of the dangers of being a perennially dominant team in a one-bid conference. As good as Vermont had been all season, there was no way the know-nothings on the NCAA basketball committee were going to give it an at-large bid if it didn't win the conference tournament.

In addition to dominating the America East, Vermont had beaten a number of very solid teams in nonconference play and had lost at Kentucky by *four*. But the committee would see only computer print-outs that would, for various reasons, rank Vermont behind big-name programs with built-in advantages a mid-major can never have.

And so, as the game rocked back and forth, the pressure on the home team continued to build. Vermont took a 35–28 lead late in the first half, but UMBC closed on a 9–0 run, ending with a Lyles three just before the buzzer.

Vermont then opened the second half on a 12–2 run to open the lead to eight and pushed it to 57–48 with 8:21 left. It appeared that the Retrievers were going to get "valiant effort" points, but little else, for their trip north.

But with the finish line in sight, Vermont began to take quick shots and, once again, UMBC worked its way back into the game. Maura tied it at 58 with 5:13 to go with a three, and from that point on every possession felt critical—which made sense since an entire season of effort was on the line for both teams.

Lyles tied the game again, this time at 62, with a short jump shot with 1:02 left.

Vermont coach John Becker opted not to call time-out to set up a play. He had an experienced team and knew exactly what he wanted to do: get the ball into the hands of two-time America East player of the year Trae Bell-Haynes and let him create.

Bell-Haynes saw an opening and drove to the basket, appearing to have a layup. But Joe Sherburne came to help at the last possible second and blocked the shot. Max Curran grabbed it for UMBC and, stunningly, with under thirty seconds to play the Retrievers had the ball with the game tied and the shot clock off.

No way was Odom going to call time to let Becker set up his defense. Like Becker, he wanted the ball in the hands of his best player—Lyles—who already had 24 points in the game.

Lyles dribbled the ball outside the key as the clock wound down. Bell-Haynes was on him, not wanting to go for a steal that would create an opening for Lyles. Becker opted not to double-team to try to get the ball out of Lyles's hands, because he didn't want to chance putting Lyles on the foul line.

Lyles dribbled the clock down. With three seconds left, he began to make a move to clear space for himself, backing his dribble off just a little. Too late, Bell-Haynes realized what Lyles was doing and lunged at him, hand in the air.

But Lyles had space and was squared up. He released the shot from beyond the three-point line, and it cleanly swished as the clock hit zero.

Shockingly, UMBC, which hadn't led for the game's final 19:26, had won. The Retrievers were going back to the Dance for the first time since 2008 and had finally ended their twenty-three-game losing streak to Vermont.

It was an improbable victory, the kind that would go largely unnoticed away from the UMBC campus and outside the orbit of the America East Conference. The Retrievers would go on the board the next evening as a No. 16 seed, lined up to have forty minutes of semi-fame and then simply be added to the list of sixteenth seeds who had been victims of power-school top seeds.

But for the UMBC players, not so far removed from 7-21 and from being invisible on their own campus, this was a moment they would carry with them forever, regardless of what came next. For them, this was a true shining moment, just without the schmaltz of the song blaring from a PA system inside an NFL stadium.

Patrick Gym seats about three thousand people. Most were stunned when Lyles's shot went in. But as the UMBC kids celebrated, they all knew they'd been part of something special.

I wasn't in Patrick Gym that morning—for several reasons. I was at the Palestra for the Ivy League semifinals. In 2017, the Ivy League had become the last conference to play a conference tournament but—naturally—didn't go all the way, allowing only the top four teams to advance to the tournament.

I was at the Palestra for the *Post* because there were a number of potentially good columns, but also because the America East championship game was on ESPN. That meant the network brought in its own "talent" to do the game. Even if ESPN had decided to use the play-by-play/color men who did the games in the league all season, it would have been Vermont's game anyway.

So, I stood around a TV in the Palestra's media room—normally a room used for Penn season-ticket holders during the regular season—and watched the last few minutes.

I'm a fan of Vermont's John Becker; I think he's one of the most underrated coaches in the country. I'm also good friends with Tom Brennan, who had first brought Vermont to national prominence with three straight America East titles and a stunning first-round upset of Syracuse in the 2005 NCAA Tournament.

"I'll never have to buy another meal in Burlington the rest of my life," Brennan had joked after the Syracuse game.

He wasn't far wrong. He had retired after that 2005 season and was unofficially the mayor of Patrick Gym. Officially, the court had been named for him.

If Vermont made the NCAA Tournament, there was almost no doubt I'd be rooting for the Catamounts to pull a first-round upset like the one they had pulled off thirteen seasons earlier.

But in the instance of the Vermont-UMBC game, I'd be lying if I said I wasn't grinding my teeth, hoping UMBC would pull off the upset that day. By then, I'd been doing UMBC games on TV for two seasons. I'd gotten to know and like all the coaches and players and had become a huge fan of Freeman Hrabowski.

And so, as the final minutes melted down, I stood in front of the TV, then walked away—paced for a bit, drank a Coke (bad for me in every possible way)—and then walked back.

As Lyles dribbled the clock down in the final seconds, I knew exactly what was going to happen. Lyles was going to take the last shot. Looking at Vermont's defense—the lane jammed, Bell-Haynes giving Lyles some space—I knew Lyles was going to take a jump shot just before the buzzer.

And I was convinced he was going to make it. I hoped no one could read my mind as the clock went under five seconds. I was afraid if anyone knew I was thinking, *He's going to make it,* it would be bad karma for UMBC.

And then Lyles made the shot. "Holy s——," I said aloud. "They did it. They really did it."

The next night I was in the newsroom at the *Post,* as I always am on Selection Sunday when the brackets are unveiled. In the back of my mind, I was thinking I might go to Dayton if UMBC was sent there for the "First Four," as the NCAA now calls the four play-in games played there on Tuesday and Wednesday of week one of the tournament.

If the Retrievers played another No. 16 seed for the right to play a No. 1 seed, I would have the chance to see them play a winnable game. From there, I could drive to Pittsburgh for the first- and second-round games on Thursday and Saturday.

UMBC didn't get sent to Dayton. Instead, it was sent to Charlotte for a first-round game Friday night against Virginia. For Ryan Odom, it was a bittersweet matchup. He would be facing the school he'd grown up rooting for in the city where his coaching career had bottomed out three years earlier.

I knew UMBC had no chance to win. Stay close for a while if it could make shots from the outside? Perhaps. But win? That wasn't going to happen.

I'd written about lower-seeded teams often in the past, and I knew the drill. For the players, the highlight might be the open-practice day prior to the first round. They would work out on the same court as the glamour teams and go to the same interview room. Ryan Odom would sit in the same seat where Tony Bennett would sit. The players would look into the myriad TV cameras and explain that they had all the respect in the world for their opponent but expected to win the game. The players would be awed when they were introduced to the network-TV types who would be doing the game.

In Charlotte, Odom and his players were introduced to Jim Nantz, Grant Hill, and Bill Raftery. For them, it was like meeting royalty.

The mentality of most 1-16 meetings was summed up best in 1998 when Navy, a No. 16 seed, met North Carolina, a No. 1 seed, in the Hartford Civic Center.

Sitapha Savané was Navy's starting center. "When I walked out to jump center with Antawn Jamison, I didn't know whether to shake his hand or ask for an autograph," he said after his team had lost, 88–52. "I'd seen him play on TV so many times, it was a thrill just to stand next to him."

I knew UMBC shot the ball well enough that if it had a hot-shooting night from three-point range, it might keep the game competitive. But sooner or later, the Cavaliers pack-line defense would start to extend to the three-point line; there would be a 15-2 burst, and that would be that. The Retrievers would go home to relive their miraculous morning in Patrick Gym.

And so I opted for Pittsburgh, which made perfect sense. Easiest trip—drive under four hours. Perfect logistics—hotel across the street from the arena. Plenty of column potential: Villanova, which I thought was the best team in the tournament; Duke, always writable; Trae Young, Oklahoma's freshman sensation; and a semilocal team for the *Post*—Radford, which *did* go to Dayton and won the right to play Villanova in another 1-16 matchup.

Plus, I was pretty certain the second-round games Saturday would be in the afternoon, meaning I could get home Saturday night.

And then I sat in my hotel room late Friday night and watched UMBC play Virginia. I was going to stay up as long as the game was competitive. Once Virginia began to pull away, I'd go to sleep.

Except it never happened. It was 21–21 at halftime, in many ways a typical Virginia game. The Cavaliers always played at a slower-than-slow pace, and sometimes it took a while for their pack-line defense to wear a team down.

I actually dozed off during the endless twenty-minute halftime and woke up just in time to see Joe Sherburne make a layup while being fouled at the start of the second half to put UMBC ahead 24–21. No one knew it at that moment, but Virginia would never catch up.

Lyles was unconscious. He finished the game with 28 points on 9-of-11 shooting (3-of-4 from three-point range) and seemed to make a basket every time UVA appeared ready to start a run. Virginia, a team that made it a habit to squeeze the life out of teams with second-half runs, never scored on *two* straight possessions in the final twenty minutes.

Astonishing.

More astonishing: against one of the best defenses in the country, UMBC shot just under 68 percent in the second half, and Maura repeatedly beat Virginia's guards up the floor to set up UMBC's offense.

"Lyles was great, absolutely great," Virginia coach Tony Bennett said, months later. "But the kid we absolutely couldn't handle was Maura—at both ends of the court."

The Retrievers became instant national celebrities, the upset compared to the 1980 U.S. hockey team at Lake Placid, unknown Buster Douglas knocking out Mike Tyson in 1989, and the New York Jets and Joe Namath in Super Bowl III.

In basketball there was no tournament upset to compare it to, since a No. 16 had never beaten a No. 1. The game brought up most often was the December 1982 contest between Chaminade, an NAIA team, and—yes—Virginia, ranked No. 1 in the country at the time and led by three-time national player of the year Ralph Sampson.

Terry Holland's top assistant coach at the time? Dave Odom.

The Retrievers, no doubt exhausted from celebrating, lost their second-round game two nights later, 50–43, to Kansas State. But nothing could change what they had done. Odom became a celebrity, especially in the Baltimore-Washington area. His name was bandied about for a number of jobs, but none appealed to him enough to leave UMBC—especially after Hall got him a big raise.

When Notre Dame coach Mike Brey was at Delaware in the 1990s, he described the life of a mid-major from a one-bid league this way: "For us, winning our conference tournament and getting to the NCAA Tournament is like a power school getting to the Final Four," he said. "If you win a game, it's like winning the national championship."

College basketball has changed since then, and experienced mid-major teams now have a better chance to compete with freshmen- and sophomore-laden power school teams. George Mason, Butler, VCU, and Loyola Chicago have all made the Final Four—Butler the national championship game twice.

But for UMBC, a school playing in the NCAA Tournament for the second time in history, the Virginia win wasn't just historic, it was like getting to the Final Four—at least.

"I woke up the next morning," Hrabowski said, "and thought to myself, 'Did that really happen?'"

It had. Now it was eight months later, and Ryan Odom felt he had one mission for his 2018–19 team: "No looking in the rearview mirror," he said. "Eyes on the road ahead."

That would be easier said than done.

THE REARVIEW
MIRROR

And so it was that I walked into the Retriever Events Center on the night of November 12, knowing everything was now different for UMBC.

The two new banners hanging from the rafters were tangible evidence of the changes. They had been raised ten days earlier during "Retriever Madness," an annual preseason event similar to the ones many college teams hold to try to get their fan base fired up for the coming season.

Once, when college basketball teams could not begin formal practices until October 15, they were known as "Midnight Madness," first created by then–Maryland coach Lefty Driesell and copied nationwide. Now, with there being essentially no rules governing when practice can begin, fewer teams hold "madness" events, and they are almost never at midnight.

Each black-and-gold banner had a UMBC logo at the top of it with a rendering of the Retriever mascot (a Retriever is an Egyptian-bred dog). One banner, on a yellow background with black lettering, said: "Men's Basketball . . . 2018 America East Champions . . . 25-11."

The other, on a white background with blue lettering, said: "Men's Basketball . . . 2018 NCAA Tournament Second Round . . . #16 UMBC-74 . . . #1 Virginia-54."

If the banners weren't enough evidence of the new world UMBC was living in, my conversation earlier that day with Manhattan coach Steve Masiello made it even clearer. Manhattan was the opponent that night and, as I always do to prepare for any game I'm working on television, I had called both coaches.

"A year ago, I'd have had to convince my players that this was a good team," Masiello said to me. "They'd hear UMBC and say, 'What's that spell?' Now I don't have to say a word about that. They know exactly who UMBC is and how good a team we're facing."

Of course, the UMBC team Manhattan would be playing that night was considerably different from the one that had hung those two banners. The star guards who had keyed the team's run in March, Jairus Lyles and K. J. Maura, were gone. So was the team's sixth man and third guard, Jourdan Grant.

That was a lot of talent and experience gone, especially in a sport where guards tend to rule. Size has become a bonus for teams, but it is not a necessity in what has become a perimeter-oriented game.

Ryan Odom had recruited another K.J.—K. J. Jackson, a junior college guard from Texas—to step into the starting lineup. He'd also added two freshmen he thought had potential: R. J. Eytle-Rock, who, like sophomore center Dan Akin, was from Great Britain, and Jose Placer, who had grown up in Orlando, but whose parents were originally from Puerto Rico, which had allowed him to play on Puerto Rico's nineteen-and-under team the previous summer.

Odom knew it would take a while for the new guards to feel comfortable on the Division 1 level, but he was hoping the experience he had in the frontcourt, with everyone returning and transfer swingman Rickie Council (who had played at Providence for two years) eligible, would balance the loss of the three guards.

Against Manhattan, there were few signs of trouble. The Retrievers routed the Jaspers, 75–52. It wasn't until later that everyone realized that Manhattan, which would finish the season 11-21, just wasn't as good as Masiello's teams had been in the past.

The first tangible evidence of Odom's belief that this team was going to have growing pains came in a loss at home to American on the Saturday after Thanksgiving. In a tight game, the absence of Lyles and Maura in the endgame was noticeable. It happened again a couple of weeks later against a not-very-good Towson team, when UMBC blew a late lead and lost in double overtime.

Odom knew this was all part of the process. He had hoped Jackson could run the team but was finding he was probably more effective playing off the ball. In a win at Drexel in early December, he played Eytle-Rock, the freshman, at the point throughout the second half and Jackson went off, scoring 27 points.

When conference play began, UMBC was 8-7, identical to its record a year earlier, but a little bit deceiving. The 2017–18 team had lost competitive games at SMU, Arizona, and Maryland and had played three games without Lyles while he sat out with a concussion.

The 2018–19 team had played two teams from power conferences, Marquette and Penn State, and had lost badly in both games.

Conference play, as always, would be the test. The Retrievers had been picked third in preseason behind Vermont and Hartford, whose top seven players were all seniors.

The start was hardly encouraging. UMBC had to come from thirteen points down in the second half to win at home against Maine—which had been picked last in the league.

Then came a disastrous trip to Hartford and UMass Lowell. There was no shame in losing on the road to a good Hartford team, but UMBC appeared to have the game won late. It had turned a nine-point halftime deficit into a five-point lead with under two minutes to go, but missed free throws and a mental error by Joe Sherburne, arguably the highest-basketball-IQ player on the team, gave Hartford a chance. Sherburne fouled Hartford's J. R. Lynch with three seconds to go and the Retrievers leading 59–57. Lynch calmly sank both free throws and the Hawks won in overtime.

"It was disappointing because we had the game won," Odom said later. "But we didn't play badly. We just missed some free throws, which you can't do against a good team, and then Joe made a mental mistake—which you don't expect.

"Okay, one we let get away. Move on."

Except when they moved 115 miles north and east to Lowell, they didn't move on. "Didn't show up," Odom said. "Beginning to end."

Lowell led the entire game en route to a 64–53 victory. In the locker room afterward, Odom didn't rail, but he let his team know that what had just happened was unacceptable.

"You need to understand that you can't just play with urgency some of the time," he said. "You have to play every possession with urgency, not just in games, but in practice. You better come to practice on Monday prepared to really get after it. What we've got here right now simply isn't good enough."

Odom's not a screamer. When he does raise his voice, his players notice. He's more analytical, more likely to point out mistakes on tape than to throw things around the locker room. But when he walked onto the practice floor Monday, he didn't like what he was seeing or feeling. When practice started, he knew his instincts had been correct.

"It wasn't that they lacked effort," he said. "There was dread, almost fear on every play. They were dreading what was going to happen. It was a basketball practice—nothing terrible was going to happen to them. It's not as if I go off every time we lose a game or even a couple of games. But they were playing scared—in a practice."

He shrugged and smiled. "There was only one thing left to do," he said. "I went off on them—really let them have it. I told them what was going on had to stop, that there were no excuses left, and that we were a long way from last year in every possible way.

"I think I got their attention. Things started to change after that. We weren't perfect by any means, but we started playing the way we had to play to have a chance to compete."

UMBC was 9-9, 1-2 in conference play. There was a lot of season left.

6

SAFETY SCHOOL

The night after UMBC easily beat Manhattan, Harvard traveled eighty-five miles west on the Massachusetts Turnpike to play the University of Massachusetts.

The game was Harvard's third of the season. They had played their now-traditional opening game a week earlier against MIT, which has an excellent Division 3 program. The Engineers (what else could you possibly call their teams?) had been coached for twenty-four years by Larry Anderson. They had been to the D-3 tournament eight times in the previous ten seasons and had reached the Final Four in 2012 and the elite eight a year earlier.

The two schools are located more or less side by side in Cambridge. Rockwell Cage, the former airplane hangar where MIT plays, is less than three miles from Lavietes Pavilion, which is just across the Charles River from Harvard's campus. All of Harvard's athletic facilities are actually in Boston, and athletes routinely walk across the Anderson Memorial Bridge for practice each day.

For MIT, the game is a chance to test itself against a solid Division 1 opponent to start the season. For Harvard, it means it can play an opener at home. Getting non–Ivy League teams to come to Lavietes is extremely difficult—especially now that Harvard has become a tough out.

What makes the game unique for Harvard is that MIT may be the only school on its schedule that can claim to be at least as challenging academically as Harvard. Each November, a handful of MIT students make the trip to Lavietes for the game.

"The highlight," said Harvard coach Tommy Amaker, "is when their students chant 'safety school' at our guys. It's great."

Amaker was starting his twelfth season at Harvard. He'd been the only junior starter on Mike Krzyzewski's first Final Four team at Duke in 1986, a cerebral point guard who was as good an on-the-ball defender as any college point guard I'd ever seen.

That 1985–86 season was the one I spent at Indiana researching *A Season on the Brink*. On a Monday in February, Bob Knight gave his players a day off after a Sunday game and I drove to Notre Dame to see Maryland play the Irish. Two days earlier, Maryland had lost at Duke and point guard Keith Gatlin had sat the game out with a bad back. Duke won easily in spite of Len Bias scoring 41 points.

When I walked into the Joyce Center that night, the first person I saw was Maryland coach Lefty Driesell, pacing the hallway outside his locker room. I asked whether Gatlin was going to be able to play that night.

"Oh yeah," Lefty said. "He's fine."

"But I heard he hurt his back and couldn't play at Duke Saturday."

Lefty laughed. "He just had a case of Amaka-back."

A lot of point guards had Amaka-back during Amaker's four-year Duke career, during which he started every single game. He was drafted in the third round of the 1987 NBA draft, but was a late cut by the Seattle Supersonics. His size—six feet and 165 pounds dripping weight—and the fact that he wasn't a great shooter made him an NBA long shot in spite of his superb college career. After three days with a CBA team in Wyoming, he decided the life of a journeyman basketball player wasn't for him, and he returned to Duke to pursue an MBA.

Two years later, Krzyzewski hired him as a graduate assistant while he was finishing his MBA. Not certain whether he wanted to coach when he began working for Krzyzewski, Amaker ended up staying nine years and eventually became Krzyzewski's top assistant.

He was hired as the head coach at Seton Hall in 1997 and four years later took over at Michigan in the midst of the "Fab Five" scandal that led to two Final Four banners being taken down by the school and the Wolverines being declared ineligible for postseason play in 2003.

He was 108-84 in six years at Michigan but never made the NCAA

Tournament, just missing on a couple of occasions, while winning the NIT in 2004. At Michigan that wasn't good enough, and after going 19-13 in 2007, he was fired.

Which turned out to be one of the best things to ever happen to him. That spring, Harvard was looking for a new coach. Frank Sullivan had coached the Crimson for sixteen seasons and had won more games—178—than any other coach in school history. In a league dominated by Penn and Princeton (one or the other won the Ivy League title all sixteen of those seasons), he had twice finished tied for second and had kept Harvard respectable, even though Harvard's academic admissions minimums for basketball players were higher than the Ivy League's minimums.

The Crimson had been 8-8 that winter, 1-1 in the Ivy League, when they lost their best player, seven-foot-tall Brian Cusworth, because of a Harvard rule that required athletes to graduate in eight semesters. Cusworth had sat out his sophomore season with a stress fracture in his foot and had left school second semester because it was almost impossible for him to get around campus.

Even though both NCAA and Ivy League rules allowed him a fifth year to complete his eligibility, Harvard's rules said he had to graduate in eight semesters. He had been on campus for seven at the start of the 2006–07 season and had to choose whether to play first or second semester. He chose the first because it meant he got to play sixteen games instead of twelve. Without their best player, the Crimson went 4-8. A player like Cusworth—who played professionally overseas for six years—would no doubt have helped Harvard win several more games.

Athletic director Bob Scalise told Sullivan prior to Harvard's final two games that his contract wouldn't be renewed. Other than his wife Susan, Sullivan told no one, including his players. The day after Harvard finished the season, Sullivan went to see each of his players individually to tell them he'd been fired.

"I came into their lives when I recruited them individually," he said. "I thought I should go out of their lives the same way."

I had become close to Sullivan during his time at Harvard. We had even talked about a book project that would have involved me spending a year as a volunteer coach on his staff. Even my woeful presence might have helped, since Frank had only two full-time assistants at a time when most staffs had four assistants.

Given that Harvard had more stringent academic standards than the schools it had to regularly compete with and Frank had kept the team respectable year in and year out, I was furious with the firing. I even scolded Harvard publicly during a commentary on *The Sports Reporters*.

The next day I got a call from Amaker—who I had known since high school. He was a DC kid, who had gone to W. T. Woodson High School in northern Virginia. I had first written about him in a piece about how a high school star chooses his college for the *Post*'s Sunday "Outlook" section.

"I think I might have a chance to get the Harvard job," he said. "What do you think?"

I was torn. Part of me thought Amaker would be perfect for Harvard. He wasn't your typical college coach in many ways. He had an MBA, was well-read and thoughtful, and, I believed, would work well with the kind of players Harvard might recruit.

But I also knew if he coached under the same conditions that Sullivan had coached under, he'd be taking on a Sisyphean task. I explained that to him and what had happened to Frank.

"Do you think," he asked, "Frank would be willing to talk to me? I'd like to know more from someone with firsthand knowledge."

I told him I would ask Frank. Let's be honest: a lot of coaches who had been thrown overboard by a school wouldn't give a damn what happened there next; might very well root for his old team to lose every game it ever played.

That's not Frank Sullivan.

"Of course I'll talk to him," he said. "I want the kids I recruited to have the best possible coach going forward."

They did get the best coach possible—Amaker. After talking to Frank, Tommy took the job. Technically, Harvard's academic standards didn't change. But he got the school to agree that admissions would look at the players he presented on a case-by-case basis, not just turn them down based strictly on numbers. The football and hockey teams were already receiving that benefit of the doubt.

Sullivan had left behind some good players—notably Jeremy Lin, a guard from California overlooked by the big-time programs. Harvard steadily improved as Amaker brought in better and better players.

The Crimson were 8-22 his first season, then 14-14, and 21-7 in his third—Lin's senior year. They finished 10-4, third in the Ivy League (behind Penn and Princeton), and accepted a bid to the CIT. It was the school's first postseason bid of any kind since it had played in the 1946 NCAA Tournament.

That was the start of a string of six straight seasons with at least twenty wins. Harvard tied Princeton for first place in 2011, both schools going 12-2. In those days there was no Ivy League Tournament, so the NCAA bid was decided by a one-game playoff on a neutral court—in this case Yale's John J. Lee Amphitheater. Princeton won the game on a buzzer-beating jump shot, and Harvard had to settle for the NIT.

A year later, there was no tie at the top of the standings. Harvard again finished 12-2, won the title outright, and returned to the NCAAs for the first time in sixty-six years. There was one player from the 1946 team still living, Louis Desci Jr. Amaker found him retired in Florida and invited him to make the trip to Albuquerque to watch the Crimson play. Harvard, seeded twelfth, lost to fifth-seeded Vanderbilt, 79–70, but it was clear a new day had dawned for Harvard basketball.

The Crimson won the Ivy League and represented the league in the NCAAs the next three seasons—winning first-round games against high seeds two years in a row: first beating No. 3 New Mexico in 2013, and then beating No. 5 Cincinnati a year later.

Harvard's success helped spark a basketball renaissance in the Ivy League. Other schools realized they too could compete if they had the right coach and a reasonable budget. Beginning in 2008, when Cornell won the first of three straight Ivy titles (reaching the sweet sixteen in 2010), five different schools won the Ivy League championship during a ten-year stretch. The Princeton-Penn axis had finally been cracked.

Harvard had again tied for first in the Ivy League in 2018 but had lost the championship game of the tournament to cochampion Penn. The game had been played at the Palestra, Penn's home court, but the biggest difference in the game undoubtedly came when sophomore Seth Towns, who had been the league's player of the year, went down with a knee injury with eight minutes left in the game. Penn won, 70–67, and Harvard went to the NIT.

By then, after the conference tournament had been played in the Palestra for two years, a number of coaches and administrators were complaining that playing there gave Penn an unfair advantage.

One person not complaining was Amaker. "You have to have an appreciation for the history of the sport and what's best for the entire league," he said. "Of course the tournament should be played in the Palestra. I mean, come on, it's *the Palestra*.

"It might give Penn a slight advantage—or it might not. I still think if Seth doesn't get hurt we win that game, regardless of where it's played. If you're the best team, you win. Penn won. They deserved to win."

But Amaker's voice was lost in a forest of political correctness. The league's athletic directors voted during the off-season to let each of the other seven schools host the tournament during the next seven seasons. That meant that a different school would have home-court advantage each March—if it qualified by making the top four during the regular season. It also meant going to smaller venues than the Palestra without a drop of the history.

After Harvard had played the role of "safety school" on opening night and beat MIT, it lost a tight game to Northeastern, a very good team that would go on to make the NCAA Tournament.

The Crimson weren't anywhere close to healthy. Towns and point guard Bryce Aiken, who had been injured fourteen games into the previous season, still weren't healthy. Amaker was hoping to get Aiken back by the start of Ivy League play but wasn't nearly as certain about Towns.

"He wants to play if there's any way possible," Amaker said. "But we aren't going to push it or take any chances."

Towns wasn't going to redshirt. He was planning on getting his degree in four years—regardless. There is absolutely nothing about Towns that is typical of a basketball player—especially one who has the potential to play in the NBA.

He'd grown up in the inner city of Columbus, Ohio. Both his parents—James Towns and Melissa Smitherman—had gone to Ohio State, though they had divorced when Seth was very young.

By the time Towns was a high school junior, he was six feet seven and was being recruited by a slew of big-time schools, including Ohio State and Michigan. But he was also an excellent student, and Amaker saw an opportunity.

"There are always a handful of kids every year who are good enough to play in the Big Ten or the ACC or the Big East, who also have the grades and the boards to come to Harvard," he said. "What we try to do is identify those who might like the idea of combining very good basketball with being able to say they went to Harvard.

"It's never a long list. Most kids, naturally, want to go to the big-name basketball schools more than a big-name academic school. Seth was one of those kids I thought might like the idea of Harvard."

He smiled. "Beyond that, I thought his mother might like the idea."

Amaker knew that when Seth was ten, Melissa Smitherman had taken him, along with his younger brother Gabe, to visit Harvard. She wanted them to see what the school looked like and felt like, to understand that there was nothing wrong with setting a goal to go to college there.

"She wanted them to see what they could aspire to," Amaker said.

Amaker's biggest problem in recruiting Towns was getting to his house. On four straight Mondays during the winter of 2016, he had trips scheduled to Columbus to visit Towns and his mother.

"Four straight Mondays, four straight canceled flights," he said. "That was the winter when it never stopped snowing in Boston. I just had to keep trying."

Amaker finally made it to Columbus. He went through the recruiting ritual, explaining all the reasons Towns should come to Harvard. Finally, because he thought he needed to say something that would get the attention of both mother and son, looking first at his mother, he said, "With all due respect"—then looking at Seth—"if you don't come to Harvard you're fucking crazy."

This was not your typical recruiting pitch, and it certainly wasn't the way Amaker approached *anyone*. There are few people in the world more polite or low-key—except on the practice court and in the locker room—than Amaker. Now, for a moment, the locker room in Amaker came out.

"I knew saying it was a risk," he said. "What if I offended the mother with my language? As soon as it was out of my mouth, though, I could tell by the look on Melissa's face that I'd said the right thing."

"She loved it," Towns said, laughing, a couple of years later. "She was thinking the same thing—although probably without the F word. But when Coach Amaker said that, I got what he was saying.

"To me, basketball isn't the endgame or goal. It's important to me and I love to play. If I can play in the NBA someday, that would be great. But to me, basketball is a means to an end. I know it sounds corny, but I want to do something in my life that helps people. I want to have an impact in some way on the world. I honestly believe I can do it, and I also believe as an African American with a Harvard degree I can have a leg up on all that.

"There are a lot of bad things going on in the world, a lot of people not getting a fair chance to succeed, a lot of people suffering. I'd like to find a way to help."

Sadly, Towns was speaking from firsthand experience. His best friend in high school, Abou Diawara, had been killed in a drive-by shooting while sitting on his front porch. Two years later, another close friend was killed during a home invasion. Towns's life has been considerably different from that of the typical pampered basketball star.

As part of his recruiting pitch, Amaker likes to say to people: "Look, I'm not putting down any other school, but there's only one Harvard."

In truth, he *is* putting down other schools by saying they aren't Harvard. He's also telling the truth.

About a month after Amaker had finally gotten to Columbus, he got a phone call from Towns. "Coach," he said, "I want you to know I'm not fucking crazy."

Amaker was very glad to hear that. Towns knew almost as soon as he arrived on campus that he had made the right decision. Early on, he attended a monthly breakfast at Henrietta's Table in Cambridge that Amaker had started early on in his tenure, which involved Harvard professors, students, and outsiders *not* from the sports world who would come in and speak.

One of the invited guests at Towns's first breakfast was Dr. Harry Edwards, the longtime civil rights activist. The older man and the younger man talked at length when the breakfast was over.

"He's really become my mentor, to tell you the truth," Towns said. "We talk often, whether by phone or email or text. I feel like I'm learning as much from him as I am from my classes."

Towns played well as a freshman, but it was as a sophomore that he truly blossomed. He averaged just under 16 points and 8 rebounds a game during the regular season and was voted Ivy League player of the year, only the third player ever chosen for the award as a sophomore.

He had 24 points and 11 rebounds in Harvard's semifinal win in the Ivy League Tournament over Cornell, causing Amaker to shake his head postgame as he looked at the stat sheet.

"I was all over him at halftime because I didn't think he was involved enough," he said, laughing. "Now I look at the stats and he's got twenty-four and eleven. Problem is, he makes the game look so easy sometimes that you forget he's giving you all he's got."

There were no laughs the next day. Playing on Penn's home court, the Crimson led early, then fell behind at the start of the second half. With 8:20 left, Towns went to the basket for a layup, got bumped, missed, and went down, grabbing his right knee in pain.

As it turned out, he had torn the MCL in the knee. His teammates rallied without him to actually lead 63–60 with 4:30 to go, but a 9–0 Penn run proved decisive. The Quakers won 68–65, two potential tying three-pointers in the final seconds missing as the clock went to zero.

A lot of coaches would have pointed to Towns's injury and having to play on the road in the aftermath. Amaker did neither.

"We had our chances down the stretch, and they were the ones that made the plays," he said. "This is a great venue for this tournament. This is one of college basketball's jewels, and it's part of our league. I hope we don't stop playing the tournament here. This is where it belongs."

In 2019, the Ivy League Tournament would be played at Yale. Amaker thought Yale had the most talented and the most experienced team in the league.

That, however, wasn't his concern in November 2018. Trying to get his team healthy and keep it afloat in the preconference schedule was his concern.

"The good news is some of our younger guys are getting experience they wouldn't be getting if Bryce and Seth were healthy," he said. "But we need them. I just don't know if we're going to get them back."

Harvard beat UMass that night. Center Chris Lewis scored 16 points; Christian Juzang, filling in for Aiken, had 10 points and 4 assists, and freshman Noah Kirkwood chipped in with 9. UMass guard Luwane Pipkins single-handedly kept his team in the game with 36 points.

Four months later, when the Minutemen went to New York to play in the Atlantic 10 Tournament, Pipkins wasn't in the lineup. He had announced a week earlier that he was going to leave UMass to be a graduate transfer the following season.

Officially, he didn't play in New York because of a minor injury. In truth, Coach Matt McCall had allowed Pipkins to play his final home game but couldn't see any reason to have him play on a team he had publicly renounced already.

He wasn't wrong.

Pipkins's case was as much rule as exception. More and more, players at mid-major schools who either graduate in three years or have a fifth year of eligibility because of redshirt or injury are looking to transfer, and bigger programs are more than willing to swoop in and take a player who has already played three years of college ball.

Amaker was glad to see Pipkins in the rearview mirror. His team's first two months would continue to be a rocky ride with his two best players out.

The highlight came on a trip to Atlanta to play Mercer. Amaker is a believer in making his players do more than practice and play when on the road, so he scheduled a trip to the Jimmy Carter Presidential Library during the Mercer trip.

When library officials heard that the Harvard basketball team wanted to visit, one called Amaker: Would the team like to meet President Carter during their visit?

"It was a rhetorical question," Amaker said later. "Of course we all wanted to meet President Carter. It was a thrill and an honor."

Beating Mercer—a team that had upset Amaker's alma mater in the 2014 NCAA Tournament—was a bonus.

That victory made the Crimson 6-5. But an expected loss at North Carolina to start January, followed by an unexpected loss at Dartmouth to start conference play, dropped them to 6-7. The heart of the season lay ahead.

Aiken was close to playing again. Towns was not. Amaker had no idea what to expect in the two months to come.

7

THE ROCK AND A VERY
HARD PLACE

On the first day of September, soon after they had returned to school to start the fall semester, Old Dominion basketball coach Jeff Jones met with his players to talk about preseason practices, their need to keep up with their schoolwork, and the upcoming season. The Monarchs had won twenty-five games the previous winter but had fallen short of winning the Conference USA Tournament, which was the only way to get to the NCAA Tournament in a one-bid league.

Jones had seen college basketball from all sides: he'd been a big-time recruit who played at a big-time school—one that was frequently ranked No. 1 in the country while he was there—and reached the Final Four in his junior year. He'd coached at Virginia, his alma mater, and been one step shy of reaching the Final Four.

He'd gone on to coach at American, a school that had *never* reached the NCAA Tournament and had taken the Eagles to that version of the promised land twice. And now, he was at Old Dominion, in a one-bid conference where you could win one hundred games in a thirty-one-game regular season and not make the tournament unless you won the Conference USA Tournament.

Jones also had one other matter to discuss with his players on that September day: the recurrence of the prostate cancer he had first been diagnosed with in 2015. Then, he had gone through surgery and radiation treatments that had knocked the cancer out of his body.

But a year earlier, in the summer of 2017, the cancer had come back. Because prostate cancer is often very slow-moving, doctors had hoped at first to manage it without chemotherapy. But by June 2018, they had told Jones he needed chemo in the form of a shot he would receive four times in twelve months.

"They said they'd try it this way for a year and then assess where we were," Jones said. "It was more about trying to manage it than trying to cure it."

The good news was that Jones didn't have to stop working to undergo a frequent regimen of chemo. The bad news was that the doctors warned him there would be side effects that would be impossible to hide: hot flashes and, on occasion, a quick loss of his temper.

That was a major reason Jones decided to let his players know what was going on. "I wanted to be sure they heard it from me and understood what was involved," he said. "I didn't want them noticing symptoms or, worse, hearing about it from someone outside our program.

"I told them it wouldn't affect the way I coached them at all—that, for sure, I wouldn't be any nicer. I told them the cancer had been back for a year and I hadn't been any different until now."

The difference, Jones knew, would be the side effects. A week after telling his players, Jones announced publicly that his cancer had returned. He did it for two reasons: the first the same as his reasons for telling his players—that he knew the side effects would be impossible to hide.

The second reason was that, just as he had done in 2015, he wanted to make people aware of the importance of being tested in order to catch the disease early enough to be treated. This went against Jones's instincts—he tends to be a private person who would much rather talk about basketball than about himself—but he understood that he had a platform that could be used to help people who might have to deal with the disease.

Basketball has been an important part of Jones's life for as long as he can remember. His father, Bob Jones, won a Division 2 national championship as the coach at Kentucky Wesleyan in 1973—when Jeff was twelve. He was a highly recruited guard coming out of Owensboro, Kentucky, finally choosing Virginia over North Carolina.

For years, Carolina's legendary coach Dean Smith told people that losing Jones was one of his biggest recruiting disappointments. Little did Jones or Smith know at the time that they would end up coaching against each other.

Jones had a sterling college career at Virginia. He was a four-year starter, played with Ralph Sampson for three seasons, and was the point guard on the 1981 Virginia team that reached the Final Four.

He was Terry Holland's coach on the court, a calming influence at all times. During Jones's freshman year, his parents separated, calling him soon after Christmas to let him know. They also called Holland so he would be aware of what was going on. Holland asked Jones to come see him so he could find out how he was dealing with what was going on.

"I'm fine," Jones said. He then went back to his dorm, found a basketball, and, in subfreezing weather, went out to shoot on an outdoor court nearby. He didn't come inside until a friend found him and convinced him he was going to get sick if he didn't end the shooting session.

Later, when a reporter asked Holland how Jones was dealing with the impending divorce, Holland said, "JJ's a rock."

Only, JJ wasn't a rock. He was devastated. Nothing ever affected his basketball, though. His senior year was a disappointment. Even with Sampson winning national player of the year honors for a third time, the Cavaliers, playing without Othell Wilson, Jones's backcourt mate, lost in the round of sixteen in the NCAA Tournament, a crushing loss after their Final Four run a year earlier.

Jones made a brief stab at playing in the NBA the following fall, but when he was a late cut by the Indiana Pacers, he returned to UVA as a graduate assistant. Eight years later, when Holland retired because of recurring stomach issues at the age of forty-eight, he became the head coach at twenty-nine—making him the youngest head coach in ACC history. The youngest coach prior to Jones? Dean Smith, who got the North Carolina job in 1961, four months after turning thirty.

Jones held the UVA job for eight seasons—reaching the NCAA Tournament five times, including a trip to the elite eight in 1995. But he went through a divorce of his own, one that was much whispered about in small-town Charlottesville.

No one seemed much bothered by the separation between Jeff and Lisa Jones during the 1994–95 season. Lisa, a photographer, still came to games at University Hall to take pictures. Jeff was living ten minutes away in a town house and saw the couple's three children often.

More important—at least in the minds of most Virginia fans—was the fact that the Cavaliers finished tied for first in the ACC, reached the NCAAs for the fourth time in Jones's five seasons as coach, and upset top-seeded Kansas in the sweet sixteen to reach the elite eight before losing to Arkansas—the defending national champion.

The next year, Jones had his first losing season, the Cavaliers going 12-15. There were off-court problems involving several players that led to a poor season on the court and louder whispers about the divorce. UVA bounced back the next season to make the NCAAs again, but an 11-19 record in the winter of 1998 sealed Jones's fate in Charlottesville.

"What bothers me," he said to me one night late in that season, "is that people are going to say I got fired because I got divorced. Everything was fine when we won twenty-five games while I was getting divorced. But when we stopped winning, then everything wasn't fine."

I had known Jones since his playing days at UVA. He was eminently likable, honest almost to a fault, with a sneaky, dry sense of humor. I'd spent a good deal of time with him during the 1996–97 season while researching a book on ACC basketball.

Coming off the 12-15 record a year earlier with the divorce rumors all over Charlottesville, it had been an exhausting, draining season for Jones. The Cavaliers went into their final home game needing a win to unofficially clinch an NCAA Tournament spot. They rallied late to win.

While his seniors were speaking to the crowd, Jones walked into the locker room. When I noticed he'd left the court—to make sure the focus was on the seniors—I walked into the locker room.

Jones was sitting on a chair, tears rolling down his face, a combination of exhaustion and relief bringing out the tears. This was a side of him the public almost never saw. To most, JJ was a rock.

A year after being fired at Virginia, Jones was hired as an assistant at Rhode Island and spent two seasons there before being hired as the coach at American in the spring of 2000. By then, he was happily remarried to Danielle Decker, a journalist who would become the editor of *Politico* while the Joneses were living in Washington.

American was a school with a good deal of basketball tradition. It had been a Division 2 power for years, and in 1973 senior Kermit

Washington had averaged 20 points and 20 rebounds a game for the entire season. No Division 1 college basketball player has done that in the ensuing forty-six years.

Plus, American was a cradle of great coaches: Tom Young, who would go on to take Rutgers to the Final Four in 1976, had recruited Washington, who wasn't even a starter as a high school senior. Jim Lynam, who went on to take St. Joseph's to the elite eight and coach the Philadelphia 76ers, succeeded Young. Then came Gary Williams, who would later win a national championship at Maryland and be voted into the basketball Hall of Fame. Ed Tapscott, who later became the first African American general manager in the NBA, followed Williams.

Tom Davis, who went on to great success at Iowa, was Young's lone assistant, and Fran Dunphy was an assistant under Williams.

Lots of coaching talent and plenty of wins. But the Eagles had never reached the NCAA Tournament as a Division 1 team. Twice, under Jones, they made it to the Patriot League Tournament championship game—one win away from the promised land of the Dance.

Twice, they lost close games. Then, in 2008, they got another chance and this time, after trailing late, beat Colgate. As fans and alumni stormed the Bender Arena court, Jones wept into a towel.

The towel was there because he had developed an annual in-season cough that forced him to keep a towel handy at all times. On that March afternoon, the towel was used to much better effect.

I had sat in an empty hallway with Jones prior to the game, and he had talked about how much it would mean to win this game because he knew how much it would mean to everyone connected to AU.

I sat down next to him and put an arm around him. He looked at me and said quietly, "This is the best moment I've ever had in basketball."

The Eagles made the tournament again the following year and even led Villanova by fourteen in the second half in a game played in Philadelphia. But the Wildcats rallied, won the game, and went on to the Final Four.

In the spring of 2013, Old Dominion athletic director Wood Selig, whom Jones had known since his days at Virginia, needed a basketball coach.

He had been forced to fire the hugely successful and popular Blaine Taylor in February, with the Monarchs 2-20 and rumors everywhere that Taylor, who had been arrested on a DUI charge while coaching at Montana in 1995, was drinking again.

Assistant coach Jimmy Corrigan took over the team and managed to go 3-5, remarkable under the circumstances. Selig then went after Jones and convinced him to make the move to ODU in part because of their friendship and in part because he was able to offer Jones a substantial raise.

In Jones's first season, ODU went 18-18—a major turnaround after the previous season's 5-25. A year later, the record improved to 27-8. The Monarchs missed getting an at-large bid to the NCAAs and instead went to the NIT—losing in the semifinals.

It was that summer that Jones was first diagnosed with cancer. He had surgery and underwent radiation treatment—never missing a game during the following season. He also stepped out of character, talking often about the need for men over fifty to have their prostates tested.

ODU reached the Conference USA championship game the following spring, losing at the buzzer to a Middle Tennessee team that would go on to upset second-seeded Michigan State in the first round of the NCAA Tournament. The Monarchs played in—and won—something called the "Vegas 16" tournament, yet another pay-to-play event that had been created to make money for a marketing company.

"We're not doing that again," Jones said when it was over. "Either we make one of the real tournaments [NCAA, NIT] or we go home."

He was as good as his word. Even though ODU won twenty-five games again in 2018, it didn't play in postseason after losing in the conference tournament and not being invited to the NIT.

Jones's decision to speak openly about his second cancer diagnosis raised his public profile in a way he wasn't thrilled with—but understood. He was starting his sixth season at Old Dominion and his twenty-eighth season as a college head coach.

With a veteran team returning, he thought it was time—beyond time—for the school to return to the NCAAs for the first time since 2011. To do that, ODU would almost certainly have to win the conference tournament, a three-day crapshoot held in Frisco, Texas—outside Dallas.

Like Temple, ODU had made a conference change that hurt basketball in the name of football. Old Dominion didn't play football for sixty-eight years, from 1941 until 2009. But the school brought the sport back in 2009, and it has been remarkably successful since then. It reached the Football Championship Subdivision playoffs in both 2011 and 2012 before deciding to make the jump to the Football Bowl Subdivision, which it did in 2014.

To do that, Old Dominion had to leave the CAA, which had evolved into an excellent basketball conference, but played football at the FCS level. So it bolted to join Conference USA. The move made no sense geographically or for basketball. The CAA had become a league that often received two NCAA bids and had even gotten three bids in 2011: ODU, George Mason, and VCU, which went to the Final Four.

In a three-year period, though, all three of those teams, all from Virginia, left: ODU to pursue football glory; George Mason and VCU to pursue bigger TV dollars in the Atlantic 10.

Now both the CAA and Conference USA are one-bid leagues, meaning only the tournament champion is guaranteed a place in the NCAA bracket. In 2018, two-time defending champion Middle Tennessee went 16-2 in league play and 24-6 overall. The Blue Raiders had won NCAA Tournament games the previous two seasons—beating Michigan State and then Minnesota a year later. But when they were upset by Southern Mississippi in the quarterfinals in Frisco, they had *no* chance at an at-large bid.

Middle Tennessee's loss had seemingly opened a path for Old Dominion, which was the No. 2 seed. But ODU lost to Western Kentucky in the semifinals. The Hilltoppers were ODU's kryptonite that season, inflicting three of their seven losses.

"We've been good enough and we've been close," Jones said. "But in our conference, close isn't good enough. We're looked at as a one-bid league, that's the way it's been since we made the move and, until someone proves different, that's the way it's going to be."

Jones was sitting in a seat next to the runway that led from the court inside the Ted Constant Center to his team's locker room. It was two hours before tipoff in Old Dominion's annual game with VCU. Once, the two schools had played two and sometimes three times a year when both were in the CAA. Now they play once a year, in late November or early December.

Many of the things Jones does as a coach were passed down to him from Terry Holland, who coached him at Virginia and who was his boss there for eight years when he first got into coaching.

Like many teams, ODU takes a moment for a pregame prayer. But unlike most, no one leads the prayer and there is no specific religion attached to the prayer. Jones simply says, "In your own way," allowing each player to pray—or not pray—silently for a moment before the team leaves the locker room.

That was the way Holland did it, and that's the way Jones does it.

Holland also used to sit in the empty arena in a corner seat until his players left the court for the first time during pregame warmups. Jones has done the same thing—first at Virginia, then at American, and now at ODU.

Most coaches not only enjoy ritual, they crave it. It gives them comfort on game days—which are rarely comfortable.

Jones inherited one other thing from Holland that he would rather not have acquired: a nervous stomach. It was stomach problems he couldn't completely kick that pushed Holland into premature retirement.

Jones has stomach issues and a perpetual cough throughout each basketball season, which date to his early days at Virginia. He doesn't even attempt to eat on game day. "At most I might try to eat something light in the morning," he said. "But pregame meal? No way."

As Jones sat in the arena on the evening of November 28, he was a picture of calm on the outside, in spite of what was going on inside his stomach and his mind. He had been through two rounds of chemo since June and, while he insisted he felt fine, the side effects, especially the hot flashes, were noticeable even as he sat in a relaxed mode well before game time.

Sitting next to him, I asked him if he was okay a couple of times when I saw his face redden and some sweat begin to bead on his forehead. He laughed.

"This is normal for me, not a big deal," he said. Then he smiled. "The good thing about the games is that when I have a hot flash nobody really notices. I sweat a lot during games anyway, so if I have a hot flash I don't really look all that different."

All that said, Jones was wired for this game.

ODU and VCU are ninety miles apart—Virginia Commonwealth in downtown Richmond, Old Dominion in downtown Norfolk. The schools began playing each other in February 1969—the first season that VCU fielded a team—and had played a total of ninety-four times.

The VCU Rams led the series 50-44, having won seven of the teams' last eight meetings.

In a twist, ODU had beaten VCU twice in 2011, including the CAA championship game in the Richmond Coliseum, which is located about a mile from the VCU campus. The Rams made it into the NCAA field as an at-large team, being sent to the newly born and newly branded "First Four" in Dayton. That was the first year the NCAA Tournament expanded to sixty-eight teams, and VCU got in as one of the last four at-large teams.

From there, they stunned the college hoops world by making it to the Final Four, blowing out top-seeded Kansas in the regional final. Their run ended in the Final Four when they lost to Butler—which had beaten ODU in the first round on a buzzer-beating layup.

Old Dominion hadn't been to the tournament since that 2011 loss. VCU had made the field in seven straight seasons before an 18-15 record in 2018, Mike Rhoades's first season as the Rams' coach.

Jones was 1-4 against VCU, the only victory coming at home four seasons earlier.

"They're hard to play against, especially now because Mike [Rhoades] has been able to go back to the 'Havoc' style that Shaka liked to play," Jones said. "They'll run nine or ten guys at us and press whenever they can. We've got to make it a half-court game as much as we possibly can."

"Havoc" was the style that Shaka Smart had made famous at VCU—ninety-four feet of pressure defense the entire game. It had helped make the Rams successful and had made them one of the most entertaining teams in the country.

Smart had stayed at VCU through the 2015 season. In six years, he never won fewer than twenty-six games. If he had decided to run for mayor of Richmond, he would have won by acclamation. The Siegel Center, VCU's home arena, had started a sellout string during the 2011 season that would reach 134 straight games by the end of the 2018–19 season.

The building seats 7,637, just about the perfect number for a school like VCU. I had been convinced the streak would end five seasons earlier when I had driven to Richmond for a VCU–George Washington game in the middle of a snowstorm. I almost turned back halfway down I-95 because the forecast for that night was for lots more snow. I called Ed McLaughlin, VCU's athletic director, and asked for a weather report.

"Just barely starting down here," he said. "You'll be fine. Not supposed to be too bad."

McLaughlin is a fine human and an excellent athletic director. He's a terrible weatherman. By the time I hit the Richmond city limits, the snow was coming down mercilessly. By then, there was no turning back. I made it to the Siegel Center and wondered if I should get a hotel room for the night.

I figured most fans would be smart enough to stay home. Maybe they had also called McLaughlin. At tipoff the building was full—not announced full—really full. The streak lived.

Of course no one at ESPN paid any attention to that game or the streak living through a blizzard. Dick Vitale has never screamed about what a uniquely wonderful place the Siegel Center is to see a game— sometimes I think Cameron Indoor Stadium and Allen Field Houses are the only two places he's ever been to for a game.

But the streak is one of those little-noticed facts about college basketball that set the sport apart from the place the preening administrators look to for their billions. It's about players who don't need to be called "student-athletes"; a school proud of the legacy it has created and a city that has embraced it.

It's just flat-out cool. I made it home from the GW-VCU game, a trip that normally took under two hours, in a little more than four. It was okay. I enjoyed the night in the Siegel Center. And I might even forgive McLaughlin someday.

As luck would have it, Jones and I were both with McLaughlin on the night Shaka Smart left VCU. It was during the 2015 Final Four in Indianapolis. Jones annually puts together a dinner at the Final Four for friends, coaching pals—including his current staff—and assorted stragglers . . . like me.

McLaughlin had been an assistant athletic director at American during Jones's early years there, and they'd remained friends. As the night progressed, McLaughlin frequently left the table to go outside and take cell phone calls.

Everyone knew that Smart had been offered the Texas job and that the money was a lot more than VCU could hope to pay. Intellectually, McLaughlin understood all this. He had often said since arriving at VCU that the toughest day he would have on the job would come when Smart—inevitably—left for a Power Five school. It wasn't as if Smart had jumped at the first chance to make big money: he had turned down chances to go to UCLA and North Carolina State, among others.

Smart was making $1.2 million a year at VCU. Texas offered $3.2 million a year for six years. "He'd be crazy to turn it down," McLaughlin said.

He didn't. Shortly before midnight, McLaughlin took one more phone call. When he walked back into the restaurant, Jones saw the look on his face and didn't really need to ask: "Gone, right?" he said.

McLaughlin just nodded and asked for another glass of wine.

McLaughlin hired Will Wade, who was thirty-two—the same age Smart had been when he'd come to VCU in 2009. Wade had been a Smart assistant for four years before becoming the head coach at Chattanooga, where he'd won twenty-two games in his second season. Wade took the Rams to two more NCAA Tournaments, but left for LSU—again, big money coming into play.

McLaughlin then hired Rhoades, another former Smart assistant, who had aspired to the VCU job since his days as the head coach twenty miles down the road at Division 3 Randolph-Macon.

"I think this time I've hired a coach who is going to want to stay here," McLaughlin said. He had been caught off guard when Wade left as quickly as he did.

Going 18-15 in his first season had been a downer for Rhoades—and for VCU's fan base, which had grown accustomed to twenty-five-plus victory seasons and NCAA trips. The school had made the Dance every year since 2011. But Rhoades thought he had the kind of team he wanted to coach in the fall of 2018.

Wade had backed off from Smart's Havoc style, and even though the team had been successful, the team he left Rhoades behind wasn't deep enough to press for an entire game and had players not built to play that style. Rhoades thought he now had the depth and the right players to return to Havoc.

"I feel a lot more comfortable with this group than I did last year," he had said in the fall. "We can play the way I want to play."

They had played well in their first six games, including an impressive win over Temple. Their only loss had been to St. John's in overtime in New York. If the Rams had a weakness, it was outside shooting. Rhoades could live with that as long as they played good defense.

In the first half, in front of a sellout crowd in the Ted Constant Center, known to everyone in Norfolk as "The Ted," Rhoades got everything he could possibly have wanted—and more.

VCU was smothering Old Dominion's offense. The Monarchs couldn't make a shot, most notably leading scorer B. J. Stith, who made one of his first eight shots, his only make coming on a layup. In the game's first seventeen minutes, ODU scored fifteen points. In the meantime, the Rams were making three-point shots look easy: they made six of their first nine and had a 32–15 lead with 2:37 left.

Jones wasn't happy with the score, but he didn't feel as if his team was playing that badly. "We were running good offense, just not making shots we would normally make," he said later. "And they were making everything. I honestly didn't think they could continue shooting that well or we would continue shooting that poorly for the whole game."

He was right. Stith finally made a three to cut the margin to 32–18, and ODU scored the last five points of the half to escape down by just 32–20.

The second half was 180 degrees different. The Rams didn't make another three-point shot—they were 0-for-10 in the last twenty minutes. Shots began to fall for ODU, notably for Stith, who finished with 21 points, and point guard Ahmad Caver, who had 18, along with 5 rebounds and 4 assists.

It was the Rams who only scored 20 points in twenty minutes once the second half began. ODU scored 42, more than doubling its first-half output. The final was 62–52. Very much a Tale of Two Halves.

"Yeah," Rhoades said when I used that line on him a couple of days later. "We played the best of halves, followed by the worst of halves."

You have to love a literate basketball coach.

The win was a big deal for Old Dominion and for Jones. It was a comeback that turned the crowd of 8,172 from nearly silent to roaring against an archrival. It also sent a signal to Jones that his veteran team could take a punch against a good team and get up off the floor.

Few coaches in basketball could relate to that notion more than Jones. There would be more to come.

8

LAST FRAN STANDING

December 2, 2018, Easton, Pennsylvania

On a sunny Sunday morning, I was in my car by 8 a.m. heading north and east in the direction of Easton, Pennsylvania. This was a trip I had made so often I could probably drive it blindfolded.

During the 1999–2000 basketball season I had written a book about Patriot League basketball called *The Last Amateurs*. Lafayette had been the best team in the conference back then, and Fran O'Hanlon, the coach, was as bright and funny as anyone in the sport. Plus, he had a group of kids who were fun to be around.

And they could play.

Even after writing the book, I had continued to return to Lafayette frequently. I did Patriot League games on TV for several years, and even when that gig went away, Lafayette continued to bring me back to Kirby Sports Center a couple of times a year to do color on their regional telecasts.

I loved having any excuse to go to Lafayette. The drive was three hours and fifteen minutes each way. I had worked with seven coaches while researching *The Last Amateurs*. The only one left was O'Hanlon.

"Last man standing," he liked to joke. "And that's just barely."

O'Hanlon was now in his twenty-fourth season at Lafayette. He had been late to coaching because he was a good enough player to make a living playing in Europe for a number of years after playing for one season in the ABA with the Miami Floridians.

He was a Philadelphia guy, living and coaching an hour from where he had grown up. O'Hanlon was a legendary shooter in Philadelphia's summertime Baker League. Everyone in the league had a nickname, and O'Hanlon's was "Rainbow Johnson," the Rainbow coming from the way he shot the ball. He had played on very good Villanova teams, starting on a team that reached the elite eight of the NCAA Tournament in 1970 when he was a senior.

Then he began his odyssey—a year in the ABA, where his biggest challenge was often getting into arenas because guards refused to believe he was a player. "I looked about seventeen," he said. "It wasn't as if we carried ID cards."

He then played in Sweden for eleven years for a team called "Hageby Basket." He also played under a different name there for a while, because Europe had very hazy rules about who was eligible to play and who was not. He adopted the name "Francis Francis," which eventually became "Francis Francis Dribbler."

"They had a scouting report on me that said, 'Francis Francis—dribbler,'" O'Hanlon said. "Somehow in the game program that became my name. So I just stuck with it."

He coached in Israel for several years—with one year as the women's coach at Temple in between. He finally came home to Philadelphia to coach at Monsignor Bonner High School before getting his first college job as an assistant to Fran Dunphy at Penn in 1989. Six years later, he succeeded John Leone at Lafayette. O'Hanlon was forty-six when he got the job and liked to joke that "I'm off to a late start in my quest for the Hall of Fame."

He did turn the school's basketball fortunes around. The Leopards went from two wins in Leone's last season to seven in O'Hanlon's first, then eleven and 19-9 and a tie for first place in the Patriot League in his third season. After losing the Patriot League championship game to Navy in 1998, Lafayette won the conference tournament the next two years, reaching the NCAAs for the first time since 1957.

There were no athletic scholarships in the Patriot League when O'Hanlon first arrived and began building his program. The league had been founded in 1990 on the Ivy League model that athletes could receive financial aid but no scholarships just for being good at a sport.

That utopian notion began to crumble at the end of the century: Holy Cross was the first school to decide to bring back athletic scholarships, and it was soon followed by Lehigh and Colgate. By the early

2000s, Lafayette and Bucknell were the lone holdouts, since Army and Navy gave full scholarships to all their students.

When Bucknell began giving scholarships, Lafayette was the last man standing—so to speak. It wasn't until March 2006 that the school voted to allow athletic scholarships again. By then the Leopards had gone from 24-7, including an NCAA trip in 2000, to 11-17 in 2006.

"Even after we got scholarships, it took a while for us to recruit the kind of players that allowed us to compete," O'Hanlon said. "It wasn't an easy road back."

O'Hanlon never complained about the lack of scholarships. Complaining wasn't his way; self-deprecating humor was. When his team was successful, he was quick to point out that his players and assistants had done a wonderful job overcoming his presence.

Nothing could have been further from the truth. O'Hanlon was about as respected as any coach in the college game. The Leopards finally won the Patriot League Tournament again in 2015, only to draw a first-round matchup in the NCAAs with Villanova—O'Hanlon's alma mater. In their previous trip to the tournament, Lafayette had played Temple—another Philly school, a place where O'Hanlon had once worked, a team coached by a close friend of his, John Chaney.

Pure coincidence, of course.

O'Hanlon had turned seventy in August and had a young team for the 2018–19 season. "Young team, old coach," he said. "Probably not a great combination."

Even though the previous three seasons had been difficult and he was facing another winter with a young team—one senior—O'Hanlon had no thoughts about cashing his coaching chips.

"I still love doing it," he said. "I enjoy working with the kids, I enjoy getting ready for games. It's what I do. Maybe because I got a late start doing it I still haven't lost any enthusiasm."

Actually, there were other coaches in O'Hanlon's age group who had started earlier than he had who still seemed to have their zest for coaching: Jim Boeheim was seventy-four; Cliff Ellis was seventy-three; Mike Krzyzewski was seventy-two; Leonard Hamilton was seventy, as was Fran Dunphy.

Once, it was unheard-of to coach into your seventies. John Wooden retired at sixty-three; Dean Smith at sixty-six. Adolph Rupp was *forced* to retire by Kentucky when he was seventy.

"Coach Smith told me he retired too soon," Roy Williams often said. "He made me promise not to do that. That's why I'm still going [at sixty-eight]. It helps that I still love it."

It also helps that coaches make a lot more money nowadays than in the past. O'Hanlon wasn't close to the multimillionaire status of Boeheim or Krzyzewski or Williams or Hamilton. But he comfortably made about $350,000 a year—plenty to live on in Easton—especially with both children grown.

But it isn't the money that keeps the older coaches coaching. It's all the things that come with coaching. Some simply can't imagine a life without the perks and attention. Some just love going to practice every day. Others crave the forty minutes.

"There's nothing about coaching I couldn't give up," Jim Valvano once said. "Except for the forty minutes. So much about the job isn't real. But *that's* real. You give everything you have to try to win, and when it's over a W is a W and an L is an L. No *if this* or *if that*. It's one or the other. That's as real as it gets."

O'Hanlon certainly wasn't still coaching for the perks or the attention. He loved the relationships with his assistant coaches and the players and, like Valvano, he loved the forty minutes.

"I still get a nervous stomach before every game," he said. "Never changes."

He was sitting directly across from his team's bench in the Kirby Sports Center about two hours prior to his team's game with Sacred Heart. Sitting in maroon sweats, legs crossed, one arm stretched over the seat next to him, he looked comfortable and relaxed. He greeted people as they came into the empty gym—athletic department staffers; security guards; members of the TV crew—as if they were all getting together to watch an NFL game at one o'clock.

They weren't. This would be one of those games his team could win, but it wouldn't be easy. Sacred Heart was 3-5 but talented enough to have beaten Army and Hartford—both solid, veteran teams. What's more, Sacred Heart had just lost at Boston College three days earlier—by eight.

"If we play smart and make plays we can win," O'Hanlon said. "But we've got no margin for error. We almost never do."

The Leopards were 2-4 at the moment, their best win coming at La Salle (by one) in the second game of the season, their most frustrating losses coming at St. Peter's in overtime and, three days earlier, against Cornell—also in overtime. That was what O'Hanlon meant about no margin for error. Most losses would be like that. So would most wins.

About an hour before tipoff, O'Hanlon headed upstairs to change into a dark jacket, white shirt, gray pants, and a blue-and-gold silk tie. The jacket was unnecessary. O'Hanlon has never kept a jacket on beyond a game's first possession in his career.

"I like to look good walking on the court," he said, laughing. "Or at least as good as I can look."

As with every team, there was one more review of the scouting report. O'Hanlon is one of those coaches who like to make sure their players have paid attention to the scouting report.

As they go through details one more time, he might ask a quick question about a particular player: "Myles [Cherry], what do you have to remember most about [Jarel] Spellman?" . . . "E.J., how many assists a game is [Cameron] Parker averaging?"

The players know these questions are coming, so they've done their homework and are prepared. Which is the point of the exercise.

Cherry is from Australia, one in a long line of international players O'Hanlon has been able to recruit thanks to the many contacts he made while playing and coaching overseas.

He's a six-foot-eight-inch junior, a solid player averaging 10 points a game. He had 18 points and 12 rebounds in the La Salle game.

He was also a teammate in Australia of Ben Simmons, who played one year of college ball at LSU before becoming the No. 1 pick in the NBA draft in 2016. At six-ten, Simmons has guard skills and has become an important part of the rebirth of the Philadelphia 76ers.

I asked O'Hanlon why he ended up with Cherry and not Simmons. He smiled. "Guess I took the wrong guy," he joked.

Lafayette certainly could have used Simmons—especially early, when it missed its first four shots, all threes. No one says "three-point shot" anymore. Everyone says—and everyone takes—threes.

The rule was first put in back in 1986, and the line was so close back then that Valvano said, "I'm not saying the line is short, but my mom came to practice the other day and hit nine of ten."

The line back then was nineteen feet, nine inches from the basket. It had been moved back to twenty feet, nine inches, and after the conclusion of the 2019 season, the NCAA rules committee voted to move it back to twenty-two feet, one-point-seven-five inches—which is the distance used in international basketball.

No rules change in history, except perhaps the one that eliminated the jump ball after every made basket, has affected basketball more. In 1986–87, the first season the three-point shot existed, only 16 percent of shots attempted were threes. In the 2018–19 season, 37.5 percent of shot attempts would be threes. Even that number didn't fully explain the importance of the three, since many shots from two-point range came off offensive rebounds. Teams running their offense will often shoot more threes than twos.

Lafayette, like a lot of mid-majors who aren't likely to recruit inside players—the big-time schools will die to get anyone over six-eight who can run down the court without tripping over the foul line—shoots threes early and often most nights.

There's a reason why the phrase "live by the three, die by the three" is heard often: many, if not most teams, do just that.

On this NFL football Sunday afternoon, with a crowd of 1,322 inside Kirby (which seats 3,500 when packed), the Leopards came out misfiring—missing their first four threes and quickly trailing 5–0. By halftime, they had made just 3-of-17 from beyond the arc (seventeen being exactly half the shots they had taken) and trailed, 35–27.

While the players cooled down, O'Hanlon and his coaches stood in a narrow hallway outside the locker room discussing ways to come from behind.

The hallway leads to the swimming locker room, and there were rec swimmers standing a few yards away, either getting ready to swim or getting dressed after their swims. O'Hanlon leaned on a Suitmate—a machine that dries bathing suits—as he glared at a stat sheet as if burning a hole through it with his eyes would change the numbers.

Fortunately, no one needed to dry a bathing suit at that moment.

The lead quickly grew to ten early in the second half when Sacred Heart's Aaron Clarke hit a jumper, but Lafayette hung in, playing better defense and getting to the offensive boards. Not surprisingly, those were the two things O'Hanlon had talked about during the break. He never brought up the poor shooting.

"There's no point telling players to shoot better," he said later. "They know they need to shoot better. If they're taking bad shots, that's different. But we weren't. We just couldn't make anything."

Lafayette took the lead 49–48 on an E. J. Stephens tip-in with just under eight minutes to play. Kinnon LaRose answered right away with a three for Sacred Heart, making it 51–49. The lead had lasted eleven seconds.

But then Lafayette put together a surprising 11–3 run, keyed by back-to-back baskets by impressive six-four freshman Isaac Suffren, who would finish with 12 points and be the only Leopard to make at least half his shots (6-of-8) from the floor. A three by Stephens made it 60–54, and when the Leopards got a stop at the other end with the clock ticking under four minutes, the crowd was as loud as 1,322 can get and things looked good for the home team.

But this was a home team that still didn't know how to finish. Stephens missed a three that could have stretched the lead to a possibly insurmountable nine with 3:44 left. Cherry missed inside. Lafayette had a third chance to stretch the lead, but with the shot clock down, Alex Petrie missed a jumper with 2:08 left.

Given new life, Sacred Heart promptly scored twice to make it 60–58, but Stephens answered with a layup with just under a minute left and it was 62–58.

Lafayette didn't score again. Clarke missed a jumper, but Spellman rebounded the miss and scored to make it 62–60. Another empty Lafayette trip and then Suffren fouled LaRose, who made both shots to tie the game with forty-three seconds left.

Again, the Leopards ran the shot clock down, and Petrie—their best three-point shooter—missed one more shot. The Pioneers didn't call time to set up a last shot. Instead, Cameron Parker drove to the basket—and missed. But Spellman was there *again* to tip in the miss with three seconds to go for a 64–62 lead. Justin Jaworski got off a shot before the buzzer, but it rimmed out.

Final: 64–62. O'Hanlon, jacket draped over his arm, did the post-game TV interview he does after every home game, win or lose. He loved his team's effort, didn't love the last two minutes.

Lafayette had been outscored 10–2 in the final two minutes. It had held a team averaging 87 points a game to 64—and lost. It had rebounded well, until allowing Spellman's two critical put-backs in the final minute. The case could easily be made that horrific three-point shooting—6-of-31—had done the Leopards in. O'Hanlon didn't see it that way.

He tossed his jacket on the Suitmate while he and his coaches gave the players a minute to recover inside the locker room. "Offensive rebounds killed us in the end," he said, again staring a hole through the stat sheet. "We certainly played well enough on defense to win. What'd they have, nineteen points the second half until the last two minutes?"

He shook his head and turned to lead his coaches into the locker room. The players all clapped as they entered. There was a moment of acknowledging what everyone had put into trying to win the game.

O'Hanlon emphasized the positive: the second-half comeback; the defense; the plays that had led to the lead. Then he reminded them that a possession isn't over until the basketball is rebounded.

He told them that all he would ask of them in three days, when they played a guarantee game at Connecticut, was the same kind of effort. He might have added that better shooting would help—but he didn't.

He walked outside the locker room and leaned against a wall for a moment.

"I'm getting too old for this job," he said, softly.

I told him I knew he didn't mean that.

"You're right," he said, smiling. "I loved today." He paused. "Except for the last two minutes."

I felt the same way. Coaches like O'Hanlon and places like Lafayette are, in many ways, the reason I still love the college game so much. O'Hanlon never aspired to be a multimillionaire TV coach wearing $2,000 suits. There's a song in the iconic musical *A Chorus Line* in which the show's main character—Cassie—sings, "All I ever need is the music, the mirror, and the chance . . . to dance."

All Fran O'Hanlon has ever needed is a team, a gym, and the chance . . . to compete.

God love him—and the school that's given him that chance—for that.

I OWN A COLLEGE—
IONA IS IONA

December 2, 2018, Richmond, Virginia

During my talk with Manhattan coach Steve Masiello prior to his team's game at UMBC, I asked him how he thought his team's conference—the Metro Atlantic Athletic Association, aka the MAAC—stacked up for the coming season.

"Rider should be the favorite," Masiello said. "They were good last year and have a lot back. Quinnipiac is better, and I think Siena is too. We've got a lot of new players, but I hope we can compete by February and March."

He paused. "And of course, Iona is Iona. Always."

Iona is one of those schools most basketball fans can't possibly locate (it's in New Rochelle, New York) and probably can't tell you what conference it plays in.

But basketball fans *do* know Iona.

They know it because Jim Valvano famously coached there from 1976 to 1980, leading Iona to its first two NCAA Tournament bids in 1979 and 1980. The 1980 team was led by six-eleven center Jeff Ruland, who would go on to a lengthy NBA career. Valvano had stunned most of the college basketball world by convincing Ruland, who had grown up on Long Island, to eschew big-time programs like North Carolina and Indiana to stay close to home.

Valvano always liked to tell (and retell) the story about the first party he attended in New Rochelle after being hired at Iona.

"I was so excited about getting the job," he said. "All night I kept introducing myself to people and saying, 'Hi, I'm Jim Valvano, Iona

College.' Finally, this woman looks at me and says, 'Aren't you awfully young to own your own college?'"

Valvano *did* own Iona by the time he left for North Carolina State in 1980. The Gaels had gone 29-8 that season and had beaten Louisville—the eventual national champion—77–60 in Madison Square Garden. Valvano, who had always dreamed of coaching in "the nine o'clock game in the Garden"—had his team cut down the nets after that victory.

That season was sullied when Valvano left and Ruland, who had another year of eligibility, did too—shortly after news broke that he'd hired an agent during the season.

Pat Kennedy, Valvano's top assistant, took over and went to two more NCAA Tournaments before leaving himself to go to Florida State.

Iona continued to have a solid program under up-and-coming coaches. Tim Welsh went to the NCAAs in 1998 and then left for Providence. Ruland returned as coach and won consistently (three more NCAA bids) until a 2-28 season in 2008 got him fired.

In came Kevin Willard for three seasons, until Seton Hall offered him the chance to coach in the Big East.

Which was when Iona turned to Tim Cluess.

In New York City basketball circles, the name Cluess is a revered one. Tim Cluess was the last of four brothers who had played at St. John's: Hank, Greg, Kevin, and, finally, Tim. The middle brothers—Greg and Kevin—had been stars. They had also both died tragically young: Greg in 1976 from lymphoma; Kevin ten years later at thirty-three from leukemia.

Tim had played his senior season at Hofstra and then been a high school coach on Long Island for sixteen years. He had coached successfully at the Division 2 level at C.W. Post (now known as Long Island Post) and turned fifty feeling perfectly happy coaching at that level.

And then, a year later, Iona knocked on his door. "My first instinct was to say no," he said. "I loved doing what I was doing, and we were having success. Eventually, though, I decided it was worth taking a shot. I was fifty-one. If I didn't do it then, I was never going to do it."

Cluess was now in his ninth season at Iona. In his first eight, the Gaels had never failed to win twenty games and had made the NCAA Tournament five times. In 2012, they had won twenty-five games and had done what was unheard-of in the MAAC, getting an at-large bid to the NCAAs after being upset in the semifinals of the MAAC Tournament.

They then made a little bit of unwanted history: blowing a twenty-five-point lead to Brigham Young playing in the First Four in Dayton.

They had won the MAAC Tournament and made it back to the NCAAs four times since then—including the three previous seasons. Thus, Masiello's "Iona is Iona" comment. The MAAC Tournament would be played in 2019 in Albany's Times Union Center, which was Siena's home court. Everyone in the MAAC knew, though, that the road to the NCAAs still led through New Rochelle.

Three days after losing at Old Dominion, VCU returned home to the Siegel Center to face Iona. Cluess's Gaels came in 2-4, but had played a ridiculous schedule. They had opened at home with a win against Albany and then had played their next five games away from home. In fact, they would play exactly *one* more nonconference game on their home court, and that would come December 30 against Holy Cross.

They had played at New Mexico; two games in a neutral site event in Las Vegas; at Providence; and at Ohio.

"It's been a little much," Cluess admitted on the afternoon of the game, shortly after his team's shootaround. "I mean, we're going to go fifty-one days between home games. That's tough on any team. But this team probably could have used a couple of winnable home games to go with all these other games."

Cluess knew his team was going to walk into one of college basketball's best—and toughest—atmospheres that night.

"I've heard a lot about it," he said with a laugh. "The sellouts, the band, how loud it gets. Part of me is looking forward to it. Part of me isn't certain we're ready for it at this stage."

Cluess wasn't playing the role of poor-mouth coach. There is a lot of blunt New Yorker in him. His best player was Rickey McGill, a senior point guard who had been second team All-MAAC a year earlier and had played a key role in the Gaels winning the MAAC Tournament again.

Cluess had coached some very good guards at Iona, notably A. J. English and Lamont Jones. I asked if McGill was that kind of player.

He laughed. "Absolutely not," he said. "Rickey's a good player, and he's come a long way from his freshman year to where he is now. But he's not in the same class with those guys. He'd be the first one to tell you that."

As it turned out, Cluess knew what he was talking about when he said his team wasn't ready for the primetime spotlight of the Siegel Center.

The building was first opened in 1999 and named for local businessman Stuart C. Siegel, who donated $7 million of the $30 million it cost to build. In 2015, a local construction company, E.J. Wade, had signed a ten-year deal with VCU for naming rights, so the building is now officially known as "The E.J. Wade Arena at the Stuart Siegel Center."

Everyone still calls the place "The Stu."

What makes the Stu unique isn't just the fact that the stands are close to the court or that it has a low roof that holds noise. It's also the VCU band—known as "The Peppas." They play well, they play often, and they play loud. Along with the students—who sit at the same end of the court—they make sure the place is almost never quiet.

Throw in the fact that VCU has had consistently good teams since the building opened in 1999 and the 134 straight sellouts, and you have a place that visitors both enjoy and fear. The enjoyment comes from playing in an electric atmosphere, the kind most players crave. The fear comes from the understanding that a VCU run can blow the roof off the building and blow the game open very quickly.

"You can't be afraid to call time-out in an atmosphere like that," Cluess said. "In fact, you have to be prepared to do it before the game gets away from you."

Cluess twice called time-out early in the first half to try to stem the VCU tide. It didn't help. The Rams trailed 8–6 early, but went on a 12–0 run to lead 18–8. Then, after a Cluess time-out and a McGill three, they went on another 12–0 run. In all, they outscored Iona 24–3 during a six-minute stretch to make it 30–11.

Game over. It was 46–27 at halftime and the lead grew to thirty-four in the second half before Rhoades cleared his bench. The final was 88–59. Cluess had been right: his team wasn't ready for either VCU or the Stu. I was doing the game on television. I had a lot of time to tell Valvano stories during the second half.

The loss dropped Iona to 2-5. The Gaels wouldn't win another nonconference game—even losing to Holy Cross when they finally got to play another home game on December 30. That meant they went into MAAC play at 2-9. But they weren't finished—not even close.

After all, Iona was still Iona.

10

LIVING ON
THE EDGE

Philadelphia's Big Five should be the role model for local college basketball rivalries. Not only do the schools play one another every year, they also play Drexel, the city's sixth Division 1 school, not annually but at least sporadically. Both La Salle and Temple were on Drexel's schedule during the 2018–19 season and in 2019–20.

The complete opposite of this approach is Washington, DC, where the area's two power schools—Maryland and Georgetown—have rarely played each other during the last forty years and Georgetown won't play George Washington—once its archrival—at all.

The mid-majors are far more willing to play one another, but without the cooperation of the two power schools, it has been impossible to organize anything resembling the Big Five in DC.

Which is a shame, given the quality of college basketball programs in the area. Georgetown, under the legendary John Thompson, went to three Final Fours in four years between 1982 and 1985, winning the national title in 1984. In 2007, Thompson's son John Thompson III took the Hoyas back to the Final Four.

Maryland first became a national power under Lefty Driesell in the 1970s and went to back-to-back Final Fours in 2001 and 2002 under Gary Williams, winning the championship in 2002.

Thompson the elder, Driesell, and Williams are all in the Basketball Hall of Fame. Quite a legacy.

But there's more: George Mason, under Jim Larrañaga, wrote one of *the* great Cinderella stories in hoops history in 2006 when it beat

Michigan State, North Carolina, Wichita State, and Connecticut en route to the Final Four. American went to back-to-back NCAA Tournaments under Jeff Jones and then made it there again in 2014 under Mike Brennan. George Washington has had quality teams, dating to the 1970s when Bob Tallent was the coach. Navy had great moments when David Robinson took the Mids to the elite eight in 1986 during a three-year string of NCAA bids. Don DeVoe won three Patriot League titles in Annapolis in the 1990s.

Then there are the pseudolocals, teams that the DC media claims as their own when they have success: VCU was a DC darling during its Final Four run in 2011; Virginia Tech has received considerable attention in recent years under Buzz Williams; and Virginia has become an adopted home team in recent years, especially in the spring of 2019 when it won the national championship.

That's a lot of good to great basketball. And yet, there's nothing even close to the Big Five.

The one local school that hasn't had many great moments is Howard, best known for academic success and athletic failure.

Howard is located in northwest Washington, not far from Children's Hospital. It is one of the country's historically black colleges and universities and competes in the Mid-Eastern Athletic Conference (MEAC), which is one of two Division 1 conferences—the other being the Southwestern Athletic Conference (SWAC)—that is made up of HBCUs. There are eleven members of the MEAC—after Hampton bolted for the Big South in 2018—and ten members of the SWAC.

In 1981, Howard was the first team to represent the MEAC in the NCAA Tournament. That was the first year the conference received an automatic bid, and the Bison received a respectable No. 12 seed. They lost to Wyoming, 78–43. Since then the school has won the MEAC once—in 1992—and was a No. 16 seed. It had to face No. 1 Kansas and got crushed, 100–67.

Howard hasn't been back to the NCAAs since then. It did reach the MEAC championship game in 2002 but was badly beaten by Hampton.

Howard faced serious NCAA sanctions in 2001 and then again in 2014. In 2012, after initiating the investigations that led to the NCAA sanctions two years later, Howard shut down its entire spring sports calendar because things had gotten so out of control.

This from a school that is often referred to as "The Harvard of the HBCUs." The school annually produces more African American PhDs than any other in the country. Its list of distinguished alumni is remarkable: Thurgood Marshall; Toni Morrison; Stokely Carmichael; David Dinkins; Kamala Harris; Ta-Nehisi Coates; and Sean Combs, just to mention a few.

And yet, the school is frequently in turmoil. As recently as 2018, more than a thousand Howard students staged a sit-in to demand an injunction over the way the school was spending funds. Shortly thereafter the faculty voted "no confidence" in the school president, provost, COO, and board of trustees.

On the other hand, the school's graduation speaker in 2016 was President Barack Obama.

Kevin Nickelberry knew what he was getting into when he became the basketball coach in 2010. Nickelberry had grown up in Prince George's County and was well aware of the many ups and downs Howard had gone through. He had been a Division 3 basketball player at Virginia Wesleyan and then began a coaching odyssey. He had been an assistant at Howard under Mike McLeese from 1995 to 1998 and then, when McLeese was fired, had moved on to Monmouth, Holy Cross, and Clemson as an assistant coach.

He got his first shot as a head coach at Hampton in 2006. That lasted three years. He then coached in Libya for a year—"I needed to work," he said with a laugh—before coming home to take the Howard job in 2010.

Since winning the MEAC title in 1992 and finishing 17-14, Howard had experienced one winning season—2002, when it had gone 18-13 under Coach Frankie Allen. In five seasons under Nickelberry's predecessor, Gil Jackson, the Bison's *best* record was 9-22. Plus, the basketball team was on NCAA academic progress rate (APR) probation—handed down for lack of progress among athletes toward a degree.

"It was a mess," Nickelberry said. "Fortunately for me, the administration understood that this was going to require a massive rebuild and would take time."

It took until Nickelberry's fifth season to find respectability. Nickelberry's reputation has always been that of a tireless recruiter, and he solidified it at Howard. The problem, as is often the case with mid-major programs that have been down, is that players frequently established themselves at Howard and then transferred to schools with a better basketball pedigree.

In Nickelberry's fifth season, Howard went 16-16—its first non-losing season since 2002—and finished fourth in the MEAC. The team was led by a pair of young guards, James Daniel and J. T. Miller. A year later, as a junior, Daniel became a genuine star, leading the country in scoring. Part of the reason he had to score so much was injuries to other players that forced too much of the scoring load onto him.

Still, with Daniel back in 2017 and Miller also back, there were high hopes. They never came true. Daniel was injured and played only two games. At Howard's level, losing your best player is devastating. Miller played very well, but the record slipped to 10-24.

Still, both had a fifth year of eligibility. They both used that fifth year at other schools as graduate transfers—Daniel at Tennessee, Miller at Missouri State.

Nickelberry was now in his ninth season at Howard and was in the final year of his contract. After the debacle of 2014, Howard had gone outside the box to find a new athletic director, hiring Kery Davis, a longtime HBO executive with an Ivy League (Dartmouth) pedigree. Davis was smart, tough, and demanding.

Nickelberry knew he needed a good season to get a new contract, and he thought he had put together a team capable of doing just that. The backcourt was formidable with sophomore R. J. Cole, junior C. J. Williams, and redshirt junior Chad Lott. The frontcourt was young—two freshman starters—but talented. None of the team's three seniors played major minutes. The Bison were probably a year away from potentially being very good. Nickelberry knew he didn't have the luxury of waiting till next year.

The Bison were 6-3 when they arrived at George Washington's Smith Center—named, not for Dean Smith, but for Charles E. Smith, a former GW trustee—on a frigid Friday night.

The game was an important one for both teams and both coaches. Howard had beaten American the previous Saturday, and a second win over a local rival would go a long way toward establishing credibility for the team—not to mention giving it a confidence boost.

George Washington needed a win—period. The Colonials had opened the season at home against Stony Brook and bolted to a 22–0 lead, only to end up losing the game, 77–74. They were 2-8 coming into the game with an even younger team than Howard—four sophomores and a junior started, and the only senior was a walk-on.

The argument could be made that GW coach Maurice Joseph had been shoved into one of the most difficult jobs in the country when he had taken over two years earlier for Mike Lonergan.

Joseph, born and raised in Canada, had started his college career at Michigan State, under Tom Izzo. He had transferred to Vermont in search of more playing time and had found it. When Coach Mike Lonergan left the school after his senior season to take the GW job, Joseph went with him.

Lonergan had done excellent work at GW, reaching the NCAA Tournament in his third season with a 24-9 record and then winning the NIT in 2016, his fifth season. For a school like George Washington, winning the NIT was a big deal.

But Lonergan's relationship with athletic director Patrick Nero had cratered. The two men were constantly at odds, and after much whispering around campus, the whole thing blew up in the summer of 2016 when the *Washington Post* published a long story rife with anonymous quotes from former players and assistant coaches about Lonergan's coaching style. He was accused of being verbally abusive and of questioning—among other things—Nero's sexuality while talking to his team.

Even though those quoted were no longer at GW, the *Post* granted them all anonymity, which made the reporting questionable—at best. It didn't matter. Not long after the *Post* story broke, Lonergan was fired. Nero lasted fifteen more months before being allowed to resign.

Lonergan sued the school for the $3 million he was still owed on his contract and eventually reached a settlement reported to be for $1 million, in return for a confidentiality agreement that does not allow him to talk about the events that led to his firing.

Lonergan's firing took place in September with players back on campus and already practicing. Joseph, who was all of thirty-one, was named the new coach, even though he was the least experienced of GW's three full-time assistant coaches. The players liked him. After the Lonergan controversy, the school wanted a coach the players liked.

Regardless, Joseph walked into a buzz saw. The locker room was split over the entire Lonergan-Nero episode, and being asked to take over a team that had lost three key seniors would have been difficult under any circumstances.

The good news was that Lonergan had recruited very well and two excellent players—Tyler Cavanaugh and Yuta Watanabe—were still in school. Led by those two, the Colonials went 20-15 and Joseph had the "interim" removed from his title.

Recruiting was very difficult, though, especially during that first season when GW was seen as a program in chaos and Joseph couldn't promise players he was recruiting that he'd be the coach the following season.

Cavanaugh graduated, but with Watanabe still around, the Colonials were a respectable 15-18 in Joseph's second season. Once Watanabe departed, it was back to square one.

Everyone on campus knew that the school's boosters were already pushing for a better-known, more experienced coach to replace Joseph, regardless of the record in his third season. As if all that wasn't enough, the team's one experienced big man, junior Arnaldo Toro, went down for the season with a hip injury before a single game had been played.

Other than that, Mrs. Lincoln . . .

The game wasn't pretty. Both teams played tight—and shot tight. For Howard, the stage was bigger than what they were accustomed to—a five-thousand-seat gym that was a little more than half-full (2,630) was more than the crowds they played in front of most of the time.

GW *needed* a win, and everyone in a white uniform knew it. The Colonials shot 35 percent in the first half and *led* by ten. The Bison shot 8-for-34 and were 0-for-8 shooting threes. Cole, averaging 21.4 points per game, was 0-for-7 and had 1 point.

The highlight of the first half was actually a fan. In forty years as a reporter, I haven't said that more than a half-dozen times. Maybe not that often.

Most of the time when fans shriek at the officials, especially when they do it on every call, I want to turn around and plead with them to shut up—especially since officials get their calls right at least 95 percent of the time. I keep my mouth shut because I know engaging is the worst thing I can possibly do.

This fan was different. He was funny.

"Isn't this game bad enough without you guys missing so many calls?" he asked at one point.

Later, after a call went against GW, he yelled: "Fake news!"

Then, in the interest of being fair, after a call went against Howard, he said in a voice heard all over the gym: "Do you guys realize you're reffing down to the level of this game? Didn't think it was possible."

His name was Wayne Simmons, and he wasn't at all happy with the Colonials, even with a ten-point halftime lead.

Nickelberry wasn't any happier.

"If they had tied a rope around us, we couldn't have been tighter," Nickelberry said later.

That was his halftime message in the Smith Center's basement locker room: just play basketball. "You're good enough to beat this team if you just play."

They did better in the second half, closing the margin to 48–46 midway through the half. The shooting wasn't much better—Cole would finish 4-for-19 for the game without ever making a three, and the Bison would shoot 3-for-18 from three-point range as a team—but their defense improved, and with a win in sight, the Colonials' shooting got worse.

Finally, after a put-back by Lott had closed the margin to 67–64 with thirty-nine seconds left, Howard needed a stop and GW needed a basket.

The Bison weren't going to foul, and the shot clock ran down with GW looking for a shot. Finally, the ball swung to Terry Nolan Jr., one of the four sophomore starters, and with the shot clock at two, he calmly drilled a three.

Ball game. The final was 70–64.

"That was a rock fight," a clearly exhausted Joseph said. "Sometimes, you have to learn to win ugly, and that's what we did tonight. We weren't sharp offensively, but we held their three leading scorers to twenty-four [combined] under their averages.

"Right now we have to get better every time we play—win or lose."

Joseph was relieved to get a win. Any win. Nickelberry was upset because he knew an opportunity had been lost.

"That's a game we should win," he said, walking in the direction of his team's bus. "If we're going to be any good, we have to win those games."

There was lots of season left. But both teams and their coaches knew they needed to get better—and soon.

DAY—AND NIGHT—
IN THE CATHEDRAL

On the Saturday before Christmas, I was up, showered, coffee'd, and on the road by 7 a.m. absolutely bursting with energy for the day ahead.

I was going to spend roughly eight hours inside the Palestra watching two basketball games, all in the guise of doing research for this book. About the only thing better would be if there were three games.

Once, the Palestra did host the occasional tripleheader. More traditional, though, were the Big Five doubleheaders, which usually featured a nationally known team playing a Big Five team in the opener followed by two Big Five teams facing each other in the nightcap.

One of those doubleheaders was my first experience in the building known as "The Cathedral of College Basketball." It was my junior year of college, and Duke played St. Joseph's in the opener. Then Villanova and Temple played in the second game.

From the street, the Palestra is hardly imposing. It sits behind Penn's tennis courts and next to Franklin Field, set back from Thirty-Third Street as you drive by it. Because its façade is reddish-brown brick, it is easy to miss—especially in the dark—if you don't know to look for it.

I probably drove past it four times before I stopped someone on the street and said, "Where in the world is the Palestra?"

"There," the guy answered, pointing at the building that was right in front of me.

Once I found it, I fell in love almost instantly. In those days, the media seating was right behind the scorer's table in a row raised high enough so that you had a great view of the court. Since I was there representing the Duke student newspaper, I was seated almost directly behind the Duke bench, meaning I could look right into Bill Foster's huddle.

Naturally, I stayed for the second game and was enthralled by the atmosphere: the streamers tossed by the students after their school's first basket; the "rollouts," each student section produced mocking the other in some way and—most of all—the intensity of the game and the fans.

Once I went to work at the *Washington Post,* I made a point of making at least one trip to the Palestra every season, even after the number of Big Five games was cut way back; even after the doubleheaders all but disappeared. Even after the NCAA, in its wisdom, came up with a rule that made it mandatory for referees to call a technical foul on any student body that tossed streamers onto the court.

The rule was there to keep angry fans from throwing *anything* onto the court, but it didn't give officials the discretion to say, "This is tradition and its harmless, so we aren't going to call it."

I grew up in New York and I've lived in Washington my entire adult life, but Philadelphia is where I feel most at home when it comes to college hoops. Some of my closest friends in the business are Philadelphia legends: Jack Scheuer, who covered Philly sports for the AP for forty-five years, and Dick (Hoops) Weiss are two of them.

Hoops was given his nickname early on in his career by an editor named Sandy Padwe, not just because of his love for the game, but for his encyclopedic knowledge of it. He grew up in Philadelphia and attended his first game in the Palestra in 1960 as a teenager. He went to Temple and then worked at the *Philadelphia Daily News*. Even after he took a job as the national college writer for the *New York Daily News,* he continued to live in Philadelphia and remained a staple at Big Five games.

Thirty-two years ago, I drove to Philly for a Villanova–St. Joseph's game in the Palestra. It was a triple-overtime classic. When it was over, Dan Baker, then the executive director of the Big Five, set Hoops and me up in his office so we could write in a comfortable spot. I finished, did a radio hit, and was ready to make the drive back to DC.

The *Philadelphia Daily News* was one of the great afternoon papers in the country, and with no real deadline to deal with, Hoops was, shall we say, deliberate. When I finished, he decided he'd go home to finish his story. We walked out of Dan's office to the exit.

It was locked. There was no other way out.

Fortunately, Hoops had Dan's home number and reached him there.

"I'll have to call security," Dan said. "They'll send someone to let you out."

It took an hour. Hoops and I sat in the hallway because we'd locked ourselves out of Dan's office when we left. Hoops sat on a step and wrote. I just sat.

Years later, my wife insisted that being locked inside the Palestra was a dream come true for me. "If you ever disappear," she often tells me, "I'll know you've left me to move into the Palestra."

That's a stretch, but not by much. I *do* feel absolutely at home whenever I walk inside the building. The first thing I do is walk down the main concourse to "the sign."

Everyone who knows college hoops knows the sign. No one knows who actually said it or wrote it, but I can't see it—or write it—enough: "To win the game is great . . . to play the game is greater . . . but to love the game is the greatest of all."

I stand there, reading it for the millionth time, and smile. Maybe I get a little misty-eyed. Then I touch the plaque it's on and head off to buy a pretzel before I walk down the ramp to the floor. I get chills every single time I hit the bottom of the ramp.

December 22 was a doubleheader day in the Palestra . . . sort of.

In today's world, every college program tries to soak in every dollar possible, so the doubleheader would be split—both by time and money.

The first game would be Temple and Drexel with a one o'clock tipoff—a Drexel home game. The second game would be Loyola of Chicago—last season's Cinderella Final Four team—playing St. Joseph's. It wouldn't start until five, which would be enough time to clear the building and then let in a different set of fans with a different set of tickets.

It didn't make much difference to me. The roughly two hours between games would mean I'd have time to talk to players and coaches from Drexel and Temple, get a bite to eat, and be ready to go for the five o'clock tipoff.

First, though, I would drive downtown to have breakfast with Loyola coach Porter Moser and then spend some time with his team before getting to the Palestra in plenty of time for Temple and Drexel.

For me, a dream day.

It is almost impossible to miss a basketball team walking through an airport, a restaurant, or a hotel lobby, if only because the sight of a dozen young men ranging in height from about six feet tall to seven feet tall—with a number of six-sixes to six-eights mixed in—can usually mean only one thing: basketball.

In fact, there are players who are described as "airport players," because they're very tall, impossible not to notice in an airport, but can't really play.

And so it was, early on a Saturday morning in Philadelphia's downtown Marriott hotel, that the Loyola basketball team made its way to a meeting room to eat game-day breakfast, followed by a walk-through to prepare for their game later that afternoon against St. Joseph's.

Heads turned, as they do, although most people weren't exactly sure which team it was in the maroon-and-gold sweats. It wasn't as if Zion Williamson was in the group. Of course, if he had been, he no doubt would have been surrounded by security.

Even though a number of the Loyola Ramblers had done something Williamson would never do—play in a Final Four—they needed no security.

But someone did recognize them: a hotel employee.

"Hey," he said as the players walked past him, "that's Sister Jean's team."

It was an apt description. During Loyola's remarkable run to San Antonio the previous March, the team's star hadn't been Coach Porter Moser or any of the players. It had been Sister Jean Dolores Schmidt, the team's ninety-eight-year-year-old chaplain.

Sister Jean wasn't some kind of publicity stunt. She'd been at Loyola since 1991 and had been the team chaplain since 1994. She was revered on campus. The school had actually produced a Sister Jean bobblehead in 2011 and had held a Sister Jean Day a year later. She'd been awarded an honorary doctorate by the school in 2016.

But when the Ramblers began winning NCAA Tournament games

and the media learned that their team chaplain was a ninety-eight-year-old nun—one who knew her hoops—she became an overnight star nationally.

She was sharp as a tack, funny, and willing to talk about her beloved team and players. The media couldn't get enough of her.

"What made it so appealing," said Moser, "was that she's the real deal in every way. You met her, you liked her. You listened to her, you learned."

Loyola is a Jesuit school with a great basketball history. It won the national championship in 1963 and took part in what is known as "The Game of Change," when it faced Mississippi State in the round of sixteen that year. The Bulldogs had to literally sneak out of Starkville to fly to East Lansing, Michigan, to play in the game. They were under a court order to not play because an unwritten state law forbade state schools from playing against integrated teams.

Prior to the game, Loyola captain Jerry Harkness and Mississippi State captain Joe Dan Gold met at the center jump circle to shake hands—a photo that became famous in college hoops history. When Gold died in 2011, Harkness, who had become a friend, attended his funeral.

But Loyola hadn't been a factor nationally since 1985, when it had reached the sweet sixteen before losing to defending national champion Georgetown.

Moser was a Chicago kid—he'd been born in Naperville about fifty miles outside the city—but was a dyed-in-the-wool fan of all Chicago teams growing up. He'd played basketball at Creighton and then gone to work there for his college coach, Tony Barone. He'd followed Barone to Texas A&M.

He was thirty-two when he got his first shot as a head coach, at Arkansas–Little Rock. He turned the program around there and was rewarded with the Illinois State job—better league (the Missouri Valley) and closer to home.

But things didn't go well there. It wasn't as if the Redbirds were terrible: they were 17-13 in Moser's second season and 15-16 in his fourth. But overall they were 51-67 and Moser was fired, a moment he later described as "miserable and life-changing."

The biggest life change was his next job: working as an assistant to Rick Majerus at St. Louis. Majerus, who died in 2011 at the age of sixty-four after years of heart problems, had a reputation in the media as being funny (which he was), roly-poly (also true), and an always happy guy.

That wasn't true. He was almost obsessively competitive and drove his players and staff hard. Moser, who is as genuinely upbeat as Majerus appeared to be, was often the liaison between the hot-tempered coach and his players.

"I loved working for Rick," he said. "It wasn't easy by any means, but I learned a lot from him about basketball and about coaching. We had turned it around there, and I was completely comfortable in the number two role there.

"When Loyola called, I was actually torn. I'm a Catholic kid from Chicago, it's a Jesuit school. It made all sorts of sense. But I wasn't sure I wanted to leave St. Louis or Rick. Finally, he [Majerus] said to me, 'You're going. You have to go. This isn't an option.'"

Loyola was still playing in the Horizon League when Moser arrived, the same league that had produced Butler, which had just gone to back-to-back national title games and used that exposure to jump first to the Atlantic 10 and then to the Big East.

Two years after Moser arrived, the school applied to join the Missouri Valley, which needed to add a team after Creighton had jumped to the Big East. Longtime MVC commissioner Doug Elgin was intrigued by Loyola because it was in Chicago and he thought his league could use a major media market.

"The other thing was, the first time I visited, it looked as if the entire campus was under construction," Elgin said. "It was clearly a school that was building—literally and figuratively."

Elgin might have been concerned with Loyola's more recent basketball history: since the sweet sixteen run of 1985, the Ramblers hadn't been back to the NCAA tournament. In fact, they'd had four winning seasons in twenty-seven years. But Elgin was convinced the school had hired the right guy in Moser.

"It wasn't just the enthusiasm," Elgin said. "You meet a lot of coaches who are enthusiastic. He had a plan. I felt like he knew what he was doing."

Loyola was 10-22 in its first season in the MVC, and there were those who thought they'd outkicked their coverage. But a year later, they went 24-13 and won the CBI—one of the "pay-to-play" postseason tournaments. For Loyola, that was a big deal.

And then, three seasons later, Loyola exploded. The Valley—as everyone in the Midwest calls the MVC—was wide-open going into 2017–18, since Wichita State, which had been the league's dominant team after Creighton left, had jumped to the American Athletic Conference.

Loyola had all their key players back from a team that had gone 18-14. Loyola was picked third in the preseason poll. Moser thought his team had a chance to be better than that. An early win over then-fifth-ranked Florida convinced him he was right.

Moser had made solid recruiting inroads in Chicago, but he had two senior guards from Overland Park, Kansas—which borders Kansas City. Ben Richardson and Clayton Custer had started playing together in the third grade (seriously) and had been teammates right through high school.

They'd gone in different directions coming out of high school: Custer had been a more coveted recruit and chose Iowa State over Big 12 rivals Oklahoma State and Kansas State. Kansas had also shown some interest before backing off because it was guard-rich.

Richardson, who was more a combo guard than a point guard—like Custer—was more of a mid-major recruit, choosing Loyola over schools like UMass and Indiana State.

It hadn't worked out for Custer at Iowa State. He played little as a freshman and, as many players do nowadays, he transferred—deciding to reunite with Richardson at Loyola.

After sitting out a year, he had become Richardson's backcourt mate, which also allowed Marques Townes more freedom to play without the ball.

Custer missed five games with an injury in late December and early January. The Ramblers lost the last of those games 61–57 to Indiana State—giving up the last seven points of the game. They were 11-4 at that moment. From that point on they won twenty-one of their next twenty-two—the only loss coming at Bradley in late January.

It wasn't as if the nation had Loyola fever as the winter unfolded. The attendance in the Joseph J. Gentile Arena on the Loyola campus for the Indiana State game was 1,501—which was fairly typical in the five-thousand-seat arena at that stage.

The Ramblers were never ranked in the top twenty-five during the regular season. I voted for them in the AP poll on February 19, as did one other voter. By Selection Sunday, the day of the last poll, they received twenty-seven votes and came up just shy of making the top twenty-five.

They finished off the season by beating Illinois State—the school that had fired Moser eleven years earlier—to win the Missouri Valley Conference tournament and the automatic NCAA bid.

The NCAA basketball committee, which rarely does mid-majors any favors, made them a No. 11 seed—which means that if Loyola had *not* won the tournament, it would not have received an at-large bid.

Which once again shows how little the committee knows about basketball.

Loyola then proceeded to win three straight tournament games by two points, one point, and one point: In the opener against Miami, Donte Ingram hit a *long* three-pointer from well beyond the key at the buzzer for a 64–62 win. Two days later, it was Custer's turn—he hit a buzzer-beating jumper that seemed to climb up and over the rim to beat Tennessee, 63–62. Then, in the sweet sixteen, Townes drained a long three with the shot clock down and Loyola clinging to a 66–65 lead that clinched a victory over Nevada.

By now, Sister Jean had become a national folk hero and it appeared that God *was* on the Ramblers' side. They didn't need any extra help in the regional final, dominating Kansas State (which had upset Kentucky) almost from start to finish in a 78–62 victory.

All of a sudden, Loyola was America's Team and Moser was America's Coach. The other three Final Four teams—Villanova, Kansas, and Michigan—must have felt invisible when they arrived in San Antonio. The ride ended against Michigan in the semifinals, but the love affair didn't.

"It started to get crazy when we made it to the sweet sixteen," Custer remembered. "When we came home from Dallas, we got a hero's welcome on campus. After that, it never really stopped—even after we lost to Michigan. It was an amazing feeling, [to] know that we'd accomplished something no one—except us—thought we could accomplish. It was just a great ride, a life-changing ride for all of us."

Moser, whom most college basketball fans couldn't have picked out of a lineup in February, was in demand from media, from corporations as a speaker, and from anyone looking for a celebrity at an event.

"I wasn't in Sister Jean's class," he said, laughing. "But it was amazing how my life changed. I understood it. We were an appealing story, with an appealing group of kids."

Almost missed amid all the adulation was that Loyola had finished behind only Duke in academic rankings.

Moser knew the joy ride that had been March was going to feel completely different when November arrived. Richardson would be gone; Ingram would be gone . . .

Getting into the homes of big-name recruits would be easier. No more explaining that yes, Loyola of Chicago was different from Loyola of Baltimore and Loyola of New Orleans.

There would also be the issue of being a target game on opponents' schedules. Moser decided he needed advice from someone who had gone through it, so he flew to Boston to spend time with Celtics coach Brad Stevens, who had taken Butler to the national championship game in 2010 and then—perhaps even more remarkably—again in 2011.

"Brad told me the first couple of months of the next season were the most miserable he ever had," Moser said. "He'd lost Gordon Hayward, and yet every time they lost a game it was 'What's wrong, why are you guys losing?' Of course, they turned it around late and got on a run again in March, but Brad said it was the best and worst learning experience he ever had as a coach.

"Matt Howard, who'd been a starter on both Final Four teams, was there that week and I spent a lot of time talking to him. He said the first three months of his senior year [2011] were absolutely miserable. It was one thing to be recognized everywhere you went on campus when you were winning, but not nearly as much fun when you weren't."

Stevens, who is about as cerebral as anyone in coaching, had given a lot of thought to what had happened the season after the Hayward miss.

"We lost our anonymity," he said. "Before the first Final Four run we were one of those mid-majors that people might pick to win a game or maybe two in their pools. We were a solid NCAA team every year, but it wasn't as if we were a TV team every night. We were still playing in the Horizon League.

"Then the perfect storm happens. Not only do we get to the Final Four, but it's Indianapolis a few miles from our campus. And then we play Duke in the final and almost pull off the most dramatic finish in history.

"For a while, most people treated it as if the shot had gone in, not just missed. It felt that way a little—for a while. Now we're a media darling, we're on TV all the time. And we're not very good. I remember being at wit's end when we lost to Youngstown State. We were 14-9 and going nowhere.

"And then we just stopped losing. I wish I could say I waved some kind of magic wand, but I think it was more about the guys figuring there was nothing to lose at that point and starting to enjoy basketball again. I can tell you one thing for sure: it wasn't an easy ride to get there. That's what I tried to explain to Porter. He shouldn't feel as if he was doing something wrong if it wasn't an easy ride."

Stevens is still only forty-three but is in his seventh season as coach of the Boston Celtics. He is considered one of the NBA's best coaches but knows he may not be in Boston forever. He has no idea what he might do next.

"I love coaching here," he said. "I've enjoyed it. But if there came a time where they didn't want me anymore, I don't know if I'd stay in the NBA or go back to college. I really don't."

There's one job he's certain he'll never take. When he was still at Butler, Stevens was often mentioned on the very short list of possible successors to Mike Krzyzewski.

"Never happen," he said, laughing. "Because I couldn't coach in that gym and look at that [2010] banner every day. I'd insist they take it down. I don't think they'd be willing to do that."

Talking to Stevens was helpful for Moser. But he knew that all the research in the world wasn't going to make up for the loss of three starters: Richardson, Ingram, and Aundre Jackson. And there was going to be the noise factor.

"That's what we all noticed right away," said Custer, who along with fellow senior Marques Townes had to fill the leadership void left by the three who had graduated. "A year ago, if we played Furman at home in November and lost, there would have been less than two thousand people in the building and almost no one outside of our families who would have noticed.

"This year, we lose to them—and they're really good—and it's a national story."

Furman *was* really good. A week after beating Loyola it played at Villanova—the defending national champions—and also won.

Like any successful mid-major coach, Moser had put together a tough preconference schedule, hoping to put his team in a position to get an at-large bid if it didn't win the MVC Tournament in March. He was fully aware that his team wasn't as experienced as it had been a year earlier, but he wanted to leave no potential stone unturned.

And so, there were games in an exempt tournament in Fort Myers, Florida, against Richmond (a win) and Boston College (a loss) and then a loss to sixth-ranked Nevada, a team that came to Chicago on a mission after losing to the Ramblers the previous March. You can't "get revenge," as the media often reports for losing an NCAA Tournament game, but you can get satisfaction from a fourteen-point win the following November.

It was in the Nevada game that sophomore guard Lucas Williamson, who had stepped into Richardson's starting spot, broke his hand and was ruled out until January.

A loss in Baltimore to Maryland followed by expected home wins over Norfolk State and Benedictine brought the Ramblers to Philadelphia with a 7-5 record. The noise hadn't abated.

"We all knew it was going to be different this year, feel different too," Custer said. "I miss Ben every day—on and off the court. Except for that one year when I was at Iowa State, I've had him next to me on the court since third grade. Even my transfer year I was with him in practice every day.

"I think we understand how special last season was." He stopped and smiled. "Truth is, even now, I'm not sure it's completely hit me what we did. I'm sure it will when my college career is over; when we come back for reunions, things like that.

"The one thing I know and that we've discussed is that no matter what happens going forward, our legacy is secure; we're a part of Loyola's history forever and basketball history forever. That's pretty cool."

He paused for a moment. "Of course, it would be even cooler if we could do it again."

I watched the Ramblers go through their walk-through in a Marriott ballroom. It was very precise. Managers had painstakingly put tape on the floor so that players could see the end line, foul line, and three-point line.

Moser was very detailed about what needed to be done, and the assistants reviewed the scouting report on St. Joseph's. I noticed one thing that was different, at least to my ears: when he wanted to work on inbound plays, he called them "end-outs." I hadn't heard that before. Maybe it was a midwestern thing, like calling soda "pop."

Once the walk-through was over, I jumped back in my car and drove to the Palestra, walking in at noon.

I stopped at the sign, walked down the ramp, and headed to the Temple locker room.

When the Palestra was renovated several years ago, the changes were all about seating—fan comfort. The locker rooms, except for the home locker room, weren't changed. They are as tiny now as ever.

Fran Dunphy was standing in front of a whiteboard in one of the visitors' locker rooms (there are three) diagonally across the court from the locker room he called home for seventeen years as Penn's coach.

The board was filled with all sorts of notes on individual players—"left-handed"; "will always look to drive"; "shooter"—the kinds of notes that are the staples of basketball scouting reports. Dean Smith always put a + next to someone who was a shooter, to indicate he needed a hand in his face at all times. Occasionally he went to ++, but that was rare.

"Len Bias," he said when I asked him who had gotten the ++ designation. "David Thompson. Bob Verga [a Duke star of the 1960s]. Christian Laettner, his last two years."

It was a short list.

Dunphy was poker-faced less than an hour before tipoff in a building he had played in first as a high school star and then for La Salle and had coached in as the home coach before returning a couple of times a year after moving to Temple.

The Palestra *is* the Big Five. Dunphy—after playing for La Salle, getting a master's at Villanova, and coaching for thirty years at Penn and Temple—was Mr. Big Five.

"Feeling anything?" I asked, knowing this would be his last appearance as a coach in the Cathedral.

"Not really," he said. "It's a game we need to win. That's most of my focus. It has to be."

Zach Spiker was in his third season at Drexel, and the Dragons had steadily improved. They were 6-6, with an impressive win over

St. Joseph's on their résumé. They were still young—one senior would start—but playing Temple in the Palestra would be a big deal, and Dunphy knew his team had to be ready to play or it could be a long afternoon.

"Be ready to bring everything you have emotionally," he told his players. "Because I promise you they will."

Temple was 9-2, the two losses being to VCU and at Villanova in a tight game. Dunphy liked what he had seen so far, but he knew every win was crucial because the Owls were likely to be a bubble team come March.

As it turned out, the most emotional moment of the afternoon came before tipoff. After the teams had been introduced, the coaches were introduced. Normally, the visiting coach—Dunphy—would be introduced first. But not on this day. Spiker was introduced to a nice round of applause from the Drexel fans. Then public address announcer Jeff Asch—who worked for Drexel—introduced Dunphy.

"And please welcome, coaching his final game in the Palestra, the winningest coach in Big Five history with five hundred and sixty-six victories, Fran Dunphy."

Instantly, the entire building—Temple fans, Drexel fans—were all on their feet, applauding. Not raucous cheers the way you might hear for an important basket, but loud applause. It continued for a couple of minutes. Dunphy waved his thanks. The applause continued. Dunphy waved again, then put his palms down as if to say, "That's plenty." The applause continued, no one really wanting to stop. Everyone on the Drexel bench was clapping too. Finally, after more than four minutes, after Dunphy had *again* asked them to stop, they stopped.

The start of the game was something you can see only in Philadelphia. Spiker and Dunphy had agreed that, in honor of the occasion, the tradition of throwing streamers should be brought back. The students at either end of the court were given streamers and told not to worry about being called for a technical foul for tossing them.

When Drexel's Troy Harper made the game's first basket, the Drexel students threw the streamers. Technical foul, ruled a "class B" technical, so no free throws were shot. The Temple students reciprocated a moment after that.

Dunphy's players gave him the emotion he was looking for. The Owls took the lead for good at 15–13 and finished the half on an 8–0 run for a 41–30 lead. Drexel crept to within 60–54 on a Harper jumper with 8:55 left, but the Owls responded with a 7–0 run and eased to an 82–64 win. Shizz Alston Jr. played the way a senior star is supposed to play, scoring 25 points, and sophomore Nate Pierre-Louis made 9-of-11 shots for 22 points and added 9 rebounds.

Temple looked like an NCAA Tournament team that could handle itself in an emotional game.

An hour after the final buzzer, as he was leaving the building, Dunphy ran into Porter Moser coming in for his game. The two men chatted for a while. I walked over.

"Did he tell you about the ovation?" I asked Moser.

Moser looked quizzically at Dunphy. "He said his guys played really well," he said.

"Four-minute standing ovation when they introduced him," I said.

"Stop it," Dunphy said. He turned to Moser. "It wasn't that long."

"You're right," I said. "It was actually four minutes and fifteen seconds. I timed it."

"You're too much," Dunphy said—a line he uses often on people.

Moser grinned. "Four fifteen?" he said. "Not long enough in my book."

I couldn't have agreed more.

There were two good things to be said about the Loyola–St. Joseph's game: it was close and it had a dramatic ending. Beyond that . . . not so much.

St. Joseph came into the game with a 5-5 record that was better than it looked. Phil Martelli, in his twenty-fourth season as head coach—he'd been an assistant for ten years prior to that—thought he was going to have a good team, so he put together a tough nonconference schedule.

St. Joe's had wins over Old Dominion, Wake Forest, and Princeton—all solid teams. It had lost to UCF (which would come within inches of beating Duke in March), Temple, and Villanova. There was one bad loss: at William & Mary. A good Atlantic 10 team should not lose to a middle-of-the-pack CAA team, even on the road.

Martelli had been extremely successful at St. Joe's—coming within a bounce of the ball of reaching the Final Four in 2004 and taking the school to seven NCAA Tournaments—most recently in 2016, when the Hawks had gone 28-8 and won the Atlantic 10 Tournament. Martelli had been voted coach of the year by the writers who covered the Big Five.

At the annual Big Five awards dinner in April, Martelli accepted the award and then said: "Once again I am going to save the Big Five media from itself. This is very kind of you. But Jay Wright just won the national championship. How can he not be the coach of the year?"

He then called Wright to the podium and handed him the plaque.

St. Joe's had a down year in 2017 and had gone 16-16 a year earlier. The school was changing. In 2015, Mark Reed had been named president—the first lay president in the school's 164-year history. The previous spring, Don DiJulia had decided to retire after thirty-five years as athletic director.

DiJulia was a St. Joe's graduate—class of 1967—and had played basketball and baseball. He'd been a basketball coach for years before becoming AD. He was, like Martelli, a lifelong Philly guy with an abiding love for the game—he often showed up at other Big Five games just to watch and to interact with the coaches, all of whom were his friends. Perhaps no athletic administrator anywhere understood coaching the way DiJulia did.

DiJulia's successor was Jill Bodensteiner, a classic twenty-first-century athletic director hire. Bodensteiner was a lawyer and a career administrator. She was a Notre Dame graduate who had worked her entire professional career at the school. Her bio was filled with all sorts of NCAA committees she'd served on. In short: a bureaucrat, who would undoubtedly be an excellent fund-raiser—which is the most important thing ADs do nowadays.

She had never coached, and her presence in DiJulia's place made many Big Five hoops people nervous.

"She's going to feel pressure from some of the alumni," my pal Hoops Weiss said soon after Bodensteiner had stopped to say hello to him and to introduce herself to me. "A lot of them think they should be competing regularly with Villanova. That's their complaint with Phil. They don't understand, they're *not* Villanova."

Martelli wasn't worried. He thought he was going to have a good season and, new AD or old AD, who was going to run him out going into his twenty-fifth season?

The Palestra was close to full for the five o'clock tipoff. Neither team had any success on offense: Loyola would finish the game shooting 34 percent from the floor and 5-of-19 from three-point range after going 0-for-9 in the first half. St. Joe's was worse: 32.8 percent from the field and 5-of-24 from three.

Even though the game was anything but pretty, I enjoyed myself. Hoops sat to my right and Jack Scheuer to my left. If there's a writer in Philly *more* legendary than Hoops, it is Scheuer. He covered Philadelphia sports for the AP for forty-five years and is the leading scorer in the history of the Palestra.

That's because he organized and ran the weekly noon hoops game played by media members every Wednesday forever. Jack played Division 3 basketball and was a superb shooter well into his seventies. He also ruled the noon hoops game with an iron hand.

Once, when Fran Dunphy was still coaching at Penn, he forgot it was Wednesday and scheduled a 1 p.m. practice during semester break. When the Quakers walked onto the floor, Scheuer looked at Dunphy and said, "Dunph, are you kidding?"

"Sorry, Jack," Dunphy said. "We'll go inside and watch film until you're done."

Scheuer was now eighty-six, but his memory was as encyclopedic as ever, and sitting next to him wasn't just a hoops history lesson, it was like listening to a basketball professor explain the game. He also had a key to the back door of the Palestra, which was a good thing because he'd had hip surgery and walking wasn't easy. Being able to pull up to the back door and walk inside from there was very helpful.

Several years earlier, in the midst of a snowstorm, Jack had pulled into his spot and walked to the door.

"Hey, pal, that door's locked, you can't go in there," a security guy had said.

"I have a key," Jack answered.

"Yeah, right, you have a key to the Palestra," the guard said. "You have a key, be my guest."

Jack opened the door, waved at the stunned guard, and walked inside.

All three of us—Hoops, Jack, and I—were relieved when St. Joseph's Lamarr (Fresh) Kimble hit a step-back three at the buzzer to give the Hawks a 45–42 victory.

"No offense to Loyola, Porter's a friend," Hoops said. (Hoops describes everyone in college hoops as a friend.) "But this game needed to be put out of its misery."

Loyola was now 7-6 heading into conference play.

"Plenty of time to get on a roll," Custer said just before going to greet his parents. "We know we're better than this. The difference is, now a lot of people will be watching to see how much better we can be."

ROCK-AND-ROLL
HEAVEN

December 21, 2018, Conway, South Carolina

I f I were to ask you to name coaches with more than eight hundred career wins, I'm sure you could quickly come up with Mike Krzyzewski, Jim Boeheim, Bob Knight, Jim Calhoun, Dean Smith, Adolph Rupp, and Roy Williams.

But how about Cliff Ellis?

In all, there are twenty-six coaches with eight hundred wins at all levels of college basketball: Divisions 1–3 and NAIA. The seven named above are the only ones who have won more than eight hundred games at the Division 1 level. Bob Huggins, currently coaching at West Virginia, won seventy-one games at Walsh, an NAIA school, before going on to win another 788 in Division 1, meaning he has a total of 859 wins.

And then there's Ellis. He also started his career at an NAIA school, going 78-12 at Cumberland (Tennessee) College before becoming a Division 1 coach. Since then, he's won 764 games, giving him a total of 848 wins.

Which isn't bad for a guy who thought his life's path was as a musician when he graduated from Florida State in 1968. He was the lead singer in a group called the Villagers, and the first record they cut in Nashville was a major success.

"I thought that was going to be my life's work," he said. "I loved music. Still do. But basketball kept pulling me in. I couldn't quite get it out of my system."

He continued with the Villagers but also began coaching high school basketball. Then, in 1972, he was offered the job as coach and athletic director at Cumberland College in Tennessee. After that, music became a hobby.

His eye-catching record at Cumberland got him a Division 1 job at South Alabama. He coached there for nine seasons, then went to Clemson for ten and Auburn for ten. He took South Alabama to two NCAA Tournaments and then made basketball winners out of schools known almost strictly for football.

His Clemson team won the ACC regular-season title in 1990, the only time the school has ever finished first in conference play. During that season, someone made the mistake of asking Ellis if he thought perhaps the ACC was a little bit down.

Ellis is about as congenial as anyone in coaching. His answer to that question was not.

"You're only asking that because Clemson's in first place," he said. "If Duke or North Carolina were in first place, you wouldn't bring it up. I'll tell you what, the league's as good as ever, it's just hard for a lot of you people from North Carolina to accept the idea that Clemson's pretty good."

Ellis still likes to point out the uniqueness of that school year: "Duke won the conference title in football and Clemson won it in basketball," he said with a laugh. "Think that will ever happen again?"

Two teams from that "down" ACC—Duke and Georgia Tech—made the Final Four that season. Ellis still believes it could just as easily have been his "pretty good" Clemson team.

The Tigers made it to the sweet sixteen and met top-seeded Connecticut in the Meadowlands. They came from way behind to take the lead, 70–69, with one second left. After a time-out, Jim Calhoun put Scott Burrell, a baseball pitcher, on the end line to throw the inbounds pass.

Burrell threw a strike to Tate George, who caught the ball in the right corner and in one motion buried an eighteen-foot jump shot to give Connecticut a 71–70 win.

"They made a great play and the kid made a tough shot," Ellis said. "But I will always believe if we had replay back then, it would have shown that he didn't get the shot off. No way to prove it, but that's what I believe."

We were sitting in a restaurant in Conway, South Carolina, a few days before Christmas. Ellis was now in his twelfth season at Coastal Carolina and, as at Clemson and Auburn, he had been very successful—twice taking the school to the NCAA Tournament; twice winning twenty-eight games—but, having failed to win the Atlantic Sun Conference tournament those years, had played in the NIT.

Now Coastal was in the Sun Belt Conference, a move made—surprise—because the school wanted to play football at the FBS level.

"I'm fine with it," he said, shaking his head. "It might take us a year or two [the Chanticleers were in their second season in the conference], but we'll figure it out. I'm too old to get upset about things like that. Nothing I can do about it anyway."

After taking Auburn to two sweet sixteens, Ellis had been fired in 2004 and had figured—to quote Jim Phelan—he had enough. He didn't need to work; he had written three books on coaching, and he still had his music. So he and his wife, Carolyn, settled down in Auburn and felt perfectly comfortable. Carolyn even ran for the state legislature.

Then, in the summer of 2007, he got a phone call from David A. DeCenzo, who had just become the president of Coastal Carolina. He was looking for a basketball coach, and he knew Ellis had won everywhere he'd been.

Ellis wasn't sure. Like his friend Tubby Smith, he'd grown accustomed to chartered airplanes while at Clemson and Auburn, and he was perfectly happy not coaching.

He called two old friends from his days in the ACC: Les Robinson and Mike Krzyzewski. He called Robinson because he had transitioned from the big time (NC State) to the not so big time, the Citadel. He called Krzyzewski because, well, he's Krzyzewski.

"They both said the same thing—coaching is coaching, doesn't matter how big the gym is or how much you're getting paid. Mike asked me one other question: 'What's your gut telling you? Do you think you want to go back?'"

The answer was yes, he wanted to coach again. When Ellis called DeCenzo to say he'd like to come in and talk to him about the job, DeCenzo told him he'd received a pretty strong recommendation that made him sure he wanted to hire Ellis.

It was from Krzyzewski.

"I never asked him to make a call," Ellis said. "He never told me [he] was going to call. He just called."

"I owed it to him," Krzyzewski said, laughing. "All those years at the ACC meetings, he'd get up and sing at night and I told him he was terrible. Fact is, he was really good."

And so, Ellis went back into the gym—and has never looked back. He had just turned seventy-three when I went to visit him, and he led me around campus and through the almost-new HTC Center, the sparkling five-thousand-seat arena Coastal now plays in, like a kid showing off his backyard.

He admitted he still had one goal he wanted to accomplish before he walked away and he and Carolyn did some traveling.

"My best friend in coaching is probably Lefty [Driesell]," he said. "He's got seven hundred and eighty-six wins. I want to get past him so I can spend the rest of our lives giving him a hard time about it.

"I'll never be the coach he was—and thank God they finally put him in the Hall of Fame—but I'd love to have that one on him."

His eyes twinkled. As always, Ellis was enjoying himself. I had the sense he had *always* enjoyed himself.

The Chanticleers were off to a 6-5 start and had already lost two key players to injury. Ellis wasn't happy, but he knew he could deal with it.

"We'll be okay," he said. "And next year, watch out."

I believed him.

CHRISTMAS GIFTS AND
CHRISTMAS COAL

One thing that's tough about being a college basketball player is you don't get to go home at all for Thanksgiving and your Christmas break is extremely brief.

Everyone plays over Thanksgiving weekend—some teams play tournament games *on* Thanksgiving—and even though coaches try to let players go home briefly for Christmas, the break is usually three days, perhaps four. Many teams resume play on December 27, and coaches almost inevitably want them back for a Christmas night practice—especially if they have to travel for that first game after the break.

Perhaps the most inspired performance I've ever seen by a basketball team came on December 21, 1985, in Bloomington, Indiana. On a Saturday afternoon, Indiana played Iowa State in Assembly Hall.

The plan was for the players to leave for Christmas break right after the game and return on Christmas night to prepare to play Idaho on December 27. Everyone knew the plan was subject to change.

"We lose to these guys and we might practice twice a day right through Christmas," assistant coach Royce Waltman said.

"Could be three times," said Ron Felling, also an assistant.

Iowa State was a very good team—one that would go on to upset a second-seeded Michigan team in the second round of the NCAA Tournament and reach the sweet sixteen.

The final score that December afternoon in Bloomington was Indiana 86, Iowa State 65. It really wasn't that close.

In the locker room, you'd have thought Indiana had won the national championship.

Most teams don't face that kind of pressure, but everyone wants to head home for Christmas in a good frame of mind—coaches included.

When Jim Valvano was still coaching at North Carolina State, his wife, Pam, begged him to schedule an easy game as the last one before Christmas.

"If he lost that game, it would ruin Christmas," she told me several years ago. "I'd have to go upstairs on Christmas morning and make him come down to open presents with the girls. He really just wanted to stay up there and sulk."

Nowadays, more and more conferences are going straight into conference play out of Christmas break. This is because, with conference expansion, most are playing at least eighteen conference games. The major conferences are starting to go to twenty-game conference schedules because the more games they have involving two conference teams, the happier their TV networks are. A lot more ads can be sold on, say, a Wake Forest–Clemson game than Wake Forest–UNC Asheville or Clemson-Wofford.

The coaches hate it because it cuts down on their scheduling flexibility: some would rather have a couple more guarantee games; others want more opportunities to build their nonconference résumés with nationally televised games.

The commissioners and athletic directors could care less. Show them the money. Period.

Both George Washington and American had one nonconference game to play coming out of Christmas and had decided to play each other on Saturday, the twenty-ninth. That meant they could let their players have all of Christmas with their families and bring them back to practice on the afternoon of the twenty-sixth.

"They deserve it," American coach Mike Brennan joked. "They put up with me enough without having to do it on Christmas."

Actually, Brennan is one of the more reasonable coaches in the game. Maybe it's because he played for Pete Carril at Princeton. Carril was one of the game's great coaches and could spin himself into a Danny DeVito–like mess during a game, but there was a cerebral element to him—perhaps because he coached cerebral players.

He ran an offense that was built on players who could pass—especially the center—and on using the aggressiveness of a defense against it. The Princeton offense is built on backdoor cuts, smart screens, and—these days—good three-point shooting. If you are impatient playing against it, you'll get burned consistently.

Never was this more evident than in 1989, when No. 64 Princeton played top-seeded Georgetown to the buzzer in a first-round tournament game before losing 50–49 when an official swallowed his whistle in the final seconds after Princeton center Kit Mueller was fouled by Georgetown center Alonzo Mourning.

Georgetown survived. Seven seasons later, UCLA was the defending national champion and drew Princeton in the first round. The Bruins weren't as lucky as the Hoyas.

Princeton slowed the game to a crawl, rallied from seven points down late, and, on a backdoor pass—naturally—from sophomore Steve Goodrich to freshman Gabe Lewullis, pulled the upset, 43–41. The headline in Princeton's student newspaper, *The Princetonian,* said simply, "David-43, Goliath-41."

That turned out to be the last of Carril's 525 victories. He had decided to retire during the season and had told his players about it after they'd beaten Penn in a one-game playoff for the Ivy League title.

Mitch Henderson, who was a sophomore on that team, is now Princeton's coach. He is one of eleven Carril products who are head coaches at the Division 1 level. Brennan, who graduated in 1994, worked for seven seasons as an assistant coach at his alma mater, then spent three seasons at American working for Jeff Jones before moving to Georgetown to work for John Thompson III—son of the Hall of Fame Georgetown coach and another Carril product, having graduated in 1988.

When Jones left American for Old Dominion, Brennan succeeded him and promptly won the Patriot League Tournament in his first season. He was aided greatly by the fact that Jones had recruited a transfer from Stephen F. Austin a year earlier named Darius "Pee Wee" Gardner.

Gardner was generously listed as five feet nine and 165 pounds. Not only did he not mind the nickname Pee Wee, he insisted on being called that in his official bio. Darius didn't live there anymore.

Brennan was willing to call Gardner anything he wanted to be called. He almost never came off the court. He averaged 37 minutes a game as a junior and 38.5 as a senior. He sat only when in foul trouble or if a game had been decided.

Beyond that, he reminded Brennan of Sidney Lowe, who had been the point guard on Valvano's 1983 NCAA championship team. Early in the season—there was no shot clock—Lowe was trying to dribble out the clock in the final minutes of a tight game.

At one point, he got close enough to Valvano to yell, "Coach, I think I need a blow!"

"You'll get one, Sidney, I promise," Valvano responded. "Just as soon as your eligibility is used up."

That was Gardner. When AU needed a basket, Gardner either took the shot or set up a backdoor cut (Princeton offense, remember?) for a teammate. The Eagles went 20-13 and won the league title his junior year; they were 17-16 and lost in the championship game a year later.

Carril came down to watch AU play and practice several times a year. He would also spend time at Georgetown, watching Thompson III's team.

Not surprisingly, he loved Gardner and mentored him whenever he got the chance—which was absolutely fine with Brennan. "Pee Wee loves him," he said. "If you don't want to listen to him, who would you listen to?"

Carril also loved a seven-foot freshman named Gabe Brown, who was so thin he looked as if any gust of wind might blow him away. Carril called Brown "The Impossible Dream" and told Brennan he could evolve into a good player.

Sadly, the dream died when Brown—after scoring 13 points in two seasons—transferred to Rockhurst University, a Division 2 school outside Kansas City, after his sophomore season. There, he averaged 4 points per game as a senior.

Unfortunately for Brennan, Gardner also left after the 2015 season—his eligibility *was* used up—and he graduated. That fall, I had lunch with Brennan, and he walked into the restaurant looking markedly thinner than he had when I'd last seen him.

"Pee Wee withdrawal," he explained.

He was kidding. Sort of. American had losing seasons the next three years—injuries were a big factor—but in the fall of 2018, Brennan clearly had his best team since the Pee Wee days.

They had opened the season by going to George Mason and winning in overtime, their best victory in a long time. They'd also won at UMBC, a much bigger win than it would have been a year earlier. They came into GW's Smith Center with a 6-4 record, their best nonconference mark in a long time.

Their best player was point guard Sa'eed Nelson, a six-one junior who many thought could be the Patriot League player of the year when all was said and done. Just as important, center Mark Gasperini was healthy. A year earlier, on the first official day of practice, Gasperini had caught an elbow in the head. He hadn't played a minute all season, never able to get out of concussion protocol.

At the mid-major level, it is almost impossible to survive the season-long loss of a player as talented as Gasperini. There's simply no one capable of stepping into a void like that.

Now a redshirt sophomore, Gasperini had returned in the fall, and even though it took him a while to get his basketball-playing legs under him again, the Eagles were markedly improved.

They even had some depth, something they'd sorely lacked in recent years. Brennan often had to play his five starters thirty-five-plus minutes a game, and it wasn't a coincidence that they tended to run out of gas late.

Now Brennan could go to his bench for young talent, notably a freshman named Jacob Boonyasith, who played without any fear, driving right at big men, catching-and-shooting without hesitation. He reminded me a little of a kitten, relentlessly jumping on a fully grown cat just because it seemed like a fun thing to do.

Patriot League teams are not supposed to beat Atlantic 10 teams. The Patriot League has improved immeasurably since all ten teams—Boston University and Loyola of Baltimore joined the league six years ago—began giving athletic scholarships again.

The conference has had some remarkable NCAA Tournament moments: Bucknell stunned Kansas in the first round in 2005, then beat Arkansas a year later. In 2012, Lehigh—led by future NBA all-star C. J. McCollum—went into the tournament as one of those classically underseeded teams from a one-bid conference and—as a No. 15—shocked second-seeded Duke.

Some have called that game Mike Krzyzewski's worst loss. It wasn't even close. Lehigh was a good team. The home loss to Wagner in 1982, a team that finished 11-20, was much worse.

But the Patriot League is still a one-bid league. Although Bucknell has established itself as a perennially solid team and the conference has acquitted itself well in postseason more often than not, the committee simply yawns and says, "Who won the tournament?"

On the other hand, the Atlantic 10 is perennially a multi-bid league. It was known as the Eastern Collegiate Basketball League when it first started play in 1976, but that was quickly shortened by most to Eastern Eight. After Villanova and Pittsburgh jumped to the Big East in the early eighties, the league added Temple, St. Joseph's, St. Bonaventure, and Rhode Island and changed its name to the Atlantic 10.

Now it has fourteen teams but is still called the Atlantic 10, a misnomer not unlike the Big Ten (fourteen teams) or the Big Twelve (ten teams). Only three of the original Eastern Eight are left: Duquesne, Massachusetts, and George Washington.

For several seasons, the quality of the Atlantic 10 had been so high that it was receiving multiple NCAA bids that came close to the number the Power Six schools (the Big East is regarded as a power conference in basketball) were receiving. In 2013, the league got five bids; a year later it got six. Since then it had dropped off somewhat, but it had still received three bids in each of the last four seasons.

American had already proven that it could compete against an A-10 team with its opening-night victory over George Mason, which had been picked in preseason to finish in the A-10's top four.

GW was 3-9 coming in and, with the conference opener at St. Joseph's a few days away, badly needed to win at home against a Patriot League team.

GW got the victory, but it certainly wasn't easy. In fact, I walked out of the building that afternoon feeling as if AU had let the game get away.

The case can be made that GW won because six-nine sophomore Javier Langarica played the game of his life, scoring 15 points and grabbing 12 rebounds. The case can also be made that Sa'eed Nelson played the worst game of his college career. He shot 3-for-10, had just 1 assist, and committed 7 turnovers.

If Langarica had been merely good or Nelson had been ordinary, American would have won.

But that didn't matter. The game was tight throughout—the biggest lead of the second half and overtime was a GW 45–40 margin that went away almost instantly when the Eagles went on a quick 7–0 run.

The rest of the game was like pulling teeth back and forth. Nelson finally made a basket with 1:09 left to tie it, and then neither team could score in the last sixty-nine seconds. The overtime was similar. The winning basket came when GW's Justin Mazzulla missed a shot with the score tied at 64 with thirty-two seconds left, got his own rebound, and scored to make it 66–64.

Sam Iorio, who was AU's best player on the day—20 points—then turned it over with nineteen seconds remaining, and the Colonials made their free throws to hang on for a 72–67 victory.

This was a game that would be little noted nor long remembered—even by the 2,096 who showed up to watch.

But for the teams and coaches, the outcome was significant. Everyone knew that Maurice Joseph was fighting to save his job at GW, and every win mattered, especially one at home against a midlevel Patriot League school that was also a local rival.

For American, it was an opportunity lost, a chance to get a second win over an Atlantic 10 rival from the DC area and to go into Patriot League play 7-4. AU's number one goal—of course—was to win the Patriot League Tournament and play in the NCAAs. But if that didn't happen, seventeen wins might give it a chance to play in the CBI or the CIT.

Nowhere close to the Dance, but at least a night out on the town. At the mid-major level, that's no small thing.

SECOND-YEAR LAW
STUDENT

The college basketball season is played out in three parts: First comes the nonconference season, when the big boys play TV games and guarantee games and the not-so-big boys pick up guaranteed money and try to schedule enough winnable games to have a respectable record and their players in a good frame of mind when the New Year—and part two—begins.

Part two is conference play. For the big boys, the goal is to finish in the top half of their league because that will virtually assure them of an NCAA bid. For the smaller conferences, finishing first means they'll at least play in the NIT, and it'll give them an advantage in their conference tournament.

And then, there's part three: March Madness (trademarked, of course, by the NCAA), which begins with thirty-two conference tournaments: Big boys play for pride and seeding; everyone else plays for the one guaranteed NCAA bid.

For many mid-major conferences, the entire basketball season—starting with off-season workouts in June—comes down to those three or four conference tournament days in March.

If you are in a one-bid league, your NCAA fate is almost always decided by your conference tournament. There are thirty-two conferences in Division 1. Most of the time twenty-one of them will receive only one bid. There are *rare* exceptions. In 2019, Buffalo would have received an at-large bid had it not won the MAC Tournament. Wofford, which went 18-0 in the Southern Conference and was 29-4 overall, also would have received an at-large if it hadn't won the conference tournament.

Both those teams easily won their first-round games against teams from Power Five conferences. Buffalo beat Arizona State by twenty-one and Wofford beat Seton Hall by sixteen. Buffalo then lost to Texas Tech—which almost won the national championship and Wofford lost to Kentucky—by six.

Think those teams were a bit underseeded?

Belmont, which tied for first with Murray State in the Ohio Valley Conference, received an at-large bid, albeit to Dayton as one of the "First Four." There, the Bruins beat a very solid Temple team before losing late to Maryland—having traveled well into Wednesday morning to get to Jacksonville, then playing early on Thursday.

Fairness, thy name is the NCAA.

Most one-bid conference coaches understand that they have almost no chance to ever get an at-large bid.

"We win in Charleston [site of the CAA conference tournament in 2019] and we go," said Hofstra coach Joe Mihalich after his team won the regular-season title. "We lose, it's the NIT. Period."

The issue, then, is how to make your players understand that the regular season matters. In some conferences—the CAA, for example—it affects only seeding. Naturally, it's better to play the lowest seed you can possibly play in each round of the tournament. And many conference tournaments play their championship game on the home court of the highest remaining team—a sop to ESPN, which wants a lively atmosphere when it televises the final.

Some conferences have gone to playing all tournament games at the home of the higher-seeded team. That isn't the greatest thing logistically, but it does provide incentive for the regular season.

"Playing at home doesn't guarantee anything," said UMBC coach Ryan Odom. "But it sure makes you feel better about things."

Odom's UMBC team had pulled one of the biggest conference tournament upsets in years in 2018, traveling to Vermont for the conference championship game and beating the Catamounts—a team that had gone 15-1 in America East play and had easily beaten UMBC twice.

Vermont had a string of impressive wins over good mid-major teams and had lost *at* Kentucky by four. It was 27-7 after losing to UMBC. Did it have *any* chance to get an at-large bid? None. In fact, it didn't even get a home game in the NIT—which is run and controlled by the NCAA.

Everyone in the one-bid leagues knows that. One of the hardest things for a coach whose team wins the regular season in a one-bid league but loses in the conference tournament is to convince his players they should get fired up for the NIT.

"I have no idea how I'm going to do that," Norfolk State coach Robert Jones said after his team, 2019 regular-season champions in the MEAC, lost to North Carolina Central, 50–47, in the tournament championship game. "All year long, we've played with the idea that our goal was the NCAAs." He shrugged sadly. "I'll have to try to come up with something."

Jones and Norfolk State proved to be a rare exception to the rule. Sent to play at top-seeded Alabama, they pulled out an 80–79 overtime win. As a reward, they were sent to Colorado—*not* by private jet—where they lost.

Regardless of what is to come in March, conference play *feels* different. There's a familiarity and, because they often play twice and occasionally three times in a season, there's an intensity that's different than nonconference play.

The players know one another; the coaches know one another. The coaches are often friends—they socialize with one another at annual conference meetings and are often united in trying to make things better for the conference.

"The only person you want to beat more than a friend is your brother," said Towson coach Pat Skerry.

Skerry was in his eighth season at Towson. He had done a remarkable job, taking over with the Tigers in the midst of a twenty-one-game losing streak while also landing on NCAA academic probation.

There's an old saying among coaches: if you're going to recruit bad players, make sure they're at least good students. Towson had done neither.

In Skerry's first season, Towson went 1-31, finally snapping what had become a record-breaking forty-one-game losing streak with a win over UNC Wilmington.

A year later, having recruited good players who turned out to be good students, Skerry saw his team jump to 18-13—the single greatest jump from one season to another in NCAA history—while going 13-5 to finish second in the CAA. But the team was ineligible for the CAA Tournament because of the lingering academic probation.

Towson had won at least twenty games three times under Skerry, but he hadn't been able to break through and win the CAA Tournament.

He had known from the start this was going to be a difficult season. Four important seniors had graduated and two key starters had transferred, both looking to "move up" to bigger schools in more glamorous conferences. In all, Skerry had eight new players.

Tony Shaver's William & Mary team was also young, but he believed it had the potential to be solid by March and *really* good in a year when just about every key player returned and a talented transfer would be eligible.

"It could easily be the best team I've had here," Shaver said.

Shaver was sixty-four and had done remarkable work at William & Mary. The case could be made that his rebuilding job had been even more daunting than Skerry's at Towson when Shaver first arrived at the second-oldest college in the country—founded in 1643—in 2001.

Shaver had been wildly successful at Division 3 Hampden-Sydney and was caught off guard by how low the talent level had sunk at his new school. "We had four players on my last Hampden-Sydney team who would have started for my first William & Mary team," he said.

Slowly but surely, he rebuilt the Tribe into a competitive team. William & Mary was one of four schools that had played in Division 1 since it was initially formed in 1947 that had never made the NCAA Tournament, along with St. Francis Brooklyn, Army, and the Citadel.

But it had come painfully close to breaking through that barrier. Four times William & Mary had reached the finals of the CAA Tournament—and four times the Tribe had come up short. The most painful loss had come in 2014, when they had led Delaware by seven points with a little over a minute to go, only to lose by one.

Shaver literally tears up when he talks about that night.

Now he had a young team that he thought was probably a year away from having a serious chance to win the CAA and finally get to the Dance.

One senior played: Paul Rowley.

There was literally no one in college basketball like Rowley. Among the many players who were playing as graduate students, he was one of the few seriously pursuing a graduate degree, not just enrolling in a program so he could play basketball.

And he was the only one who was in his *second* year of law school.

Rowley was six feet eight and could make threes. He was also an almost freakishly good student, who had graduated from high school at seventeen and had been recruited by just about every academically minded mid-major. He had finally chosen William & Mary over Harvard and Bucknell—all excellent academic schools, all playing good basketball when he was a senior at Loudon Valley High School (the same school that had produced legendary William & Mary football coach Jimmye Laycock) in 2014.

"In the end, I just loved everything about William & Mary," he said. "I really liked the players and the coaches. I loved the campus, and it was only two hours from home. It felt like home when I visited."

Rowley had sprained an ankle two weeks before the start of his freshman season. Knowing he'd miss a good chunk of the season and that he probably wasn't going to play very much behind senior Terry Tarpey, he decided to redshirt.

That didn't slow him down academically. After his third year at William & Mary—and his second season playing—he was ready to graduate. The question was, what next?

"I knew I wasn't ready to be done as a player," he said. "In fact, I'd had a good enough year that some bigger schools were trying to convince me that I should be a grad transfer for them. I had no desire to leave.

"My sister, Tess, was in her second year at the law school. I had spent a lot of time with her friends and I really liked them. I guess it was the geek in me coming out. So I decided to apply to the law school."

One person not sure if that was a good idea was his coach.

"My first thought was the first year of law school and Division 1 basketball is a lot to handle," Shaver said. "Law school's really a full-time job. And he had become an important player for us by then. We needed him to play well. But when I met with him and we talked about it, I finally said to him, 'Paul, if there's anyone who can pull this off, it's you.'"

Rowley's grades and boards made him an easy admit to the law school. Still, there was also some concern on the academic side. A couple of years earlier, a golfer with eligibility left had been accepted to the law school. Within a couple of weeks of starting school and fall practice, he quit the team. It was all just too much.

It wasn't too much for Rowley. He graduated magna cum laude with a double major in computer science and finance, averaging a little more than 6 points a game (shooting 48 percent from three-point range) as a part-time starter/sixth man.

In his first year as a law student, his basketball numbers were about the same, and his law school numbers were impressive: a 3.7 GPA that ranked him fourteenth in a class of 186.

He got an internship that summer at a law firm in Norfolk, which went well. Unfortunately, he developed a sports hernia that required surgery and forced him to miss all of preseason and the first five games of his 2L (second-year law) season. By then, his role had evolved. On a young team, he was a respected leader. Shaver counted on him to get on the younger players and encourage them when needed.

"The funny thing is the challenge hasn't been law school," Shaver said. "He's killing it there. The challenge has been keeping him healthy."

Rowley finally made it back into the lineup for game six—against St. Joseph's—and scored 12 points in an upset win for the Tribe. He had 12 in the next game against Marshall and then got sick soon after that, a bad case of the flu.

He kept playing, but his shooting suffered. Finally, in the conference opener against James Madison, he shot 0-for-3 in the first half, got sick all over the locker room at halftime, and then made two critical threes late in a 79–74 win.

Towson came to town two days later on Sunday for game two of the conference season on a rainy winter afternoon.

Kaplan Arena, where William & Mary plays its home games, is one of the more charming midsize (seats five thousand) arenas in college basketball. Because the Tribe has been consistently good in recent years, the team draws well from the town of Williamsburg, meaning that, even with the students on break, a solid crowd—3,348—showed up on the last day of the NFL regular season.

The Tribe led for most of the game, using a 10–0 run late in the first half to open a 34–20 lead. Rowley came in at the first TV time-out and didn't score, but he played a key role in the first twenty minutes because center Nathan Knight got into early foul trouble.

Shaver moved Rowley, at six-eight, 200 pounds, to center on the defensive end, where he found himself guarding Towson's six-foot-nine-inch, 270-pound Alex Thomas.

"I came in here as a three [small forward] and sometimes I've played four [power forward], and now there are times I play five [center]," Rowley said, laughing. "I mean, look at me. I have to be the least physical player you've ever seen, but I loved mixing it up with a football-player-sized guy who just wants to hammer me into the floor."

Rowley would end the afternoon without scoring, but would have 4 rebounds, 1 block (yes, a block), and 3 assists—one perhaps the most critical of the game.

Towson had cut the lead to 48–44 midway through the second half. Under Skerry, the Tigers have had a penchant for digging in and rallying against teams from way behind. They'd done it to William & Mary at times in the past.

With the crowd getting restless, the ball went to Rowley in the low post—not his strength on offense—and he was double-teamed. Recognizing the double-team instantly, he found leading scorer Matt Milon in the corner, and Milon buried a three to stretch the lead to 51–44 and gave the Tribe a much-needed chance to take a breath.

Towson didn't go away, but never got even. The final was 71–61.

One of the cooler Kaplan traditions is for the players, after finishing the postgame handshakes with their opponents, to cross the court after a victory and run by the stands to exchange handshakes and high fives with the fans. The biggest heroes that afternoon were Milon (19 points) and Justin Pierce, who had 18. Leading the team across the court, huge grin on his face? Rowley.

"Hey, my shot didn't fall today, it happens," he said. "We won, that's all I care about—seriously. Look, when I was in high school if you'd have told me I'd be a fifth-year senior in college who would be an off-the-bench, cheerleader, lead-by-example guy, I'd have laughed at you.

"I mean, I was a *hooper*. Everything in my life was hoops. I dressed like a hooper, I acted like one, I liked hoops music [hip-hop]. Basketball was my life.

"Still is, to some degree. I suspect basketball will always be part of my life no matter what I go on to do. I mean, I've got a game made for weekend rec-league basketball.

"I read a story about Longwood's coach [Griff Aldrich] that said he practiced law for twenty years and then decided basketball was his first love and got into coaching. I could see something like that happening to me."

First, though, he had a third year of law school and the rest of his final season at William & Mary. He had high hopes for his young, improving team. "When we were 2-6," he said, "I swear we were the most confident 2-6 team you ever saw."

After the win over Towson, they were 6-8 but, more important, 2-0 in conference play.

"I've been coaching a long time, and I can honestly say I've never met anyone like Paul," Shaver said. He smiled. "I think we've been good for each other. I think he's learned from me that sometimes you need to get after things a little bit more, be a little more intense, competitive. And I think he's taught me to step back every once in a while and enjoy things, see the glass not just half-full, but more than half-full."

He shook his head. "My *only* complaint with him in five years is the whistling."

Rowley had a habit, both in practice and in games, of whistling while he played. "I don't even know when I'm doing it most of the time," he said. "I'm just enjoying myself so much, I start to whistle. I've got as great a life as you could hope to have, why wouldn't you whistle if you were me?"

Shaver understood, but really wished Rowley would cut it out. "I know he's trying," Shaver said with a shake of his head. "After a while though you just say, 'If this is the worst thing one of your kids does, why complain?' It's awfully hard to get mad at him. He's a unique kid in every possible way."

And the only L2 in college basketball.

January 5, 2019, Catonsville, Maryland

The America East Conference has only nine teams, meaning its conference schedule is sixteen games, a pure round robin in an era when many conferences have too many teams to have a pure round robin.

(See: ACC, Big Ten, Pac-12, SEC, all of which have expanded in the pursuit of TV money—mostly in football—at the expense of deciding their regular-season champion by the fairest method: home-and-home for all teams.) Nowadays, those titles are often decided by who gets to play the most games against bottom-feeders or who draws the home game when top teams meet only once.

This isn't a problem in the America East. And so, conference play began on the first Saturday in January. The league's defending champions, the previous season's miracle team—UMBC—hosted Maine in the opener for both teams.

Maine is one of those schools where competing in basketball has always been a struggle. The school has never been to the NCAA Tournament. Actually, the women's team has made the tournament eight times. The men, never.

The last coach to have any success at Maine was John Giannini, who had four winning seasons in eight years at the school, including a 24-7 record in 2000 and a 20-10 mark in 2004. That success got him the job at La Salle.

Since then, the Maine winters have been very cold inside Memorial Gym, which is where the Black Bears play their home games. Giannini's last year, 2004, was the last time Maine had a winning record. It was also the last time Maine won a *game* in the America East conference tournament.

In 2011, Richard Barron was hired as Maine's women's coach. Barron had been a Division 3 basketball player at Kenyon and had decided to take some time after graduation to decide whether to go to law school or the seminary.

He was an assistant high school coach—and science teacher—for a year before getting hired as an assistant women's coach at Sewanee— also known as the University of the South—in Sewanee, Tennessee.

The plan was to stay one year and then make a decision on what to do next.

At Barron's going-away party at season's end, Sewanee's athletic director suggested he stay on and become the women's coach. The job was open.

"I think he was joking," Barron said. "Or at least half joking. But I'd had fun that year. I figured, why not? I was in no rush."

He stayed four years and built a winning program. That led to an offer to become the coach at Princeton. He wasn't as successful there—one NCAA bid in seven seasons—and then landed at Baylor, working for Kim Mulkey for two years. Then it was on to NC State for two more. By then, Barron was an established women's basketball coach, married with three children. Law school and the seminary were both in the rearview mirror.

And so, when Maine offered him the women's job in 2011, he jumped at it. The Black Bears had fallen on hard times—4-25 the previous season. Barron rebuilt. In 2015 and 2016 they won America East regular-season titles, only to lose in the conference tournament and play in the women's NIT. Still, he had completely turned the program around and had become a very popular figure in the state.

On the morning of December 4, 2016, Barron woke up feeling as if he had water in his ear. "I couldn't hear out of it," he said. "When I tried to stand up, something was wrong with my equilibrium. Everything was slanting to the left. I felt like I was going to fall over."

Doctors prescribed a heavy dose of steroids, which did nothing—except make his weight balloon and produced bouts of 'roid rage. He kept trying to coach until early January, when he had to take a leave of absence.

By then, he was completely miserable. Almost any noise at all sounded like a bomb going off in his head. Someone putting down a coffee cup made him put his hands to his ears.

"I could literally *hear* my toes wiggling," he said. "I could *hear* my eyes blinking. I couldn't be in a room with more than one of my kids at a time and, even then, they had to whisper."

He went to the Mayo Clinic in Rochester, Minnesota. They had no answers and recommended he try the Mayo in Jacksonville because the doctors there would run different tests.

By then, he was in a state of panic. He was forty-eight with three young kids, and he was convinced he had some mysterious disease that was going to kill him.

"I was racked with guilt," he said. "If I died, we didn't have enough insurance to carry my wife and the kids through. We didn't have any relatives in Maine, so they'd almost certainly have to move so my wife could get help with the kids with me gone. All their friends were in Maine.

"It wasn't so much that I was afraid of dying, I was afraid of what it was going to do to my family."

The last doctor he saw at the Mayo in Jacksonville was an ear doctor. By then, he'd all but given up hope. The next morning the ear doctor asked him to come back and see her.

"She had it," Barron said. "I had something called semicircular canal dehiscence. In English, I had a hole in my head—literally."

It was a tiny hole above the right ear. That was why he was hearing things so acutely and painfully. It was also why he had equilibrium issues.

He had surgery in Los Angeles in July—the hole being spackled shut. Almost from the minute he came out of surgery, his life began again.

The question then was, where was it going to lead him? He had turned the coaching job over to his top assistant, Amy Vachon, and she'd taken the next step—getting Maine to the NCAAs in 2018.

"No way was I going to take the job back from her," Barron said. "That would have been patently unfair."

Athletic director Karlton Creech suggested he work in administration—fund-raising mostly—at least until the end of the basketball season. That was fine with Barron. He and his family loved living in Orono and had been touched by the outpouring from the community when he'd been sick.

The men's team was suffering through another difficult season. Bob Walsh was in the fourth and last year of his contract. He was highly respected by everyone in the America East because his teams were almost always outmanned but always competed. Still, going 6-26 was as frustrating for Walsh as it was for everyone else at Maine, and he decided not to ask for a new contract, resigning on March 5.

That's when Creech found his new role for Barron: coaching the men.

There was precedent in Division 1 for a women's coach taking over a men's team, but not much of it. Speedy Morris had been the women's coach at La Salle for two seasons when athletic director Bill Bradshaw called him on the morning of the conference championship game in March 1986 and offered him the men's job. Morris had a fourteen-year run at La Salle and took the school to four NCAA Tournaments, going

30-2 in 1990, led by national player of the year Lionel Simmons. He was fired after the 2001 season and returned to coaching high school basketball, and he was still at it in 2019 at the age of seventy-six.

The only other coach to move from coaching women to coaching men was Army's Pat Harris. A graduate of the school—he played for Mike Krzyzewski—Harris was named interim coach for the women's team in 1997. That spring, he was given the job as the men's coach. He stayed for five years and was fired by athletic director Rick Greenspan in 2002—even though he'd just been voted the Patriot League coach of the year by his peers.

That was the list—Morris and Harris. Creech was convinced Barron was the right man to coach his men.

Not surprisingly, Maine had struggled in nonconference play and came into the REC (Retriever Events Center) at UMBC with a 3-13 record. There were, however, some hopeful signs. Three of the losses had been in overtime, and there had been a win over Fordham—granted a bottom-feeder Atlantic 10 team but, nevertheless, an Atlantic 10 team.

Barron had decided to redshirt all his freshmen, and, much as Walsh had done, he was looking for transfers and international players. Maine isn't exactly a basketball hotbed, nor is New England. Barron would have to cast his net far and wide and hope to catch the occasional big fish or, more likely, an overlooked one.

UMBC hadn't torn up the preconference season either. It was a new world for Ryan Odom and his players, being a target game for teams rather than a yawner for big-time teams and a winnable game for others.

With the two senior guards who had made most of the big plays in close games—Jairus Lyles and K. J. Maura—gone, the Retrievers had lost a couple of close games at home—to American and Towson— and had been trounced by Florida Gulf Coast at home and Northern Kentucky on the road. Overall, they were 8-7, three of the wins over Division 3 teams.

On a comfortable Saturday afternoon, with the temperature approaching fifty and a small crowd of 1,081 in the REC, it was Maine that looked like the team that had played in the NCAA Tournament a year earlier for the first twenty-five minutes.

The Black Bears were up 31-19 at halftime. UMBC, which had struggled shooting the ball from outside all season, continued to do so in the first twenty minutes. Maine even extended its lead early in the second half, taking a 37–24 lead on an Andrew Fleming layup with 16:21 left. Fleming was the best player on the court all day, finishing with 18 points, 10 rebounds, and 5 assists.

But in the end, it wasn't enough. The difference was depth. Barron got a total of 5 points from his bench. Odom got 13 from sophomore Brandon Horvath and another 9 from junior Arkel Lamar.

Maine hung in, trailing just 53–52 with 5:45 to go after Sergio El Darwich made two free throws, but was out of gas by then. UMBC didn't exactly light it up down the stretch, but Maine didn't score again after the El Darwich free throws, and UMBC won, 61–52.

Neither coach was happy. Barron wasn't looking for moral victories, and Odom knew his team had been lucky to escape. "We got away with one," he said. "Credit to them, they played well. But we're going to have to play a lot better than that to contend in this conference."

Three nights later, Maine hosted Vermont. The schedule makers had done them no favors, opening on the road against the conference champs, then bringing the conference favorites to town for the conference home opener.

Vermont crushed the Black Bears, 73–49. Barron saw the sunrise the next morning because he was awake most of the night trying to figure ways to get his team to play better.

"I saw the sunrise," he said, "and realized I'd been up most of the night stewing."

The good news was that he was alive and healthy when the sun rose. News that was almost as good came three days later, when the Black Bears made the trip to Albany and shocked the Great Danes, 66–62.

The four-hundred-mile bus trip back to Orono flew by for Barron. He was healthy and doing what he loved: coaching. The sex of his players didn't matter even a little bit.

PHILLY KID

January 9, 2019, Richmond, Virginia

For the past six years I've had the privilege—and I say that with absolute sincerity—of doing color on about five or six Virginia Commonwealth games a year.

Because VCU has been viewed as a big-time team since its trip to the Final Four in 2011, many of its games are part of various network packages: CBS, ESPN, and the Atlantic 10 conference package, which shows up on both NBC's and CBS's cable outlets. That usually leaves a handful of games that the school produces itself.

Which is why I found myself making the familiar trip down I-95 south en route to Richmond on the afternoon of January 9 to see VCU host La Salle. It was unseasonably warm for January, temperatures in the fifties. All that mattered to me was that it wasn't snowing.

As anyone who has ever driven it knows, I-95 on a weekday afternoon is miserable—at best; a complete nightmare if there's any sort of accident or bad weather. For a seven o'clock game at the Siegel Center, I leave at two o'clock. If all goes well, I'll walk in the building by 4:30, which leaves me lots of prep time and time to do some other nongame work. If all doesn't go well, I'll still be there in plenty of time before tip.

The ride home will take about an hour and forty-five minutes—if it's not snowing.

On paper, this game was a mismatch. VCU was clearly much improved after its down (18-15) season a year earlier. The Rams were 10-4 coming in, and three of the losses had been to St. John's (by one, in Brooklyn), Virginia, and Old Dominion. All three of those teams would make the NCAA Tournament. One—Virginia—would win it. Five of the ten wins had been over teams that would make the NCAAs. There had been just one clunker—a loss to College of Charleston, not a bad team, but not one VCU should be losing to at home.

The opponent on this night would be La Salle. The Explorers were on a three-game winning streak. Which meant they were 3-10.

"For a while, I thought I might go down in history as the only coach to never win a single game," La Salle coach Ashley Howard said with a laugh. "Right now, I might be the happiest 3-10 coach in history." Howard had been a standout at Drexel in 2002 (see chapter one) who was sidelined by a heart condition.

I'd seen La Salle play at Temple on opening night, and even though the Owls won a close game, I'd been impressed by the Explorers. There were a lot of new players, a clear senior leader in sixth-year player Pookie Powell, and the kind of enthusiasm you see with a new coach.

And then?

"Teams got a look at us on tape after the Temple game," Howard said. "Gave them an idea how we played. We lost a couple we shouldn't have lost, but the schedule didn't do us any favors either."

That was an honest assessment. There were two home losses that really hurt: to Lafayette, three days after the Temple game, and to Drexel, the one D-1 Philly school that isn't part of the Big Five. Drexel lives to play—and to beat—Big Five schools, and the win over La Salle was a big deal.

The schedule *was* a bear: at Florida, Miami, and Northwestern in an exempt event; Villanova in the Palestra; Bucknell—a very solid team every year; and Penn. How good was Penn? Good enough to beat Villanova, Temple, and St. Joseph's and win the Big Five.

La Salle finally got a win just before Christmas by beating Alabama A&M in Atlantic City, then doubled down the next night with a win over Towson, also in Atlantic City.

"Made Christmas at home a lot more enjoyable," Howard said. "Truth is, it was my kids who got me through those first thirty-six days without a win—not that I was counting—but going home to them made it all bearable.

Howard and his wife, Ariana, had two young children: their

daughter, Journey, was four, and their son, Ace, had been born just prior to the start of the season.

"I heard it from other coaches before I had kids, but now I understand it," Howard said. "When you coach, every day is competitive—in some way. To come home and be with two people who adore you regardless is a joy and a relief at the same time."

He smiled. "Especially when you're 0-10."

As the losses mounted, Howard leaned on three people: his dad and two former bosses.

Mo Howard had been an excellent player on very good Maryland teams in the 1970s and had been the thirty-second pick in the 1976 NBA draft. He's still a revered figure in Philadelphia, and Ashley has always looked to him for basketball guidance.

"When I was little, people told me how good my dad had been," he said. "I knew he was just about the only guy out of Philly to leave and go to play in the ACC. But it wasn't until I got older and became a player myself that I realized just how good he had to be to do the things he had done."

He also talked to Jay Wright, whom he had worked for the previous five seasons at Villanova. Wright had become an iconic figure in college basketball after winning national championships in 2016 and 2018. During the five seasons Howard worked for Wright, the Wildcats had gone an astonishing 163-21. Howard had lost almost half as many games in five weeks as he'd been part of in five *years* at Villanova.

"Jay reminded me that it hadn't been easy for him when he first got to Villanova," Howard said with a grin. "He wasn't 0-10, but he did wonder at times if he was going to make it."

Wright's first three seasons at a school that took NCAA Tournament bids almost for granted had produced a record of 52-46 and three NIT bids. In his third season, Villanova was 18-17 overall and finished eleventh in the Big East.

"We weren't exactly killing it at that point," Wright said.

Howard had known he was going from the penthouse to the basement—or darn close to it—when he took the La Salle job, but ten straight losses is a shock to anyone's system.

Finally, Howard called Bruiser Flint, who had never gotten to coach him at Drexel because of the cardiomyopathy that had ended his college career after his sophomore season. Flint was now an assistant coach at Indiana.

Howard still thought of him as his basketball mentor. "I think I must have driven him crazy, calling almost every night. I needed someone to vent to—Bru was the guy. I was the happiest guy in the country when we finally won, but Bru was probably second because he had a chance to breathe."

Howard liked the improvement, but also knew the going wouldn't be easy in the A-10. Starting A-10 play with a road victory over Massachusetts, though, was encouraging.

Going into the Siegel Center to face VCU four days later would be difficult. And yet, Howard was looking forward to it. "That kind of atmosphere is certainly potentially dangerous for the road team, especially when they get on a run—I know that," he said. "But I also think if you don't get an adrenaline surge from playing in there, you shouldn't be playing basketball."

La Salle had plenty of adrenaline in the first half. With VCU struggling to make shots—the Rams shot under 30 percent from the field—La Salle jumped to an early lead and then, up 16–10, went on a 12–0 run to lead 28–10 with 8:38 left in the first half. The sellout crowd—the 126th in a row—was quiet, the kind of quiet that comes when people can't quite believe what they're seeing. Wasn't the opponent 3-10? Hadn't VCU just blown Fordham out in the Bronx, 86–60, shooting almost 67 percent for the game?

The answers were yes and yes.

"I told the guys they were better than their record," VCU coach Mike Rhoades said later. "I guess they had to see it to believe it."

VCU closed the gap to 37–28 by halftime and then worked its way back into the game in the second half, taking the lead when La Salle went completely cold, missing twelve of thirteen shots during a seven-minute stretch. Powell, the closest thing Howard had to a glue guy, couldn't hit during that stretch. He would finish with 15 points but would be only 7-for-19.

La Salle never completely went away, trailing by just four in the last minute, but VCU's depth—four players finished in double figures—and the Rams' hounding defense—they forced twenty turnovers—were the difference.

"I said if we had less than fifteen turnovers, we could win the game," Howard said. "I was probably right."

The loss was disappointing, because the chance to get what would have been a massive road win had been there. As it turned out, VCU didn't lose a home game in conference play all season. But Howard could see the progress his team had made since November, and that made him happy.

Was he the happiest 3-11 coach in the country? Perhaps; perhaps not. But at least Bruiser Flint might get a night or two off from the phone going forward.

GRAY DAYS

Jimmy Allen was in a good mood on the morning of January 12, a bright Saturday in Baltimore.

His Army basketball team had been through a number of ups and downs since its almost magical afternoon at Duke in November, but he felt as if it was now pointed in the right direction.

A three-game round robin event in Providence the weekend after the Duke game had been a disaster—three losses, two in eminently winnable games.

The trip had started badly and only gotten worse. On the trip to Providence, the Black Knights got caught in a November snowstorm and their bus simply died going up a hill. Everyone—players, coaches, managers—had to get out and push.

Even with a group of strapping young men in military shape grinding away, it took an hour to get the bus up the hill and off the road until help could arrive to restart the bus.

"We couldn't just push it to the side of the road because it was sliding backward," Allen said. "It wasn't just exhausting, it was dangerous."

A one-point loss to Sacred Heart might have been avoided if not for the night in the snow. Then came a tight loss to UMass Lowell and, finally, a blowout loss to a good Brown team.

The Black Knights had rebounded with a couple of home wins and had then gone to Air Force for a gratifying road win.

The conference opener was at home against two-time defending league champion Bucknell. The Bison had lost several key players but were still the team that most in the Patriot League believed you had to go through to win the title.

"If we can play with them, we can play with anyone in the league," Allen said.

For twenty minutes, Army didn't just play with Bucknell; they embarrassed the Bison. The halftime score in Christl Arena was 37–13. That's not a typo. The lead even stretched to twenty-six early in the second half. And then Bucknell began to come back. Teams that are consistently good and win a lot of games year in and year out almost never feel as if they're out of a game.

By contrast, teams that haven't won with any consistency for a while start looking over their shoulder when they see the more-decorated team coming. Bucknell center Nate Sestina more or less took over the game in the second half. He was 7-of-7 from the field and had 17 points—in a stretch of fourteen minutes.

The Bison went on a 46–18 run and, with just under five minutes to play, took the lead at 59–57. Army didn't fold at that stage and actually got the lead back, 63–62, with the ball and forty seconds to play.

Army point guard Tommy Funk had to take a long three just before the shot clock ran out. Sestina rebounded and got the ball to Avi Toomer, whose layup with three seconds left gave Bucknell the lead, 64–63, and, as it turned out, the game.

As heartbreaking as that loss was, Army had come back to win its next two—against Lafayette at home and on the road against Boston University. That put the Black Knights at 2-1 in the conference, with a game at Loyola that would be followed by three home games.

"We've got a lot of home games early," Allen said. "We need to make hay in those because, obviously, that's gonna mean a lot of road games late. But this is a road game we need to get."

Loyola was in the midst of a rebuild. The school had fired G. G. Smith—son of Tubby Smith—the previous spring after going 11-21. Smith's five-year record in north Baltimore was 56-98. The school hired Tavaras Hardy, who had been an assistant at Georgia Tech under Josh Pastner, to replace Smith.

Hardy was thirty-nine and had spent his entire career as a player and as a coach at power schools: he'd played and coached at Northwestern and had moved on from there to Georgetown and then Georgia Tech. The Patriot League was a new experience for him.

The Greyhounds had lost seven players from the previous season—five to graduation, two to transfer. They didn't have a single scholarship senior on the team and were 4-11 in all games and 0-3 in the conference. Which was why Allen considered this a must-win: road wins are tough to come by; you have to take advantage of a down team when you get a chance to beat them on the road.

Allen and his assistants reminded their players that a desperate team was a dangerous one during morning walk-through and that no team was more dangerous than a team winless in conference that was playing at home.

As the players finished their breakfast and listened to the coaches, I noticed something I'd never seen before at a pregame meal: coffee.

"At West Point, everyone drinks coffee," Allen said with a laugh when I noted the presence of the coffee. "It's part of surviving. They'll drink a lot less here because, relatively speaking, they got to sleep in this morning."

The bus was leaving at 11 a.m. from the Lord Baltimore Hotel—an iconic, ninety-one-year-old downtown landmark that included a grand piano in the lobby—for the fifteen-minute drive to north Baltimore, which is where Loyola is located.

Allen arrived in the lobby, freshly showered and ready to go. He stopped to thank the front desk staff for their hospitality and then threw his hands up in frustration.

"My suit," he said. "I left it upstairs."

This is one of the perks of being the head coach: if you're a couple of minutes late for the bus, it isn't leaving without you. Given that I'd spent an entire season with a former Army coach who never wore anything but red sweaters on game day and remembered watching George Raveling and his entire Iowa staff coach in sweats, I suggested Allen might consider just showing up in sweats.

"When I win as many games as Knight did, I'll think about it," he said. "For now, I'll stick with a suit."

As it turned out, the forgotten suit was a harbinger. Loyola *was* a dangerous team, even playing in front of a less-than-roaring crowd of 818 people in Reitz Arena.

Army went completely cold the last six minutes of the first half, and Loyola pieced together a 16–4 run that put the Greyhounds up 39–28. Allen was pretty close to beside himself at halftime.

"I don't think we could have played worse if we'd been wearing our shoes on the wrong feet," he said later. "It was as if we walked right into their trap."

The lead ballooned to thirteen briefly in the second half before Army methodically got back into the game. Both Tommy Funk and Jordan Fox were struggling to shoot—Funk would finish 2-of-10 from the field and Fox 4-of-12, but Matt Wilson was playing well inside (14 points and 10 rebounds), and several of the so-called role players chipped in too.

Twice, Army cut the lead to one point, both times on jumpers by Tucker Blackwell, the first a three, the second from the corner. That one made the score 56–55 with plenty of time—four minutes to play.

The Black Knights got a stop at the other end and came down looking to take the lead for the first time since midway in the first half. The ball went to Wilson, who drove, shot, and appeared to get fouled—hard. No call. Allen was close to losing his mind. Army never got another chance to take the lead. Isaiah Hart made key free throws in the final two minutes, and the Greyhounds hung on to win, 66–64.

Army didn't lose the game because of the officiating. It lost because Funk and Fox had poor shooting days and Loyola played, undoubtedly, the best game it had played all season.

But when Allen found out that one of the officials, Chris Balunek, was working his first game ever in the Patriot League, he was upset. Balunek had made several questionable calls throughout the game, including the noncall on Wilson. One of the other officials on the game admitted afterward that he felt the need to "have a talk" with Balunek about his approach if he was going to officiate at the Division 1 level.

"It's unfair because that game's important to both teams and you have a guy who's over his head," Allen said. "We earned the loss, don't get me wrong. But boy was it frustrating."

At the Patriot League level, Wednesdays and Saturdays are the toughest days for the officiating supervisor. On other nights, officials who work in higher-level leagues are available because most college refs loathe a night off. When the schedules are thinner, more officials from the bigger conferences are available. On Wednesdays and even more so on Saturdays, when schedules are packed, it's a scramble to find officials in leagues like the Patriot, the Ivy, the America East, the MEAC—and others.

Which is why coaches in those leagues have frequently advocated going to a Thursday–Sunday or Friday–Sunday schedule. The leagues, though, are often ruled by television. They play when TV wants them to play. Army-Loyola was on Stadium TV, a digital outlet. One would think Stadium could have done the game on Sunday at one instead of Saturday at one. Army could have traveled on Saturday—no school, less traffic—and been home in plenty of time Sunday to be ready for wake-up on Monday morning.

And the officiating crew probably would have been more experienced.

Makes sense, doesn't it? Which is probably why it didn't happen that way. Regardless, Allen and his players got on the bus for the trip home in a bad mood.

At West Point, January and February are known as "the gray days," because it seems everything is gray: the buildings are gray; the uniforms are gray; and the skies seem to be gray most of the time.

The loss to Loyola would make the gray days even grayer.

17

LET'S PLAY TWO!

I've always loved doubleheaders, dating to when I was a kid. Growing up in New York, there was a doubleheader either at Shea Stadium or Yankee Stadium almost every Sunday. It was $1.30 for a general admission ticket at Shea; $1.50 at Yankee Stadium. Two games for that price.

Most people don't remember that before the NBA exploded in popularity, it wasn't uncommon for Madison Square Garden to host Tuesday night doubleheaders. I first saw the great Boston Celtics teams play in the 6:30 game in the Garden against the fledgling Chicago Bulls. The Knicks game started at 8:30. When I was young, my dad insisted we go home at halftime of the Knicks game since it was a school night, but I'd get home in time to listen to Marv Albert call the last few minutes on the radio.

In those days, the Knicks usually lost. Sort of like these days.

As a young reporter at the *Washington Post,* I loved being in the Research Triangle area on a Saturday for a different kind of doubleheader: a game at Duke, North Carolina, or North Carolina State in the afternoon, then a game at night at one of those schools. I'd go to the afternoon game, grab an early dinner with friends, and then drive the ten miles between Duke and North Carolina or the twenty-five miles between those two schools and State in time to get to the night game.

Hoops heaven.

I still try to pull off hoop doubleheaders when I can on Saturdays, and on the third Saturday in January, I had a unique opportunity. At one o'clock, UMBC hosted Albany in an important America East game for both teams. At seven o'clock, sixty-seven miles up I-95, Delaware was hosting Towson in a CAA game.

I was doing both games on television. There was plenty of time to get from Catonsville to Newark and arrive in plenty of time for game two—unless it snowed. Naturally, there was snow in the forecast.

Hoping for the best, I arrived a couple of hours before tip at UMBC.

This was one of those games that wasn't going to attract much attention beyond the two schools, but was key for both teams.

Albany hadn't had a losing season since 2010. Will Brown had been named the interim coach at the school in December 2001 at the age of thirty and been given the job full-time at the end of that season. In the sixteen-plus seasons since, he had built one of the better mid-major programs in the country.

The Great Danes had won the America East Tournament five times and had gone to postseason (CBI, CIT) on three other occasions. Albany had won at least twenty games the past four seasons, and that included an 83–39 win over UMBC a year earlier in Albany.

That game had been one of the low moments—perhaps *the* low moment—of Ryan Odom's tenure at UMBC. Albany always played very physically and could push a team around if the officials allowed them to do so. On that day, they had hammered the Retrievers in every possible way.

"If the officials decide they're going to let the players play when we face them, we have no chance," Odom said. "They're just much too strong for us."

Odom was to the point with his team after that game. "We're going to put this one behind us right now," he said. "We're just going to flush it completely."

Then, as the players filed out, he loudly flushed a toilet to make his point.

The tactic worked. A month later, when the teams met in the second game played in the new REC, UMBC rallied in the second half to win, 68–60—a critical victory because Albany had been such a tough out for UMBC in the past and—more importantly—four weeks earlier.

This, however, was not a typical Will Brown team. It was still rugged and physical but lacked experience, in large part because the two players who would have been the Great Danes' best players had both left as graduate transfers in the spring of 2018.

Brown was neither surprised nor disappointed when David Nichols left for Florida State. Nichols was talented and no doubt would have put up good numbers as a senior, but Brown thought he was as much a headache as he was an asset. He had actually considered throwing him off the team during the season but had held off because he *was* a good player and because he didn't want to hurt his chances of finding a place for him to land the following season.

The shocker was Joe Cremo. He had been the team's leading scorer at just under 18 points a game and was, without a doubt, the team's leader and go-to guy. If he had stayed at Albany, he would have been a candidate for America East player of the year.

But Cremo left for Villanova, which had just won the national championship and would again be a national contender even though four players had left for the NBA.

The transfers hurt both Albany and the two players. Nichols averaged seventeen minutes off the bench for Florida State and 6.4 points per game. Cremo played sixteen minutes a night for Villanova and averaged 4 points per game, but by postseason he was down to six minutes a game as younger players improved.

Without his starting backcourt, Brown was forced to rely on freshmen—five of his top eight players were freshmen, including three from Australia—which wasn't the norm for Albany. The Great Danes had struggled in the preconference season, going 5-10, and were off to an 0-3 conference start. In the previous fourteen seasons, Albany had finished below .500 in the America East twice—the last time being in 2010.

"That season was like this one," Brown said. "When that group were seniors, they went to the NCAAs."

Brown loved the potential of his freshmen, but that wasn't making life any easier in the winter of 2019.

Odom was having his share of ups and downs too. After his "Come to Jesus" practice blowup following the losses at Hartford and Lowell, UMBC had played its best game of the season two days later against Binghamton, blowing out the Bearcats, 70–49.

But UMBC was now hurting inside—the area Odom had counted

on to be the team's strength. Sophomore center Dan Akin had missed the first eleven games recovering from knee surgery. Akin had come back in mid-December and had steadily improved as he got his basketball legs back under him. He had been one of the few bright spots in the loss at Lowell, scoring 11 points and grabbing 15 rebounds.

Two days later, not long after Odom had read his team the riot act, Akin went down, untouched, reaching for his knee. It turned out he had torn the MCL in the right knee—the same one he'd injured the previous summer. He was done for the year.

Two nights later, in the easy win over Binghamton, Brandon Horvath walked to the bench shaking his left hand early in the second half. Horvath was a six-ten sophomore with a soft shooting touch whom Odom loved to bring in off the bench because he almost always gave the team an offensive jump start.

The injury didn't appear too serious, but he was in street clothes for the Albany game. Suddenly, Sam Schweitz was the starting center and senior Nolan Gerrity—who had hardly played all season—was his backup.

The game was close throughout. The biggest lead all day was seven—Albany went up 40–33 early in the second half—and the Great Danes appeared in control even though the game was tight going into the final minutes. The only reason UMBC stayed close was Jose Placer, the freshman guard from Miami who had played limited minutes in the first eighteen games. But with two of the team's top six players reduced to cheerleading and Providence transfer Rickie Council struggling, Odom reached deep into his bench and gave Placer extended minutes for the first time all season.

"We knew when we recruited him he could score," Odom said later. "I can't say I expected him to score that much in a game that important that soon." He smiled. "He really had no choice. If he doesn't score that way, we lose the game."

UMBC's starters—with the exception of K. J. Jackson—were offensively challenged the entire afternoon. Joe Sherburne, their most reliable shooter, was 1-for-8. Arkel Lamar, their most explosive scorer was 3-for-14. Jackson had 17 points; the other four starters combined for 21.

Council had been a starter early in the season. After playing in the

Big East at Providence for two seasons, Odom was hoping he would replace some of the firepower lost when Jairus Lyles and K. J. Maura departed.

But, as often happens with transfers, he'd struggled—notably with his shooting. There's just no way to mimic game speed in practice. Odom had started bringing him off the bench, hoping to take some pressure off him.

It wasn't working against Albany. In the first half, Council got off one shot—a miss—in seven minutes.

He was nailed to the bench in the second half. Placer had 8 points by halftime and wasn't coming off the court in the second half. Every time it looked as if Albany was about to sail away with the game, Placer hit a shot. After Devonte Campbell made a three to make it 55–50, Placer answered by making a layup while being fouled and made the free throw with 1:20 left to cut the lead to 55–53.

Ahmad Clark, Albany's leading scorer who had been in foul trouble most of the day, missed a jumper—but got his own rebound with forty-three seconds left. Brown called time to set up a play since his team couldn't run the clock out.

But with Clark dribbling at the top of the key to kill time before starting the play, Lamar suddenly lunged at the ball and knocked it loose. He chased it down and tied the game with a layup with fifteen ticks left. The Great Danes didn't get off a last shot.

Overtime.

Albany bounced back from the shock of losing the lead and led 61–57 after Rayshaun Miller made a three with 2:19 left. The Retrievers went back to Placer, and he answered with a deep three to make it 61–60 eleven seconds after Miller's shot.

The teams then went cold, exchanging missed shots and turnovers until Placer—of all people—lost the ball in traffic with twenty-two seconds left; Aussie freshman Cameron Healy—brilliant all day with 24 points—coming up with the loose ball.

Schweitz fouled him instantly, and Healy calmly swished both free throws to make it 63–60. One more time, Placer answered with a jumper. Two seconds later, with no choice, Sherburne fouled Campbell with the clock at fourteen seconds. Campbell missed the first, then made the second.

Brown called time to set up his defense—a move coaches make all the time nowadays. In the old days, only the offense called time in the final seconds; now, more often it's the defense.

It was at that moment that Odom made a move that came straight from his gut—because it couldn't have come from his head. Council hadn't played a second in the last twenty-five minutes because Odom couldn't afford to take Placer out at all.

Now, needing another shooter on the floor—even one who hadn't made a shot all day—Odom put Council back in the game. At the very least it meant there was one more shooter Albany had to be aware of, although it seemed far more likely that Placer, Sherburne (even on a bad day), or Lamar (same thing) would be the one taking the shot.

That's exactly what Odom was counting on. As soon as Placer took the inbounds, instead of dribbling quickly into scoring position (fourteen seconds is an eternity plus another eternity in basketball), he picked up his dribble short of midcourt and rifled a pass to Council in the right-hand corner, right in front of the UMBC bench.

There was no one from Albany near Council. The thinking—which made sense—was that he'd see the ball only if the clock was down and everyone else was guarded. Even then . . .

Instead, he caught the perfect pass in rhythm and was in the air before anyone could even think to move at him. The ball splashed through the net with nine seconds left. Healy raced downcourt and got off a well-guarded three as the buzzer sounded. It wasn't close.

Suddenly, shockingly, UMBC had won, 65–64. Council's line for the day: seven minutes, 1-of-2 from the field, 3 points. It was exactly enough.

"As tough a loss as I can remember," Brown said. "We let that one get away."

Or did UMBC *take* it away? "Rickie's a shooter," Odom said. "Sometimes you just have to have faith in your players to make a play. He made one."

Because the game went overtime, it was 3:40 when I walked to my car. The sky was overcast, but there was no sign of snow. I would make it to Delaware in plenty of time.

Towson-Delaware was exactly the same kind of game as Albany-UMBC: two teams badly needing the game. The only thing different was the league: CAA as opposed to America East. What was the same was that both were now one-bid leagues.

That hadn't been true of the CAA once upon a time. But a slew of top basketball teams—Old Dominion and Georgia State (strictly for football reasons); VCU and George Mason, both looking to improve their basketball profiles and revenues—have all left in recent years. Tom Yeager, who was the league's commissioner for thirty years, did a remarkable job holding the conference together, bringing in schools like Hofstra, Towson, Northeastern, Drexel, and the College of Charleston.

But losing three of the league's most consistent basketball programs has hurt. In 2011, Old Dominion won the conference tournament, and George Mason and VCU made the field as at-large teams. VCU went to the Final Four—the league's second trip to the last weekend in six seasons: George Mason had made it that far in 2006.

The next year, VCU won a first-round game against Wichita State. Since then, the CAA has been strictly a one-bid league, and its only NCAA Tournament win came in the First Four in Dayton in 2016 when No. 16 James Madison beat No. 16 LIU Brooklyn for the right to play top-seeded Indiana in the first round of the East Regionals. Indiana won, 83–62. The win over LIU is the last one the CAA has had.

Delaware had won the conference tournament in 2014 under Coach Monté Ross. But back-to-back losing seasons followed after the core of that team graduated, and Ross was fired at the end of the 2016 season after going 7-23. The presence of a new athletic director didn't help either—if you have a new AD, you better make it impossible for him/her (in this case) to fire you.

Delaware's new coach was Martin Ingelsby, a Notre Dame graduate who had spent thirteen years on Mike Brey's staff there. Brey is still a revered figure at Delaware. He had coached there for five seasons, going 99-52, including 69-24 in his last three years. The Fightin' Blue Hens (as they like to be called) had gone to two NCAA Tournaments and an NIT during those last three seasons.

Brey's recommendation of Ingelsby carried a lot of weight. He even threw in the fact that he'd be willing to come and play at the Bob Carpenter Center as an added incentive.

Ingelsby's first day on the job was remarkably productive. He got a commitment from Ryan Daly, a six-four guard who had been largely overlooked by Division 1 schools. Daly was a graduate of Archbishop Carroll—the same school Ingelsby had graduated from in 1997. Ingelsby and Daly's father were friends, so the connection was very real.

Daly's entire family had connections to St. Joseph's—starting with his grandfather, Jim Boyle, who had been the coach there for eight years. Both his parents had gone there. But when the Hawks didn't recruit him, he committed to Hartford and then decommitted before signing with Delaware.

Daly doesn't look like people think a star basketball player should look. He's almost chunky and doesn't appear quick enough to be hard to guard.

But he *is* hard to guard: he has a deceptive first step and doesn't need to be squared up to make a shot from outside. He was the CAA's rookie of the year in 2017 and had averaged 17.5 points and 6.2 rebounds as a sophomore.

Ingelsby was slowly building his program around Daly and Eric Carter, a six-ten back-to-the-basket center (a rarity these days) who had planned to transfer after Ross was fired but decided to stay. When Ingelsby added a talented shooter, Ryan Allen, to the mix for his second season, it looked as if the Blue Hens were close to taking off.

They were 14-19 in that second season, but with the core three returning and several now-veteran players in the mix, Ingelsby thought season three could bring a major turnaround.

"It had taken a while," he said. "The one thing I learned from Coach Brey was that unless you're Duke or Kentucky or Kansas, the first goal is to get old and stay old."

In other words, recruit players who might not be stars right away but can develop into stars as juniors and seniors. Carter would be a fifth-year senior in 2019, Daly was a junior, and Allen was a precocious sophomore who had succeeded Daly as the CAA's rookie of the year.

Except Ingelsby never got the chance to coach that core trio. Shortly after the 2018 season ended, Daly announced he was transferring to St. Joseph's. In one sense, it was understandable given his family's connections to the school. But Ingelsby was caught off guard. The Hawks hadn't recruited Daly coming out of high school, and he had become a star at Delaware.

Now, having shown that he was a better player than most college coaches had thought him to be coming out of high school, he was leaving when Delaware was on the verge of turning things around.

"I don't even like to talk about it," Ingelsby said, months later. "It definitely hurt and, even though it wasn't personal and I got that, I took it kind of personally. I had to move on, though, and keep working with the kids who wanted to be here."

The Blue Hens had been very up and down the first two-plus months of the season. They had gotten off to a 7-2 start, the only losses being at Maryland—by just 73–67—and to a UNC Greensboro team that would win twenty-nine games.

Then the roller-coaster ride began: a solid double-overtime road win at Columbia, followed by a fifteen-point home loss to Navy. The nadir had come in a loss to in-state rival Delaware State. The Hornets had won four games a year earlier. They had a new coach, Eric Skeeters, and were improved, but not *that* much improved.

The start of conference season was also remarkably good and remarkably bad. It opened with an embarrassing 91–46 loss at Hofstra. Three nights later, the Blue Hens went to Northeastern to play the team picked to win the league title—and won, 82–80.

They were 5-2 in conference with Towson coming to town, after a win over James Madison two nights earlier in a game in which Allen and Carter had combined for 55 of the team's 76 points, shooting 20-of-29 from the field to hold off the Dukes after a fourteen-point lead had been whittled to three. Allen made four free throws in the final minute to clinch the victory.

Towson was a bigger mountain to climb than one might have thought, given their record. The Tigers had lost no fewer than eight players—five to graduation; three to transfer from a team that had gone 18-14 the previous season. Two of the transfers, Zane Martin and Justin Gorham, had been the team's two leading scorers. Martin had gone to New Mexico and Gorham to Houston, leaving Coach Pat Skerry with a lot of holes to fill.

"We knew this year would be a rebuild," he said. "You try to be prepared, but when you throw in transfers with graduation, it's tough. We've got eight new players, and even if they're talented, it's going to take them a while to mesh. Just have to put my head down and make them understand how hard we have to work to compete."

Skerry's teams had always been competitive since his arrival eight seasons ago. He had taken over in about as bad a situation as any coach could possibly walk into: the Tigers had gone 4-26 in Pat Kennedy's final season, losing their last nineteen games and going 0-18 in the CAA. What's more, they were on NCAA academic probation for two years, bad for the school's image, bad for recruiting.

Skerry knew all this when he took over, but starting 0-22 to extend the losing streak to an NCAA record forty-one straight losses before finally beating UNC Wilmington and going on to a 1-31 record was no fun.

Skerry regrouped. He hit the recruiting trail hard, going after transfers, JUCOs (junior college students), and freshmen. A year later, Towson was 18-13, which was not only the biggest turnaround in terms of games won from one season to another but Towson's first winning season since 1996. The Tigers would have been invited *somewhere* with that kind of story to tell, but they were still on probation and couldn't even play in the conference tournament.

As a consolation prize, Skerry was voted CAA coach of the year. A year later, the Tigers moved from the dilapidated Towson Center next door to the sparkling-new SECU Arena. They won twenty-five games that season and made it to the CIT quarterfinals. After a down season in 2014–15 they had bounced back with three straight winning seasons. Skerry had been given an eight-year contract two seasons earlier in part because he deserved it, in part because the school wanted to make sure he wasn't tempted by another job offer.

But this had been the winter of Skerry's discontent. It had started in the opener, a humiliating 73–42 loss at Virginia.

"I told the players that one was on me," he said. "I needed a guarantee game, but scheduling those guys was a mistake—especially with a brand-new team. My fault—a hundred percent."

They had limped through the preconference schedule, their most impressive win a come-from-behind double-overtime win at UMBC. Brian Fobbs, a JUCO transfer from New York City, was the best of the new players. He had hit the winning shot in Catonsville, a three-pointer with ten seconds left—the last of his 32 points. But the key to the victory had been rebounding—which had been Towson's calling card under Skerry. The Tigers outrebounded the Retrievers, 46–33, and that, as much as anything, was the difference.

They had started the conference season with a win over Elon, but had dropped six in a row—five in the conference, one to Cornell—since then. One thing made them dangerous: their rebounding and their tenacity. It certainly wasn't their shooting or their quickness.

The rebounding was what worried Ingelsby most. He was 0-4 against the Tigers, and rebounding had been critical in all four games.

"It's not a stretch to say that sometimes their best offense is throwing it up on the glass and going and getting it," Ingelsby said. "We can't allow that."

They didn't allow Towson to do much of anything—including rebound—for most of the first half. There aren't that many rebounds to be had when your opponent seems to be making every shot. After Towson's Jordan McNeil hit a three on the first possession of the game—a rare thing for the Tigers—Delaware went on a 14–0 run. It was 14–3 with 13:15 left when Towson finally scored again. The lead ballooned to 37–19 before Towson scored the final three points of the half to make it 37–22.

I've seen a lot of basketball games in my life, and I think I've become pretty good at reading body language. Watching Delaware leave the court—still up fifteen—I thought they looked more like a team down fifteen. They walked slowly, Ingelsby even pausing to look over his shoulder as if he thought there might be a (Towson) Tiger closing in on him from behind.

My play-by-play partner on the game, Andrew Bogusch, an old friend from the days we had worked together on a CBS Sports Radio show, had been doing play-by-play on Delaware's home games all season. "This is what they do," he said when I commented to him about the body language (off air). "They play great in the first half and then get in trouble in the second half."

Bogusch knew his Blue Hens. Towson opened the second half on a 7–0 run, meaning it was 10–0 bridging halftime, and the margin was 37–29 with nearly a half to play. Carter and Allen, so unstoppable two nights earlier against James Madison, were stoppable. Allen hit his first shot of the night—an early three-pointer during the 14–0 run—and then was 2-of-11 the rest of the way, failing to make another three. Carter played solidly with 14 points and 8 rebounds, but the two combined to shoot 9-of-22, a far cry from the 20-of-29 against JMU.

Towson relentlessly closed in, not dominating the boards, but controlling them at key moments.

After Carter got loose for a dunk with 1:47 left to make it 63–61, Fobbs was fouled. An almost 90 percent free-throw shooter, he missed the second shot, meaning Delaware still led, 63–62.

But Brian Thomas swooped in to grab the offensive rebound. Thomas was a senior and an example of a kid who had never lived up to his high school hype but had hung in there to try to help his team. He had limped off in the first half with an apparent back injury but came back to play in the second half with much of the Towson frontcourt in foul trouble.

Towson quickly called time to set up a play. Almost everyone figured the ball would go to Fobbs. Instead, sophomore guard Tobias Howard, whom Skerry had benched because he lacked playmaking skills, found Thomas in the corner. It was hardly the ideal shot, the six-nine Thomas not being any kind of outside shooter.

Except this time, he made it. Towson led 64–63 with twenty-two seconds left.

Delaware got the ball to Allen, who drove the lane, missed, and grabbed his own rebound. He was fouled with 1.1 seconds left on the clock.

Against James Madison, Allen had been 6-for-6 from the line, including making four in a row in the final minute. Even on a poor shooting night from the floor, he was 6-of-8 from the line. It looked as if Delaware would escape.

Except Allen missed the first. Skerry called time to let him think about the second one. I was certain I was about to see my second overtime game of the day/night doubleheader. For the record, TV announcers don't get paid overtime. Neither do referees or sportswriters. And at this level of college ball, certainly not the players.

As the teams returned to the floor, I said to Bogusch, "Allen's not missing two in a row. We're going to play overtime."

Brilliant observation.

Allen missed. Game over. Towson had won, 64–63.

It was one of those outcomes that leave everyone stunned. The Tiger players and coaches were amazed they'd gotten out of Dodge—or in this case Newark—with a win. The Blue Hens had thought they were about to go to 6-2 in the league and be challenging for the top spot.

"We led most of the game, we had *two* turnovers all night—and we lost," Ingelsby said. "Our defense let down in the second half, but I'm still not sure how that happened."

Neither was Skerry. "Must have been the coaching," he said.

And then he burst out laughing.

He was in the midst of a difficult season, but a night like this one would keep him going and keep his players going. There wouldn't be any magical moments in March; there would be no games in packed arenas or highlight moments on *SportsCenter*. But there was a gutsy, come-from-behind win on a dank January night to hold on to for everyone getting on the Towson bus for the trip home.

It was raining—still no sign of the predicted snow—when I walked to my car. I could not possibly have been more grateful.

18

MORE THAN A GAME

Martin Luther King Day. It was very cold and sunny, and people came streaming into Burr Gym to see Howard play Harvard. I arrived very early to spend some time with Howard coach Kevin Nickelberry. In all the years I've gone to games at Howard, I've never had a media credential. I walk in and say hello to people, and nobody stops me. It's that kind of place.

The first thing you notice when you walk in the front door of Burr is the plaque that says simply, "Burr Gym, 1964."

The place feels a little bit worn but has the comfortable feel of an old gym, a place meant for basketball. It has very few of the bells and whistles that the multimillion-dollar power-school arenas have; no screaming music or giant message boards bleating out corporate ads all day long.

This is a gym. This is a basketball place.

Even the public address announcer adds to the atmosphere, as opposed to most places where one cringes almost every time the microphone is open and fans have to endure either endless corporate promos or screaming.

For thirty years, Shellie Bowers had been the voice of Howard athletics at both football and basketball games. He also did high school games all over the DC area and was a fixture during the summertime Kenner League, played at Georgetown.

Bowers wasn't like other PA voices. He had his signatures—"THREEEEEEE!" he would yell for a Howard three-pointer, and he would implore fans to "give it up" for the Bison or "show some love" to either team. He was folksy and often funny and very much a fixture when you walked into Burr Gym. He and Nickelberry even had a pregame secret handshake.

But on December 4, Bowers had died, very suddenly, at the age of fifty-five. His memorial service a few days later was filled to overflowing with people whose lives he had touched in some way.

In his place was another veteran PA announcer, Tony Lee. Like Bowers, Lee did games all over Washington, and he had occasionally filled in for Bowers at Howard. Now he was trying to fill unfillable shoes.

"I have to be myself, I can't be Shellie," he said. "I'll put a little extra emphasis on someone's name after a big shot, but I don't want to go overboard."

Lee's signature call—at least to me—was when a player made the front end of a one-and-one and he intoned, "He gets . . . anotha." It was simple, not over-the-top, and cool.

This was a special day, perhaps best explained by Clarence Armstrong, one of the three referees: "There's no place I'd rather be today than right here."

Right here was in northwest Washington, exactly four miles from the spot where Dr. King gave his "I Have a Dream" speech in 1963—a year before the building opened. Right here is also on the campus of one of the best historically black colleges and universities in the country. In fact, Howard is often referred to as "the Harvard of the HBCUs."

When Nickelberry and Harvard coach Tommy Amaker, both DC-area kids, first launched the idea of playing each other, they called it "HU North vs. HU South."

Amaker went to W. T. Woodson in northern Virginia; Nickelberry to Central High School across the river in Prince George's County, Maryland. Amaker was a star who started for four years at Duke and was the point guard on Mike Krzyzewski's first Final Four team in 1986.

Nickelberry wasn't that kind of star. He played at Division 3 Virginia Wesleyan and then began a lengthy coaching odyssey that took him to seven different jobs around the world (Libya included) before he returned home to coach at Howard in 2010.

One of the people he called when he had the chance to get the Howard job was Amaker.

"He wanted to know if I thought you could get it done at an academic school in a league where most of the other schools recruit JUCOs and transfers all the time," Amaker said. "I said, 'Look, I walk into a living room with Harvard on my shirt and I have an advantage. But with certain kids, especially those with parents who have any HBCU ties at all, Howard on the shirt is going to matter too.'"

Nickelberry took the job, even though Howard was in complete disarray. It wasn't just that the basketball team had been to the NCAA Tournament exactly twice—1981 and 1992—but that the academic-minded school wasn't even producing academically. It wasn't just that the school produced exactly *one* winning season since the NCAA trip in 1992—and it also wasn't the fact that Nickelberry's predecessor, Gil Jackson, had never lost *fewer* than twenty-two games in five seasons, it was that Howard—the Harvard of the HBCUs—was on NCAA probation—for academics.

"First day I got the job, the president said to me, 'You've got nine sophomores, they better all graduate,'" Nickelberry remembered. "My first job wasn't to win games, it was to rebuild our academic reputation."

The nine sophomores graduated. Four more twenty-plus-loss seasons were tacked on before Nickelberry's relentless recruiting began to produce results. He recruited James Daniel, a five-foot-eleven-inch guard out of Hampton who became the country's leading scorer. With other solid players in the program, Howard went 16-16 in 2015—its second nonlosing season in twenty-three years—and the future seemed bright.

Then injuries began to kick in. Daniel averaged 27.3 points a game the next year as a junior but didn't have enough support to sustain what had started a year earlier. Then he got hurt, sat out the next season, and left to go to Tennessee as a graduate transfer.

One of the most difficult things for all HBCUs to deal with is big-time schools swooping in to take talented players who had been overlooked coming out of high school. There aren't a lot of charter airplanes in the world of the HBCUs, and there are a *lot* of road games because guarantee games abound in order to keep athletic departments out of the red.

"You can understand it," Nickelberry said. "A kid plays well here, then a school comes along with a twenty-thousand-seat arena versus a twenty-seven-hundred-seat arena; they're playing on national TV; staying at five-star hotels. Who wouldn't be tempted?"

Both Daniel and second-leading scorer J. T. Miller chased the bright lights prior to the 2016–17 season, leaving Nickelberry almost back on square one for a season he had thought might be a very successful one.

"Realistically, if we can compete with the best teams in the MEAC once every three or four years, we're doing well," Nickelberry said. "We almost never take transfers or JUCOs. Everyone else in the league does that. It makes it hard to compete."

Nickelberry had actually gone so far as to suggest that Howard move to the Patriot League. The ten schools there were much closer to Howard's academic profile than the MEAC and, like Howard, the league played FCS football.

After losing Daniel and Miller, Nickelberry had regrouped and thought he had potentially the best team in his nine seasons. There were no seniors getting playing time, and if the big-time wolves could be held off, the Bison had a chance to be excellent in another year when their very young big men had a year under their belt to go with three talented guards.

The problem was that Nickelberry knew he might not get a crack at next year. He was in the last year of his contract, and athletic director Kery Davis, in his fourth year at the school, was about out of patience.

Davis's first important hire—Mike London as football coach—had worked out well. London had turned the Bison around and had gone 7-4 in his first season. But he left a year later to take the job at William & Mary. Davis had hired Ron Prince to take his place in December. Now he was ready to make decisions about Nickelberry's future, and Nickelberry knew it.

Amaker had no such issues. He had become an icon in his twelve seasons at Harvard, taking the school to places it had almost never been in the past—including four NCAA Tournament trips and two NCAA Tournament *wins*.

He and Nickelberry had first come up with the idea of playing in Washington on Martin Luther King's birthday weekend three seasons earlier.

Amaker had brought his team to Washington on Saturday night

Jordan Fox: he was going to enlist in the Army out of high school; Tommy Allen had a better idea. *Courtesy of Mark Wellman*

Army's Tommy Funk: the classic smart, tough-minded Philadelphia point guard. *Courtesy of Danny Wild, USA Today Sports Images*

Campbell's Chris Clemons was too small for college basketball—until he became the NCAA's third-leading scorer of all time. *Courtesy of Bennett Scarborough Photo*

Clayton Custer (Loyola), a year later: "Every missed shot, every turnover all of a sudden was news." *Courtesy of Steve Woltmann*

oe Sherburne—captain, leader at UMBC—and four years
vithout a B . . . or a C . . . *Courtesy of Mitchell Layton*

Ryan Odom in the spotlight he wanted his team to put in
he rearview mirror last season. *Courtesy of Mitchell Layton*

Tommy Amaker of Harvard never misses the chance to make a road trip for his team about more than playing a basketball game. *Courtesy of Rich von Biberstein/Harvard Athletics*

Harvard's Seth Towns: Ivy League player of the year in 2018 . . . Out injured for all of 2019 . . . 2020? *Courtesy of Gil Talbot*

William & Mary's Paul Rowley was the only second-year law student to play against national champion Virginia last season. Also, the only second-year law student to play against *anyone* last season . . . *Courtesy of William and Mary Athletics*

Fran Dunphy waves—again—to the crowd during the ovation that wouldn't stop, prior to his final game coaching Temple in the Palestra. *Courtesy of Mike Sperando*

Winthrop's Bjorn Broman. He might have been exhausted, but he didn't want college basketball to end. *Courtesy of TimCowiePhotography.com*

Pat Kelsey (Winthrop) made news speaking from the heart on a subject that had nothing to do with basketball. *Courtesy of TimCowiePhotography.com*

Hofstra's Justin Wright-Foreman "eyes" the basket—to great effect. *Courtesy of William Howard, Hofstra University*

Three generations of Howards celebrate the hiring of La Salle's new coach: Mo—the old pro; Ashley—the new coach; and Journey—whose future is clearly limitless. *Courtesy of Greg Carroccio, Sideline Photos*

Old Dominion's Jeff Jones wasn't going to let a second bout with cancer affect the way he coached his team. *Courtesy of Old Dominion University Athletics*

The Palestra's famous sign. Gives me chills every time I stop and read it at a game. *Courtesy of the University of Pennsylvania*

"The Cathedral of College Basketball": the Palestra, located on Penn's campus in west Philadelphia. *Courtesy of Wikimedia Commons*

and had scheduled a trip to the National Museum of African American History and Culture. But because Donald Trump's shutdown of the government was in its twenty-ninth day, the museum was closed. Since outdoor monuments were open, Amaker changed the plan and took his players to both the Lincoln Memorial and the King Memorial. It was brutally cold and windy, but there was no way the Crimson weren't making the trip.

Amaker loves to quote Dr. King. His favorite King quote is this: "The true test of a man is not where he stands in comfort or conveniences, but where he stands in challenge and controversy."

Amaker uses that quote so often that the first time he took his players to the King Memorial in 2016 and they spotted the quote on a plaque, several said, "Hey, Coach, we thought *you* said this."

"I guess I use it so often they started to think it was mine."

For both Amaker and Nickelberry, playing this game on this day had great meaning as African Americans coaching largely African American teams.

Nine of the ten starters in the game were African Americans. The tenth, Harvard's Christian Juzang, was half African American and half Vietnamese. Prior to the game, the two teams linked arms for the playing of two national anthems: first "The Star-Spangled Banner" and then "Lift Ev'ry Voice and Sing"—the black national anthem.

The words to "Lift Ev'ry Voice and Sing" were written in 1900 by the poet James Weldon Johnson. His brother John Rosamond Johnson put the words to music five years later. In 1919, the NAACP began calling the song "The Negro National Hymn." The Reverend Joseph Lowery quoted from it at length during his benediction in 2009 at President Barack Obama's inauguration, and opera star Denyce Graves sang it during the opening ceremony at the National Museum of African American History and Culture.

The Howard players, more familiar with the song and its history, lifted their fists—as did many in the stands—during the playing of the song. The two songs, played back-to-back with the players and coaches standing with arms linked, were dramatic and moving.

There were plenty of Harvard fans and alums in the building—including Supreme Court justice Elena Kagan, a 1986 graduate of Harvard Law School. She made the trek downstairs to the locker room area prior to the game to say hello to Amaker.

I have seen quite a few celebrities greet coaches prior to games in my life, but this was a first—a Supreme Court justice talking hoops (and clearly knowing her stuff) with a coach.

The game was an important one for both teams.

Howard was coming off a win against South Carolina State two days earlier, but it had gotten off to a rocky start in MEAC play and was just 2-3, 8-11 overall. Nickelberry knew that a sub-.500 record in conference play would almost certainly doom him.

Amaker had no such worries, but he wasn't thrilled with his team at that moment. The Crimson had been very up and down throughout preconference play: a loss at San Francisco was followed two days later by an impressive win at St. Mary's.

But Ivy League play had opened with a thud. Harvard opened at Dartmouth and was soundly beaten, 81–63, by the Big Green.

Amaker understood that the Ivy League was deeper now than it had been in years. He also knew that his two best players—Seth Towns and Bryce Aiken—still weren't playing, although Aiken was practicing. But Dartmouth was still a bottom-feeder in the league (it would win just one more conference game), and the loss was unacceptable.

"To say that he was angry in practice after Dartmouth doesn't really begin to describe it," Seth Towns said with a grin. "The word 'unacceptable' was used a lot.

"He always lets us know when he's not happy in practice, especially if he doesn't think we're playing hard or if we aren't focused on the task at hand. Nothing makes him angrier than not playing good defense, and our defense at Dartmouth was pretty awful. He was, let's say, emphatic in letting us know that."

In addition to "unacceptable," the players heard a lot of words not heard very often in Harvard classrooms. Amaker had decided it was time for his team to put up or shut up, and he wasn't about to shut up in delivering that message.

The Ivy League schedule is always a jumble, especially early because the schools have varied exam schedules. Teams traditionally opened by playing the same opponent back-to-back. This season was no different for Harvard—the first two games were, as always, against Dartmouth. But there was a two-week gap between the game at Dartmouth and the game at Harvard.

The only game in between was this one—nine days after the opener at Dartmouth.

Amaker went back to preseason mode in practice, working his players hard mentally and physically. Amaker is different from a lot of coaches in that he can go from quoting Martin Luther King to blistering the walls in a heartbeat.

The trainers had told Amaker that Aiken could play against Howard. That was a plus. But how much did he want to play him after he hadn't appeared in a game in more than a year?

"I'm going to start him," Amaker said. "He's the kind of kid who isn't going to go out there and be afraid or timid. He's tough-minded that way. He'll *want* to start and he'll *want* the ball."

Prior to the game, Amaker reminded his players that this was a special day, a day to think about more important things than basketball.

"I tell you all the time that every game we play matters," he said. "And they do. But this game, playing here today is meaningful. That's a different level. They all matter, only a few are meaningful.

"I always tell you there are three things in life you can't get back: time, words, and opportunity. Today's an opportunity. Don't let it pass us by."

Then he added a Dr. King quote that he thought apt for the day and for where his team was at that moment: "Life's most persistent and urgent question is, what are you doing for others?"

He finished with a basketball basic: "We need to put that Dartmouth performance behind us. That needs to be our nadir, and we start to get better right from here. The best way to do that is to remember to help your teammates out there on the court."

They did exactly that. On the game's first possession, Aiken caught the ball on the left wing and, without any hesitation, fired a three. Swish. Sixteen seconds in, he was back.

The Crimson jumped to a 9–2 lead. The Bison hung in, thanks in large part to their three excellent guards: sophomore R. J. Cole and juniors C. J. Williams and Chad Lott. Cole would finish with 21 points, 8 assists, 3 rebounds, and 2 steals. Williams had 19 and 5 boards, and Lott had 16. In short, 56 of Howard's 71 points.

But every time they closed the gap, the Crimson had an answer. Often it was six-ten junior center Chris Lewis, whom Howard's young big men simply couldn't handle. Lewis would finish the day with 16 points on 7-of-9 shooting to go with 6 rebounds. Experience does matter.

Howard got to within 28–24, but Henry Welsh, who delivered critical minutes off the bench, hit a three with 5:25 left. The lead swelled again to 45–28 before another talented young Howard player, Raymond Bethea Jr.—a freshman guard—hit a three in the final seconds to make it 45–31 at the break.

Aiken had looked as if he had never missed a game, sharing time at the point with Juzang, playing off the ball at times too. He would finish with 16 points and 5 assists in twenty-nine minutes.

Amaker's halftime message was as direct as his pregame talk: "This is who we are, fellas, this is how we should play." And then a warning: "Don't take your foot off the gas. This team is too talented to take for granted just because we've got a lead."

He wasn't wrong. Urged on by the sellout crowd—2,700—Howard kept inching back in the second twenty minutes. But the closest the Bison got was 63–56 with 6:44 to go. Even with the building as loud as it had been all day, Harvard didn't flinch.

Justin Bassey, who would finish with 18 points, got fouled going to the basket and made both free throws. Then Aiken hit another three to make it 68–56, and the Crimson cruised from there.

The final was 84–71. For Nickelberry it was a disappointing loss. His team hadn't played poorly, it had just been outplayed. The Bison were now 8-12.

"It was a great day," he said, forcing a smile. "Except for the game."

For Amaker, the entire trip had been a rousing success. The trip to the monuments, the team bonding that happens on the road, the return of Aiken, and the clear-cut win. The Crimson were back to .500. The rest of their games would be against Ivy League opponents.

And while he couldn't help but wonder how good his team might be if Towns ever got healthy, he felt he had enough talent to compete for another title.

"Yale's got the most talent and experience," he said. "We'll have to beat them if we want to win the league."

And, very possibly, they would have to beat Yale on their home court in March if they wanted to go back to the NCAAs.

As the teams exchanged handshakes and hugs after the buzzer, I watched and thought: Clarence Armstrong was right. There was no better place to be on this day than in this old gym.

19

YES, CHRISTINE, THERE
IS A FARMVILLE

Scott Griffith Aldrich goes by Griff. Orlando Henry Smith is Tubby to all who know him.

Smith got his nickname because, as a kid, he loved to stay in the bathtub. "I was also kind of chubby," he likes to say. "The nickname fit."

Scott Aldrich has always been Griff to friends and family. "My grandfather, who was a submarine captain in World War Two, went by Griff—also his middle name. So I always have, too. But I wasn't going with Griffith."

The coaching matchup between Griff and Tubby—Longwood versus High Point—on a cold, clear Thursday night was summed up best by Griff as he sat in a coffee shop near the Longwood campus after his team's pregame meal that afternoon.

"I have twelve career wins, he's got six hundred and six," he said, laughing.

Both men had written remarkable stories to get to this matchup, but Aldrich's was unique.

He had played Division 3 college ball at Hampden-Sydney, which is located six miles down the road from Longwood. There, he and Ryan Odom were teammates and roommates.

They were also best friends, and Ryan helped Griff get a job working for his dad the next year at Wake Forest. At the same time, after graduating magna cum laude, Griff applied to law schools and got into Virginia, William & Mary, Wake Forest, and Tulane.

"I got turned down by Georgetown," he said. "Shortest rejection letter in history, I think."

Ryan and Griff traveled to Milwaukee that spring (1996) to see Wake Forest play in the NCAA Tournament. Ryan had told his mother about Griff's acceptance to law schools. Soon after they arrived, Dave Odom called Griff into his hotel suite.

"The coaching offer is withdrawn," he said. "You go to law school."

Griff followed orders and went to Virginia, where he did well enough to have several job offers when he graduated. But the coaching bug was still there, so he took a job at Hampden-Sydney working for Tony Shaver, his college coach.

A year later, after a friend who worked there insisted he interview at Vinson & Elkins, a massive (eight-hundred-lawyer) firm in Houston, he was offered $110,000 as an entry salary there.

"I still had forty thousand in unpaid college loans," he said. "I figured I had to give it a shot."

Even then, he kept his hand in at basketball, coaching a local AAU team that produced a number of good players—including DeAndre Jordan—but was a local and regional team, not one of those teams that take in big bucks from shoe companies and travel the country.

Soon after he made partner, he was offered the chance to go to London for a brief stint in the firm's office there. It was supposed to last six weeks. He stayed four years. By then he was married to Julie Wareing, and while they were there, she enrolled and got her degree at Oxford.

They came home changed. Aldrich's faith is extremely important to him and, as he kept making more and more money as an oil and gas lawyer—later as the COO of oil and gas company—he felt as if he was leaving something important out of his life.

Eventually, he and Julie moved out of the fashionable River Oaks community where they lived and moved across town to Third Ward, into a home in Houston's inner city.

Aldrich founded an AAU program called "His Hoops," which was funded by a ministry called the Force for Families.

His Hoops was not your typical AAU team by any stretch. When players arrived after school four days a week, they had to read for thirty minutes and study math for thirty minutes before they were allowed to touch a basketball. If Aldrich felt a player had a chance to earn a Division 1 scholarship, he would often recommend him to a higher-level AAU team. Dinner was served after practice, sometimes brought in by a local food bank; sometimes at the Aldrich house. One player lived with Griff and Julie for two years.

Griff and Julie had also decided to start a family. They had struggled to get pregnant, so they decided to adopt. They now have three children: Ford and Scott, both seven, and Laura Lee, who is three. All are African American.

"We wanted a family, and we wanted to adopt kids who really needed a home and a place where they could be loved," Aldrich said. "These three were perfect for us, and I hope we're perfect for them."

Aldrich continued to have success in business after the move back to Houston. Not only did he start the oil and gas business, he also became CFO of an investment firm. He loved the work he was doing with His Hoops. All was well.

But something was still nagging at him.

"College basketball has always been my first love," he said. "I grew up [in Virginia Beach] loving ACC basketball. I loved playing, even though I was only good enough to be a D-3 player, and in my brief exposure as a coach, I was truly happy. Becoming a lawyer was about money. I enjoyed doing it, think I was pretty good about it, but it wasn't my passion."

And so, when his old college pal Ryan Odom became the coach at UMBC, Aldrich called him and told him he wanted to go to work for him.

Odom knew Aldrich could help him—on and off the court. He had one job open: as director of basketball operations and recruiting coordinator. The job paid $32,000 a year—about $800,000 less than Aldrich was making at the time.

"Fortunately, we had a cushion financially," he said. "The only issue really was asking Julie to move from Houston, where she'd grown up, to Baltimore."

Julie understood why her husband wanted to do this. In the spring of 2016, the Aldrich family moved east.

Of course, they had no idea they were signing on to what would become a college hoops rocket. The Retrievers went from seven wins to twenty-one in Odom's first season, and the second season produced the America East title and the Virginia Miracle.

In the meantime, Longwood president W. Taylor Reveley IV was looking for a basketball coach. Longwood had been founded in 1839 under the name Farmville Female Seminary Association and had gone through no fewer than seven name changes before becoming Longwood University in 2002.

It didn't take male students full-time until 1976, and after some success in Division 3 and Division 2, it became a Division 1 program in 2004.

Mike Gillian, who had been an assistant to Jim Larrañaga at both Bowling Green and George Mason, was given the task of making the transition to D-1.

In many ways, Gillian was perfect for the job. He was, if it was possible, *more* upbeat than Larrañaga. Longwood didn't have a league to play in when it transitioned, meaning it had no chance to play in the NCAA Tournament—which is what every college player who isn't going to be a one-and-done dreams about.

Longwood was 1-30 in its first season (2004–05) as a D-1 team. Somehow, Gillian convinced enough players to come to Longwood to go 17-14 in 2009—which was a not-so-minor miracle. Longwood finally found a league, joining the Big South in 2012, but Gillian didn't get to stick around to take the next step. After Longwood went 8-25 in its first Big South season, he "resigned."

Jayson Gee, who had had success at Division 2 Charleston University, was hired to take his place and went 42-120 the next five seasons, including 7-26 in 2017–18.

Reveley, a third-generation college president—his grandfather had been president of Hampden-Sydney and his father president of William & Mary—was willing to think out of the box. He had graduated from Virginia law school a year after Aldrich, and his unique background intrigued him.

"When I got the first call, I thought, 'Why is he calling me? They don't need a compliance guy,'" Aldrich said.

Reveley was interested in hiring him not for compliance but to coach. After the two men met over dinner in Baltimore, Reveley thought he had his guy. The only thing that delayed the hiring was UMBC's success.

"Initially I was going to go down for the formal interview the

Monday after the America East Tournament," Aldrich said. "But then we won. So we rescheduled for the following Sunday after we played Virginia on Friday. Except we won and we were playing Kansas State that day."

Only after the Retrievers lost to Kansas State did Aldrich finally make it back to the town where he'd gone to college—but to a different school this time. His contract called for him to be paid $150,000 a year—a lot more than $32,000 a year, but considerably less than what he'd made in Houston.

He was thrilled. "I never, ever dreamed this could happen," he said on the afternoon of the High Point game. "There are times I just look around and say, 'Are you kidding me?'"

Tubby Smith could be forgiven if he said the same thing—just for different reasons.

As Aldrich had noted, he had won 606 college games in a storied career that had included six years as a high school coach; three assistant coaching jobs—VCU, South Carolina, Kentucky—and head coaching jobs at Tulsa, Georgia, Kentucky, Minnesota, Texas Tech, and Memphis before coming full circle and returning to High Point—his alma mater—the previous spring.

Smith had won everywhere he'd been, but his most notable accomplishment had been winning the national championship in 1998—his first season at Kentucky.

To say that Smith had walked into a difficult situation at Kentucky was putting it mildly. The job isn't one for the faint of heart under any circumstances. Kentucky fans don't hope to win, they insist on winning as if it is a birthright.

What's more, Smith was following Rick Pitino, who had become an icon in the state for resurrecting the program after it had been on NCAA probation for two years. Under Pitino, the Wildcats had won the national championship in 1996 and had lost the title game (to Arizona) a year later in overtime. After vowing never to leave, Pitino had bolted to become president/general manager/coach and king of all things for the Boston Celtics.

Smith was coming off back-to-back sweet sixteen trips at Georgia and had been a Pitino assistant for two seasons. When Kentucky approached him about the job, he wasn't sure he wanted it.

"We were going to be good the next year at Georgia," he said. "My son G.G. was already there and my younger son, Saul, was going to come too. It was a great situation for me.

"Plus, I knew following Rick would be difficult for anyone."

There was one other thing: Smith is African American. Kentucky had never had an African American coach, and although the infamous days when Adolph Rupp's all-white team had lost to an all-black Texas Western team in the 1966 national title game were long gone, Kentucky wasn't exactly Cal Berkeley or Stanford culturally.

It was Pitino who talked Smith into taking the job.

"He said, 'Tubby, it's a hard job, but it's *Kentucky*. You succeed there, which you will, you go down as a great basketball coach when all is said and done.'"

Smith took the job. It helped that Pitino had left a number of quality players behind. Even so, the first season wasn't all that easy. I still remember driving in Florida one night late in February and picking up Smith's weekly radio show on fifty-thousand-watt WHAS in Louisville.

The Wildcats had just lost to Auburn the previous Saturday. When the host opened the phones, the first caller, no doubt trying to ease any tension, said, "Coach, I just want you to know I haven't given up on this team yet."

Kentucky was 25-4. Turned out the caller was right not to give up on the team. It didn't lose again, coming from seventeen points down in the regional final to beat Duke; it then beat Stanford in overtime in the Final Four and won the national title with a victory over Utah.

The Wildcats finished 35-4 *and* won the championship. That was good enough for Kentucky fans.

At least for a while.

Kentucky was consistently good or very good during the next nine seasons. The Wildcats never won fewer than twenty-two games. They won five SEC titles and reached the sweet sixteen five times and the elite eight three times. But they didn't make it back to the Final Four. Naturally, the whispers started. John Calipari has been to one Final Four since winning his national title at the University of Kentucky in 2012, but there are very few whispers about him.

That's because Calipari is one of the great salesmen of all time, in addition to being a superb coach. Smith was never a salesman—and he was black. It's okay to be black at Kentucky as long as you *win*—not just win, but *win*. At 25-4, some fans might give up on you.

Smith knew enough was enough after back-to-back second-round (gasp!) losses in the NCAA Tournament, and when he was offered the job at Minnesota, he bolted.

That was in March 2007. I remember being in the lobby of the coaches' hotel at the Final Four in Atlanta that spring when Smith walked through en route to a meeting.

He was stopped constantly by coaches congratulating him—many emphatically. He'd coached at Kentucky, won a national title, and sailed happily into the sunset.

Smith had success at Minnesota, making the NCAA Tournament three times in six seasons. But Kentucky isn't the only school where fans and alumni have unreasonable expectations. In 2013, after taking the Gophers to the second round of the NCAAs, Smith was fired.

He was hired almost instantly by Texas Tech and turned a moribund program into a winner, going 19-13 in his third season. He went from there to Memphis and went 40-26 in two seasons. But Memphians, remembering their two Final Four trips (both vacated), wanted to bring back the glory days, so Penny Hardaway, a star at the school in the 1990s, who was coaching a local, high-powered high school team, was hired to replace Smith.

Smith was sixty-six. He had won 596 games and a national title. He certainly deserved (and deserves) consideration for the Hall of Fame. He was ready to relax, spend some time with his grandchildren, and not lose sleep over losses anymore.

"I'd been doing it as a head coach for twenty-seven years at that point," he said. "I figured that was enough."

Then came a phone call from Nido R. Qubein, the president of High Point—Smith's alma mater. Qubein was looking for a basketball coach and he wanted Smith. He had just forced Scott Cherry, who had coached at the school for nine years, to resign. Cherry was the school's winningest coach—he'd gone 146-134 and taken the school to its first four Division 1 postseason appearances: two NITs and two CITs, going 23-10 in 2015.

But the Panthers hadn't been able to win the Big South Tournament and reach the promised land of the NCAAs, and that was what Qubein wanted. When High Point went 14-16 in the 2017–18 season, he decided it was time for a change.

Surprisingly available was a coach who had coached five different schools to a total of eighteen NCAA bids and had won the whole thing once. Plus, he was a grad who, along with his wife Donna, had already pledged $1 million toward the building of a new gym.

"Why not come here and finish your career in a building where the floor is named for you and Donna?" Qubein said. "It's a perfect way for you to finish your career."

Smith was tempted—but torn. He was comfortable with the notion of retiring, didn't feel he had anything left to prove. But it *was* his alma mater, and he could bring G.G. with him as his top assistant. Plus, because Qubein had been a very successful businessman before he became High Point's president in 2005, he had the ability to pay a lot more than a typical mid-major coach might be paid.

He called his old friend Cliff Ellis, who had gone from the big time at Clemson and Auburn to the not so big time at Coastal Carolina and seemed very happy with where he was in life.

"I told him all the same things that Mike Krzyzewski and Les Robinson had told me when I was thinking about taking the Coastal Carolina job," Ellis said. "I asked him if he still had coaching in his blood and he said yes. I said, 'Tubby, a gym is a gym and a team is a team and a game is a game.'"

Ellis smiled. "Then I asked him how much they were going to pay him. He told me. I said, 'Listen, pal, you tell that president if you don't take the job to call *me* and I'll take it.'"

Smith called Qubein back and told him he'd take the job.

"Cliff was right," he said, relaxing an hour before the game at Longwood. "Coaching is coaching, it doesn't matter where you are or what level you're at. It doesn't matter if you're inside Rupp Arena with twenty-three thousand people or here"—he gestured around Willett Hall—"with a thousand people in the place. It's basketball, it's competition, and I still get keyed up for every game."

He smiled. "There is one major difference. I spent twenty-seven years traveling to games on charter airplanes. Now I'm on charter buses. The ride up here was three and a half hours. The ride home tonight will be the same. If we're lucky, we'll get back to High Point about one thirty in the morning. *That* is different."

The game that night was exactly what Aldrich had predicted it would be: a rock fight.

Both teams tended to be offensively challenged. And both played good defense. That made for an ugly game with enough missed bricks being fired to get the new gym that Longwood was planning at least half-built.

The attendance in 1,800-seat Willett Hall was 1,481, which made the place feel full and lively.

How bad was the shooting? Longwood made 8-of-30 shots in the first half and *led* 22–19 at the break because High Point was even worse: 5-of-27. For the game, the two teams combined to shoot 11-of-53 from outside the three-point line, an astonishingly bad 20 percent.

There wasn't any doubt that Smith was coaching as hard as he ever had. "Sometimes I remind myself I have to coach these guys *more* because they aren't as talented as guys I've coached in the past," he'd said before the game. "But I also have to be more patient for the same reason."

Smith, dressed immaculately in a dark suit, white shirt, and matching pocket square, would often leap from the bench to give instructions. When the play failed or the defense didn't get a stop, his shoulders would slump and he'd walk back to the bench, shaking his head, to say something to his son G.G.

I felt as if I could almost read his thoughts: *Do I really want to be here?*

As you might expect with no one able to make shots with any consistency, the game stayed close throughout, except for an almost ten-minute span in which Longwood outscored High Point 21–7 to take a 47–34 lead with just 6:13 to play.

Given that it appeared the Panthers couldn't throw the ball in the ocean from a rowboat (old cliché, but accurate in this case), it looked as if the Lancers would throw the last rock.

But inexperienced teams often have trouble staying in the present, and they frequently struggle to close out a game—especially a game that most people aren't expecting them to win.

Jordan Whitehead started High Point in the right direction with a three-point play on a possession in which the Panthers—the Big South's best rebounding team—got three cracks inside before Whitehead scored.

From that moment on, every possession for the Lancers felt like a tooth pull. It was still 52–46 with 2:17 left, but they couldn't put the game away. Two mistakes by leading scorer Isaiah Walton—a missed three and a turnover—led to two Panther baskets, and it was 52–50 with twenty-eight seconds still left. By now, the crowd was holding its collective breath. So was Aldrich.

"It isn't as if we didn't try to give it to them at the end," he said later. Smith called time. The shot clock was off, so as soon as Longwood beat the pressure and got the ball into the frontcourt, Jamal Wright fouled Walton.

That was exactly what Aldrich and Longwood wanted. Walton was the team's leading scorer, at 18.8 points per game; he was a redshirt senior with more experience than anyone else on the team, and even though he had shot the ball poorly all night—3-of-11 from the field—he was an 88 percent free-throw shooter.

The foul was only High Point's ninth of the half. So it was one-and-one for Walton. He missed.

Smith opted not to call time, preferring to push the ball to the basket without giving Longwood a chance to set up its defense. Once, coaches always called time to set up a last play in a game-on-the-line situation. Now they rarely do.

The Panthers got the ball inside to Whitehead, who had about as wide-open a layup as you could possibly ask for. Somehow he missed, the ball rolling off the rim. Jordan Cintron grabbed the rebound for Longwood and was fouled with six seconds left.

He went to the line and missed. "I was beginning to think we were never going to make another free throw—*ever*," Aldrich said.

Fortunately for Cintron and for Longwood, the foul had been High Point's tenth. So he got a second shot. This time, he made it.

Leading 53–50, Longwood's Sean Flood intentionally fouled Wright as he crossed midcourt to prevent a potentially tying three-pointer. Wright made the first, then missed the second on purpose as his teammates crashed the boards in search of an offensive rebound and one last chance to tie the game.

But Cintron again grabbed the rebound and quickly passed the ball to Shabooty Phillips. He was fouled with three seconds left and made both free throws. Phillips had first met Aldrich when the coach had convinced him to join His Hoops as a high school junior. Phillips had agreed to join the team only after Aldrich had beaten him one-on-one "in street shoes," Phillips said when he retold the story.

After two seasons in junior college, Phillips had transferred to Longwood to rejoin Aldrich. He coolly made both free throws, and the final was 55–51.

"Boy, I really taught Tubby a basketball lesson, didn't I?" Aldrich joked. "I made sure we gave him a wide-open layup at the end. Works every time."

Aldrich was exhausted. Rock fights will do that to you.

On the other side of the building, Smith could only shake his head. "We made a hell of a comeback," he said. "We had a layup to tie the game. I can't ask them for much more than that."

I asked him if he'd be able to sleep on the bus ride home.

"Sleep?" he said, incredulous at the question. "We just lost. I don't sleep after losses. I'll watch the tape."

He stood up to walk to the bus.

Coaches, I thought, coach. It doesn't matter where—the NBA Finals, the Final Four, or a cold January night in Farmville, Virginia.

Coaches, coach. Period.

20

FROM KIRBY TO THE PALESTRA—
ANOTHER DAY IN HOOPS HEAVEN

It was another doubleheader day.

Unlike the previous Saturday, television wasn't involved. It was one of those days that set up just about perfectly for me. Army was playing at Lafayette at two o'clock, and then at seven Penn and St. Joseph's were playing in the Palestra.

As a bonus, Penn had a chance to win the Big Five title outright for only the sixth time in history. The Quakers had ended Villanova's twenty-five-game five-years-plus Big Five winning streak with a 78–75 win at the Palestra in December. Villanova coach Jay Wright, who has won two national titles and been to three Final Fours, called his team's Big Five winning streak "as big a deal as anything we've accomplished since I've been here."

Outsiders can't understand that, especially since so many of those Villanova wins were by lopsided scores. But the intensity of the Big Five and its meaning to the schools can't be underestimated. There's a saying in Philadelphia that goes like this: "They say there's no trophy for winning the Big Five. They must not be from Philadelphia."

Even though it was technically a St. Joseph's home game, the Palestra would be rocking on Saturday night.

Before that, though, I walked into a quiet Kirby Sports Center at a few minutes past noon and found the two coaches, Fran O'Hanlon and Jimmy Allen, sitting directly across from the Lafayette bench— O'Hanlon's pregame hangout spot before the gym began to fill up— talking easily.

Their teams appeared headed in opposite directions at that moment. Army was 5-2 in Patriot League play, having recovered from the disappointing loss at Loyola to win three straight home games, the most impressive a 67–57 win over a rapidly improving Colgate team; the most important a 71–62 win over Navy. Any win over Navy is important.

"Games we had to have," Allen said. "We already let one home game [against Bucknell] get away. We couldn't drop another with all the road games coming up after that."

This was the first of those road games. Army had beaten Lafayette at home earlier in the month, but Allen knew it would be different playing at Kirby.

The Leopards were 2-5 in conference play and, as you might expect from a young team, wildly inconsistent. They'd gone on the road to beat American the previous Saturday and then had lost at home to Colgate.

O'Hanlon never lets anybody see him sweat, but he knew a win against Army was vital if his team was going to stay out of the dreaded bottom four at the end of the conference season. Seeds seven through ten had to play an extra game in the conference tournament. In spite of the Holy Cross Miracle of 2016, no one wanted that.

The crowd that afternoon would be a rather sedate 1,133. When Lafayette was rolling around the turn of the century, the 3,500-seat building was almost always sold-out or close to sold-out, and the place rocked when the Leopards got on a roll. Now, not so much.

Still, home court is home court, and Lafayette was clearly ready to play.

O'Hanlon had made a lineup change, deciding to bring second-leading scorer Alex Petrie off the bench to give his team a spark. The notion of bringing one of your best players off the bench dates to the great Red Auerbach, who believed bringing his second- or third-best player off the bench after six to eight minutes gave his team an offensive spark and an energy boost.

Auerbach's first "sixth man" was Frank Ramsey, and although Ramsey had a Hall of Fame career, it was John Havlicek who made the "position" famous in the 1960s. Today the NBA gives out a "Sixth Man of the Year Award," and most coaches employ the concept.

It isn't used as often in college because college players tend to have fragile egos and they aren't being paid. But O'Hanlon thought bringing a gifted shooter like Petrie off the bench might help his offensively challenged team. The Leopards, who liked to shoot threes and play up-tempo, had scored only 47 points against Colgate.

O'Hanlon's move paid dividends in the first half. Petrie scored 13 points and keyed a run that gave Lafayette a 21–12 lead. Army came right back with an 11–0 run of its own, but Petrie hit a late three and the Leopards led 33–29 at the break.

They stretched the margin to a dozen on a couple of occasions, the last on a three by talented freshman Justin Jaworski that made it 48–36 with 15:42 left. Army began to creep back, led by sophomore Lonnie Grayson, who came off the bench to provide desperately needed offense—18 points on 8-of-11 shooting, including 3-of-5 from three-point range.

His performance probably saved Army, because both Fox and Funk were in shooting funks. Funk had jammed a finger on his shooting hand and, even though he wouldn't complain about it, was clearly not himself, shooting 0-for-11 from the field. Fox was going through a very up-and-down stretch: he'd been 5-of-7 (4-of-6 from three) against Colgate; then a horrific 0-for-10 against Navy, followed by 4-of-8 against Holy Cross.

Against Lafayette, he was 1-of-6 from the field, the basket on a pretty backdoor play that cut the margin to 50–49. Lukas Jarrett answered with a layup to make it 52–49 with 10:09 left. And then the Leopards hit the wall.

O'Hanlon had talked before the game about avoiding empty possessions—those that ended with a turnover or a bad shot. It was important not only to the offense, but also to the defense. Turnovers and bad shots often lead to easy baskets for the opposition.

After Jarrett's basket, Lafayette failed to score for almost six minutes. During that stretch the Leopards had five turnovers and four missed shots. They never got an offensive rebound, and every time Army got the ball back it felt as if the Black Knights came flying down the court as Lafayette scrambled to get back.

The run was 13–0. John Emezie, whose mother was a surgeon at Duke hospital, hit a three to tie the game. Then he made a layup on a pass from Funk to give Army its first lead since the first half, 54–52. By the time Jaworski hit a jumper with 4:26 to go, the margin had grown to 62–52.

From there, Army made most of their free throws, and the closest Lafayette got was 69–63 on a Petrie drive (he finished with a game-high 20 points) with forty-one seconds to go. The lead had been 69–60, but Emezie's foul allowed Petrie to go to the line and cut the margin to six. Allen was briefly apoplectic about Emezie's foul, but he couldn't get too upset since Emezie had come off the bench to score 11 points and had also had 2 assists and grabbed 2 rebounds.

"He was great," Allen said later. "But what was he thinking?"

Neither team scored again, and 69–63 was the final. For Lafayette, a difficult loss to take after having a double-digit lead in the second half. For Army, a critical road victory, especially coming from behind on the road; especially on a day when Funk and Fox combined to shoot 1-for-17 from the field.

Lafayette's archrival, Lehigh, would make the sixteen-mile trip from Bethlehem on Wednesday. Army would make its longest and most difficult bus trip of the year to Colgate that same day.

I was on my way to Route 22 and the Pennsylvania Turnpike for the seventy-eight-mile drive to the Palestra about twenty-five minutes after the final buzzer. I was tingling with anticipation the entire ride.

I pulled into the parking garage behind the Palestra at 5:40. Ideally, when I go to the Palestra, I like to arrive at least two hours before tipoff. It gives me extra time to see friends and to enjoy being inside the building when it's still empty. It also allows me some time to walk around and look at the different displays on the concourse. I've done it many times, but always find something I've missed before.

Because Army-Lafayette hadn't tipped until 2 p.m. I didn't get on the road until 4:25. Still, I made good time, even though I hit some of the inevitable traffic on the Schuylkill Expressway heading into downtown Philadelphia.

It was cold and dark by the time I arrived, and one of the security guards—they always seem to know me in Philly—said, "Mr. Feinstein, you can go in the back way if you want."

I thanked him but walked around to the front entrance. Why? Because that's what I always do at the Palestra. Plus, I had to make my pilgrimage to the sign.

I stopped at a concessions stand and bought three Philadelphia pretzels at five bucks apiece—one for me, one for Hoops Weiss, and one for Jack Scheuer. I walked down the ramp, found Jack and Hoops, and handed them the pretzels.

"No mustard?" Jack said.

Jack's eighty-six and has a difficult time walking these days. I went back up the ramp and got him mustard. And a Coke.

All was right with the world.

The building was a few hundred shy of a sellout—8,173—meaning most of the corners were filled. It was an old Palestra tradition to have Scheuer declare on the PA, "We have corners!" when the building was packed.

Both teams were clearly tight early. St. Joseph's was trying to get on track in what was quickly becoming a disappointing season. Phil Martelli had high hopes before the season started, but his team had been very up and down since November—good enough to beat Old Dominion and Davidson—bad enough to lose to William & Mary and start the conference season with back-to-back home losses to not-so-good George Mason and not-good-at-all George Washington.

Then, in a one-point loss to Duquesne a week earlier, the Hawks had lost two key players: second-leading scorer Lamarr (Fresh) Kimble—who'd hit the game-winning shot against Loyola in December to spare us all overtime—and leading rebounder Checco Oliva. Kimble had a fracture in his right shooting hand and would miss a month. Oliva had a knee injury and was done for the year.

The game was much bigger for Penn. The Quakers had pronounced themselves back the previous season when they had won their first Ivy League title since 2006—Fran Dunphy's last season as coach. Glen Miller, who'd had success at Brown, had been hired to replace Dunphy and hadn't been able to sustain what Dunphy had built. After five seasons he'd been replaced by Jerome Allen, a star under Dunphy in the nineties. Allen had lasted four seasons, going 9-19 in his final winter at Penn.

Enter Steve Donahue. Unlike Miller, he was a Philly guy, which almost always matters in the Big Five. He'd been a Dunphy assistant for ten years before taking over Cornell and breaking the Penn-Princeton stranglehold on the Ivy League by winning it three straight years from 2008 to 2010.

He built his program on overlooked players. He didn't find Louis

Dale, his point guard; Dale found him. His mother sent Donahue a tape of her son, asking him to take a look. When he saw Dale on tape, he invited him to visit campus.

"He arrived with a filled-out admissions form and a check for the fee," Donahue said. "He had about fourteen hundred on the boards. Didn't take a genius to know he was someone we wanted."

Ryan Wittman was the son of former NBA and Indiana star Randy Wittman, but most of the big-time programs didn't think he had the game for the Big Ten or the ACC. So Wittman landed at Cornell, where he scored more than 2,000 points and left as the fifth-leading scorer in Ivy League history.

And then there was center Jeff Foote. Donahue had rushed to the hospital after practice one day when one of his players took a very bad fall. When Donahue introduced himself to the emergency room nurse, she said, "You know, I have a son who plays basketball."

Donahue really wasn't in the mood to listen to a mother tell him about her five-foot-ten-inch son with a vertical leap of twelve inches. Then she said, "He's at St. Bonaventure right now. But he's not very happy."

Cornell rarely takes transfers. But then she added, "He's seven feet tall."

At that moment, she had Donahue's attention.

Jeff Foote transferred to Cornell, sat out a year, and became a key cog for the Big Red, especially in 2010 when they won that third Ivy League title and then upset Temple and Wisconsin to become the first Ivy League team since Penn in 1979 to reach the sweet sixteen.

There they lost to Kentucky, but only after rallying from a huge deficit to within five with plenty of time left. "I thought we had them," Donahue said later. "I really did."

He left Cornell for Boston College after that because the money and the lure of the ACC were too tough to turn down. The night Donahue took the job, Hoops Weiss, who had known Donahue since his Penn days, said to me, "I wish I could have talked him out of it. This is a mistake. BC is a football school first and a hockey school second. And now it's in the ACC with fifteen teams. Steve's used to recruiting a certain kind of Ivy League kid. That won't get it done in the ACC."

As usual, Hoops was right. BC had its moments under Donahue

but was 54-76 in four seasons. Donahue was fired. He took a year off before Penn came running to get him after Allen had been fired.

It had taken two years to turn it around, but the Quakers had gone 24-9 in his third season and now were poised to win the Big Five.

"You have to understand what a big deal this is to us," Donahue said. "We sell ourselves to recruits as a Big Five school that plays in the Ivy League, not the other way around."

The Big Five had been far more daunting than the Ivy League. Penn had won the Ivy League twenty-six times. It hadn't won the Big Five since 2001–02.

But the Big Five streak-breaking win over Villanova (which also broke a fifteen-game Penn losing streak to the Wildcats) had given them a chance. They'd beaten La Salle and won at Temple. Only St. Joseph's stood in their way.

That may explain why neither team shot especially well in the first half. "The building deserves a better game than this," Scheuer commented at one point.

The best player on the court was a freshman, Penn's Bryce Washington. He made back-to-back threes late in the first half to give Penn a 31–25 lead, and it was 35–31 at the half.

St. Joe's simply couldn't make a three all night, shooting an almost impossible 3-for-24 from behind the line. Penn built the lead to 56–43, but with the Hawk mascot flapping furiously, the Hawks refused to die. (For those who don't know, St. Joseph's rallying cry is "The Hawk will never die," and the Hawk mascot, who is on scholarship, *never* stops flapping his wings during a game—including time-outs.)

The Hawk who really didn't die was redshirt sophomore Charlie Brown. Unlike the *Peanuts* character, Brown could play. He couldn't make a shot from deep (1-of-8) but figured that out and kept scoring in the lane, finishing with 27 points and 12 rebounds on the night, playing all forty minutes. Martelli was forced to play four of his five starters for at least thirty-six minutes because the two critical injuries had left him with almost no bench.

Twice, Brown cut the lead to three by driving and twisting and making baskets while getting fouled. The second made it 70–67, and you could feel the Penn crowd getting nervous. This was supposed to be a night to celebrate. Brown was trying to make it a night to bemoan what might have been.

Enter Antonio Woods and Jake Silpe.

Both were seniors. Woods was a starter, but not much of a scorer. In fact, at that moment, with 2:09 left in the game, he hadn't scored. Silpe had started twenty games as a freshman, but Donahue had recruited over him and his playing time had dwindled from twenty-three minutes a game as a freshman to seven minutes a game the next two years.

Instead of either quitting or transferring, he spent summers working on his shot. Donahue wanted guards who could shoot. Silpe made himself into one.

Now, with the game on the line, Penn ran the shot clock to under ten seconds before Woods started into the lane and then flipped a quick pass to Silpe in the left corner. Silpe was into his shooting motion as soon as he caught the pass. The ball hit the bottom of the net with one second on the shot clock and 1:40 on the game clock. As it turned out, that was the wooden stake Penn needed. The final was 78–70.

The Penn students didn't storm the court the way they had after the Villanova win. When you beat the defending national champions who you have lost to fifteen straight times, you storm the court. When you beat a team that is 9-11, even if it means winning an important title, you jump up and down and hug one another, but you don't storm the court.

Big Five fans get it. Instead of storming, the students threw red streamers onto the court, a reminder of the Big Five's tradition of tossing streamers.

Penn's players, notably leading scorer A. J. Brodeur, talked about Donahue showing them a documentary on the Big Five in which Penn hardly seemed to get a mention. "We were an afterthought," Brodeur said. "We wanted to change that."

They had done just that. As I walked across the court with the streamers still flying, I scooped one up and put it around my neck.

"Looks good on you," Donahue joked.

It sits, right now, a few yards from my desk, wrapped around a writing award from years ago.

After I had talked to the players and coaches, I made my way up the ramp, stopped by the sign for a moment, and headed to my car. No doubt I had a huge smile on my face all the way home.

It had been that kind of a day.

THE OLD COACH AND
DIVISION 3

January 31, 2019, West Hartford, Connecticut

Jim Calhoun sat in the small cluttered office a few steps from the court inside the O'Connell Athletic Center, which is where the University of St. Joseph plays its basketball games. He was thirty miles from Gampel Pavilion, where he had been one of college basketball's kings as the coach at the University of Connecticut, winning three national titles in twenty-six seasons.

Those thirty miles might as well have been a million miles in the basketball universe.

St. Joseph's is an 1,100-student Catholic school that was founded in 1932 by the Sisters of Mercy as a college for women. The school had admitted its first class of men—about one hundred of them—in the fall of 2018.

Which is where Calhoun came in.

He had retired from UConn in September 2012 after a series of health scares and injuries that dated to 2003, when he'd had surgery for prostate cancer and returned to the bench sixteen days later. There had been another cancer scare in 2008, this time squamous cell carcinoma—a serious form of skin cancer. He'd fallen off a bike in 2009 during a charity race and broken a hip, and then he had spinal stenosis and a hip fracture in 2012.

He turned seventy in May of that year and knew it was time. He passed the reins to Kevin Ollie, a former UConn player who had been his top assistant, and went off to spend time with his grandchildren and work on his golf game.

Except, not exactly.

He still had an office in Gampel Pavilion and was often seen prowling around at practice. "I still had the itch," he said. "It never went away."

Still, given all the health issues, the three national titles, and the spot in the basketball Hall of Fame that had come his way in 2005, he resisted the urge to scratch.

Until the fall of 2017, when he got a call from an old friend, Bill Cardarelli, who had been the athletic director at St. Joseph's for twenty-five years. The school was about to admit men in the fall, and Cardarelli wondered if Calhoun had any thoughts on who might coach the basketball team.

Calhoun had plenty of protégés he could have recommended. But the more he and Cardarelli talked, the more he kept coming back to one name.

"Me," Calhoun said with a laugh. "The more I thought about getting back in the gym, working with the kids, competing—even at a completely different level than the one I'd coached on at Northeastern and UConn—the more I liked the idea."

So he threw the name out at Cardarelli, who initially thought he was joking.

He wasn't.

Because Calhoun was still on the payroll at UConn as a consultant, he couldn't be named a full-time employee until the following September. That didn't slow him down that winter. He saw sixty-three games as a scout, and nineteen players enrolled at St. Joseph's in the fall as basketball players. On September 18, the school officially named him as the men's basketball coach.

During his initial press conference, school president Rhona Free—after some babbling about "student-athletes"—talked about the "Calhoun effect" that had drawn not only basketball players to the school, but also students in general. It had been a known fact the previous winter that Calhoun was going to coach at St. Joseph's.

There was no way Calhoun was going to return to coaching in anonymity—or anything close to it. The *New York Times* had a reporter on campus before his first game, and ESPN planned about a fourteen-part series on his return. I knew I was going to go up and see him at some point, but I wanted to wait until the initial hoopla had died down a little. The best time to get a sense of how a basketball season is going is during the hoops dog days in January and February.

As I drove to West Hartford on the morning of January 31, there was no doubt my timing was right. According to my car, it was three degrees outside when I crossed into Connecticut, and there was snow from a storm earlier in the week piled high everywhere I looked.

It took me two tries to find the O'Connell Center. St. Joseph's is built around two quadrangles and—naturally—I picked the wrong one. Actually, I thought there *was* only one, and I had to call Calhoun to get him to talk me in.

His office was a few yards off the lobby and down a short hallway. It was smaller than the offices his assistants had occupied at UConn, but he didn't seem to mind. I noticed Dick Vitale's latest book sitting on his desk and asked if he'd read it.

"Only a little," he answered. "I read his Mount Rushmore of coaches." He paused as if deciding whether to go on. "Wooden, Krzyzewski, Knight, Smith—okay. But Roy Williams? Don't get me wrong, Roy's a great coach. But he's won all his games at Kansas and North Carolina. You can't coach at those schools and not win. Can't be done.

"Wonder if he checked to see where Northeastern and Connecticut were when I took over?"

The comment wasn't made because of ego. It was made because Calhoun is one of those people who can't stop competing—at anything.

Northeastern was in Division 2 when Calhoun took the job in 1972. It became a D-1 school in 1979 and in five of Calhoun's last six seasons reached the NCAA Tournament. He took over a moribund Connecticut program in 1986. In seven seasons in the Big East, the Huskies had never finished over .500 in conference play. There was talk among alumni that it should find a conference it could compete in, since clearly the school didn't belong in the same league with national powers like Georgetown, Villanova, Syracuse, and St. John's.

Connecticut won the NIT in Calhoun's second season. That drew mostly yawns from UConn fans, but two years later the Huskies were 31-6 and a last-second Christian Laettner jump shot from reaching the Final Four. From that day forward, they were a national contender most years.

"The years we weren't as good were my fault," Calhoun said. "I've always been a believer in creating chaos. Some years I let the chaos get out of control. Those were the years we weren't very good."

Calhoun is a voracious reader, and he'd read a quote from Albert Einstein: "Genius comes out of chaos."

He embraced that concept, but the truth is, he couldn't possibly coach any other way. He'd grown up in Braintree, Massachusetts, the oldest of six children, and when his father passed away, he'd gone to work at the age of fifteen. He'd gone to Lowell State as a basketball player but dropped out for twenty months to work because his family needed the money. He returned to American International and graduated just after turning twenty-six in 1968.

Calhoun was from a hardscrabble background, with the emphasis on *hard*. He believed that you challenged players to make them tougher, and if you made them tougher you made them better. Never once did he back away from a fight or an argument with anybody.

When Gary Williams, a fairly intense competitor himself, was at Boston College, the two men went at each other during games like dogs locked in a small pen. One night, Williams called Calhoun a profanity—a very unflattering one—during a heated argument. When the game ended and the two men shook hands, Calhoun looked at Williams and said, "You ever call me a name like that again, I don't care where we are or what's going on, I'll take you down."

Williams was stunned. I've been around him often enough to know he will say things while wound up during games that he literally won't remember at game's end. This was one of those times.

"I would never talk that way to another coach," Williams said, truly baffled.

Calhoun, as the old saying goes, forgave, but he never forgot. He and Williams remained fierce rivals even after Williams left BC, first for Ohio State and then for Maryland.

"Gary and I are a lot better now," Calhoun said. He smiled. "Of course, we don't compete against each other anymore either."

It's often that way with Hall of Fame coaches. Dean Smith and Mike Krzyzewski traded barbs for seventeen years before Smith retired in 1997. Then it all changed. When Smith died in 2015, Krzyzewski was one of the few people not affiliated with North Carolina in some way who were invited to his funeral.

Perhaps Calhoun's desire to come back had something to do with the way his UConn career ended. He had won a third national title in 2011—coming from nowhere in March to do so. The Huskies finished tied for ninth in the Big East that year, won five games to win the Big East Tournament, and then won the title, beating Kentucky in the national semifinals and Butler in the championship game.

If Calhoun had known what was to come, he probably would have thrown down the mike after accepting the national championship trophy and walked out of the building for good. But he didn't, and the next season was a nightmare: Calhoun had to sit out a three-game suspension at the start of Big East play because a former manager turned agent-wannabe had been caught trying to steer a high school player to UConn. Then he had to have back surgery in February for spinal stenosis and missed another week. The Huskies squeaked into the NCAA Tournament with a 20-13 record as a No. 9 seed and were soundly beaten in the opening round by Iowa State, 77–64.

Calhoun has never been one to run from adversity. He's a big believer in the old saying that adversity reveals character. But in August he had yet another bicycling accident and fractured a hip. He knew it was time, so in September he announced his retirement.

But he didn't feel finished or complete, in spite of the 873 victories and all the success and the plaque in the Hall of Fame. Which is why he sat midafternoon on the last day of January eating his "pregame meal" out of a brown paper bag brought to him by his son Jeff, one of his assistant coaches. Calhoun may be the only D-3 coach in history with a staff of four assistants—former Brown and Penn head coach Glen Miller; son Jeff; Rashamel Jones; and Ryan Olander.

St. Joseph's is also—without a doubt—the only D-3 program in history to have its games broadcast on a fifty-thousand-watt radio station—WTIC in Hartford. Which was why Joe D'Ambrosio, UConn's radio voice throughout Calhoun's twenty-six years, ambled into the office at about five o'clock to tape Calhoun's pregame show.

"I think this is the eight hundred and fifty-third one we've done," D'Ambrosio said, laughing.

There's no joking around when it comes to coaching and competing. Not when Calhoun's involved. During his pregame show he gave D'Ambrosio a detailed breakdown of Johnson & Wales personnel, having been through the scouting report provided by his staff in detail. To him, prepping for Johnson & Wales was no different from prepping for Syracuse, Georgetown, or Villanova.

The St. Joseph's Blue Jays were 12-8 heading into that night's game. They had started 3-0 but had been up and down since then, not surprising for a team with one junior (who averaged 2.8 minutes a game), one sophomore, and seventeen freshmen. In D-3 there's no limit to how many players you can have on a roster, since there are no scholarships.

Prior to the start of the season, Calhoun had yet another bout with cancer. This time he'd undergone surgery to remove almost 60 percent of his stomach. It had barely slowed him down at all.

He'd come flying out of the box in the opener against William Paterson, drawing his first technical foul of the season sixteen minutes in. A month later, in a neutral site game in Florida against LaGrange, he'd been tossed after picking up two techs. It had to be another first: a Hall of Fame coach thrown out of a Division 3 game.

"I need these guys to understand that I take this every bit as seriously as I took Final Four games," he said. "It's not fair to them if I don't do that. If I'm asking them to be all in, then I better be all in."

He sat in the locker room as his team prepared to play, clasping and unclasping his hands repeatedly. "This is entirely different," he said. "And exactly the same."

The O'Connell Center is about what you'd expect for a D-3 gym. It seats about six hundred when the bleachers are rolled down and has a track upstairs running around the court. That was where D'Ambrosio called the game from. The scorer's table was too small to fit him and his radio equipment.

If you love basketball, you loved the Johnson & Wales–St. Joseph's game. It went double overtime and had just about everything a basketball game could possibly have. Jamie Benton was Johnson & Wales's coach. He'd been at the school for ten years and had been very successful. He had also played for Gary Williams at BC during Calhoun's early days at Connecticut.

"I remember the two of them going at it," he said with a laugh. "Sometimes you kind of had to look away because you might lose track of the game."

Part of Benton couldn't help but be awed by the presence of

Calhoun on the other bench. Part of him still saw the young Calhoun, up on every play, jawing with the officials and getting on his players for mistakes.

Which he did—early and often. Calhoun sits on a high stool during games, because it's easier on his lanky body to stretch his legs out when sitting. But he doesn't sit very much. Dressed in a yellow shirt with a blue sweater, khakis, and black loafers, he looked dapper and calm as he walked down to shake hands with Benton before the game began.

Once the ball went up, Calhoun was on the officials almost nonstop. At one point he stalked onto the court and screamed, "One thing I know for sure is they aren't going to leave here tonight feeling like they got a home job!"

At another point he yelled, "If you guys don't start calling them when they foul my guys on rebounds, you're going to have to throw me the hell out of here!"

The officials didn't want to throw Calhoun out of anywhere. They didn't even want to tee him up. Some young officials might want to tell their grandchildren they once teed up the great Jim Calhoun. This group—Ryan Corbett, Kevin Kobelski, and Michael Medina—was mature enough to want no part of that. Corbett often worked D-1 games, and Kobelski often did important D-2 games in the New England area. They had enough experience to know that a night with Calhoun was not going to be like working with, say, Bobby Cremins.

Years ago, I asked Rick Hartzell, then one of the top officials in the country, to talk to me about the (then) nine ACC coaches and what it was like reffing a game for them. (Officials always talk about working *for* coaches.) Hartzell saved Cremins, then at Georgia Tech, for last. "If Bobby Cremins says you missed a call," he said, "you missed the call."

Not quite so with Calhoun. The fact that if you combined the ages of the three refs that night, they'd barely add up to Calhoun's seventy-six might have had something to do with it. They constantly ran to Calhoun to try to steer him back to the coach's box, all the while explaining they were doing the best they could. Which they were.

The game was a wild roller-coaster ride. St. Joseph's led 38–31 at the break. With his team up 32–28, Calhoun stood to signal for a time-out. No one saw him, and a turnover led to a Donovan Maxfield three-pointer seconds later. Calhoun almost always has a water bottle in his hand. This one crashed against the wall behind the bench, water flying all over.

Directly behind me, one of the ESPN crew members said, "We've learned to stand over here out of the way of the flying water bottles."

The Blue Jays stretched the lead to 40–31 to start the second half, but then Johnson & Wales went on a 34–16 run that seemingly put the game away, leading 65–54 with 5:14 left.

But Calhoun's chaos had clearly toughened his young team. They rallied and, even trailing 72–68 with 14.9 seconds left, tied the game at the buzzer on a three by Delshawn Jackson Jr. No one gets yelled at by Calhoun more than Jackson.

"Because I think he can be a terrific player," Calhoun said simply.

When Jackson hit an off-balance jumper with one second to play in the first overtime to put St. Joseph's up 88–86, it looked as if all the work was going to pay off.

There's no TV replay available at a D-3 game, so the officials huddled up, took a guess, and put 1.6 seconds on the clock.

After a time-out by each team, Brian Hogan-Gary, Johnson & Wales's leading scorer, caught an eighty-foot inbounds pass cleanly twelve feet from the basket, turned, and calmly swished a shot that was clearly good to tie the game again, at 88–88.

I heard myself murmur "Tate George" as the shot went in, remembering Connecticut's miraculous 1990 sweet sixteen victory over Clemson in the Meadowlands, when Tate George caught a length-of-the-court inbounds pass from Scott Burrell with one second left and hit a corner jumper as time expired for a stunning 71–70 win.

In those days, the clocks didn't have tenths on them. Cliff Ellis, who was coaching Clemson in those days, insists to this day that if the clocks had been more precise or if there had been replay, the shot wouldn't have counted.

But it did—and my literary agent, Esther Newberg, who lives and dies with UConn basketball, named a cat Tate George.

Hogan-Gary's shot didn't end the game the way George's had, but did put it into a second overtime. It also brought about the demise of another water bottle.

The second overtime was much like the first, the lead continuing to change hands. This time, St. Joseph's had the ball for the final possession, trailing 98–97. But the evening was finally out of miracles.

Calhoun's Blue Jays got three shots off, two from nearly point-blank range, and couldn't convert.

Calhoun walked off the court head down, taking the loss as hard as he might have taken UConn's Final Four loss to Michigan State in 2009. He and the coaches sat on their side of the locker room in silence for a few minutes, staring holes through the stat sheets.

Finally, Calhoun looked up and said, "Well, fellas, we came, we saw, we lost. That's all there is to it."

His message to the players was along those lines. He appreciated the effort, but "I told you at the beginning that I expect effort all the time."

He left them with a final thought: "We have practice tomorrow at three, then we're on the road Saturday. And we had *better* win there. You had better come ready to compete."

He walked out the door. The players knew one thing for sure: their coach would come ready to compete. He had never known any other way.

WHERE HISTORY WAS—
AND IS—MADE

February 1, 2019, Cambridge, Massachusetts

As I pulled onto I-84 on the morning after the St. Joseph's–Johnson & Wales donnybrook, it occurred to me I'd gotten very lucky with the weather. The high temperature in Hartford on Thursday had been twelve degrees, but the weather report for Boston said temperatures would rocket into the twenties on Friday and maybe even crack the freezing mark on Saturday.

Most important, there was no snow in the forecast.

I breezed into Boston in plenty of time to get to Lavietes Pavilion during Harvard's pregame shootaround. I turned into the gate that leads to the athletic facilities a couple hundred yards before I would have reached the Charles River and wound my way past ancient Harvard Stadium (built in 1903) and the hockey arena before finally reaching the backdoor of Lavietes.

This would be my weekend for games played in ancient gyms. Only Fordham's Rose Hill Gym has hosted college basketball games for longer than Lavietes. Rose Hill opened in 1925; Lavietes in 1926. Even the Palestra, which opened on New Year's Day in 1927, is a pup compared to those two.

Friday night I would watch Yale play Harvard at Lavietes. The next afternoon, I'd be at Matthews Arena on the campus of Northeastern, which is *the* oldest arena in the United States. Matthews, though, was built as a hockey arena and didn't host its first basketball game until 1931. Only when Northeastern moved its basketball games to Matthews in 1972 did it become the full-time home of a college basketball team.

Matthews also has one distinction none of the others have: it was the site of the 1912 Democratic National Convention. The nominee that year was Woodrow Wilson.

When people think of Harvard-Yale, they think of football. The Game, as it is called, has been contested 136 times, dating to 1875, with Yale leading the series 68-60-8. It ranks behind only Rutgers-Princeton (1869) and Yale-Princeton (1873) in age and behind Lafayette-Lehigh (155 games) and Yale-Princeton (141) in frequency.

It also may have produced the most famous newspaper headline in college football history. After Harvard had scored two touchdowns and converted a pair of two-point conversions in the last forty-two seconds of the 1968 game, the *Harvard Crimson*'s headline was: "Harvard Beats Yale, 29-29."

The basketball rivalry isn't nearly as storied, in large part because the basketball programs don't have the history that the football programs do.

The rivalry began to heat up when Tommy Amaker arrived at Harvard in 2007. Until then, Harvard had reached the NCAA Tournament once—in 1946 before the Ivy League was formed, with a win over Yale to qualify. Frank Sullivan, who coached the Crimson for sixteen seasons prior to Amaker's arrival, kept a small trophy in his office that was the only evidence of Harvard's one appearance.

James Jones had arrived at Yale eight years before Amaker came to Harvard in the spring of 1999. Slowly, he'd built Yale into an Ivy League contender. This was during the period when the Ivy League consisted of Penn, Princeton, and six other teams whose main purpose appeared to be to show up to give Penn and Princeton a full schedule.

Beginning in 1969, a year after Columbia had beaten Princeton in a one-game playoff to earn the league's NCAA bid, either Penn or Princeton represented the conference in the NCAAs in thirty-seven of the next thirty-nine seasons. Penn was the rep twenty-two times, Princeton, fifteen. Only Brown—in 1986—and Cornell—in 1988 broke the two-school stranglehold.

That changed beginning in 2008 when Cornell won the first of Steve Donahue's three straight league championships. Princeton beat Harvard on a buzzer-beater in a one-game playoff in 2011, and then, beginning in 2012, the Crimson went to the tournament for four straight seasons.

Harvard won first-round games in both 2013 and 2014. Then, in 2015, the Crimson beat Yale in a one-game playoff in the Palestra in one of the most intense basketball games I've ever seen in person.

Amaker had called it before the game. "I have no idea who is going to win," he said to me, standing outside his locker room. "But I promise you it won't be pretty."

He was right. It was a scrape-and-claw game for forty minutes, every pass defended, every rebound fought for, every shot contested. Harvard finally won 53–51, or by the roll of a basketball. Steve Moundou-Missi, who had been the Ivy League defensive player of the year, made an eighteen-foot jump shot with 7.2 seconds left to give Harvard the two-point lead.

Yale raced the ball downcourt—Amaker had wanted a time-out to set up his defense but couldn't get anyone's attention—and Javier Duren drove past Wesley Saunders into the lane. Moundou-Missi came to help, and Duren had to twist his body to the left just a tad to get the shot off. It rolled off the rim. Justin Sears tried desperately to tip it in, but the ball fell harmlessly to the floor as the buzzer sounded.

For Harvard, it was a miraculous fourth straight NCAA trip. Eight days earlier, Yale had beaten the Crimson at Lavietes to seemingly wrap up the league title—taking a one-game lead to Dartmouth for the season finale. But an hour after Harvard had beaten Brown in its season-closing game, players, coaches, and families all watched together as Dartmouth's Gabas Maldunas hit a shot with under a second to go to give Dartmouth a stunning 59–58 win.

Jones is the dean of Ivy League basketball coaches, having come to the school in 1999. He'd done the impossible in 2002—gotten his team into a three-way tie for the league title with Penn and Princeton—and even though there had been some ups and downs, Yale had become a more-than-respectable program.

Still, the Bulldogs hadn't been to the NCAA Tournament since 1962, and the losses to Dartmouth and then Harvard were devastating. Even so, Jones knew he and his players had been part of something special.

"All due respect to the Palestra," he said, "I would have watched this one if it had been played outside."

The next night when the brackets went up for the NCAA

Tournament and for the NIT, Harvard was the No. 13 seed in the West Regional. Yale was . . . nowhere.

Since Harvard and Yale had tied for first place, the NIT wasn't obligated by rule to offer the loser a bid. Only if a team won the regular season outright and didn't get an NCAA bid was an NIT bid automatic.

What's more, Yale couldn't even get a bid to the CIT or the CBI, because those tournaments had filled their fields before Harvard and Yale played on Saturday. I had seen Yale play up close. I knew how good the Bulldogs were. In those days, I had a daily radio show on the CBS Sports Network. I spent several minutes on the show that morning blistering the NIT for not taking Yale.

That night, my phone rang. It was James Jones.

"I just wanted to thank you for what you said today," he said. "I appreciate it." He paused and then said, "The worst part is, what do I tell my kids? This is so unfair to them."

It was unfair. It was also typical of the way college hoops often works. Yale was not going to be as big a TV draw as a team from one of the power conferences. Among those selected by the NIT were a twelve-loss Miami team (ACC); thirteen-loss teams from Stanford (Pac-12) and Illinois (Big Ten); fourteen-loss teams from Pittsburgh (ACC), Alabama (SEC), and Connecticut (the 2014 national champion from the AAC); and, best of all, a 17-15 Arizona State team.

The committee just *had* to have all those teams, even though many if not most of the players at those schools would just as soon have gone home. The NIT would have been a big deal to the Yale kids, who had finished 23-7. The committee didn't care.

A year later, Yale ended Harvard's four-year stranglehold on the Ivy title, and the fifty-four-year NCAA drought ended. In the first round of the tournament, the Bulldogs beat sixth-seeded Baylor. Then they took Duke, the 2015 national champion, to the final minute before losing by six.

Please don't tell me the best of the Ivies can't play with the big boys.

Now, in 2019, Harvard and Yale again appeared to be the best teams in the Ivy League. Amaker was number two in Ivy seniority to Jones, and their rivalry was about as intense as the rivalry between the schools.

Amaker's arrival at Harvard and the rise of his program had made

Jones's job a lot tougher—not only on the court but in recruiting. The two men respected each other but couldn't be called friends. And both knew what was at stake when they played each other.

Yale had swept Brown in its opening conference series and was 2–0 coming into Lavietes. Harvard had used the Howard game to springboard to an easy home win over Dartmouth. That game didn't wipe the taste of the first Dartmouth game from Amaker's mouth, but it told him his team had bottomed there and was now headed in the right direction—especially with Bryce Aiken back in the lineup.

Amaker believed Yale was the most talented team in the league. The Bulldogs had a genuine star in senior Miye Oni, a six-foot-five-inch swing man who could score inside and outside and would go on to succeed Seth Towns as the Ivy League player of the year. They had a very good backcourt and, as with all of Jones's teams, they could guard.

The game would be much like the one in 2015 that Amaker had predicted wouldn't be pretty.

Amaker knew his team might have to play at Yale twice more before the season was over—the return game in the regular season and a tournament game in March, since the geniuses running the Ivy League had decided to move the Ivy League Tournament out of the Palestra and rotate it to the other seven schools. Yale's John J. Lee Amphitheater was up first.

That would come later.

Lavietes was packed on a Friday night, the students out in force. This hadn't always been the case. The success of the basketball team had become a unifying force on campus—a largely white student body rallying behind a largely black basketball team.

"That's been as gratifying as anything," Amaker said. "The way our team has helped people cross racial divides on this campus."

The game was also gratifying for Harvard.

On the first possession of the game, Justin Bassey hit a three from the left wing to make it 3–0. As it turned out, Yale never caught up. Every time the Bulldogs looked like they were about to get back in the game, someone in white-and-crimson seemed to make a three. Aiken hit one soon after Bassey. With the score 14–9, six-ten sophomore Robert Baker hit back-to-back threes from the top of the key to extend the margin to 20–9. Sophomore Danilo Djuricic came off the bench to hit a three—Harvard's seventh of the half—and then rebounded a missed shot and dunked at the buzzer for a 35–20 halftime lead.

There's nothing a coach hates more than talking to his team with a big halftime lead. Everything you've told the players about how dangerous the opponent is has gone out the window. Which is why Amaker harped on the theme of making sure his players were ready for Yale's run when it came.

Except it never came. Yale never got the lead into single digits. Harvard's defense was sterling. The lead grew to 42–23 at one point, and the final was 65–49. Oni was held to 11 points on 3-of-15 shooting and 0-for-6 from behind the three-point line. Baker and Bassey led Harvard with 13 points apiece, but the defense was the story of the night.

Which made Amaker happy . . . briefly.

The Ivies are the only D-1 conference in the country that plays a weekly Friday–Saturday schedule. Brown would be in town in twenty-four hours. It was time to start worrying about that game.

The next afternoon, I was at Matthews Arena on the Northeastern campus more than two hours before the 4:30 tipoff between Hofstra and Northeastern. When going to a place I've never been, I always leave time to get lost.

I didn't, though, and found the building locked when I arrived. Fortunately, one of the refs working the game had already gotten inside and was lost himself—looking for will call to leave tickets for a friend. He let me in.

Frank Sullivan arrived a few minutes later. Because he'd coached in the building while at Harvard, he knew the way in through a back door. Sullivan looked tired. I asked why.

"Didn't really sleep last night," he said. "We got beat, and I've never slept well after losses."

"We" was the girls basketball team at Newton Country Day School of the Sacred Heart. Sullivan had decided he'd had enough of college basketball administration the previous spring and had retired from his job as associate commissioner of the America East, where he had been the league's supervisor of officials for eleven seasons. He'd also been the liaison between the league's coaches—men and women—and the league office. Which meant he spent a lot of time putting out fires and trying to appease angry coaches.

In February 2017, Sullivan had been watching a game at New Hampshire when he saw that he had a text from UMBC's Ryan Odom—a surprise, because Sullivan knew that Odom's team was playing at that moment.

His first thought was that it had been a pocket dial. Or perhaps it was from hours earlier and was, for some reason, popping into his queue at that moment. Then he read the text, Odom railing against veteran official Ray Perone.

"I'm thinking, 'Is he so mad he's texting from the bench during a time-out?'" Sullivan said, laughing. "Finally, I figured it out: Ryan had been tossed and was sitting in the locker room texting. The whole thing caught me off guard because Ryan wasn't a complainer. And I thought he'd be too busy coaching to be texting me."

Sullivan looked at the tape the next morning and apologized to Odom. It looked as if Perone had overreacted and turned a minor debate into a major one.

"I should have known that if Ryan was that mad, there was something to it," he said later. "He's one of the easier coaches to work with."

Once he'd had enough of mollifying coaches—and officials—and dealing with NCAA politics, Sullivan decided to retire and just go to games for fun.

But the chance to coach the girls at nearby Newton County Day had come up in the fall, and he'd decided to do it. "First day I was there, I realized how much I'd missed being in the gym," he said. "I felt as if I'd never left."

Coaching girls high school ball was a few steps down from Division 1 men's ball, but Sullivan didn't mind. He loved teaching again, trying to help the girls get better—regardless of won-lost record. But losing still ate at him. Coaches never stop being coaches.

I left Frank to relax and read the game notes and went to find Northeastern coach Bill Coen. I've always found that most coaches either don't mind talking before a game or *want* to talk before a game because it helps kill the time. Bob Knight always wanted someone to talk to before a game because he had so much nervous energy running through him. For one season that person was me.

With the assistant coaches on the floor with the players, I was the only sounding board left. Every few minutes, he would look at me and say, "Do you think we're all right?" as if I had any clue. As if anyone ever has any clue before the game—any game—starts.

I found Coen in a room marked "Club hockey coaches" and was reminded again that Northeastern was a hockey school first and Boston was a college hockey town.

Like Sullivan, Coen is one of the nice guys in coaching. This was an important game for his team. Hofstra was 9-0 in conference play and had won sixteen straight games. Northeastern was in second place. If the Huskies wanted to make it back to the NCAAs for the first time since 2015, they were going to have to go through Hofstra.

I mentioned to Coen that Sullivan was in the building. "Where is he?" Coen asked.

"He didn't want to bother you before the game," I said. "Plus, he's sulking a little."

I explained about the loss the night before. Coen laughed. "Of course he's upset. This is what we do. Where is he?"

I pointed Coen in Sullivan's direction and didn't follow. I figured they'd both enjoy a coach-to-coach talk without a non-coach intruding.

I was right.

The Hofstra Pride—when I was a kid they had been known as the Flying Dutchmen—arrived just before three o'clock for the 4:30 tipoff.

My dad had always liked Hofstra because he had decided that the Flying Dutchmen nickname was an homage to the Wagnerian opera of that name. It wasn't: the school had been founded on land that had been owned by a man named William S. Hofstra, who was of Dutch descent. The nickname was changed in 2004 so as to include male and female athletes. The school's mascots are now a pair of lions—Kate and Willie Hofstra.

Hofstra's best player was Justin Wright-Foreman, who was averaging 26 points per game and, even though he was barely more than six feet tall, was getting attention from NBA scouts.

When Hofstra coach Joe Mihalich introduced us before practice one afternoon, my first comment was, "No way you're six-two."

Wright-Foreman was listed as six-two and was clearly no taller than I am. I'm six feet—barely. He's six feet—more barely.

Wright-Foreman grinned and said, "I'm tall enough."

He was right about that. Wright-Foreman is one of those basketball stories that get overlooked because they aren't sexy enough for ESPN or for Dick Vitale to be screaming about him. He doesn't play at Duke—or any other power—and he doesn't do 360 dunks that will be replayed a million times in twenty-four hours.

When I watch Wright-Foreman play, I think of something Mike Krzyzewski—who does coach at a place sexy enough for ESPN and Vitale—said years ago when I asked him if a player he was recruiting was more of a "two" (shooting guard) or a "three" (small forward).

"He's not a number," Krzyzewski said. "We don't recruit numbers. We recruit basketball players. He's a basketball player."

Wright-Foreman's a basketball player with, as Mihalich puts it, "a gift for shooting the ball."

Because of his size and because he played at Construction High School in Queens—not exactly a high school hoops hotbed—Wright-Foreman was largely overlooked going into his senior year. Mihalich was at an AAU tournament in Los Angeles when he noticed a kid in the game who was unguardable.

"He had forty points and he made it look easy," Mihalich said. "I told my coaches—we gotta get this kid."

Only in the insane world of high school/AAU hoops could a coach from Long Island discover a kid from Queens in Los Angeles.

Hofstra got the kid at least in part because no one else was seriously chasing him.

"There were other schools interested," Wright-Foreman said. "Some from bigger conferences. But I knew Hofstra really *wanted* me. That made my decision pretty easy."

His freshman year wasn't easy. It wasn't that he couldn't score, it was that he couldn't guard. Mihalich didn't feel comfortable with him on the floor for extended periods. Plus, he had two senior guards ahead of him.

It changed the next year. The senior guards were gone, Wright-Foreman's defense had improved, and he went from 4.1 minutes a game to 28 and from 1.6 points a game to 18—quite a jump.

A year later, he averaged 24.4 points a game, and NBA scouts began showing up at Hofstra games to watch him. He noticed the scouts and was intrigued.

"I know I want to play in the NBA someday," he said. "I believe I'm good enough. I wasn't sure if I was ready, though, so I asked Coach what he thought."

Mihalich was fairly certain that Wright-Foreman needed another year—at least—to become an NBA player or to at least get a fair shot to make an NBA team. But he didn't want to be the naysayer, and he thought it couldn't hurt for Wright-Foreman to get an idea of where he stood in the eyes of scouts who had seen him play.

"I told him he should put his name into the draft, knowing if he didn't feel like there was enough interest he could pull his name out," Mihalich said. "I probably could have called some people to get him into some individual workouts, but I wanted to save my powder. I didn't want to call in chits until I really needed them. This year will be different."

Realizing he almost certainly wouldn't be drafted and would most likely be headed for Europe or the Triple-A-level G-League if he turned pro, Wright-Foreman decided to return to Hofstra. He knew the Pride would have a very good team if he came back, and he also wanted to get his degree. He was on track to graduate in the spring with a major in applied rhetoric and a minor in linguistics. When you talked to him, it was apparent that if he didn't make a living with his jump shot, he could make one with his mouth.

The decision to return had proved to be the right one. With Wright-Foreman, fellow six-foot senior guard Desure Buie, and junior Eli Pemberton leading the way, the Pride arrived in Boston with a 19-3 record and a 9-0 mark in CAA play. Their three losses had all been on the road: at Marshall, Maryland, and VCU—in overtime—the latter on the Saturday after Thanksgiving. They'd gone undefeated in both December and January.

What was most impressive about Wright-Foreman was that he didn't score just by taking shot after shot. He was shooting 51.1 percent from the field—unheard-of for a high-scoring guard in today's game—and 42.5 percent from three-point range. He was *not* a volume scorer. He took good shots and knew when to shoot and when to pass.

The Pride was not a physically dominating team. They had only one player over six-five who played serious minutes—six-ten Purdue graduate transfer Jacquil Taylor. Their strengths were their guards, their experience, and their coach. They had won a lot of close games, including a triple-overtime game at William & Mary in which Wright-Foreman played all fifty-five minutes.

Mihalich was another coach from the Philadelphia school of hoops. His father—Joe Sr.—had been a professor at La Salle, and Joe had grown up a block away from the campus. He had gone to La Salle as a walk-on and, after graduating in 1978, went to work for the great Morgan Wootten at Dematha Catholic in Hyattsville, Maryland. After that, he'd returned to La Salle, where he'd spent seventeen years as an assistant—first under Lefty Ervin and then under Speedy Morris.

He finally got his first shot to be a head coach in 1998 at Niagara and had stayed fifteen years, going 265-203 and reaching postseason four times: two NCAAs, two NITs.

By then, all three of his sons were coaching. Tony was now a track-and-field coach at Iona; Joe was an assistant under Steve Donahue at Penn; and Matt was working for John Gallagher at Hartford.

While Mihalich was building the program at Niagara, Hofstra was enjoying excellent success under Jay Wright (two NCAA bids before leaving for Villanova) and Tom Pecora, whose 2006 team was 26-7, won two out of three from George Mason—which went to the Final Four that season—and somehow didn't get an NCAA bid. Pecora won twenty games four times before leaving for Fordham in 2010.

That decision proved disastrous for both Pecora and Hofstra. Fordham is a coach-killer job, over its head in the Atlantic 10 Conference, and Pecora had four twenty-loss seasons in five years before being fired.

Hofstra hired Tim Welsh, who'd been successful at Iona and at Providence. But Welsh never coached a game at Hofstra. He was charged with DUI one month after being hired and resigned soon after. Assistant coach Mo Cassara stepped into the breach, but there were numerous off-court issues with players and the program fell apart. When the Pride went 7-25 in Cassara's third season, he was fired.

Enter Mihalich, coaxed to Long Island if only because it *had* to be warmer than Niagara and was considerably closer to Philadelphia. In Mihalich's second season, Hofstra went 20-14. A year later, it went 24-10 and tied with UNC Wilmington for the CAA regular-season title, only to lose in the conference tournament championship game to UNC Wilmington in overtime.

This was clearly Mihalich's best team. But he knew that the 9-0 conference record was a little deceiving, and he also knew that

Northeastern, which had been the preseason favorite to win the conference, had played a tough nonconference schedule and that Coen's teams tended to peak in March.

Mihalich's mind wasn't on playing in, as the banner in the rafters said, "Historic Matthews Arena" when he walked onto the floor. The building had been given a $12 million renovation a couple of years earlier that included a massive video board, a new (and very loud) sound system, and a new floor. The Northeastern logo on the floor covered almost the entire court.

"Sort of like putting lipstick on a pig," Mihalich said to CAA commissioner Joe D'Antonio, who was in town for the game.

Mihalich might not have loved it, but Coen certainly did. Especially that afternoon.

The first half was tight until Wright-Foreman picked up his second foul with 7:37 left as he went to the basket and was called for a charge. Mihalich went semi-nuts. The call, like most block-charges, could have gone either way. It was also the kind of call that stars usually get. Not this time.

Northeastern then finished the half on a 7–0 run to lead 37–29 at the break. As it turned out, Hofstra never recovered from that spurt. With Wright-Foreman as cold as he had been all season (5-of-14 from the field, including 2-of-8 from beyond the arc), Northeastern steadily built the lead while all of us watching waited for Hofstra to make a run. The closest thing to a run by the Pride came when Mihalich, frustrated by the entire day, ran out onto the court long enough to get himself teed up late in the game.

By then, Northeastern was in complete control, and the only question was whether Wright-Foreman would be denied double digits for the first time since December of his sophomore season—a streak that stood at seventy-five straight games. He hit two late threes to finish with 15. That was the closest thing to good news for the Pride all day.

Hofstra had been lucky to beat Northeastern the first time they'd played in January. The Pride still had control of the regular-season race, but the CAA plays its conference tournament at a neutral site—in 2019 it was in Charleston—so the regular-season title meant little, except for pride (no pun intended) and a guaranteed NIT bid if the NCAAs didn't happen. Northeastern would clearly be a tough out, come March.

Even when playing away from historic Matthews Arena.

THE COUNTDOWN
BEGINS

February 3, 2019

When the calendar turns to February, everyone in college basketball begins looking to March. Some of it is for the same reason everyone looks to March: warmer weather on the horizon, even though there's no guarantee in many places that there might not be some snow still to come.

Snow or no snow, the third Sunday in March is always Selection Sunday—college basketball's Christmas Day, though some teams are inevitably left with the coal that is the NIT or—worse—nothing in their postseason stocking.

I woke up on February 3 knowing it was six weeks until Selection Sunday. The countdown was now under way: there would be constant updates from the so-called bracketologists on who was on the bubble, who was off the bubble, and who the top seeds would be.

Joe Lunardi, who has worked at St. Joseph's for thirty-two years in various public relations and marketing jobs, invented bracketology and has turned it into a cottage industry. Many others have since copied him, but Lunardi's the best—if only because he might take what he's doing seriously but doesn't take himself too seriously.

I have often likened bracketologists to weatherpeople. If you make a prediction that looks wrong, you change the prediction. In February, the bracketologists are constantly updating their brackets based on who just won and who just lost. I laugh out loud at headlines that say things like "Loss to Duke drops Virginia to second line." Or "North Carolina win puts Syracuse into last four in."

There might still be eight games left to play, but *at that moment,* that's where the bracketologists have those teams ranked. The only rankings that matter are the ones that come out on Selection Sunday when the NCAA field is announced. That's why the bracketologists "update" until just before the selection show begins. That way they can claim to have gotten "sixty-seven out of sixty-eight teams right!"

Well, of course they get sixty-seven or sixty-six or maybe even sixty-eight teams right. Give me until fifteen minutes before the brackets are announced and I'll get most of them right too.

It's also worth noting that the bracketologists aren't trying to tell you who *should* be in the field, but whom they think the ten-member committee, made up of commissioners and athletic directors who often know little about basketball and depend on computer printouts and staff assistance to select the field, will select.

They know that, nine times out of ten, given a close race between a power conference school and a mid-major, the power conference school is getting in. That's why St. John's, in a weak Big East, was in the 2019 tournament and—for example—29-7 UNC Greensboro was not. St. John's comes out of New York and had a Hall of Fame player as its coach, Chris Mullin.

It is also why two Big Ten schools with losing conference records—Minnesota (9-11) and Ohio State (8-12 . . . yes, seriously)—got in and teams like Hofstra (twenty-seven wins), Lipscomb (twenty-nine), and Furman (twenty-five, including a road win *at* Villanova) did not.

"It's frustrating at times," said Loyola Chicago coach Porter Moser. "As good as we knew we were a year ago, we knew we weren't getting a bid if we didn't win the conference tournament. You're a number one seed in a so-called one-bid conference, the pressure is incredible. There's no safety net if you have one bad day or someone else has one hot one."

Loyola Chicago, which would *not* have received an at-large bid in 2018, went to the Final Four.

In 2019, two non–Power Five schools received at-large bids: Belmont, which was sent to the First Four and won there; and Nevada, which had gone to the sweet sixteen a year earlier and was 29-3 before losing to San Diego State in the Mountain West championship game.

That was the list.

February goes by very fast in college basketball—especially for the one-bid conference teams whose conference tournaments begin the first week in March. The start of March Madness was four weeks away. That was when conference tournaments would begin.

While I was in Boston spending the afternoon at historic Matthews Arena, all hell was breaking loose in northwest Washington.

Norfolk State, unbeaten in the MEAC at 7-0, had come to Burr Gym to play Howard. The Bison had won two conference games in a row since the loss to Harvard, and they came in feeling confident that they were about to get on a roll. They were 4-3 in conference play and second place—at worst—felt very possible.

For twenty-two minutes, Howard played almost perfect basketball, leading 55–31 with 17:33 to play. R. J. Cole, on his way to 29 points, 6 rebounds, and 5 assists, was having a superb day, and Howard was doing a good job of keeping Norfolk State, easily the league's most physical team, off the boards. The Bison actually outrebounded the Spartans, 15–13, in the first half.

But Norfolk State's size and strength began to wear on the Bison, and as the lead dwindled, Howard began making mistakes. The Spartans had eighteen second-chance points in the last eighteen minutes and forced eight Howard turnovers, leading to easy baskets. A follow dunk by Jordan Butler got the game tied at 78–78 with 1:31 left, and after Cole and C. J. Williams had missed at the other end, Norfolk State ran the clock down until Mastadi Pitt was fouled going to the basket with one second to go. Calmly, he made both shots, and Norfolk State had escaped, 80–78.

Unfortunately, the blown lead was only the beginning of Howard's problems. Not surprisingly, emotions were running high when the buzzer sounded while Cole's half-court fling was going wide. When the teams went to shake hands, there was a good bit of chirping on both sides. Then it became shoving. And then, quickly, it became a semi-riot: players throwing punches while fans poured out of the stands.

Coaches from both teams came running to try to break things up, even as campus police came onto the court. Howard coach Kevin Nickelberry was in the middle of it, yelling at players from both teams to "get to the stairway," which led to the basement locker rooms for both teams.

A cell phone video would later show Nickelberry yelling at Norfolk State's Nic Thomas from about ten feet away to get to the staircase, pointing as he did so. At that moment, several people grabbed Nickelberry and wrestled him away from the scene.

The story in the next day's *Washington Post*—the game probably would have gotten about one paragraph if not for the postgame fight—described Nickelberry as "being dragged away."

Looking at the video, seeing Nickelberry being pushed back, one might have thought that was what happened.

"I wasn't dragged away, I wasn't going after anybody," Nickelberry said. "I was telling the kid to get out of there, to get to the stairs. That's what I was trying to do with everyone—my players, their players. That's all."

When the league looked at the video and heard from both sides, it apparently agreed with Nickelberry. Six players were suspended for one game—three from each team. The league took no action against Nickelberry or against Norfolk State coach Robert Jones.

But Howard president Wayne A. I. Frederick saw it differently. On Monday, Nickelberry was summoned to the president's office and told he was being put on indefinite paid administrative leave.

Nickelberry walked through what had happened with Frederick and pointed out that the league had taken no action against him. According to Nickelberry, Frederick said, "Perception is reality, Kevin. The *Washington Post* describes you as being held back from going after a player. We can't let that pass without taking some action."

When I asked athletic director Kery Davis later if Frederick would speak to me so I could hear his side of the conversation, Davis laughed. "He's not going to talk to you about that," he said. Talking to the media is often beneath college presidents.

The only break Howard caught in the whole fiasco was that the three suspended players weren't starters. The Bison traveled to Florida A&M and Bethune-Cookman the next weekend with Keith Coutreyer, Nickelberry's top assistant, in charge. They won both games to get to 6-4 in the league.

When the team returned from the Florida trip, Nickelberry was allowed to rejoin his team.

"It was a long week," he said. Then he laughed. "We lose Saturday, you *know* who's going to get blamed."

Howard lost that Saturday to North Carolina A&T in another hard-fought game, but one without the chippiness of the Norfolk State game.

"If they're the second-best team in the league and Norfolk State is the best team in the league, I'm not afraid to play anyone," Nickelberry told his players afterward. "You know we can play with them. Now we have to prove we can beat them."

Howard was now 6-5 in the conference. There were five games left until the MEAC Tournament. Nickelberry knew his job was on the line. So did his players.

February 6, 2019, Catonsville, Maryland

The first Wednesday in February was another TV night for me: Hartford coming to play UMBC in, as Ryan Odom had christened it, "The REC" (Retriever Events Center), as opposed to the old "RAC" (Retriever Athletic Center).

The America East is one of those leagues that play their entire conference tournament on home courts. The higher you finish, the more likely you are to play at home. The two teams had played in the conference tournament semifinals the previous season, and UMBC, playing at home, had won to advance to the championship game at Vermont, where it had pulled off its stunning upset of the Catamounts.

The loss had been especially tough to take for Hartford coach John Gallagher, because he was convinced his team was capable of winning at Vermont. He had reason to think that, since the Hawks had won in Patrick Gym in mid-February. That was Vermont's only conference loss in the regular season.

"We were peaking at the right time," Gallagher said. "We were experienced at that point and healthy." He smiled. "The only problem was Ryan's team was peaking too. They were just better than us that night."

Prior to the start of that season, Gallagher had been given an ultimatum by a new athletic director, Mary Ellen Gillespie: win at least fifteen games or she was going to make a change. Gallagher was entering his eighth season at Hartford and had some ups—seventeen wins and a CIT bid in 2013—and downs—nine wins in 2016–17.

Hartford is not an easy place to win. The University of Connecticut probably gets about 95 percent of the state's media coverage for basketball—men *and* women—and recruiting to a place where it snows early and often in the winter is never easy—unless you are a basketball power.

Even with the semifinal loss to UMBC, Hartford won nineteen games—a school record—that season. Gallagher got a two-year contract extension, really not much by today's standards. But he was relentlessly upbeat, another Philadelphia-born-and-bred coach.

(For the record, I didn't set out to chronicle Philly basketball coaches in this book—there are just a lot of them out there.)

Gallagher had played under Phil Martelli at St. Joseph's in the late nineties, then worked as an assistant at La Salle, at Lafayette (under Fran O'Hanlon), at Hartford, and then at Penn. When Steve Donahue got the Boston College job in 2010, he hired Gallagher as his top assistant. Two weeks later, he was offered the head coaching job at Hartford. Donahue told him he had to take it.

Hartford's season had been very up and down for three months. The Hawks' top *seven* players were seniors, meaning this was a season to do some serious damage. But they got off to a disappointing 2-6 start, and Gallagher thought his players were pressing, feeling as if they had to be *better*.

They'd finally beaten a good team, winning at home against Bowling Green—which would go on to win twenty-five games—before traveling to Duke for a $70,000 guarantee game.

For a change, they were playing a game with absolutely no pressure: they were supposed to lose by a hundred. Instead, they hung with the Blue Devils for almost thirty minutes, trailing just 47–39 before the inevitable onslaught buried them. But they came out of the game believing that if they were good enough to compete with Duke, they were good enough to beat most of the teams they would be playing for the rest of the season.

They won four of their five remaining nonconference games, culminating in a 79–78 win at Boston College. The win wasn't quite on the level of UMBC's historic win over Virginia the previous March, but it was a shocker. America East teams aren't supposed to beat ACC teams—not in March, not in January, heck not in July if they scrimmage someplace. Certainly not on the road.

Buoyed by that victory, the Hawks had rallied late to win their conference opener at home against UMBC. The joyride got derailed when they went to Patrick Gym and found Vermont more than ready to play, clearly remembering Hartford's win up there a year ago.

And so they came into the REC with a 4-4 conference record, still riding the roller coaster Gallagher had hoped to avoid with such an experienced team.

UMBC was 6-2, not having lost since the two losses on the New England swing in January. "Ryan's doing a better job this year than last, if that's possible," Gallagher said of Odom on the day of the game.

He wasn't blowing smoke the way coaches often do before a game. UMBC had lost its two best big men—Dan Akin and Max Curran—for the season, early in January. Their next-best big man, Brandon Horvath, was also out, meaning the guys who had been fourth and fifth on the inside-depth chart—Sam Schweitz and Nolan Gerrity—were now one and two.

Odom had altered his lineup, at times playing with three guards and six-foot-six-inch Joe Sherburne at the four spot. (Apologies to Mike Krzyzewski for using a number to describe a player's position.)

Sherburne was the only senior starter, an excellent three-point shooter, and a very good rebounder for someone his size. He was the classic quiet leader, never really showing much emotion on the court, but about as intense as they came.

He had graduated from UMBC in three years and had never gotten a B in college. In fact, during his sophomore year, he had been the "scholar of the game," a sponsored bit that was part of every America East telecast. Gary Stein had read Sherburne's résumé while an on-screen graphic showed a photo of him and noted that he had a 3.75 GPA.

"Impressive," Gary said as he finished reading.

"And he can shoot too," I added.

A couple of weeks later, Sherburne's parents, Jan and Paul, came to town for a game. Before the game, Paul Sherburne introduced himself and told me how much he and his wife enjoyed our telecasts.

"There's just one thing," he said, "if you don't mind me bringing it up."

My first thought was that he was going to ask me not to refer to his son as "Cool Joe" anymore. I had started calling him that because of his always calm demeanor and ability to hit shots under pressure. It also seemed to make sense since Joe Flacco, who played quarterback for the Baltimore Ravens about six miles down the road from UMBC, was known as "Cool Joe."

I quickly learned that Sherburne, a rabid fan of the Green Bay Packers and Aaron Rodgers, wanted nothing to do with being called Cool Joe. A Rodgers-related nickname would be fine, but no thanks to Flacco. Actually, he didn't say it quite that politely.

That wasn't what Paul Sherburne wanted to talk about.

"You guys [Stein and I] have been great to Joe," he said. "But the other night you did that 'scholar-athlete' thing on him." He paused, a little embarrassed. "Thing is, you said he had a 3.75 GPA. It's actually 4.0."

Whoops. There was no point in telling him that Stein had been reading from the material he'd been handed. Hey, we got it wrong, we'd fix it.

Paul Sherburne was classic Midwestern polite. "Don't misunderstand," he said. "We really love the telecasts."

I told him we'd correct it that night—which we did. I made the point that I had also had a 4.0 GPA in college—*total* in four years. Or something close to that.

The season hadn't been easy for Sherburne. The graduation of Lyles and Maura had changed his role in a myriad of ways. He was now the captain, the unquestioned leader. Lyles and Maura had both been extroverts; Sherburne was more introverted. More important, his role on court had changed considerably. Because the two seniors had been so hard to guard, Sherburne often found himself open on the perimeter when one of them would draw a double-team and kick the ball to him.

Sherburne on an open catch-and-shoot was almost automatic. Now there weren't as many open shots, and he had worked an effective shot fake into his repertoire that got him to the basket more often. He had also had to rebound more—going from 3.9 rebounds a game to 5.6, a considerable jump.

UMBC had gone to Vermont after its miraculous escape against Albany and had again won in Patrick Gym, an almost unheard-of feat in the America East—back-to-back wins at Vermont.

"All of a sudden it feels like they've got our number," said Tom Brennan, the ex-coach for whom the court was now named. "What'd we beat 'em, like a hundred times [actually twenty-three] in a row? Then they come up here and steal our NCAA bid and walk in here again and make it look easy."

The final was 84–71, clearly UMBC's best performance of the season. The Retrievers had reached the halfway mark of the conference season 6-2, trailing only Vermont and tied with Stony Brook, the league's surprise team. Hartford was 4-4 and looking for something to jump-start its season.

It got exactly that on a remarkably balmy February day and evening, the midafternoon temperatures reaching into the fifties.

Early on, it looked as if UMBC's hot streak would continue. The Retrievers jumped to a 17–7 lead in the first eight minutes, amping up the crowd of 1,888. In the REC, that number meant the building was less than half-full. People often forgot that when Odom arrived three years earlier, the old RAC, which seated about 1,800 was rarely half-full.

Gradually, Hartford found its legs. Experienced teams rarely fold just because an opponent comes out hot, even on the road.

Gallagher had pieced together a fascinating group of players. John Carroll, the power forward, was from Dublin and had announced before his junior year that, in order to lose weight and add quickness, he was giving up beer. "For someone from Ireland," he said, "this is a big deal."

George Blagojevic had been born in Serbia, raised in Australia, and didn't play basketball until he was a teenager. He had found a home playing basketball in Hartford.

The Hawks' best player was J. R. Lynch, a five-ten point guard from the unexotic town of Hoboken, New Jersey, which was most famous for being the hometown of Frank Sinatra but in the basketball pantheon for producing Jim Spanarkel and Mike O'Koren in back-to-back years at Hudson Catholic High School. Spanarkel had become Duke's first 2,000-point scorer, and O'Koren had been a four-year starter and star for Dean Smith at North Carolina. Lynch was also a Hudson Catholic grad and had an uncanny knack for getting to the basket.

UMBC led 33–32 at halftime after Hartford climbed back into the game. The Retrievers were up 33–28 with 3:47 left but didn't score again for the rest of the half. Walking off the court, Odom had that feeling that coaches get in the pit of their stomachs sometimes that this wasn't his team's night.

If he had been Miss Clavell, the famous teacher from the *Madeline* children's books, he would have been thinking, *Something is not right.*

His gut turned out to be correct. Carroll began the second half by making two free throws to give his team its first lead of the night at 34–33, and the Hawks took the lead for good at 43–40 on a Jason Dunne three-pointer. The lead grew steadily from there to 57–47, and UMBC couldn't put together a run. Every time the Retrievers made a basket that looked like it might launch a rally, there was Lynch, beating Odom's young guards, getting to the basket, and getting fouled. He finished with 28 points, including 15-of-16 from the line. By himself, he got to the line as often as UMBC did. That, and a 36–31 rebounding advantage—UMBC had only two offensive rebounds the entire night—decided the game.

For Hartford, it was a key win. Vermont still led the conference with only one loss—to UMBC—and Stony Brook, the surprise team in the league, was now second with two losses. UMBC was still third, but just a game ahead of Hartford. If the two teams finished tied, Hartford would have the tiebreaker by virtue of having won both games head-to-head.

"Long way to go," Gallagher said after the game.

Actually, that wasn't the case. The end of the regular season was three and a half weeks away.

DOG DAYS AND VERY
COLD NIGHTS

Waking up on a miserably rainy Saturday morning in Washington, it was difficult for me to believe that conference tournaments would be starting in a little more than three weeks—specifically on Monday, March 4.

The newspapers and the Internet were full of stories about pitchers and catchers beginning to report to spring training camps, a sure sign that March Madness wasn't far away.

A word on the phrase "March Madness." The NCAA is zealous about trademarking every phrase it can possibly make money from, including "The Final Four," "Elite Eight," "Selection Sunday," "First Four," and "Big Dance." Someday soon I'm pretty certain they will trademark the word "basketball" and insist that anyone who wants to use the word pay them a licensing fee.

There's some dispute about where "March Madness" comes from. Most historians credit it to a man named Henry Porter, who was an executive working for the Illinois High School Association and wrote in 1939, "A little March madness may complement and contribute to society and keep society on an even keel."

That was a reference to the annual Illinois high school basketball tournament—not the NCAA Tournament, which, by sheer coincidence, was launched that year.

There are some who claim there were "March madness" references made during the Indiana high school tournament as far back as 1931, but Porter's specific paean to the Illinois tournament generally gets the most credit.

As far as anyone knows, the first time March madness was referenced as part of the NCAA Tournament was in 1982 when Brent Musburger, then with CBS, used it during a down-to-the-wire game.

It grew from there.

Then, in 1996, a video game company tried to use it and the Illinois High School Association, which had actually trademarked the term years earlier, stepped in to stop it. By then, the NCAA was using it all the time, and the two groups agreed to take on the video game company together, forming—wait for it—"The March Madness Athletic Association." Seriously.

The court ruled that the trademark belonged to both the Illinois group and the NCAA. Since then, the NCAA has made a practice of chasing down anyone who publicly uses the term "March Madness" to try to sell product—unless it's been paid.

Nowadays, however, it goes even further than that. No one who works for the NCAA refers to the "NCAA Basketball Tournament." For one thing, political correctness requires them to say, "NCAA *Men's* Basketball Tournament." Beyond that, though, they don't make any money from calling it merely the basketball tournament.

If you buy a program (for $15) at any NCAA regional site, there is no mention of a basketball tournament on the cover. It merely says, "March Madness." The Final Four program (which costs $20) is different. It has the logo of that year's Final Four—different for each city and year—and photos of players from each of the four teams, along with the team logos.

Take a look at the microphones the sideline reporters use throughout the tournament. What do they say? "March Madness."

Apparently, those who work for the NCAA have been well schooled in pitching their product. When I walked into Dayton on opening night of the First Four, one of the first people I encountered was Dan Gavitt, whose official title is senior vice president of basketball—which in English means he runs the tournament.

As Gavitt and I shook hands, he said, "Happy March Madness." I'm sure he said that to all the boys . . . and girls.

But February can feel as if it's a long way from March. Which is why a Saturday afternoon game in northwest Washington, DC, at American University felt critical to both teams: Army, which was trying to break a three-game losing streak, and American, which had won four of five but was coming off a disappointing loss at Navy. Both teams were 6-5 in the Patriot League and scrambling for seeding position in the conference tournament, which—like the America East—is played at home sites, making seeding vital.

Both schools had finished in the league's dreaded bottom four the past two seasons—Army eighth both years; American ninth and tenth—meaning they had been forced to play first-round games in the league tournament, rather than getting a bye to the quarterfinals.

Both were clearly improved this season and hoping to find their way into the top four, which would assure them at least one home game.

"The less you travel late in the season, the better off you are," Army coach Jimmy Allen said. "Everyone's tired by then. It isn't so much playing in the other guy's gym as it is riding the bus to get to that gym."

Army had been 6-2 after its come-from-behind win against Lafayette, but hadn't won since. The losing skein had started—predictably—with a trip to Colgate. There may not be a tougher trip in college basketball than going to Colgate, because it always involves driving back roads to get there.

When I was doing my book on Patriot League basketball in the winter of 1999–2000, I made the often harrowing drive up Route 11 to Route 12B from Binghamton a half dozen times. My memories of those drives are consistent: it always snowed; there were always cars slowing—understandably—to a crawl. Even in July, Google Maps will tell you it will take an hour and twenty-four minutes to drive sixty-eight miles. In January, it might take twice as long.

When I talk about that season and describe getting to Colgate, I say this: "You drive to the end of the earth and turn right. Then you drive about another fifty miles, and when it starts snowing you know you're almost there."

I used that description during a telecast one night, and Matt Langel, Colgate's coach, happened to be watching. The next day I got a text from him: "You're killing me," he wrote.

I called him and apologized. "I exaggerated, I know," I said.

"Yeah," Langel answered with a laugh. "But not by much."

The trip in 2019 was made a lot more difficult by the fact that the

Raiders had become the surprise of the league. Bucknell and Lehigh had been picked—as they almost always were—to finish one-two in the preseason, but Colgate was proving to be a serious threat.

After Army's 6-2 start, the Raiders blew Army out when the Black Knights finally made it up 12B into Hamilton. Losses to Lehigh and Holy Cross had followed. Allen was concerned. His team hadn't finished well in February and March in several years, dating to the days when he was still Zach Spiker's assistant.

He knew how tough the winter was at West Point. But he also knew he couldn't just accept that as excuse. And so, he arrived in Washington in a much different mood than he'd been in walking to the bus at Lafayette two weeks earlier.

"We need a win, it's that simple," he said. "We're better than we've played the last three games. They're playing well right now. It won't be easy."

Briefly, it looked as if it might not be all that difficult. American started the game colder than the icy rain falling outside Bender Arena, and Army had an early 21–12 lead.

The game had started with Jordan Fox missing inside, but Jacob Kessler grabbing the rebound and scoring. Allen had no way of knowing that those would be the only two points he would get from Kessler and Alex King, both starters who were averaging a little more than ten points per game—none in the game's final thirty-nine minutes.

The Eagles, who had made one basket in the first eight minutes, finally began to make some shots, but Army still led at halftime, 33–29.

The lead didn't last very long in the second half. American freshman Jacob Boonyasith, given a start by Brennan, was having the game of his young career. Every time his team needed a basket, Boonyasith made a play, frequently going to the basket to score or get fouled. He would finish with 20 points (on 8-of-11 shooting) and 5 rebounds.

"We knew he was talented," Allen lamented later. "But we didn't expect him to be that aggressive. He just killed us."

Boonyasith's hot hand might have been survived and Sa'eed Nelson's near triple-double (11 points, 11 assists, 9 rebounds) might have also been survived if not for one thing: Army could not have thrown the ball into the ocean from a hovering Army helicopter.

I just thought that was a more apt cliché than my usual rowboat line.

For the day, Army took sixteen three-point shots—twelve in the second half. A good-shooting three-point team would make at least six or seven of those shots. An okay-shooting team might make five; a poor-shooting one perhaps four. Army was a mediocre three-point-shooting team, making 31.5 percent of its threes for the season, which would mean on an average day it would shoot 5-for-16.

Not on this afternoon. The Black Knights didn't make *one* three-point shot all day. Fox, their best three-point shooter, was 0-for-5. Lonnie Grayson, the team's three-point shooting specialist off the bench was 0-for-4.

As the bricks from the team in black piled up, American took the lead and pulled away, building a 57–45 lead on a Nelson steal and layup. It was still 65–55 at the under-eight-minute TV time-out, and AU looked to be cruising.

But the Army kids, whether they could shoot straight or not, had no quit in them. They began forcing the ball inside and scoring. Center Matt Wilson scored 14 points, and Aaron Duhart came off the bench to chip in 11.

John Emezie made two free throws to cut the lead to 67–66 with 1:20 to go, but Boonyasith answered—again with a drive to the basket to up the lead to three with forty-eight ticks left. Knowing he was shooting blanks, Fox smartly used a shot fake to get to the basket and get fouled. He made both. It was 69–68, under twenty seconds to go.

Army had to foul. It sent Stacy Beckton Jr. to the line. Beckton was having one of his best games in three years as an Eagle. His two free throws gave him 15 points and made it 71–68.

Sixteen seconds left. Plenty of time, but Army needed a three. With the clock ticking down, Brennan opted not to foul—who could blame him?—and the ball finally came to Emezie on the left wing with three seconds left.

An open three. Another miss. Appropriately, Boonyasith got the last rebound.

It was a huge win for American, because it pushed its record in the conference to 7-5—a big jump given that the Eagles had won eight conference games *combined* the previous two seasons.

For Army, it was another frustrating loss on a day when even less-than-average three-point shooting probably would have resulted in a victory.

Allen was so frustrated that he took a shot at Nelson during his postgame radio show. "It's a lot easier to be a great player when the officials let you carry the ball all the time," he said.

Allen knew better than that. He knew his team had let a very winnable road game get away. The Black Knights had now lost four in a row and were 6-6 in the Patriot League. There were still nineteen days—and five games—left in February.

February 10, Fairfax, Virginia

I was in the car and pulling out of the garage at American about twenty minutes after the game ended. I was headed to the Marriott in Fair Oaks, Virginia—a few miles from the George Mason campus in Fairfax.

I was meeting Ashley Howard for a pre-team-meal cup of coffee in the hotel's quiet lobby. It had been a month since I'd seen La Salle play very well and lose close at VCU, and a lot had happened to the Explorers since then.

After the loss to VCU, La Salle had lost its next three games to drop to 1-4 in the Atlantic 10 and an ugly 3-14 overall. They had started to turn things around with a win at Fordham that had started a four-game winning streak, which included road wins at Richmond and at St. Joseph's. Even though the Hawks were having a down year, any win over a Big Five rival was a big deal for La Salle right now.

Howard was enough of a realist to understand that the A-10 wasn't as deep as it usually was and that his team's 5-4 conference record was a reflection of that. But he also knew that the team he was coaching in February was a lot better than the team he'd been coaching in November.

"That's the important thing, that we keep getting better and learn to play in tough situations," he said. "We're losing Pookie [Powell] next season, but the rest of these guys are back. We add a couple of pieces to what we've got, and we could be a tough out a year from now."

Perhaps almost as important, Howard now felt better about Howard—as a head coach.

"Look, it's very easy to talk about how tough our schedule was— which it was—or how we could have won a couple more games with a break or two—which we could have," he said. "If Saul [Phiri] hadn't sat out first semester, we almost certainly would have won a couple more games—at least.

"But when you're sitting there ten games into your first season as a coach and you're 0-10, it shakes you. If it doesn't, something's wrong."

That was why writing "0-10" on a piece of paper and then burning that piece of paper had been cathartic. "It was as if, at that moment, I said, 'Okay, it happened and now it's over, move on,'" he said. "My timing was probably pretty good doing it before a game I thought we should win [Alabama A&M], but since then we've been competitive in just about every game."

They were 7-4 since the ritual burning and now had a very realistic chance to at least stay away from having to play the first day of the A-10 Tournament in Brooklyn.

With expansion, many conferences have been forced to go to a five-day format in order to allow every team to play. The ACC has fifteen teams; the Big Ten and the SEC have fourteen, as does the A-10. That means teams eleven through fifteen in the ACC and eleven through fourteen in the other conferences have to show up a day earlier than everyone else to play their way into the first round.

There's a red-*A*-on-the-forehead quality—or perhaps it's a red *L* for loser—to playing the first day of a conference tournament. The buildings tend to be mostly empty, except for the most loyal fans—and family—of the teams playing. I still remember walking into the first day of the ACC Tournament when it was played in Washington in 2016 and seeing the upper deck of what was then Verizon Center covered with tarps to mask all the empty seats. This at an event where during one stretch there was no public sale of tickets for thirty-five years.

La Salle was now closer to the top four in the conference standings and the cherished "double bye"—which allowed a team to sit out the first *two* days of the tournament and not play until the quarterfinals—than it was to the bottom four.

That made Howard happy.

"The best thing is I've really enjoyed this group of kids," he said. "Even when we were 0-10 they were showing up ready to go in practice every day. There was no whining, which wouldn't have been surprising under the circumstances. Now they're seeing results, and that makes every day more enjoyable."

One of the teams La Salle was chasing was George Mason, which, after an up-and-down nonconference season, had burst out of the blocks in conference play to a 7-1 start, including some impressive routs of St. Joseph's (85–60 in Philadelphia) and Rhode Island (84–47).

The Patriots were in their sixth season in the A-10, having jumped there from the CAA in 2013 in search of more TV money. The move had not worked out very well at the outset. GMU went 11-20, 4-12 in its first season in the league and 9-22, 4-14 in its second. That led to the firing of Coach Paul Hewitt and the hiring of Dave Paulsen. Paulsen had been able to squeeze 9-9 conference records out of the Patriots in the past two seasons, a major improvement. In GMU's last fifteen seasons in the CAA—thirteen under Jim Larrañaga and two under Hewitt—its *worst* conference record had been 9-9, and that had happened only once.

Sunday was as nice a day as Saturday had been a miserable one. The sun was out, and even though it was still cold, the bright day lifted my spirits as I steered the car down I-66 toward George Mason.

Going to George Mason always put me in a good mood. The first time I saw David Robinson play was in the school's old field house in 1984 when he was a Navy freshman.

Robinson didn't start that night, but he came off the bench and scored 24 points and had 9 rebounds. I was sitting with Jack Kvancz, who was Mason's athletic director at the time. As soon as I saw Robinson explode off the floor a couple of times, I turned to Kvancz and said, "Who the hell is that kid?"

Kvancz smiled wanly. "He grew up just down the street from here. We could have had him. But [Coach] Joe [Harrington] didn't really want him. He was better off at Navy anyway. His father's an old Navy guy, and he wants to be an engineer."

It should be noted that Robinson was only six-six at the time. During the off-season between his freshman and sophomore years he grew to seven-one while not losing any of the quickness or coordination he had when he was six-six. The rest, as most people know, is basketball history.

It was under Larrañaga that George Mason made its own history. Larrañaga had come to Mason in 1997 from Bowling Green, where he'd been very successful. In his second season, the Patriots had won the CAA Tournament and made it to the NCAAs, where they had been crushed in the first round by Cincinnati.

They made it back two years later and came within one slightly misfired pass of upsetting Maryland in the first round. Mason center George Evans, who had been almost unguardable in the low post all day, had Maryland center Lonny Baxter sealed near the basket in the final seconds with the Terrapins leading, 81–80. But the pass to him was a little bit low, and he couldn't quite reach down to get it. The ball went out-of-bounds to Maryland, and the Terrapins made two free throws and won the game, 83–80. From there they went on to their first Final Four.

That same first weekend regional, held in Boise, Idaho, also produced Lefty Driesell's last great moment on the national stage. By then, Driesell was coaching at Georgia State, a commuter school in downtown Atlanta.

Once again, though, he'd worked his recruiting magic and Georgia State had gone 28-4, winning the Atlantic Sun Tournament. Georgia State was the fourth school (Davidson, Maryland, James Madison) that Driesell had coached into the NCAA Tournament.

On the same afternoon that Maryland escaped George Mason, Georgia State stunned Wisconsin, 50–49. During his postgame press conference, someone asked Driesell if he could talk about the difference between coaching at a power school—like Maryland—and coaching at a mid-major, as he was doing at Georgia State.

"Mid-major, mid-major?" Driesell repeated, incredulous. "I ain't ever been mid-nothin'. Go over there and ask Wisconsin if we're mid-major."

Mid-majors like George Mason and Georgia State lived for the chance to knock off power schools like Maryland and Wisconsin. Georgia State lived the dream that day; Mason—barely—did not.

Five years later, in 2006, the Patriots lived the dream—and then some.

After they lost in the semifinals of the CAA Tournament to Hofstra, they knew they were sitting on the outside of the bubble—or so they thought. What's more, Larrañaga had announced after the loss to Hofstra that point guard Tony Skinn would be suspended for the team's next game—whether it was in the NCAAs or the NIT.

In the game's final minute, with Hofstra up 53–49, Skinn had delivered a sucker punch to the groin of the Pride's Loren Stokes. As soon as he saw Stokes crumple, Larrañaga knew what Skinn had done.

Unlike most coaches, who will say they need to review the tape or talk to their player or wait to see if their league will take action, Larrañaga made the announcement that Skinn would be suspended right after the game.

"I didn't need to see tape," Larrañaga said later. "I knew what had happened."

Skinn did look at the tape the next night during the telecast of the UNC Wilmington–Hofstra championship game (won by UNC Wilmington) and was horrified. "I knew I'd made an awful mistake," he said. "But actually seeing it, made me feel kind of sick."

The NCAA basketball committee was chaired that season by Craig Littlepage, who had been an outstanding player at Penn and then had coached at Penn and Rutgers. In other words, he understood basketball. For once, the committee actually treated mid-majors fairly, including George Mason.

The Patriots were the No. 11 seed in the East. The only school that had a legitimate complaint about that was Hofstra. The Pride had beaten Mason twice in the last few weeks of the season.

The committee would never admit it took one team from a conference over another team from a conference, but that had clearly happened. Mason had finished 15-3 in the CAA; Hofstra 14-4. But what probably put the Patriots in was an impressive win a couple of weeks earlier *at* Wichita State. The winning shot in the game had been hit by Tony Skinn.

The postbracket interviews conducted with the committee chairman on CBS are usually lovefests. "Mr. Chairman, your committee has done another wonderful job this year. . . ."

Not this time. Jim Nantz and Billy Packer went after Littlepage, and their main bone of contention was the inclusion of George Mason. "Can you show me what on this résumé," Nantz said, holding up Mason's schedule, "makes this team worthy of a bid?"

Littlepage handled the questions calmly and noted that several other schools—Air Force, for one—with similar résumés had made the field.

George Mason, with Skinn in street clothes, went on to beat Michigan State in the first round of the tournament that Friday and then stunned third-seeded North Carolina two days later after falling behind 16–2. Given that the school had never won an NCAA Tournament game, to beat two powers—both had been in the Final Four a year earlier, and Carolina was the defending national champion—like that in two days was extraordinary.

For everyone in the program—players, coaches, staff—to come home as a sweet sixteen team almost felt like winning a national championship. Players talked about having to remind themselves that there were more games still to be played; that what they had accomplished the previous weekend was not a climax but a step.

"A pretty amazing step, though," Skinn admitted that week.

By winning, GMU advanced to the sweet sixteen in downtown Washington, DC—Verizon Center being twenty-one miles from the Mason campus. Their semifinal opponent would be Wichita State—a team the Patriots had beaten on the road three weeks earlier.

Now on a roll, Mason rolled the Shockers and, amazingly, they were in the elite eight. If winning *one* game in the tournament was the Mike Brey equivalent of a national championship, what was winning three games?

Earlier in the week, prior to Mason's round-of-sixteen game against Wichita State, I'd gone to Larrañaga's house to write a column on what all this meant to him. He was fifty-six and, in nineteen previous seasons as a head coach in Division 1, had never won an NCAA Tournament game. Now, suddenly, he'd beaten two of the game's powers and two future Hall of Fame coaches in less than forty-eight hours.

He was sitting on the couch talking about the weekend: about the calls and emails and about being asked to go on *The NewsHour with Jim Lehrer* the night before. I asked if there was one moment that stood out.

There was a long pause.

"You know, I have two sons," he said, choking up.

Both had played for him at Bowling Green. Jon was now working in Washington and had been in Dayton for the games the previous weekend. Jay was playing in Italy and had apparently been in constant touch with Jon during the North Carolina game, including bugging his brother to walk to the bench to give his father some advice.

"After the game, Jon and I walked upstairs to the lobby, which was empty by then," Larrañaga said. "From there, we called Jay and . . . we shared the moment."

The tears were now coming in a gusher. Liz Larrañaga walked into the room and saw her husband in a puddle. "You're talking about calling Jay, aren't you?" she said with a smile.

He nodded helplessly. "There's no crying in the sweet sixteen, is there?" he said, revamping Tom Hanks's famous line from *A League of Their Own*.

The joyride was sure to end in the regional final against top-seeded Connecticut. On Saturday, the off-day in between the sixteen's and the elite eight, I had breakfast with my agent, Esther Newberg, and her sister and brother-in-law—all absolutely fanatical Connecticut fans who gave money to both the men's and women's programs. They were making plans to travel to the Final Four in Indianapolis.

If only to be a contrarian, I said, "Don't overlook George Mason. If they're good enough to beat Michigan State and Carolina, they're good enough to beat you guys."

That notion clearly annoyed them. Which was my intent. I didn't honestly think the Patriots could win.

Only, they did. They were down 6–0 before most people were seated and trailed 43–34 at halftime. I could see Esther and her family smirking from across the court. But Mason rallied and actually led 74–70 late before Denham Brown made a layup at the buzzer to send the game into overtime.

So close, I thought, so close.

But the Mason kids never blinked. They led the entire overtime, although it wasn't over until Brown's three-point shot at the buzzer clanged off the rim. Mason had somehow won: 76–74.

As I stood courtside watching the celebration unfold, Larrañaga ran past me. He stopped, grabbed my arm, and said, "I can't wait to see Nantz and Packer in Indianapolis!"

Three nights later, I was having dinner at the famous St. Elmo Steak House in Indy with a friend when Nantz and Packer walked in the door. I knew that Larrañaga and his team were having dinner in a private dining room downstairs. When the two of them stopped at the table to say hello, I said, "You know, George Mason's having dinner downstairs. I know Larrañaga would love to see you guys."

Nantz understood exactly what I was saying. "I'm going to go down there and congratulate them," he said. "And apologize."

He headed in that direction. Packer sat down with us.

"Aren't you going?" I asked.

"What for?" Packer answered.

"To apologize?"

"I have nothing to apologize for," he said. "I said what I believed and I stand by saying it."

"But maybe you were wrong?"

Packer smiled and shrugged. "Maybe," he said. "Maybe."

Those memories all flood back every time I walk onto the floor at what is now called EagleBank Arena. I still remember the Mason band playing "Livin' on a Prayer" during the first TV time-out of the second half of every game. Gives me chills.

So does looking up at the Final Four banner, which hangs in a corner on the same side of the building as the team benches.

Larrañaga is gone, having left the school for Miami in 2011 (following another NCAA trip) after a dispute with athletic director Tom O'Connor, not so much over how much Larrañaga was being paid as how much his assistants were being paid. Three years earlier, Larrañaga had turned down Providence—his alma mater—so the sense was, at sixty-one, he would retire at Mason. O'Connor thought that too. It turned out everyone was wrong.

O'Connor hired Paul Hewitt, who had taken Georgia Tech to the national championship game in 2004, and, for two years, Mason hummed along. Then came the move to the Atlantic 10.

Now, in 2019, year eight AL (After Larrañaga) and year six in the A-10, the Patriots had finally found solid ground again—or so it seemed.

After losing two in a row, they badly needed a win at home against La Salle, and they quickly jumped to a 13–4 lead. Howard called an early time-out. "Settle down," he told his players. "They're making some tough shots. Won't last forever."

He was right. An Isiah Deas layup off a steal gave the Explorers the lead at 18–17, and a Phiri three with eleven seconds left put them up 39–37 at halftime. A third straight road win over one of the league's better teams would be huge.

But with a third straight loss suddenly very possible, Mason didn't panic. Running extremely patient offense, it built a 58–50 lead, only to see La Salle take another deep breath and come back to lead, 62–61.

The Patriots got excellent games from center Jarred Reuter, who scored 16 points—9 over his average—and from sophomore guard Javon Greene, who scored 21—12 over his average—and also pulled down 7 rebounds at six feet two.

Not surprisingly, the key basket of the game came from junior Justin Kier, who had become the team's leading scorer and (at six-four) rebounder. At season's end he would be voted the Atlantic 10's most improved player.

The day hadn't begun especially well for Kier, since he started the game on the bench, having been a few minutes late for a lifting session earlier in the week. Like a lot of coaches, Paulsen is a stickler for being on time. No one was more of a stickler than Dean Smith, who once didn't start Michael Jordan in a game in Madison Square Garden after Jordan was late for pregame meal. He'd been stuck in a hotel elevator. Didn't matter, late was late.

Kier ended up playing thirty-six minutes and, with the game tied at 67–67, got fouled—made one of two—and then made a driving layup to punch the margin to 70–67. When La Salle got to within 78–76 one last time with 1:50 left, Kier threaded a perfect pass to Jordan Miller for what turned out to be the game-clinching basket. Final: Mason 84, La Salle 76.

"That wasn't easy," Paulsen said after he'd finished talking to the media. "There's no quit in that team. Ashley's doing a really good job."

Howard was in no mood to accept pats on the back or talk about moral victories at that moment. He slumped against a wall in the hall outside his locker room and did the postgame coach's stare at the stat sheet, as if the secrets to life were buried somewhere in the numbers.

"Chances were there," he said quietly. "They made plays at the end and we didn't. I can't beat them up. For one thing, they don't deserve it. We just need to be the team that makes the plays next time."

Next time was three nights later against Duquesne. This time, the Explorers made the plays late and won, 73–72. The win put them at 8-15 overall, but 6-5 in the A-10. They had come a long way from burning that piece of paper in Atlantic City.

25

FROM HIGH SCHOOL TO
HOLLYWOOD . . . OR BUFFALO

February 12, 2019, Akron, Ohio

The first time I met Nate Oats, things were not going especially well for him. He had been named the head coach at Buffalo a little more than eight months earlier, a remarkable rise from high school coach to Division 1 head coach in two years.

But before he could even think about trying to succeed Bobby Hurley—who had left for Arizona State—he lost his two best returning players. The first to leave was second-leading scorer Shannon Evans, who followed Hurley to Arizona State. That one wasn't a shock—players often follow coaches who have recruited them from one school to another.

The second one, though, was a shocker. Justin Moss had played for Oats at Romulus High School, outside Detroit. He had gone to Toledo but encountered a heart issue. When the school refused to clear him to play, he transferred to a junior college and then joined Oats and Hurley at Buffalo. As a junior, he had been the player of the year in the Mid-American Conference while leading Buffalo to the first NCAA Tournament bid in the school's history.

But he and two teammates were accused of stealing $650 from a Buffalo football player and were thrown out of school in August, just before classes were supposed to start.

"Those were basketball things," Oats said. "They happen. Transfers happen all the time. What happened with Justin was disappointing, but it was the kind of thing that can come with the job."

What happened next doesn't come with any job. Oats was sitting in his office with his assistant coaches on the morning of October 27, planning practice and catching up on recruiting since the early national signing date was only a couple of weeks away.

His wife, Crystal, called. Initially, Oats figured it was a routine call and didn't answer. He'd call back when the meeting was over. Then she called again. And again. Oats figured he'd better answer.

She had just gotten the results of a biopsy she'd had done more as a precaution than anything else. She had cancer, a rare form of lymphoma known as "double-hit lymphoma," which is every bit as bad as it sounds.

Oats bolted from the office and drove home in a state of near hysteria. "I was crying and praying all the way to the house," he said. "Longest twenty minutes of my life."

When he got home, he and Crystal cried and prayed together. Then they began planning. The doctors were proposing an aggressive cycle of chemotherapy, the kind that was so intense it required in-patient treatment. Oats's first instinct was to take a leave of absence from his job while Crystal went through the chemo.

"She said, 'No, absolutely not. You've dreamed of a job like this for years. You're going to keep working.'"

Once that had been established, they began talking to specialists to be sure the route they were taking was the right one. Hurley set them up to see a doctor at Duke, and when all was said and done, the decision was to go with the chemo.

"In a sense, it was the *only* way to go," Oats said. "Because it's so rare, this was the treatment almost any patient with it was told to try."

With his life in crisis, Oats began his career as a head coach two weeks after Crystal's diagnosis. He did take time off when she was in the hospital in order to take care of his three daughters, the oldest of whom was eleven.

"It was a scary time," he said. "I kept telling the girls that Mommy was going to be fine, but my guess is Lexie [the oldest] could at the very least understand that Mommy was really sick."

The season began with a couple of wins over D-3 teams, and then it began to be a roller coaster: good wins over Vermont and local rival Canisius. A 60–58 loss to another nearby rival, St. Bonaventure. Then back-to-back guarantee games at Duke and at Iowa State. Along the way, as Crystal was dealing with the chemo, Oats was touched by the way people responded to what Crystal was going through.

The night before the game at Duke, he got a call from Duke assistant coach Jeff Capel. The Buffalo players had been wearing lime-green ribbons on their uniforms to show support for Crystal. Capel wanted to know if it was okay if the Duke players did the same thing.

After the game, Mike Krzyzewski stopped Oats to ask how Crystal was doing and then added, "I know Bobby put you in touch with the people at our hospital, but if you need any help at all, call *me* directly." He gave Oats his cell phone number.

Creighton coach Greg McDermott called periodically to relate his experiences when his wife had gone through a cancer scare. It was all touching—but still a very frightening period.

It was during that time that I first met Oats. Buffalo was playing at VCU three days before Christmas, and I was doing the game on television. The Bulls were 7-5, rather remarkable under the circumstances.

"We've played at Duke and at Iowa State," he said. "They're both tough places to play. I'm not sure they're any tougher than VCU."

I'm very instinctual about people—I usually like them or don't like them right away. Occasionally I'm wrong—I completely misjudged tennis star Ivan Lendl years ago. I found him humorless and dull. He's very funny and very smart. There have been others.

Most of the time, though, I'm right. I liked Oats right away. He didn't shy away from talking about what he and his family were going through and talked about how he and Crystal were relying on the doctors and their faith to get them through the ongoing nightmare.

Even aside from Crystal's health crisis, I found Oats's story fascinating.

He'd grown up in Watertown, Wisconsin, the son of a minister—his father had a PhD in theology and had loved basketball his entire life. "By the time I was in high school, I knew I wanted to coach," he said.

He went to Division 2 Maranatha Baptist University and was the starting point guard for three years. Later, he would get a master's in kinesiology and exercise science from Wisconsin. He was an assistant at Maranatha and then at Wisconsin Whitewater, a Division 3 power before taking the unusual step of going from college coaching to high school coaching.

"I got talked into it by a good friend," he said with a laugh. "Part of the appeal was that I'd be the head basketball coach, part of it was that I'd be making a lot more money."

He had met Crystal at Maranatha—she was a volleyball player—and they were making plans to get married. So money mattered. The job was at Romulus High School, outside Detroit. "First exit on I-94 when you come out of the airport," he said, laughing at the memory. "Exit ninety-six, Wayne Road. Lot of college coaches took that exit to come to Romulus."

The reason for the pay raise wasn't coaching; it was for teaching math. His annual pay jumped to about $65,000 a year—including also coaching cross-country and helping run camps in the summer.

Oats loved coaching at Romulus. It wasn't an inner-city school, but it was a lower-income school. "Eleven years there I never coached a white kid," he said. "That was just the makeup of the school. We worked hard. We practiced at six o'clock in the morning. And I became obsessed with learning how to be a better coach."

When he had time off in the summer, Oats worked basketball camps—including the famous Five-Star camp—wherever and whenever he could. He sat and listened to college coaches talk, do clinics, tell stories—anything to learn. He met a lot of college coaches because they beat a path to Romulus's front door. In eleven seasons he coached eighteen players who went on to get Division 1 scholarships.

One coach he wanted to get to know and to try to spend time with was Danny Hurley. The son of a Hall of Fame high school coach and the brother of Bobby, who still holds the NCAA record for most assists in a career, Danny had played for P. J. Carlesimo at Seton Hall and had a very up-and-down college career—although he ended up scoring more than 1,000 points before all was said and done.

"Bobby was the one who had the fairy-tale college career," Danny said. "I was the one who got booed on my home floor. He had that special feel for the game that great players have. I didn't."

I asked Danny once when he knew he wanted to coach. "I was Bobby's little brother, so I went to college with aspirations of being a pro. First time we played Georgetown I went in the lane and Alonzo Mourning swatted my shot into about the third tier of the seats. The good news was I held Allen Iverson to thirty-nine. After that night, I figured I'd better think about coaching."

He'd followed his father into high school coaching—first working for him at St. Anthony's and then, after four years as a Rutgers assistant, becoming the head coach at St. Benedict's. That meant he had to face his father at times.

"Wasn't easy," he said, laughing. "Most of the time he had better players, and he was a better coach than me."

In 2008, St. Benedict's was ranked No. 2 in the country at season's end. Who was number one? St. Anthony's, naturally.

After nine years at St. Benedict's, Danny was hired as the head coach at Wagner—on Staten Island—which belonged to the Northeast Conference. The person who pushed him hardest to pursue the job was his older brother. Bobby had stayed away from basketball for a good long while after his NBA career was ruined by a serious car accident that almost killed him.

"For a long time it was just too hard to face the game," Bobby said. "I needed to mourn for my career. But eventually I realized I missed it. So when Dan had the chance to get the Wagner job, I told him to go for it, thinking I might go with him."

When Bobby told Danny he wanted to become an assistant coach, Danny said that was fine—but he would have to go through a job interview.

"Lasted about twenty-five seconds," Danny said. "I couldn't keep a straight face."

The dynamic of the older brother/star working for the young brother/nonstar worked just fine. Bobby understood that Danny was about fifteen years ahead of him in coaching experience and Danny understood that his number one assistant was, well, Bobby Hurley.

The Hurleys went 13-17 their first season at Wagner, then went 25-6 a year later—including an upset at Pittsburgh, which was ranked in the top ten at the time. People noticed, and Rhode Island offered Danny the chance to move to the Atlantic 10. Wagner wanted Bobby to stay on and succeed his brother. He decided not to break up the act.

A year later, though, the chance came for Bobby to go to Buffalo. The money was good, he saw great potential there, and so he said yes.

And his first hire was Nate Oats.

Oats had first met the Hurleys because they were recruiting one of his players at Romulus: E. C. Matthews. Oats wanted very much to sit down with Danny at some point to talk about how to make the move from high school coach to college coach.

"I called the office one day looking for Dan," he said. "Bobby answered. We must have talked for at least an hour."

They stayed close throughout Matthews's recruitment. When Bobby took the Buffalo job, Oats called Danny to let him know that, even though Bobby had done most of the recruiting, Matthews would honor his commitment to Rhode Island.

"What would you think about going to Buffalo with Bob?" Danny Hurley asked Oats.

"I was ready by then," Oats said. "I'd wanted to make it ten years at Romulus and I was at eleven. I was making eighty-five thousand by then—still teaching math and working most of the summer. I thought Bob would offer me the third assistant's job. I'd never coached in college. When he said he wanted me to be his first assistant, I was stunned."

Hurley got Oats a raise—to $90,000 a year—but there were no math classes to teach or summer camps to work. It was just coaching.

In Hurley's second season, Buffalo won the MAC Tournament and reached the NCAA Tournament for the first time ever. Hurley had now proven to the world that he wasn't just the tough-minded point guard who had helped Duke win two national titles. Arizona State had fired Herb Sendek after nine seasons and offered Hurley the job.

"If nothing else, you'd have to agree I made a great deal when it came to weather," Hurley said. "I mean, Buffalo to Scottsdale. Seriously?"

He also got a massive raise—going from being the highest-paid coach in the MAC at $650,000 annually to being one of the lowest-paid coaches in the Pac-12, at $1.4 million a year. After two seasons, he signed a contract extension that bumped his pay to $2.1 million—base—a year.

On his way out the door, Hurley recommended to the Buffalo administration that they hire Oats to replace him. Athletic director Danny White met with the players and was told essentially the same thing. Five days after Hurley left, Oats got the job.

"It was a dream job for me," Oats said. "I mean, two years earlier I was a high school coach making eighty-five thousand a year. Now I was a Division 1 head coach making five hundred thousand. I had to pinch myself to make sure I was awake."

Then, when Crystal's phone call came on that October day, he pinched himself again—hoping he was asleep. He wasn't.

Buffalo lost to VCU, 90–69, on that December night in the Siegel Center. Will Wade was in his first season replacing the iconic Shaka Smart, and the Rams were off to a semi-shaky start. They came into the game 5-5, having lost three straight games to good teams: Florida State, Georgia Tech, and Cincinnati.

Backed by their always-loud crowd, the Rams started the game hot and stayed hot. As it turned out, the win over the Bulls springboarded them to a twelve-game winning streak, and they ended up 25-11, reaching the second round of the NCAA Tournament.

"They were experienced, we weren't," Oats said later. "We didn't handle their pressure or their crowd. Looking back, we learned a lot that night. But that night was no fun."

Life got better after that. When Crystal finished her grueling chemo, the doctors told him that she was cancer free. She is tested regularly now, but—knock wood—has been healthy since the scare of 2015.

Even with a new coach and an almost-new team, Buffalo finished third in the MAC that season and then won the conference tournament with wins over top-seeded Miami and Akron, which had been the league's most consistent team over the previous ten seasons. Oats got a raise and a contract extension. After missing the tournament the following year, the Bulls became the MAC's dominant team in 2018.

They were 15-3 in league play and 26-8 after they won the conference tournament for the third time in four seasons—twice under Oats. That earned them a thirteenth seed in the NCAAs and a first-round matchup against perennial power Arizona.

They blew the Wildcats out—winning 89–68, which, at that moment, was the upset of the tournament.

"For about twenty-four hours, we were the mid-major team everyone was talking about," Oats said with a grin. "Then UMBC happened and we became invisible."

The UMBC-Virginia game was *the* story of the tournament, one of *the* stories in tournament history. Oats didn't mind. He wanted his team preparing to play Kentucky, not basking in the Arizona victory.

And then he made a mistake—sort of—in his preparation.

Talking about playing Kentucky in the second round, he brought up the difference in experience. Kentucky, as usual, was full of one-and-dones and was starting five freshmen. The Bulls had several players in their rotation who had played key roles for two or three years, although only one—point guard Wes Clark—was a senior.

Oats wasn't accustomed to the national spotlight. He hadn't yet learned the art of talking about every opponent as if it was UCLA in the late sixties and every coach as if he was John Wooden.

"I know [Kentucky coach John] Calipari's been whining about no experience," he said. "Young, young, young. Well, we don't have that problem. We have some veteran guys."

It is a fact that Calipari constantly talks about how young his team is every year—especially after a loss. His team *is* young every year because that's the way he's built his program. As he often points out, Calipari didn't invent the one-and-done, but he pretty much perfected it. Often, before one group of freshmen has played a game, Calipari has recruited their replacements because most will be turning pro the following spring. The only coach who has come close to matching Calipari in this area is Duke's Mike Krzyzewski, who came late to the one-and-done party but has also pretty much perfected the art.

It is also a fact that Calipari does an excellent job each season getting his players to come together as a team by March. This is no small feat, convincing players who are already looking for the door to focus on winning at the college level.

But Oats *was* accurate in his description. His mistake—as he himself said later—was using the word "whine." That set off the rah-rah Kentucky media and, as they like to call themselves, "Big Blue Nation."

"You should have seen some of the letters I got and the stuff on social media," Oats said, able to laugh at it all almost a year later. "They were not happy with me—to put it mildly."

Oats was asked about his comments at his Friday off-day press conference, and he backpedaled—a little. "They are young," he said. "Look, he [Calipari] is a very good coach. I was trying to make the point that we *are* experienced." He paused and then added: "That's the way the program is built. They get pros."

Exactly. The next day those pros rolled Buffalo, 95–75. Oats learned a lesson: every opponent is UCLA, and every opposing coach is Wooden.

His team's 27-9 record and the win over Arizona did get him noticed by some big-time programs looking for coaches. At forty-three, he was looked at as a hot young coach—quite a journey from someone who'd been coaching high school five years earlier. Both Xavier and Pittsburgh asked him to come in and interview. Neither offered him the job, but Oats was pretty certain he wasn't leaving Buffalo even if offered one of those spots.

"By then I was very happy exactly where I was," he said. "We had a house we really liked and Buffalo gave me another raise [to $650,000 a year] after the season. Plus, we had everybody coming back except for [Wes] Clark. I thought we could build on what we'd done and had a chance to be really good. I didn't want to leave."

Oats was right: Buffalo was really good. Early in the season, the Bulls went to West Virginia, which was ranked at the time and won in one of college basketball's toughest venues. "Fact is, we played badly that night and won," Oats said. "They had a disappointing season, as it turned out, but that was still a confidence builder to know we didn't play well and still got out of there with a win."

A few weeks later, the Bulls went to the Carrier Dome and easily beat Syracuse, 71–59. They also won at St. Bonaventure—their first win in the fifty-one-year-old Reilly Center after six losses. "We haven't played there much," Oats said. "But it was nice to say we finally got a win in that place."

The only nonconference loss came at Marquette, three days after the Syracuse game. Oats blamed himself for scheduling two games on the road against power schools back-to-back. "We had to get up at six thirty to fly to Milwaukee after only having a day at home to catch up on schoolwork. I'm not saying we would have won—they were good—but we weren't sharp."

By the time they got to conference season, they were ranked in the top fifteen and had become everyone's target in the Mid-American Conference. The MAC is, to my way of thinking, very underrated as a basketball conference. Most years it is a one-bid league, and yet most years it has somewhere between four and six good to very good teams.

The 2018–19 season was no exception. Buffalo was clearly the league's best team, but there were four other teams in the conference that would finish the season with more than twenty wins. Three received postseason bids and all had to play on the road in their first-round games: Toledo (25-8) was sent to play at Xavier in the NIT; Central Michigan (23-12) had to play at DePaul in the CBI; and Kent State (22-11) traveled to the University of Louisiana Monroe. Bowling Green (22-12), which was one of two league teams to beat Buffalo during the regular season and lost to the Bulls in the tournament championship game, was invited nowhere.

That's the life of most mid-majors.

Buffalo was doing its best to transcend mid-major status. The win over Arizona a year earlier had focused a lot of attention on the school, the team, and the coach, especially with six of the first seven players returning.

Buffalo lost at the buzzer to Northern Illinois in January and was subjected to a court-storming. Two weeks later it lost to Bowling Green, setting off another celebration.

"This is what you've become," Oats told his team on a snowy Tuesday afternoon in Akron at their pregame meal. "I think they're handing out 'Beat Buffalo' shirts here tonight. You are now everybody's biggest game." He paused for a second and smiled. "You should be proud of that."

This was very much a team that knew who it was and what it wanted out of its season. Because of its nonconference résumé, there was almost no doubt that it would receive an at-large bid even if it didn't win the MAC Tournament. Oats knew that his players knew that, so he harped on seeding. He'd been fine with a No. 13 seed a year earlier, but he was hoping if his team dominated the conference and then won the tournament again, it might get either a No. 4 seed or worst case, he thought, perhaps a No. 5.

"We want a high seed," he told his players. "But you have to go out and earn it. No way can we expect the committee to cut us any breaks."

Akron is a school with a lot of proud basketball history. Bob Huggins was the first coach to take the Zips to the NCAA Tournament—in 1986—and then took them to the NIT a year later—before leaving for Cincinnati. Keith Dambrot coached the school to three more NCAA bids in 2009, 2011, and 2013 and five NIT bids. The Zips were 305-139 in his thirteen seasons and had twelve straight seasons with at least twenty-one wins. Three other schools could make that claim during those twelve years: Duke, Kansas, and Gonzaga.

Pretty good company.

Dambrot left after the 2017 season, lured away by Duquesne—in part because his father had played there, in part because the school offered a seven-year, $7 million contract, the kind of deal a MAC school simply can't match.

John Groce was hired in his place. Groce was only forty-five, but he'd had great success at another MAC school—Ohio University—taking the Bobcats to two NCAA tournaments, including a run to the sweet sixteen in 2012 that had ended only with an overtime loss to North Carolina.

That had gotten him the Illinois job, but after going 23-13 in his first season and reaching the second round of the NCAAs, the Illini had failed to make the tournament the next four seasons. In 2017, they came into the Big Ten Tournament with a 20-14 mark, needing at least one victory to make the Dance. They were blown out in the first round by Michigan. Two days later, Groce was fired.

Akron jumped on the opportunity to bring him back to the MAC and made him the league's highest-paid coach, at $750,000 a year. The game against Buffalo had the potential to be a season-maker. The Zips were 14-9, 6-4. Buffalo was 20-3, 9-2.

The John A. Rhodes Arena in downtown Akron opened in 1983. It is known in town simply as "The JAR." It seats 5,200, and I was disappointed to see it wasn't close to full—attendance was 2,646. There was plenty of snow on the ground and there had been snow earlier in the day, but the evening was frigid and clear. The streets had been plowed.

Minutes after I walked into the building, I ran into Dan Gavitt, the NCAA vice president, who runs the tournament. Technically, the ten committee members are in charge, but Gavitt oversees the staff that does all the real work.

Gavitt is a youthful-looking fifty-two, with an easy smile and the same kind of quiet charm his legendary father, Dave Gavitt, had. Dave Gavitt coached Providence to the Final Four in 1973, was coach of the 1980 U.S. Olympic team that didn't get to go to Moscow, played a major role in the expansion of the tournament, and—most important—invented the Big East.

Four things brought about the explosion of college basketball in the 1980s: ESPN, Selection Sunday, the expansion of the tournament to sixty-four teams, and the Big East—which brought big-time college basketball to major eastern cities.

Yes, St. John's, Georgetown, Villanova (which joined after two seasons), Syracuse, Providence, and Seton Hall all played college basketball before the Big East. None had ever been true national powers. Only Gavitt's 1973 Providence team and Syracuse in 1975 had ever been to the Final Four. None had won a national title. Gavitt brought them together and put them on national television every week with "Big Monday." He did the color himself, meaning you were never going to hear a discouraging word about any of the schools, teams, or coaches.

He got hypercompetitive men like John Thompson, Rollie Massimino, Lou Carnesecca, and Jim Boeheim to understand that what was good for the league was good for all of them, even if it didn't always appear to be good for them individually.

It was also Gavitt, as chairman of the basketball committee from 1982 to 1984, who convinced his colleagues to quit fooling around with gradual expansion—thirty-two teams; forty teams; forty-eight teams; fifty-two teams—and just go to sixty-four, beginning in 1985. There were no more byes. Everyone played in the first round, and first-round upsets became a huge part of the tournament's magic.

Dan Gavitt isn't his father—and he would be the first to tell you that. His father was much more in-your-face and direct, as I found out once when I wrote a magazine piece criticizing his good friend John Thompson and Gavitt turned around and walked away from me in the coaches' hotel lobby at the Final Four that year. I was eventually forgiven, much to my benefit, because I learned a lot talking to Gavitt in his later years.

No one in the media has been more critical of the NCAA and the basketball committee than I have been through the years. I've done it in print and I've done it at the Final Four meeting between the basketball committee (four representatives), the NCAA staff, and the U.S. Basketball Writers Association on an almost annual basis.

I can still remember Mark Hollis, the since-disgraced Michigan State athletic director, literally rolling his eyes during one meeting when I had the nerve to question the committee. Joe Alleva, the since-fired LSU athletic director, and I almost ended up in a fight—a real one—several years ago when we each suggested the other should shut the hell up.

Dan Gavitt, on the other hand, would no more confront me—or anyone else—than he would try to sing the national anthem at a basketball game. He is charming and funny, and, for the most part, he will answer questions directly.

For the most part. When I walked into the JAR to see Buffalo play Akron, I asked him what he was doing there. "Just came to see a good basketball game," he said.

In English, that meant he was doing his due diligence as the guy who runs interference for the committee by showing up at a MAC game to prove the committee and the NCAA really did care about the mid-majors. And Buffalo was a team the committee needed to be aware of with Selection Sunday now less than five weeks away.

Oats and Gavitt talked amiably for a few minutes before Oats retreated to the locker room. "I wonder if he's aware of the fact that the MAC hasn't had an at-large bid for twenty years," Oats said. "I certainly am."

Oats wasn't *really* that concerned with his team getting left out of the field on March 17. He was much more concerned with seeing his team start to play better. The Bulls had lost twice in four games, and even though they had ended up beating Central Michigan by a comfortable 90–76 margin three days earlier, they had trailed by eighteen in the first half . . . at home.

"Let's hope the way you guys played once you got your act together Saturday is the way you play tonight," he said. "That second half was us. Let's see more of that tonight."

They did . . . and they didn't. They bolted to a quick 8–2 lead—pushing the ball the way Oats wanted to see. But then, with 12:39 in the half, Jeenathan Williams, a freshman who came off the bench to give the starters a rest for a minute or two, hit a three from the right wing to make it 17–10. It was the second three-pointer Williams had made all season, and, perhaps surprised to see the ball go in, he overreacted. He was right in front of the Akron bench when the shot went in and he turned, pointed a finger, and taunted the Akron players.

Bill McCarthy, an experienced official, was standing right there and had no choice but to hit Williams with a technical. That earned Williams a spot on the bench and gave Akron a boost. The Zips went on a quick 12–4 run to take the lead at 22–21. The rest of the half was tight, Buffalo taking a 30–28 lead to the locker room at the break, thanks to a put-back basket by Nick Perkins.

Oats wasn't happy at halftime, but he didn't rant. He pointed out to his players that they wear the words "Blue Collar Mentality" on their warm-up shirts, and he wasn't seeing that. The coaches chart what they call "blue-collar plays" during the game—deflections, thirty-second violations, dives on the floor, tip-back rebounds. The team wasn't close to where the coaches wanted to be in blue-collar plays after twenty minutes.

Buffalo quickly built the lead to 47–36 at the start of the second half but couldn't shake Akron, in large part because five-foot-eight-inch sophomore guard Loren Cristian Jackson wouldn't let them get away. Every time the Zips looked finished, he found a seam in the Buffalo defense and scored. A Jackson three cut the lead to 60–55 with 3:54 left, but again Buffalo created space, punching the lead to 68–58 on two free throws by C. J. Massinburg with 2:02 to go. The lead was still 71–62 with the clock under a minute, but Akron kept making shots. Jackson hit another jumper; Massinburg hit two more free throws (he would finish the night 11-of-12 and score 21 points). But Tyler Cheese made an old-fashioned three-point play with twenty-five seconds left, driving from the wing to cut it to 73–67. Oats almost pulled his neatly combed hair out when Jayvon Graves committed that foul.

Akron pressed. Buffalo—Massinburg—turned the ball over, and Daniel Utomi hit a three to make it a one-three-point-basket game at 73–70. Seventeen ticks left. The Zips fouled instantly. Massinburg made the first free throw to make it 74–70 with fifteen seconds left, then missed the second.

But before Akron could push the ball, try to score, and call time-out, Dontay Caruthers somehow got inside the Zips rebounders, grabbed the carom, and scored. That—at last—was it. Final: 76–70.

Caruthers was, in many ways, symbolic of the "blue-collar mentality" that was Buffalo's mantra. He was a junior college transfer, a fifth-year senior, who came off the bench and played about twenty-three minutes a night—often critical minutes. At six-one, he was a ferocious defender and had a knack for making key plays and getting to the ball when a blue-collar play was most needed.

Oats was pleased to win; delighted with Caruthers's game-clinching play, but not very happy with the forty minutes.

He stood in front of his players, stat sheet in hand. It was so quiet you might have thought it was a losing locker room.

"Fellas, if I told you a team had six assists and eighteen turnovers, what would you say about them?" he asked.

"That they lost," came the answer in unison.

"And if I told you a team had six assists, what would you call that team?"

"Selfish."

Oats had made his point. He knew a road win over a solid team was a good night. His team had already lost on the road twice to teams that had been fired up to make their seasons with a win. This had been a similar situation.

This time, the Bulls had won—clinching the game on a blue-collar play.

"They get it," he said while his players were heading for the showers. "February in this league isn't easy. The weather's cold, the travel's tough. But if we're going to get where we want to get, we can't hand them excuses."

He loosened his tie. It was time to get back into comfortable clothes. Blue-collar clothes. It had been a long night—but a good one.

26

THE HALL OF FAMER
THEY MISSED

I had planned to go to the Loyola-Navy game in Annapolis on Wednesday, February 19, but a snowstorm blew through the Middle Atlantic region and the game was postponed until Thursday afternoon. I couldn't make the rescheduled game.

I already had plans. I'd known Jim Phelan for thirty years, dating to 1988, the year when Mount St. Mary's moved from Division 2 to Division 1. Phelan was almost sixty when the school made the decision to move up, but he relished the challenge. After all, there wasn't much left for him to prove in Division 2. He'd won a national championship in 1962 and been to four Final Fours, all at a tiny Catholic liberal arts school that had about 1,700 undergraduates and was home to the second-largest seminary in the United States.

I had told Dottie Phelan, Jim's wife, on the phone that I wanted to spend some time with them—not at a game where well-wishers always stopped by their table in the little VIP lounge where they retreated at halftime—but someplace quiet. She invited me to come to the house.

The Phelans have lived in the same house for thirty-five years. As I made the familiar drive west up I-270 and onto Route 15, I remembered a piece I had done for CBS in 2003, shortly after Phelan announced he was retiring at season's end.

The piece had ended with me standing on "James Phelan Way," the road one turned onto from Route 15 to get to Knott Arena, the 3,500-seat building that opened in 1987 in anticipation of the Mount's move to Division 1.

It was a cold winter day, but I wore only a sports coat over my shirt and tie. That's what you did on TV. You put on winter clothing only if you were covering the Winter Olympics.

Thankfully, I nailed the tag for the piece in one take. "Standing here, on James Phelan Way, you can look north and east and, about 350 miles away, is the Basketball Hall of Fame. That's where Jim Phelan should be someday very soon."

It was a good ending. Sadly, those who vote for the basketball Hall of Fame have chosen to ignore it. Year after year they vote in college coaches with black marks on their records for violating NCAA rules, for lousy graduation rates, for being bad guys—or, in some cases, all of the above.

Phelan's been a finalist for the Hall, but never gotten the call. Herb Magee, who has coached his entire career in Division 2, is (deservedly) in the Hall. High school coaches like Morgan Wootten and Bob Hurley are (deservedly) in the Hall. Somehow, Phelan has been overlooked.

On a clear, cold February morning, I turned left at the light where Route 15 divides the Mount St. Mary's campus from the athletic facilities. I made a quick right and, about a mile down the road, found the Phelans' home.

Jim Phelan was sitting in his den in a comfortable chair with a walker nearby. "I hate the thing," he said. "I can walk fine, but occasionally I have trouble with balance. So they want me to use the walker."

Every inch of wall space in the den is covered with awards, plaques, and photos. It is a living tribute to a remarkable life. It is Dottie's doing.

"Actually, the memento I like the best is in the living room," Jim said when we all stood up to walk into the kitchen for lunch. "The Loyola people gave this to me when I retired. I was really touched."

Mount St. Mary's and Loyola are about fifty-five miles apart and once were in the same conference. They were fierce rivals. When Phelan made his final coaching trip to Loyola, the school presented him with a rocking chair. The chair itself wasn't a big deal; retiring coaches are presented with those all the time. It was the four-word plaque on the back of the chair: "From Foe to Friend."

"That meant a lot to me," Phelan said. "We went at it pretty intensely for a long time."

Phelan had first come to "The Mount," as it is universally called, in

1954 after being an assistant coach under Ken Loeffler at La Salle—his alma mater—while the school was winning the national championship.

"I got paid six hundred dollars for the season," Phelan remembered. "The budget was so tight, they didn't take me to the Final Four. When the team got back [from Kansas City] I went to the airport to meet them. I asked coach what it was like and he shrugged and said, 'Routine.'"

La Salle's "routine" 92–76 win over Bradley in the title game was keyed by Tom Gola—who had first come to Loeffler's attention while playing at La Salle College High School when Phelan, after seeing him play, recommended that Loeffler take a look at him.

Phelan graduated from La Salle in 1951—the year before Gola arrived and was drafted in the eighth round of the NBA draft by the Philadelphia Warriors. The Korean War was going on and Phelan volunteered for the Marines. Two years later, after returning, he played in three games for the Warriors.

"My claim to fame," he likes to say. "I played in the NBA."

Loeffler hired him as his assistant for the 1953–54 season. After La Salle's success, Loeffler recommended him for the coaching job at Mount St. Mary's. Phelan was twenty-five when he arrived on campus, newly married, with the first of his five children on the way.

In his first season, the Mountaineers—arguably the least-used nickname in college athletics—went 22-3 and won the Mason-Dixon Conference Tournament title. When the team came home after the tournament, Dottie asked him how it had gone.

"Routine," Phelan answered.

Before he coached his first game, Phelan decided to wear a bow tie. He'd never worn one in his life, didn't especially like them, but Loeffler had always coached in a bow tie, so, as an homage to him, he put on a bow tie.

It became the most famous bow tie in basketball history. In fact, one of Phelan's bow ties is in a display case in the Naismith Memorial Basketball Hall of Fame. The man who made the bow tie famous somehow isn't enshrined, but his bow tie is.

Phelan *is* in thirteen different Halls of Fame. He won 830 games in forty-nine seasons at the Mount, and when the school transitioned to D-1 he twice took his team to the NCAA Tournament and once to the NIT.

But Phelan is one of those people whose importance can't be explained in numbers. In 1965, Phelan recruited Fred Carter, a gifted guard from Philadelphia. In those days recruiting was much more informal, and Carter made his decision to go to the Mount without having seen the campus.

Carter liked Phelan, knew the school had a very good D-2 program, and liked the fact that Emmitsburg was only 150 miles from home. He took the train from Philadelphia to Baltimore, and Phelan picked him up to drive him to campus.

As they drove west, Carter couldn't help but notice that the city skyline had long since disappeared and they were passing through miles and miles of farmland. As they closed in on the campus, there were a lot more cows and sheep to be seen than cars.

"Coach, I have a question," Carter said. "Exactly how many black students are there at this school?"

Phelan smiled. "Look in the mirror, Fred," he said. "They're all there."

It never occurred to Phelan to think twice about recruiting the school's first black student. Carter loved the place, had an excellent career, and spent ten years in the NBA after graduating.

After Phelan retired, I made a point of making the roughly one-hour drive (depending on traffic) at least once a year from my house to Knott Arena to see the Mount play. More important, I went to see Jim and Dottie, whom I could always find sitting near the top of the stands watching. Jim always looked calm as he sat there. He was anything but.

"My stomach's usually a mess," he said to me one night at halftime. "It's true what they say about it being harder to watch than to coach or play." He smiled. "Now I know what it was like for Dottie all those years."

In forty-nine years as a coach, Phelan was teed up by officials twice.

"The second time was pretty routine," he said. "I got mad about a couple of calls, the ref teed me up. No big deal." He smiled. "The first time the ref had teed up one of my players. I said, 'What'd you do that for?' He said, 'Because he told me I stink.' I said, 'Well, he's right.' That did it."

Jim is the quiet one in the Phelan family. Dottie is the talker. She and Jim have been married for sixty-five years. Both still have excellent memories. Jim never talks up Jim. Dottie does, but not so much about his coaching—the record there speaks for itself—but about the husband, father, grandfather, and the man.

"The night we played for the national championship, we had a lot of people over to the house to listen to the game on the radio," she said. "About ten minutes before the game was supposed to start, the phone rang. It was Jim. Our daughter Carol had been sick and I hadn't told him, because it wasn't that serious and I didn't want him to worry when he was getting ready for the biggest game of his life.

"Someone had told him—I'm not even sure who it was. He said, 'How is Carol feeling?' I told him she was fine and not to worry, he had a game to coach. He said, 'Dottie, don't ever not tell me when one of the kids is sick. I don't care what I'm doing.' I never did it again."

The Phelans had five kids and have ten grandchildren. They lost their son Larry to a heart attack in 2017, and the room still gets very quiet when his name comes up. But the rest of the kids and all the grandkids still live close by, and Lynne Robinson, the Phelans' second child, has been the athletic director at the Mount since 2007. She graduated from the school in 1979—a star on the women's basketball team—coached there, and then became assistant AD in 1987.

I asked Phelan how he felt about the current state of Mount St. Mary's basketball. The Mount had enjoyed success in the six years that Jamion Christian—who played for Phelan—had been the coach, twice reaching the NCAA Tournament. But Christian had left the previous spring for Siena, and Robinson, having had success hiring young (Christian was thirty when he arrived), went young again, hiring thirty-three-year-old Dan Engelstad.

Engelstad had been an assistant at the Mount under Milan Brown, who had been Phelan's successor, and had gone on to success as a head coach at Division 3 Southern Vermont, taking the school to the NCAAs in D-3 twice.

The team was struggling in Engelstad's first year. As always, the Mount had opened the season with a number of guarantee games, but had struggled in all their games early, getting off to an 0-9 start. Now they were 8-20, 5-11 in the Northeast Conference.

"They're going to be fine," Phelan insisted. "They've gotten better as the season's gone along. Dan's a good coach." He paused and smiled. "I think the AD made a very good hire."

Phelan was a few weeks shy of turning ninety, and getting around had become difficult. But his humor and memory were both as sharp as ever. "People ask me how I'm feeling all the time," he said. "I say, 'I'm in great shape for the shape I'm in.' Why complain?"

As I stood to go after lunch, I told both Phelans—again—how much it angered me that the Hall of Fame, which is for all intents and purposes run by the NBA these days, hadn't inducted Jim.

"Most of the guys voting probably don't even know who you are," I said. "They can't see past the league or the coaches who are on TV thirty times a year. Almost every coach who has been inducted this century has been nailed for cheating by the NCAA at least once."

Phelan knew all that. He readily admits there was a time when it bothered him, but he's well past that. As he walked me to the door through the den, he gestured around the room and put his hand on my shoulder.

"John," he said. "Don't worry about it. I got enough."

I knew he was right. I also know he deserves more.

STARTING FROM
SQUARE ZERO

Two days after I visited the Phelans, I set out on a rainy Saturday morning for Dover, Delaware.

When most Americans think of Dover, they think of the Air Force base where the bodies of Americans killed overseas are returned. Movies and television shows often depict those tragic moments: a president standing at attention, flag-draped coffins being respectfully moved from airplanes to hearses. Perhaps those scenes are dramatized, but, sadly, they are very much based on reality.

The other Dover landmark is a very different one: Dover International Speedway, which once hosted Indy Racing League races and now hosts NASCAR. It seats 95,000 people—down from 135,000 after a renovation several years back—and is massive.

It sits directly across U.S. Route 13 from the campus of Delaware State, looming over the school, almost casting a shadow wherever you drive or walk.

I drove across the Chesapeake Bay Bridge to get to Dover because Del State coach Eric Skeeters had told me I'd save thirty to forty minutes by going that way rather than driving up I-95 and then driving east. The Bay Bridge is 4.4 miles long and the lanes are narrow. There are many—including my wife—who can't stand the bridge because of its length and height and the narrow lanes.

I get it. I tend to like the bridge because I like being near water—even over water—and, there are some truly pretty places along Maryland's Eastern Shore.

The last part of the trip was all back roads, but Skeeters was right about the time saved, and I pulled my car into the parking lot next to the football stadium—Alumni Stadium—in under three hours and walked the hundred yards to the back door of Memorial Hall. I was early enough that Skeeters and the Hornets were still going through their pregame walk-through prior to a four o'clock game against Maryland Eastern Shore.

Skeeters had been hired the previous summer and had quite literally started his first head coaching job on square one. The previous season, there had been 351 teams playing Division 1 college basketball. Delaware State had finished 4-28—two of the wins against Division 3 schools. That had earned them a ranking of 351st in the NCAA's RPI rankings.

It had also earned Coach Keith Walker his walking papers in February—on the same day that the school had also fired women's coach Barbara Burgess. To say that Del State's athletic department was in some turmoil was probably an understatement. The previous fall, football coach Kenny Carter had been fired after going 3-30 the previous three seasons.

Ouch.

Skeeters wasn't even a little bit skeptical about turning the program around. He was accustomed to doing things the hard way. He had grown up in Baltimore and was a good enough lacrosse player in high school to get a scholarship to Norfolk State. He'd lasted only a semester there. "I partied, I drank, and I didn't study much," he said. Then he'd come back to Baltimore and enrolled at Catonsville Community College.

His life changed radically in November 1989 when his father, David, collapsed one day and Eric had to take him to the hospital, where he was diagnosed with AIDS. He died a few months later. Soon after that, his mother, Frances, was also diagnosed with AIDS.

And then his brother Damon died of a cocaine overdose. "It wasn't that surprising," Skeeters said. "He was a dealer. The worst part was having to tell my mother what had happened and why it happened."

Skeeters was now fifty-one and had thought long and hard about turning fifty a year earlier. "My dad was forty-eight when he died," he said. "That made me think." He paused. "Martin Luther King was thirty-nine, and look at what he accomplished in such a short life. That *really* made me think."

Skeeters finished at Catonsville and went to work for several years, before enrolling at Coppin State. There he worked as a student assistant coach for Fang Mitchell and stayed on as an assistant after graduating in 1997.

Mitchell was a true MEAC legend. He coached Coppin for twenty-eight years before retiring in 2014. He'd taken the Eagles to four NCAA Tournaments, had stunned a Gary Williams–coached Maryland team in 1990, and had beaten South Carolina in the first round of the NCAA Tournament in 1997—a fifteenth seed beating a second seed.

Mitchell was also annually chosen as one of the best-dressed coaches in college basketball. He loved clothes so much, he'd opened his own clothing store. "He took me shopping one time in Pittsburgh," Skeeters said, laughing. "He said I had to own at least two suits. If we went on an overnight trip, he brought two suits with him for the trip."

Skeeters's three years at Coppin had launched a not atypical coaching odyssey. He'd gone from Coppin to Youngstown State; to Virginia Tech; to Towson; to South Florida; to George Mason; and finally, to UMBC under Ryan Odom.

Landing there had proven crucial. Everyone in college hoops knew that Odom had taken a team that had gone 7-25 the year before he arrived to the greatest upset in NCAA Tournament history two seasons later. That was the formula every struggling mid-major or lower mid-major wanted to follow. So if you couldn't have Odom, the next-best thing was to hire one of the assistants who'd been there with him during the climb from nowhere to fame.

The success of the Retrievers had helped Griff Aldrich land the Longwood job, and it had helped Skeeters win the job at Delaware State.

One might think that a school struggling to compete in the MEAC might not have coaches pounding on its door. To think that would be wrong. Among the candidates interviewed by the school were Pat Kennedy—who had been a head coach for thirty-three seasons and had once taken Florida State to the elite eight; Keith Booth, who had starred for Gary Williams at Maryland and was the top assistant at Loyola Maryland; Anthony Evans, who'd once been the head coach at Norfolk State; and Keith Johnson, the interim coach after Walker had been fired.

"I honestly had no idea how many guys wanted the job," Skeeters said. "I drove up to Philadelphia [interviews were held in a room inside the airport], did my interview, walked out the door, and bumped smack into Pat Kennedy. We're friends, since I worked for him at Towson. My first instinct was to say, 'What are *you* doing here?' But the answer was obvious: he wanted the same job I wanted. A Division 1 coaching job is a Division 1 coaching job. Period."

Skeeters got the job. He knew it would be a long road to get Del State where he wanted it to go. But the school did have some history of success—most of it under Greg Jackson, who had been the coach for fourteen years beginning in 2000.

The Hornets had won three straight MEAC regular-season titles, beginning in 2005, and had won the tournament that first year to reach their first NCAA Tournament. There, they'd played very respectably before losing to top-seeded Duke, 57–46. The next two seasons, after failing to win the tournament, they were in the NIT.

But the program faded, and Jackson was replaced by Walker late in the 2014 season. A year later, the Hornets were 18-18 and paid their way into the CBI, losing to Old Dominion. It had been downhill from there, the nadir coming in 2018.

Skeeters is one of those people who are impossible not to like—a very important quality in a recruiter. He is almost always upbeat and seems to know everyone in every room he walks into. As he and his players left the court after shootaround, he ran into UMES women's coach Fred Batchelor. The two men exchanged hugs.

"My role model!" Skeeters said. He introduced me to Batchelor and said, "He was where we are right now when he got to UMES. Now he's a legend."

Batchelor laughed. He was in his sixteenth season at UMES and had clearly built a solid program. The Hawks would finish their season 17-14 and reach the MEAC semifinals.

The ebullient Skeeters disappeared once he was in the locker room with his players. The players had eaten their pregame meal—barbecued chicken and fish on paper plates—most sitting in the small lounge area right next to the lockers.

The team had eaten pregame meal in a restaurant once: at the local IHOP on the morning of their game at Delaware.

"This is one thing we have to improve," Skeeters said. "We have to improve this area so the players have more room and can be more comfortable when they're here."

This was alumni day, and a postgame reception with many ex-players had been scheduled. The plan was to ask enough of them to chip in to raise $10,000 to improve the locker room.

Thinking about some of the luxury hotels that pose as locker rooms at power schools, I couldn't help but think about what a different world this was. Many of the big-time coaches I knew could pay for that sort of improvement with pocket money.

There were now 353 teams in Division 1—North Alabama and California Baptist were the two 2018–19 additions. There was also a new computerized process that ranked all the teams—the RPI having been replaced by something called NET, which the NCAA thought was a more complete way to analyze each team.

The new system hadn't changed Delaware State's ranking at all: the Hornets were ranked 351st going into the game—the difference being that they were now ahead of two teams, one of them UMES, which was ranked 353rd.

Once upon a time, UMES had been an NAIA power—reaching the tournament seven times, the championship game once. In 1974, after becoming a Division 1 team, the Hawks had been good enough to get a bid to the NIT—a big deal in those days because only twenty-five teams made the NCAA Tournament. There, they'd beaten local favorite Manhattan in Madison Square Garden in the first round before losing to then-powerful Jacksonville in the quarterfinals. The Dolphins were just four years removed from playing UCLA in the national championship game.

That 1970 Jacksonville team had been led by seven-foot-two-inch Artis Gilmore, who went on to the Naismith Basketball Hall of Fame, and seven-foot Pembrook Burrows III, who went on to become (almost certainly) the tallest Florida state trooper in history.

UMES was in an odd position. After going 7-25 the previous season, the school had fired Coach Bobby Collins. Rather than search for a new coach, it had named Clifford Reed interim coach—for the entire 2018–19 season.

As Skeeters and his assistant coaches went through the Hawks' personnel, it occurred to me how small the margin is between superpower college teams and mid-major, even low mid-major, teams. If I'd figured one thing out for certain during the season, it was that everyone had guys who could play.

Almost none would play in the NBA, but almost all harbored hopes of playing pro ball somewhere when they were finished with college. The reason mid-majors could pull upsets of power schools in the NCAA Tournament might have had a little to do with power school players not taking the little-teams-that-could seriously enough, but often it had to do with the road the players on the non-name teams had traveled to get to that game and that day in their lives.

Some had started at big schools and left because they weren't getting playing time. Some had been *told* to transfer. Others had been overlooked coming out of high school and had a chip on their shoulder. In most cases, they were more experienced and tougher than the stars on the big-time teams who—for the most part—had been treated as royalty dating to their high school days.

When No. 14 Mercer beat No. 3 Duke in the first round of the tournament in 2014, Mike Krzyzewski had summed the game up very simply. "When it mattered," he said, "they were men."

He didn't say his players weren't men, but the implication was obvious. Mercer started five seniors, who'd been blooded in different ways throughout their career and had waited for this opportunity all their lives. Duke had two lottery picks on their team, but neither—Jabari Parker or Rodney Hood—had ever faced any serious adversity. Neither could, as Bob Knight often liked to say, "guard the floor," much less anyone in a basketball uniform.

Delaware State wasn't nearly as good as Mercer had been, but its roster was dotted with that kind of player.

The Hornets' leading scorer was Kevin Larkin, a graduate transfer who had started his college career at Division 2 Cheyney University before transferring to Niagara, where—after sitting out a year—he had averaged a little more than 4 points per game the next two seasons. Now, at his third college, he was averaging 16 points per game.

The team's other double-figures scorer (10.5 a game) was Saleik Edwards, also a senior, who had played two years at a junior college before transferring to Del State.

"This is a game we need to win, a game we have to have," Skeeters told his players. "We're at home, and we need to make this building a place where we expect to win."

On the whiteboard prior to the game, Skeeters and his assistants had put the names of all the UMES players with notes on each one. This was standard pregame scouting.

Skeeters had also written the keys to the game. This was also standard, although each coach is different in what he emphasizes.

—Dominate the boards. (That was pretty standard.)

—Communicate. (Also standard.)

And then, the heart of Skeeters's coaching philosophy:

—Play together . . . Stay together . . . Believe.

Every coach has some kind of message like that, but each tends to come up with a different way to say it. This was Skeeters's way.

Winning home games was, clearly, a key to any team beginning to reach respectability. At that moment, the Hornets had one Division 1 victory at home—a win earlier in the month over South Carolina State. The highlight of the season, by a wide margin, had been a stunning 73–71 upset of Delaware in December. Beating their in-state rival and doing it on the road was a huge notch in this team's belt.

The attendance was 1,087, really not bad given the weather and the records of the two teams. Memorial Hall was built in 1982 and has the cozy feel of an older, smaller gym with sections of seats in red and in blue. Everyone sits close to the court.

The two schools were meeting for the 108th time. Del State led the series, 55–52, but UMES had won the last three contests.

The game was close throughout. Neither team ever had a double-digit lead. The Hornets led 28–24 at halftime, and Skeeters wasn't very happy with how they were running their offense but even less happy with their rebounding. UMES was not a good shooting team—it would finish 2-of-7 from three-point range for the day—but was getting points off missed shots.

"That is all about effort!" Skeeters said. "Where is the effort! That should be a given by now! We're second to the floor on every loose ball!" He paused. "And yet, as tentative as we've been, we're up four. Play like you mean it and we'll be fine."

UMES was leading, 49–46, with 8:57 to go when Edwards completely took over. In the next 1:42 he buried *four* three-point shots, scoring 2 points more than his per game average during that stretch.

He single-handedly outscored the Hawks 12–1, and when his fourth shot went in with 7:15 left, Del State led 55–47 and it appeared to be an apparent lock that they would make Alumni Day a happy one—not to mention set up Skeeters to make his postgame pitch for the $10,000 needed for the locker room.

Only, it wasn't a lock. Remarkably, Del State didn't make another field goal the rest of the game. In fact, it scored only one point. UMES outscored the Hornets 15–1 in the last seven minutes. The last critical basket of the game came with eighteen seconds to go and UMES leading, 58–56. With the shot clock running down, Isaac Taylor missed a jumper and Canaan Bartley, a six-foot-one-inch guard, somehow got inside all the Hornets and tipped the ball in. The final was 62–56.

It was a devastating loss. Even Skeeters, always upbeat, was almost at a loss for words. "I don't even know what to say to you guys," he said. "Whatever it is we're doing, the basketball gods don't like it. They see everything."

He was upset with himself for not benching Ameer Bennett, who had been late for shootaround. "That stops right now," he said. "You're late for anything, you don't play. I'll play with four if I have to. We gotta play at Coppin on Monday, so you better come in here tomorrow prepared to work and to figure this out. And you *better* be on time."

His only media obligation had been his postgame radio show. After circling the locker room to offer his players a few words of consolation, he headed into the rain to cross the campus for the postgame alumni reception.

There were lots of speeches from school officials and alumni about the support Skeeters needed to get the program back to where they all wanted it to be. About halfway through, I slipped out. I had a long drive home on a rainy night.

The next morning, I sent Skeeters a text thanking him for putting up with me all day and telling him I was sorry I hadn't brought better weather—or better luck.

I didn't hear back from him that day, which concerned me a little. Was he taking the loss that hard?

The next morning he texted. "Sorry," he said. "Perfect end to a perfect day. I lost my phone at the reception." Then he added: "Gotta get Coppin tonight."

Remarkably, they did, walking into Coppin's nearly new (ten years old) Physical Education Complex and beating Skeeters's alma mater, which was now being coached by Juan Dixon—the star of Maryland's national championship team seventeen years earlier.

Dixon was in his second season at Coppin, and he was coaching thirty-three miles—and a lifetime—away from Cole Field House and his glory days at Maryland.

The win returned Skeeters back into his cheerful self. "Something to build on," he texted. "And we have a lot of building left to do."

ONE CRUCIBLE
FOR ALL

February 24, 2019, Potomac, Maryland

On the morning after my trip to Delaware, I was putting together my weekly Top 25 poll for the Associated Press, when it occurred to me that Selection Sunday was only three weeks away. As soon as that thought passed through my mind, another more pressing thought came to me: March Madness was only eight days away.

While the NCAA will claim that "March Madness," one of their 434 registered trademarks, begins in Dayton with the "First Four"—another registered trademark—it begins for me and for most real basketball fans (as in those who think there are more than five teams that matter) with the beginning of the conference tournaments—especially those in the one-bid leagues. Every one of the games in those tournaments is win-or-go-home if you want to compete in "The Dance" (you got it, another NCAA trademark), and the intensity is both exquisite and excruciating.

In all, there are thirty-two conference tournaments, and only a handful don't allow everyone to compete. That means that almost all of Division 1's 353 teams arrive in March with a chance—at least in theory—to play in the NCAA Tournament. It is unusual for a team that finishes near the bottom of its league to find magic in early March and earn the automatic bid.

But it does happen. The most recent example was Holy Cross in 2016. The Crusaders finished the regular season 5-13 in the Patriot League (10-20 overall) and were the ninth seed in the conference tournament. Since the Patriot League is a home-site event, they had to win four games on the road to win the tournament.

Which is exactly what they did, beating Loyola, top-seeded Bucknell, Army, and second-seeded Lehigh to win the championship. The victory produced one of the all-time classic coach's quotes from Bill Carmody, who had taken over the program that season.

While the nets were being cut down, Carmody's opening comment in the postgame TV interview was straight out of the coach's "there's always a black cloud somewhere" handbook: "This is going to put a lot of pressure on us next season," he said.

Carmody had just gotten back to the NCAA Tournament for the first time since his 1998 Princeton team went 27-2 with a miraculous four-game run, and his first thought was about *next* season's expectations.

Holy Cross went on to beat Southern in Dayton before losing to Oregon in a first-round game.

With one week of the regular season left for thirteen of the thirty-two conferences, each game became crucial for almost every team—some playing for home-court advantage; some playing for higher seeding; a few playing just to get into the conference tournament. Six of the one-bid league tournaments were either entirely or partially played at campus sites. Almost all played their championship game at the home of the highest-seeded team remaining. The chance to play for a spot in the NCAAs on your home court was nothing short of a huge deal.

In the Patriot League, which was played strictly at campus sites, every game was crucial in the final week: Colgate and Bucknell were scrambling to win the regular-season title, and everyone else was jockeying to be either in the top four (at least one home game) or the top six—first-round bye.

Colgate had been picked third in the coaches' preseason poll behind the perennial one-two duo of Lehigh and Bucknell. But the Raiders had come a long way under Matt Langel, who had played for Fran Dunphy at Penn and then coached under him at both Penn and Temple.

I would make the case that Colgate is one of *the* toughest jobs in the country. It's an excellent school, but to say winters are tough in Hamilton, New York, is like saying hockey is popular in Canada.

What's more, Colgate is one of those schools where basketball *might* be the third-most important sport: football and hockey are clear-cut numbers one and two, and leaving campus to visit some of the really good skiing facilities not that far away might be number three. If a basketball game inside sixty-year-old Cotterell Court draws a thousand people, that's a lot. If there's noise, it's only because members of the football team have shown up to try to lend some atmosphere to the place.

Langel had suffered through six losing seasons before breaking through in 2017–18 with nineteen wins, a trip to the Patriot League championship game, and a bid to the CIT. All that was a big deal. Colgate had last played in postseason in 1995 and 1996 when it had won the Patriot League.

To call that a fluke was unfair, but there was no doubt the presence of Adonal Foyle, who would go on to be the No. 8 pick in the first round of the NBA draft and play in the league for thirteen years, certainly didn't hurt. Foyle was six feet ten and was recruited by all the big-time schools.

But he chose Colgate because the couple he had lived with after moving to the United States from St. Vincent and Grenadines were both Colgate professors.

There were no Foyles on this Colgate team. Langel and his assistants had built the program the old-fashioned way, digging deep in recruiting to find players who had been overlooked or finding the occasional transfer who was looking for more playing time.

First place and the top seed would come down to tiebreakers. In many ways, this is a wholly unfair process, because so much is at stake. Colgate and Bucknell both finished with 13-5 league records, with Lehigh a game behind at 12-6. The first tiebreaker was head-to-head matchups. They had split. No help there. The next tiebreaker was to compare records against each team, starting with the highest finisher. That was Lehigh. Both teams had swept the Mountain Hawks. Next was American. Bucknell had split with the Eagles. Colgate had swept them, winning 83–81 at AU two weeks prior to the end of the season.

No one knew it at the time, but that victory gave Colgate the regular-season title.

What did that mean? Most importantly, it meant that if Colgate and Bucknell met for the championship, the game would be played at Cotterell Court and not at Sojka Pavilion on the Bucknell campus. It also meant that if Colgate didn't win the tournament, it would automatically receive an NIT bid. Even though it had an identical record to Colgate, Bucknell would *not* receive an automatic NIT bid because Colgate had won the tiebreaker.

Langel had done just about everything but literally look under rocks to piece together a winning program. "I can honestly say there's no piece of tape we don't look at, no email we don't respond to, no kid we don't check out if we think there's any chance he might want to play for us and might help us," he said. "Let's be honest. I've never had a kid say to me that his dream was to play college basketball in Hamilton, New York. But there are kids out there who are good players and might see our place as a chance to play."

Jordan Burns, a six-foot freshman guard who was averaging 15.8 points and 5.8 assists a game, was a perfect example. Langel had seen some tape on him two summers earlier and decided to get a look at him in person at an AAU Tournament in Las Vegas. The event is huge and is divided into different playing levels, largely based on players' reputations, scouting reports from those who scout high school players for a living, and recommendations from coaches.

"Jordan was playing at what I think was called the copper level," Langel remembered. "It was about the eighth level from the top. I walked into the gym for a game he was playing and looked for the designated seating area for college coaches. They always have one. Except here they didn't, because they didn't need one. I was the only college coach in the gym."

Burns and Rapolas Ivanauskas, a six-ten transfer from Northwestern, had been added to the Colgate roster to go along with the players who had gotten to the conference final the year before. "We got to the conference final," Langel said. "But we lost to Bucknell by twenty-nine. I honestly wondered if we could get to the level we needed to in order to take the next step."

Which was why splitting with Bucknell in the regular season was a very big deal for Colgate and for Langel. Tying for first place and then having the tiebreaker go their way was an even bigger deal.

Beneath the two top teams, there was a lot to be decided in the final week. Army had finally stopped its skid by beating Loyola midweek to raise its conference record to 8-9. That meant the Black Knights could finish tied for fourth if they could win their finale at Bucknell.

Even though they would lose the tiebreaker with American—whom they had lost to twice—and wouldn't get a quarterfinal home game, finishing .500 in the league would be a big deal, as would not having to play in the first round. Making the trip to northwest Washington to open tournament play against American was also far preferable to making the shorter trip to Lehigh to play.

What was frustrating for Jimmy Allen was that his team had played thirty games and he still didn't feel as if he had figured out its psyche. "When we've been good, we've been really good," he said. "We've been, at times, the team I thought we could be, which is a team that could compete against anyone in the league. Then there have been times where we played like we couldn't *beat* anyone in the league. If I had an answer for why it's happened that way, I'd do something about it. But I don't."

After beating Loyola, the Black Knights traveled to Bucknell knowing exactly what was at stake. The game was important to Bucknell too, because if Colgate were to lose its finale at Lafayette, the Bison could still win the regular-season title and all that came with it.

Once again, Army had a very real chance to win the game. In fact, the Black Knights led 57–43 with 8:53 to go after an 11–0 run. They still led 59–47 with 6:40 left after a Tommy Funk drive. Unfortunately for Army, Tommy wasn't the only Funk in the building. His younger brother Andrew was a six-foot-four-inch Bucknell freshman who decided this was the day to have his best game of the season. He hit a three to end the 11–0 run, then answered his brother with another three to make it 59–50.

Army still led 61–55 with 3:39 to go after Matt Wilson—who would finish with 21 points—hit two free throws. And then the Bucknell bugaboo kicked in. Army didn't score again. Bucknell senior guard Kimbal Mackenzie made two free throws to give his team its first lead in the second half, 62–61, with 10.9 seconds left. Mackenzie was in many ways symbolic of why Bucknell is so consistently good. As a freshman he had averaged 4.6 points per game. By his senior year he averaged 17.6 points per game.

Army still had a chance to win the game. But when Fox started a drive to the basket, Avi Toomer stripped him. The clock ran out. Army had lost to Bucknell by one point twice, after leading virtually the entire second half in both games.

The loss knocked the Black Knights down to a tie with Navy for fifth place at 8-10 in the conference. Navy had the tiebreaker, so Army was the sixth seed, meaning it had to play at Lehigh to open the conference tournament. Navy would play at American.

"Not only could we have won both Bucknell games, we should have won both Bucknell games," Allen said. "That's the next step. Being good enough to win isn't enough. That's not the goal. Winning is the goal."

March began on Friday with all eight Ivy League teams playing. Even though Harvard had beaten Yale for a second time when the Crimson traveled to New Haven, the Bulldogs had a one-game lead going into the penultimate weekend. They were 8-2, Harvard 7-3. In the meantime, Princeton, Penn, Cornell, and Brown were fighting for the last two spots in the tournament, since only four teams would play in New Haven.

The world of the Ivy League had changed considerably since the days of Penn-Princeton and everyone else. Harvard would sweep all four games from the two league icons but would lose twice to Cornell, once to Dartmouth, and once to Brown, and would need triple overtime at home and overtime on the road to beat Columbia.

"It's all changed since I first got here," Harvard coach Tommy Amaker said. "It started, really, with Cornell and those great teams Steve Donahue coached. But then when we came in and started to win, the rest of the league decided, 'Well, if Harvard can do it, we can do it.' Now there are no walkover games in this league. None."

That was evident on Saturday when Columbia beat Yale and allowed Harvard, which was in the process of sweeping Penn and Princeton, to tie for the lead with one weekend left.

On the last Friday of the regular season, Penn would *upset* Yale—yes, that was an accurate word—on the same night that Cornell would beat Harvard. Harvard and Yale both won their finales—Harvard escaping Columbia in overtime in Levien Gym and Yale routing Princeton. Harvard won the tiebreaker for the title on the basis of its sweep of Yale. That would prove important, because it meant that if the Crimson didn't win the Ivy League Tournament, it would get an automatic NIT bid. Yale had no such luxury.

And then there was the America East, where only first-place Vermont knew exactly where it would be seeded going into the last weekend. On Saturday, New Hampshire came to play at UMBC. Since the America East is a nine-team league, one team draws a bye on each game day. UMBC's would be on Wednesday—the last day of the regular season.

The Retrievers were 10-5 and needed a win to lock up the third seed in the conference tournament. A loss would mean they would probably drop to fourth, setting up a likely trip to Vermont if they won their first-round game.

In a sense, New Hampshire had even more at stake. The Wildcats were having a horrendous season and came into the REC with a conference record of 2-12 and an overall mark of 4-23. It had been, without doubt, the worst season Bill Herrion had ever suffered through in twenty-eight years as a head coach.

Herrion was a little more than a month shy of sixty-one but admitted to feeling more like a hundred as February finally became March. "To say it's been a long winter is a vast understatement," he said on the day before the UMBC game. "I feel worse for the players, though. They only get a few cracks at this. I've had plenty and hope to have a few more before I'm done."

Herrion was one of those coaches—much like former Harvard coach Frank Sullivan—who were little known to most of the public, but highly regarded among their peers. He had coached at Drexel for eight years and taken the Dragons to three NCAA Tournaments when they were still in the America East. He'd won twenty games five times and had also been to an NIT. In 1996, led by Malik Rose, the Dragons upset fifth-seeded Memphis in the first round of the NCAAs before losing to Syracuse—which went on to play in the national championship game.

From Drexel, Herrion had moved to East Carolina, a step up, he thought, to the CAA. Except that ECU left the CAA in (surprise) a move made for football and joined Conference USA, where it was in over its head in basketball. Herrion lasted six years, but was fired after going 9-19. He landed back in the America East (by then Drexel was in the CAA) at New Hampshire and built a solid program. In a three-year stretch from 2015 to 2017, UNH won fifty-nine games and reached the CIT twice, winning a first-round game against Fairfield in 2016.

Given that the school has never been to the NCAAs or the NIT, that was impressive.

But the last two seasons had been difficult: a plummet to 10-21, followed by the swan dive of 2018–19.

Which is why the UMBC game was huge for UNH. The last-place team in the America East doesn't play in the conference tournament. There's been talk for years about starting the tournament with an 8-9 game, but it has never come to pass, in large part because athletic directors don't think it's worth the money to have a ninth seed travel to play an eighth seed when, in all likelihood, the ninth seed has almost no chance of winning the tournament.

As a result, UNH had to win at UMBC or go into its finale against Maine knowing it would not play postseason at all. Maine had won three conference games—beating New Hampshire, Albany, and UMass Lowell. UNH had won two conference games—beating Albany and UMass Lowell. UNH needed to win its last two games to finish ahead of Maine. If it lost to UMBC but beat Maine, the Black Bears would have the slimmest of tiebreakers. Even though each had beaten Albany and UMass Lowell, both Maine victories had been on the road. Only one of UNH's had come away from home. That would give Maine the tiebreak—and the last slot in the tournament.

With its season at stake, New Hampshire played as well as it had all year—for twenty-eight minutes. Every shot went in. UMBC couldn't make a thing. Even on Senior Day for Joe Sherburne and Nolan Gerrity, the Retrievers looked flat. Even the crowd—2,002—was flat. Perhaps knowing UMBC would be playing at home the following Saturday, win or lose, almost no one seemed that concerned with the outcome.

After a Mark Carbone basket with 12:48 left put New Hampshire up 48–30, Ryan Odom called time-out. He didn't rail or rant—he challenged: "We're going to find out now what you're made of," he said to his players. "You've dug yourselves quite a hole. I know you're good enough to get out of it, but let's see if you can do it."

They did it, chipping back largely on the backs of Sherburne and Brandon Horvath. Once the lead got into single digits with more than five minutes still left, I was almost certain UMBC was going to win. This was the kind of game bad teams lost because as soon as they saw the opponent coming up fast in their rearview mirror, they got tight. Shots that had been going in stopped going in.

The Wildcats hung on for dear life right until the end. A three-pointer by Nick Guadarrama extended the lead back to 53–47 with 2:25 to go, but Rickie Council answered with a three fourteen seconds later and it was 53–50.

New Hampshire played good defense the rest of the way. The problem was it simply couldn't score. A Horvath layup with fifty-eight seconds left made it 53–52. Guadarrama was called for an offensive foul. Then Horvath missed at the other end. K. J. Jackson rebounded but was called for an offensive foul with eleven seconds left. UMBC had to foul. Still in the one-and-one, Josh Hopkins missed the front end and Odom called time with ten seconds left.

The first option with the game on the line was always Sherburne, but Odom figured Herrion would order him double-teamed the minute he touched the ball. Sure enough, the ball swung to Sherburne and the defense attacked him. Coolly, he reversed the ball to Jose Placer, and, without a moment's hesitation, the freshman drilled a three-pointer from the wing for a 55–53 lead with 2.3 seconds left.

It was the only time in the second half that UMBC led. Horvath stole the inbounds pass, was fouled, and made one free throw to make the final 56–53. In the last twelve minutes, after being challenged by their coach, the Retrievers had outscored the Wildcats 26–5.

Odom was relieved, although he felt for Herrion. "I can't imagine being on the other end of a game like this," Odom said. "Especially with what was at stake for them."

Odom was also proud of his team. Having to live with the spotlight all season after what had happened a year earlier, being everyone's target all of a sudden, and adding injuries to the loss of three seniors, they'd finished 11-5 in the conference and 19-13 overall.

"You've earned at least one home game in the tournament," he told his players. "Beyond that, you've earned the right to feel proud of yourselves."

The other team that had been in the crucible all season because of what it had accomplished the previous spring was Loyola Chicago.

Porter Moser had known it was coming—that was why he'd flown to Boston to talk to Brad Stevens about his Year After at Butler. He'd known his team wouldn't be the same after losing three of the seven players who had played most of the minutes. And yet, there were moments when even he was caught off guard by his team's newfound notoriety.

"We scrimmaged Indiana preseason," he said. "And they really hammered us. Our guys just weren't ready to play a team that good that early. Afterward, when I talked to [IU coach] Archie Miller he said, 'You know, my guys were really fired up to play you tonight.'

"I thought, 'Hang on a second, you're *Indiana,* the school where Bob Knight coached, the Big Ten power. We're Loyola and *you* are the ones fired up?'

"I thought about that all the way home on the bus. Once upon a time the notion of Loyola beating Indiana was a once-in-a-perfect-storm type of thing. Now it's all different. This is who we are now. We're a Final Four team and anyone we play is going to be fired up about playing us. Actually, even though it might be hard, it's a good thing. It means we've arrived, we're on the national radar. That's what I wanted us to become. It's also what I want us to continue to be. I wanted all of us to embrace that notion."

There was plenty of evidence that Loyola was living in a different world all through the season. Some of it was good: students lining up at two in the afternoon to be sure to get into home games in Gentile Arena. "I could remember not that long ago when I could take my driver out during a time-out and hit a ball into the stands and not touch a soul," Moser said, laughing. "The only sound would be the ball bouncing off seats."

Now it was different. Moser and his players actually heard audible gasps when someone committed a turnover or missed an open shot. They lost at home to a very good Furman team and, as Clayton Custer put it, "you'd have thought the sky was falling."

Moser knew it was hard on the players, but he didn't mind it all that much. "It means we're relevant," he said.

The nadir came in the final game of nonconference play, the 45–42 loss to St. Joseph's in the Palestra, in which there were times it appeared neither team would hit a shot until the one hundredth anniversary of the building in 2027.

The Ramblers were 7-6 at that point and appeared likely to return to the middle of the Missouri Valley. But they burst from the starting gate with a 79–44 win over Indiana State. Then they found themselves on a seesaw. A bad loss at Evansville, followed by three straight wins. Then an embarrassing loss (70–35) at Missouri State, followed by two more wins. There was only one two-game losing streak—close losses at Bradley and at home against Missouri State.

Along the way they beat Drake twice, which would prove crucial. They squeaked past Northern Iowa on the road to go into the final weekend with an 11-6 conference record, meaning a win over Bradley would give them at least a share of the conference title and, because of their two wins over Drake, the first seed in the conference tournament, the automatic NIT bid, and some serious momentum going into postseason.

There had been a moment in the Northern Iowa game that was one of Moser's most gratifying. Loyola led 56–55 in the final seconds. It had been another long, tough night on the road: Senior Night, plus a "blackout" because a Final Four team was in town. Loyola was used to this by now: Indiana State had scheduled "Larry Bird night" for Loyola's visit, and every road game had been a sellout. They'd endured several court-stormings already.

But not this time. On the game's last possession, Northern Iowa ran a high ball screen to get star freshman A. J. Green open. Custer, who had struggled to shoot the ball for most of the season and had gone 1-for-10 from the floor that night, switched, got to Green—who had already scored 18 points—and forced him to change his shot. It missed, and Custer ran off the court at the buzzer, shaking his fist as if he'd hit the game-winning shot rather than just made a game-saving defensive play.

Custer had been the MVC's player of the year in 2018. But he missed his longtime backcourt mate Ben Richardson, who had graduated, and was not the same scorer he had been a year earlier.

"But it never affected his defense, his attitude, or his leadership," Moser said. "He was a great captain. I think I was almost more proud of him this year than last year because accomplishing what he accomplished was a lot harder this time around."

The regular-season finale was Senior Night at Gentile for Custer and Marques Townes. Bradley, which had beaten Loyola earlier in the season, was in town. Custer and Townes weren't losing their last home game. Townes scored 26 and Custer found his shot (5-of-7 from the floor) and had 15 points along with 5 assists. It was 48–29 at halftime, and the Ramblers cruised from there.

"To go through everything we had to go through and win the conference again was a great thing," Moser said. "We had some bad losses, and we just weren't as experienced as we had been a year earlier. But up or down they came to practice and gave everything they had every day. Nobody moped or sulked—ever." He paused. "Except maybe me, and they got me through it.

"I loved the idea that we were the top seed in the tournament. We knew we had to win to go back, and we wanted that chance desperately."

The Missouri Valley Tournament is always held in St. Louis. It is referred to as "Arch Madness." The champion receives one of the first automatic bids that is handed out—one week before Selection Sunday. The Ramblers had accomplished a lot. They knew there was still a lot left to do.

29

TALES OF JJ AND
THE LEFTHANDER

March Madness officially got underway on Monday, March 4, when the Atlantic Sun Conference Tournament began with four quarterfinal games that were played at home sites.

Like the America East, the Atlantic Sun was a nine-team league that didn't allow the ninth-place team to take part in the conference tournament. And so, last-place Stetson, which had lost to Kennesaw State, 83–82, on the last night of the season, stayed home.

The Hatters and Owls both finished 3-13 in the conference, but Kennesaw State won the tiebreaker because it had a win over third-place finisher North Florida. One of the reasons coaches object to schools being left out of conference tournaments is because it makes them an easier target for firing.

In this case, both coaches lost their jobs. Al Skinner, who'd had great success at Rhode Island and Boston College but had suffered through four losing seasons at Kennesaw State, had announced his "resignation" two weeks before season's end. Corey Williams, whose best record in six years at Stetson was 12-20, was fired two weeks after the season ended.

Kennesaw played respectably in Skinner's last game, losing to top-seeded Lipscomb, 86–71. Skinner's Owls, Jacksonville, North Alabama, and Florida Gulf Coast became the first four teams eliminated from March Madness, or "Champ Week," depending on your point of view. The only upset that night was a mild one—fifth-seeded New Jersey Tech beating fourth-seeded FGCU.

New Jersey Tech was actually a remarkable story. It had lost fifty-one games in a row at one point, going 0-30 in 2008. Jim Engles had been hired at the end of that season, and when the Highlanders broke the streak the following January, their fans stormed the court.

Engles gradually built a solid program, going to back-to-back CIT semifinals in 2015 and 2016. In 2015, when the school went 21-12, I used my vote for AP coach of the year on Engles. Shockingly (ha!), mine was the only vote he got. He wrote me a thank-you note. I'm not sure that's ever happened to me before or since.

The next night, the Patriot League Tournament began with the two first-round games, and the Horizon League Tournament also began.

The Horizon—which had produced the two Butler teams that reached the national championship game—was a strange hybrid of a tournament. The quarterfinals—two on Tuesday and two on Wednesday—were played at home sites. Then everyone took a four-day break for ESPN purposes before the semifinalists gathered in Detroit the following Monday. The semifinals and championship game were played on back-to-back nights. Eight days to play three rounds with a four-day break between quarters and semis. Makes no sense—except in TV world. If ESPN told one of the one-bid leagues to figure out a way to play its championship game on New Year's Day, that's when it would be played.

Two teams didn't make it to the Horizon League Tournament: Cleveland State and Milwaukee. Both had second-year coaches. Milwaukee's Pat Baldwin survived, no doubt in part because he'd managed sixteen wins the year before. Cleveland State's Dennis Felton held on to his job until July and *then* was fired.

I had two abiding memories related to Cleveland State. The first had come in 1986 when the fourteenth-seeded Vikings, playing in their first NCAA Tournament, had shocked third-seeded Indiana in the first round. That was my *Season on the Brink* year, and when Bob Knight walked down to the interview room, I walked with him.

Kevin Mackey, Cleveland State's coach, was still at the podium, basking in his moment of glory—as you might expect.

Knight and I stood behind a curtain. Knight was boiling over with anger as Mackey talked. "I should fire everyone on the staff for the way we prepared for their press," he said. "Starting with me."

Mackey was now talking about his days as a Boston College assistant under Tom Davis. "I discovered this new way to go about recruiting," he said. "I focused on the inner city."

Knight's eyes went wide when he heard that comment. "Is he f——kidding?" he said. "*He* came up with the idea to recruit the inner city?"

Mackey's career would bottom four years later when he was stopped for a DUI in Cleveland and a urine test showed cocaine in his system. He pleaded no contest to the cocaine charge and avoided jail—instead going to rehab for sixty days. He never coached again, but Larry Bird hired him seven years ago to scout for the Indiana Pacers.

As it turned out, that was my last moment with Knight that day. He was called to the podium a moment later, and when he was finished—he couldn't have been more gracious giving Cleveland State credit for the win—he headed straight to the team bus without going back to the locker room. I think he was afraid if he returned to the locker room he might actually fire everyone—starting with himself. Instead, he sat on the bus in the snow and stewed.

I went back and was stopped by a guard at the door. "No media in there," he said. "Coach's orders."

The NCAA requires open locker rooms after tournament games, but apparently no one was willing to take Knight on when he left instructions banning the media. I understood the guy was doing what he was told, so I said, "Look, I understand. But would you mind going in and finding one of the coaches? They'll tell you it's okay for me to be in there."

The guy smirked at me. "No media means no media, pal. Now get going."

It was about to get ugly at that point. Doing your job is one thing; being obnoxious about it is another. At that moment, Brian Sloan walked out of the locker room. He was a redshirt freshman, the son of Hall of Famer Jerry Sloan. He heard what the guard said and stepped between us.

"Hey," he said sharply to the guard, pointing a finger. "He's with us. He belongs in the locker room. Let him in right now."

Brian's about as mild-mannered as anyone you'll ever meet, but he was also six-five and did not appear mild-mannered at that moment.

"Okay, okay," the guard said.

I thanked Brian and we shook hands. I didn't see him again for years. He went on to become an emergency room doctor at a hospital in Indianapolis. A few years ago I asked him why he was still doing it after so many years—crazy hours, less money, no doubt, than he could make in private practice.

"I like to feel like I'm doing something for people who really need help," he said. "It's exhausting sometimes, but I love doing what I do."

Didn't surprise me in the least.

My other Cleveland State memory came three years later. Cleveland State had been put on two years' probation by the NCAA for recruiting violations during Mackey's tenure. When an Emery Air Express envelope addressed to the father of a Kentucky recruit fell open and $1,000 in cash fell out, Jerry Tarkanian, who had spent most of his life fighting the NCAA, said: "The NCAA is *so* mad at Kentucky it's going to put Cleveland State on probation for another three years."

Best description of NCAA justice I ever heard.

On Wednesday, before I headed to the Big South Tournament the next day, I drove to Norfolk, Virginia, for two reasons: to see Jeff Jones (JJ) and his Old Dominion team play that night against Southern Mississippi and to spend some time with Lefty Driesell.

Old Dominion had two games left to play but had already clinched first place in Conference USA. The Monarchs had gotten their season turned around in their late-November comeback win against VCU. After starting 2-3, they'd won their last eight nonconference games before stumbling out of the blocks in conference play, dropping two of three.

The case can be made that Conference USA is about as odd a conglomerate of teams that play in the same league as there is in the country. There are fourteen teams from ten different states, and they include ODU, which hugs the East Coast; two schools from the east coast of Florida; and four schools from Texas, including the University of Texas at El Paso—which is 2,010 miles from Norfolk and 802 miles from Los Angeles.

Far-flung doesn't begin to describe Conference USA. Most of the schools had joined because they needed a conference to play football in that would allow them access to second-tier Football Bowl Subdivision bowl games. Technically, the conference champion could qualify for the College Football Playoff, but that was about as likely to happen as one of the basketball teams qualifying for the NBA playoffs. More likely—but still a long shot—was the champion getting into one of the "New Year's Six Bowls," but that would happen only if that team was the highest-ranked school from the six non–power school conferences.

The league did, however, have eight guaranteed slots in bowls like the Gasparilla Bowl, the Cheribundi Bowl, and the Serv Pro First Responder Bowl (seriously, I'm not making these names up), and those spots were the reason the schools—like Old Dominion—were in the conference.

Basketball success was a cherry-on-top-of-the-dessert type of thing.

Old Dominion had moved from the CAA, a very good basketball conference that at one time had as many as five schools from Virginia in it, to C-USA in 2014, when it moved up to the FBS.

In football, where you make one trip a week and the teams fly charter and spend one night in a hotel no more than six times a year, the long trips weren't much of a burden. But in basketball, where you played on the road Thursday–Saturday, traveled commercial, and often spent three or even four nights a week in a hotel, the travel was grueling.

It was especially tough on Jones, who was still dealing with prostate cancer treatment and the side effects from chemo.

Jones was in his sixth season, and ODU had been a consistent winner in his first five seasons. But the CAA was a one-bid league, and the Monarchs hadn't been able to win the conference tournament. In 2016, they'd lost the championship game to Middle Tennessee at the buzzer and then watched as the Blue Raiders upset second-seeded Michigan State in the first round of the NCAAs. In 2018, they'd gone 25-7 and had been the No. 2 seed behind Middle Tennessee in the conference tournament. When the Blue Raiders were upset in the quarterfinals, the path seemed clear for Jones's team.

But they just couldn't beat Western Kentucky. The Monarchs had lost to the Hilltoppers twice in the regular season and lost to them again in the tournament semifinals. And so, with twenty-five victories, they played nowhere in postseason. ODU had reached the semifinals of the NIT in Jones's second season as one of the first four teams left out of the Dance that year. They had played in the CBI in Jones's first season, if only to say they were back in postseason, and in his third year they had won something called "The Vegas 16," another pay-to-play event that had (mercifully) lasted only one year.

Jones had decided after that he was done with pay-to-play. And so, when Middle Tennessee went to the NIT after losing in the conference tournament and Western Kentucky went to the NCAAs, the Monarchs went nowhere.

Jones believed he had his best team in 2019. He had experience— four seniors and a redshirt junior. The heart-and-soul players were guard Ahmad Caver and small forward B. J. Stith—both seniors.

Stith was the third member of his family to play for Jones. His father, Bryant, had played for Jones at Virginia and, after playing in the NBA for ten years, was now one of his assistant coaches. B.J.'s older brother Brandan had graduated from ODU a year earlier.

After dropping their conference opener at Marshall, ODU came home to play Western Kentucky—their tormentor of the previous season. The first seven minutes were pure torture: the Monarchs missed eleven straight shots and had four turnovers. They trailed 21–0 until Caver hit a jumper with 12:37 left in the first half.

As soon as Caver proved there was an actual basket at Old Dominion's end of the court, the game changed completely. In the next twenty-seven minutes, ODU outscored WKU 58–30 and led 58–51 with five minutes to go. From there, the Monarchs held on for a 66–63 win.

"About as remarkable a game as I've ever coached," Jones would say later. "I mean, at 21–0 we were dead in the water. I had no idea what to do. They showed what a resilient bunch they are coming back like that."

That had been evident in November in the turnaround against VCU when they had trailed 32–15 in the first half and come back to win 62–52. VCU would go on to win twenty-five games and make the NCAA Tournament. Western Kentucky ended up 20-14, not as good, but a solid team. To come back against quality teams like that said a lot to Jones about his team.

After the 1-2 start in conference play, the Monarchs had gone on a 12-1 skein and had clinched the regular-season title with a week still to play, with another escape, this one 65–64 at Texas San Antonio.

C-USA had unveiled a truly strange new scheduling format for the 2019 season. No one knew who their last four games would be against until the last weekend in February. Instead, after fourteen conference games, the teams were divided into three tiers: 1-5, 6-10, and 11-14.

Since Old Dominion was in first place, it would play its last four games against the teams that were second, third, fourth, and fifth—two home games, two road games.

The purpose of this oddball scheduling was twofold: to increase the conference's chances of a second bid by improving the NET for the top teams, keeping them away from late-season games against bad teams; and to improve the chances that the champion would get a higher NCAA seed—again by not playing bad teams late, thus improving their overall strength of schedule.

The concept was a brave one, but it did absolutely no good. C-USA had no chance to get an at-large bid. Old Dominion, which ended up winning both the regular season and the conference tournament, was a No. 14 seed, deep in the one-bid ghetto. The lowest-seeded at-large teams were No. 11s.

The first Wednesday in March was surprisingly cold—the high temperature only reaching thirty-nine. The average high for that date in Norfolk is fifty-six. It was also windy.

When Jones suggested we meet at noon, I had foolishly thought we'd be having lunch. Foolish because I had forgotten that he never ate on game day. It wasn't superstition, it was nerves—specifically a nervous stomach. He hadn't even attempted to eat anything on a game day since he'd first become a head coach in 1990.

Instead, we drove around for a while—he gave me a tour of the neighborhood where he lived and of the Norfolk shipyard. He talked about how satisfying the season had been, especially the team's ability to come through late in close games.

"We're not a great team by any stretch," he said. "We don't really have a center—so we play three. But we're a tough team, really tough."

He smiled as he said that. I don't think I've ever known a coach who didn't like having a tough team. Ask most coaches which they'd rather have—soft but talented or tough but less-talented—and they'll take the latter every time.

We finally drove back to the Ted Constant Center and walked in at two o'clock, which was when Southern Mississippi was supposed to be finishing its shootaround. ODU was supposed to have the court right afterward.

"They're late," Jones said, walking through the tunnel and seeing all the Golden Eagles still on the court. "That always bothers me. I'd never do that to another coach."

The other coach was Doc Sadler, and he was sitting in the front row of seats talking to the woman who would be CBSSportsNet's sideline reporter that night. Sadler jumped up to say hello when Jones walked in and said, "Just wrapping up here, sorry."

Jones nodded, and we walked about ten rows up in the stands and sat and watched as Southern Miss finished its work.

"I really like Doc," Jones said. "Good guy, good coach. He's got a good team. I hope we don't have a letdown tonight. The game doesn't mean anything, but I'd like the seniors to go out of here on a high note."

It was Senior Night at ODU, and since there were no home-site games in the Conference USA Tournament, this would be the final game in "The Ted," as the building is called in Norfolk, for the four seniors—unless ODU hosted an NIT game, which Jones didn't even want to think about.

The C-USA Tournament has been played in thirteen different buildings since its inception in 1996. In 2016, it was moved to a place called "The Ford Center at the Star," which was a twelve-thousand-seat building that was part of the Dallas Cowboys' headquarters—-address "9 Cowboys Way," if you were wondering.

Both the men's and women's tournaments were played there on two courts that were divided by blue curtains. Each side seated a little less than six thousand, and on the first two days, there were two games going on at once. The women played two at a time in the afternoon; the men two at a time at night.

Once again, C-USA was unique—though not necessarily better.

Once Southern Miss had left the floor and ODU started its shoot-around, I left and pointed my car in the direction of Virginia Beach to go see one of my all-time favorite basketball characters, Lefty Driesell.

I first got to know Lefty when I was the *Washington Post*'s Maryland beat writer starting in 1979. We didn't get off to a great start. The first time I went to his office to see him, his opening line was "I hear you're a Duke guy. How you gonna be fair to Murralin?" (That's Maryland in English.)

"*You* went to Duke," I answered.

"Yeah, I know, but that was a long time ago. I'm a Murralin guy now. You aren't."

I wasn't, but I explained I would have no trouble covering his team fairly. Lefty then went into a diatribe about how unfair the *Post* had been to him for years, most notably Ken Denlinger, our superb columnist who was both a mentor and a hero of mine.

At some point I made the mistake of saying that I'd never known anyone (I was a cagey twenty-three-year-old veteran at that point) in journalism who was fairer than Ken. Another diatribe followed.

"When I first got here, yo buddy Denklinker wrote a story about me with all these unanimous [anonymous] quotes from my Davidson players about how I couldn't coach; how they never listened to me; how I didn't know what I was doin'. He tried to run me outta town before I coached a game."

For several months, even as Lefty and I got to know—and like—each other, he would constantly bring up "yo buddy Denklinker" and all the "unanimous" quotes, adding, "Aah still got that story in my desk. I'll show it to you sometime."

When I asked Ken about the story, he was baffled. "I've got no memory of doing a story like that," he said, and laughed. "Of course, it's entirely possible I wrote something questioning his coaching. I *know* that's happened."

In fact, after a close loss to North Carolina State one night, Kenny had called Lefty "The Left-thinker." Lefty had offered to go outside and settle things with him when he next showed up at Cole Field House.

Finally, when Lefty mentioned for the hundredth time the story with all the unanimous quotes, I asked to see it.

"Got it right here," he said, pulling open a desk drawer and pulling out a file marked "negative publicity."

It was so heavy I could barely lift it onto the table across from his desk. Sure enough, I found a story full of unanimous quotes from Lefty's former Davidson players.

I began reading it aloud to Lefty. "That's it, that's it," he said. "Yo buddy Denklinker, trying to run me out of town."

"Lefty," I said. "This story was written by Steve Hershey. It ran in the *Washington Star*."

For a moment, Lefty said nothing. Then he stalked across to where I was standing, grabbed the story from my hand, and looked at it.

"You're right," he said. Then he paused and laughed. "Guess I owe Denklinker an apology." Another pause. "Of course, he did call me the Left-thinker, so maybe not."

Lefty *did* apologize. That was him. He would get furious with someone, then it would be over. He couldn't hold a grudge. He frequently called me early in the morning—knowing I was single and slept late—to wake me and, as he put it, "get on you."

One morning he called genuinely mad about something. He had put a couple of players who I knew were upset about their playing time "off-limits" to the media. I walked into the dorm—at twenty-three I still looked like a student—and talked to them, telling them up front that Lefty had said they were off-limits. They didn't care. "What's he going to do, bench me?" one said.

When the story ran, Lefty called, really angry. "You do that again, I'll have you arrested," he said.

"For what?" I said.

"I don't know," he answered. "I'll think of something. Meantime, I ain't never speaking to you again."

He'd never said that before. I figured I better be sure to get to practice that day to calm the waters. I walked in while the players were warming up. Before I could even sit down, Lefty came over to me.

Uh-oh, I thought, *this could get ugly.*

I braced myself. "So," Lefty said, walking up. "What's up, Feiny, you got a scoop today?"

He was smiling, almost laughing.

"I thought you were never speaking to me again," I said.

He waved his hand and said, "Oh hell, son, Aahm just tryin' to keep you in line."

Eventually, I developed a decent imitation of him. In those days, Maryland held a weekly press conference that was very well attended for two reasons: one, Lefty; two, Ledo's Pizza, which was served at every lunch. Lefty often graded the pizzas, so much so that the late Gordon Beard, then the local AP reporter, did a story once on which Ledo's pizzas Lefty liked best.

"Bacon's number one," Lefty said—and went from there.

It was at one of those press conferences that Lefty gave his "Aaah can coach" speech that became legendary.

It was also there that I asked him if he would accept the public apology Georgetown coach John Thompson had issued the day before after an incident early in the season in which Thompson had repeatedly directed his favorite word (first half "mother," second half not repeatable in polite company) at Lefty.

"'Course I accept his apology," Lefty said. "Evabody knows, to err is human, to forgive divine, and Aahm divine."

He really was divine to cover. One day Lefty walked into the press conference and said, "Faahnsteen, evabody says you do me really well."

"I'm okay," I said.

"Tell you what," he went on. "You be me and I'll be you." He pointed at the chair he usually sat in.

Everybody was urging me on.

Lefty sat in my usual seat and said, "Lefty, why you such a sorry coach?"

I said, "Well, Aah dunno, you know—"

Lefty interrupted. "What are you doing?" he said. "I never say that."

"You start every sentence with it," I said.

He shook his head. "You know, Faahnsteen, you're okay most of the time, but you zagerrate too much."

A moment later we switched places. Someone asked a question. Lefty said, "Well, Aah dunno, you know . . ."

The whole room cracked up. Lefty stopped. "Did I say it? Damn, Faahnsteen, I hate it when you're right. Good thing it doesn't happen too often."

My favorite Lefty story, the one that—to me—defines who he is, took place on Halloween Night in 1984. I was working on a magazine piece on him and went on a recruiting visit to see a kid named Sean Alvarado, who lived in Anacostia—part of Kevin Mackey's so-called inner city.

There were three of us: Lefty, assistant coach Ron Bradley, and me. As we got out of the car, about a dozen kids, all in costume, ran up to us screaming, "Trick or treat!"

Lefty pulled out his billfold and began peeling bills off, a couple at a time, until none were left. The kids ran off happily.

"How much money did you have there, Coach?" Bradley asked.

Lefty shook his head. "I have no idea," he said. "I just hope there weren't too many big bills on there."

That was Lefty. He'd give away his last dollar without a second thought.

Lefty and his wife of sixty-seven years (!!!), Joyce, lived in a lovely condo with great views of the Chesapeake Bay. Lefty had finally been inducted into the Naismith Basketball Hall of Fame in August. I'd been campaigning for his induction for years, knowing full well that the urban legends attached to Len Bias's death were keeping him out. His coaching résumé—786 wins, fourth on the all-time list when he retired—first coach to win a hundred games and take four different schools to the NCAA Tournament—should have gotten him in years earlier.

Plus, very simply, he'd made college basketball better by his mere presence.

I knew it was breaking Lefty's heart that he hadn't been inducted. Finally, realizing that no one involved with the Hall of Fame gave a damn what I thought, I decided to try a back channel.

I sent an email to David Stern, the former NBA commissioner. I told him that I didn't want to hear that he had no influence, because I knew he did. I said it was a crime that Lefty hadn't been elected while the Hall constantly elected coaches whose CVs were sullied by NCAA sanctions. Stern asked me to send him a complete list of Lefty's accomplishments—which I did. I also included information I had proving that allegations made that Lefty had suggested the idea of "cleaning up Bias's room" were completely untrue. I know exactly who made the suggestion but would probably get sued if I used his name here. I also know from people in the Maryland basketball office that day that Lefty flat-out rejected the suggestion.

"I'll see what I can do," Stern wrote back.

Whether it was Stern's intervention (and I think it was) or not, Lefty got elected in March 2018.

Lefty knew I'd been trying to get him elected—though he didn't know I'd contacted Stern—and he called to thank me—repeatedly. A few weeks before the induction ceremony he called and said, "I'd really like to invite you as my guest, but I only get ten tickets and I have eleven grandchildren."

I told him not to worry. He ended up *buying* nine additional tickets so his whole family could be there.

Since I'm part of the Hall of Fame as a winner of the Curt Gowdy Media Award, I get an invitation to the ceremony every year. For a mere $250 a ticket, I'm welcome to come.

I pass.

Lefty was wearing a Duke basketball shirt when he opened the door for me. He had gotten close to his alma mater and Mike Krzyzewski after leaving Maryland. "I wore this just for you," he said, laughing.

He was using a walker because, at eighty-seven, he occasionally has balance problems, but his mind couldn't have been sharper. We sat down in his office, which was filled with memorabilia, dating to his days as a high school coach. One thing was missing though: his Hall of Fame plaque.

"Oh yeah," he said. "I gave it to my grandson. I figured he'd enjoy it."

We talked about the old days in the ACC when he went head-to-head with Dean Smith, Norman Sloan, Terry Holland, and—later—Jim Valvano and Mike Krzyzewski.

He and Sloan had been friends, bonded by their frustration at trying to compete with Smith. Years earlier, Lefty had told me that he had become convinced that the real first name of the coach at North Carolina was "that goddamn Dean," because Sloan would call at least once a week and say, "Do you know what that goddamn Dean just did?!"

When I brought that story up, Lefty put a finger to his lips. "Be quiet," he said. "Don't let Joyce hear you. She gets mad when I curse."

In fact, I had used that quote years earlier, and Joyce had lectured Lefty about it. "I just told her, 'You know how Faahnstein zagerrates,'" he said at the time.

Fifteen minutes after I arrived, I looked up and it was five o'clock. I'd been there two and a half hours.

"You better get going," he said. "Jeff'll be mad if you're late. You gotta give the pregame talk, don't you?"

We both laughed. I knew I'd hit traffic heading back to Norfolk, but that was okay. I couldn't remember the last time I'd enjoyed an afternoon more.

Maybe I should have given the pregame speech that night.

Not surprisingly, Old Dominion got off to a shaky start. This wasn't unusual on Senior Nights, and it wasn't unusual for this team. Often it took a while for Caver and Stith to get going, and if they weren't making shots, there weren't a lot of other options.

The first half wasn't all that different from the first half of the VCU game back in November. The Monarchs were cold, Southern Miss not exactly hot, but at least warm. The Golden Eagles led 31–20 late, before ODU scored the last four points of the half to make it 31–24.

My mind shot back to November again, when VCU had led 32–15 before ODU closed to 32–20 at the break and then outscored the Rams, 42–20, in the second half.

But this wasn't meant to be, as Yogi Berra might say, "déjà vu all over again."

Old Dominion did start fast in the second half, tying the game at 34–34 with a quick 10–3 run. That brought the sellout crowd of 8,215 into the game. The Ted had been quiet throughout the first half. Now it got very loud.

But even when it looked as if the Monarchs might pull away, it never happened. They simply couldn't build a lead. Several times, they led by two but could never extend that margin. Caver gave ODU what turned out to be its last lead at 45–43 when he hit a jumper with 6:29 left. But Cortez Edwards answered that right away to tie the score, and then Dominic Magee stole the ball from Caver and fed Edwards, who was fouled. He made only one of two free throws for a 46–45 lead, but Southern Miss never looked back from there. The Golden Eagles' lead reached 52–45 before Justice Kithcart, the only Monarch to shoot better than 50 percent for the night, made a layup.

ODU didn't quit, and they closed to 55–52 one last time when Stith made his second basket of the night with 1:09 to go. But Southern Miss ran its offense perfectly and got a dunk from Edwards and two more free throws to make the final 59–52.

"Well, at least we were consistent," Jones said, greeting Jim Miller and Terry Gates, who had been teammates of his at Virginia, after his postgame press conference. "We shot poorly, we passed poorly, we defended poorly. We were just bad." He shrugged. "One of those nights."

Moments earlier, in that press conference, Jones had credited Southern Miss for outplaying his team—which it had.

The simple fact was Old Dominion wasn't likely to beat anyone on a night when Caver made 3-of-10 shots and had 5 turnovers, and Stith was worse, making just 2-of-13. The two stars combined for 16 points—18 points below their combined per-game average.

Jones wasn't happy, but he knew the game would ultimately have no bearing on his team's season. That would be decided in another week at the conference tournament, in beautiful downtown Frisco, Texas.

I headed to my car. Next stop: Buies Creek, North Carolina.

IN THE LAND OF
THE CAMELS

The Big South conference tournament had started on Tuesday—with three games played on campus sites. The league had added two teams for the 2018–19 season, South Carolina Upstate and Hampton, so it now had eleven teams. That meant three teams had to be eliminated before the quarterfinals.

One of those teams was Longwood, which had finished 5-11 in conference play, losing five of its last seven games after Griff Aldrich had to kick Isaiah Walton, his leading scorer, off the team. Walton had been Longwood's best player before Aldrich arrived and hadn't taken especially well to the discipline Aldrich was trying to bring to the place. He also had a problem with getting to class and, after pleading and cajoling, even threatening, Aldrich felt he had no choice.

He suspended him on January 30, but when Walton failed to respond what was clearly his last chance, Aldrich threw him off the team for good. Even after missing eight games early in the season with an injury, Walton was averaging 17.8 points and 6.5 rebounds a night. Very few teams can afford to lose their best player. A school like Longwood, trying to build after winning seven games a year earlier, absolutely can't afford to lose someone that talented.

"I felt like I had to do it for the sake of the kid," Aldrich said. "I hated doing it because it affected everyone on the team. But it had reached the point where it would have been selfish of me to not try to get him to get his act together."

If that sounds like coach-speak, consider this: Walton was a redshirt senior. Keeping him eligible for another month and using him to help win a few more games would have been easy. Aldrich took the more difficult route.

Without Walton, the Lancers struggled. They dropped to ninth place in the final standings, meaning they had to play a first-round game at Hampton. They didn't play poorly, losing 77–71. They finished with a 16-18 record—a disappointing finish, but still a nine-game improvement that left a lot of hope for the future.

The Big South had a tournament format unlike any other conference: after the three first-round games, the eight remaining teams would gather at the home of the top seed. In 2019, that meant no one knew where they would be on quarterfinal day until Campbell beat Radford on the final night of the regular season. The Camels' 64–62 victory meant the two schools both finished 12-4 in conference play. Campbell had beaten Radford twice—by a total of three points—and that gave the Camels the tiebreaker and home court.

The quarterfinals and semifinals would be played in the John W. Pope Jr. Convocation Center at Campbell—an eleven-year-old building that sparkled as if it had just opened. The championship game on Sunday would be played on the home court of the highest-remaining seed.

I woke up on the morning of the quarterfinals in about as upbeat a mood as I'd been in all winter, even though I had arrived at the Fairfield Inn & Suites in Dunn, North Carolina, well after midnight.

The hotel, I learned, was four years old, and *it* sparkled as if brand-new. I had a waffle for breakfast and set out for Buies Creek at about 9:30. The drive was eleven miles, most of it on back roads, but I had plenty of time since the first game didn't start until noon. The temperature was already close to fifty when I walked to my car, and I could feel spring in the air.

The weather put me in a good mood, but there was more to it than that. I have always loved the first full day of conference tournaments. I love the first game starting at noon; I love the notion of four basketball games to watch; I love the idea that every team that walks into the gym believes it has a chance to win.

"March Madness"—in any form or at any moment—isn't just an NCAA brand, it's a feeling, a culture.

The early days of March Madness, especially the one-bid conference tournaments and the first four days of the NCAA Tournament—Dayton and then the first-round games at eight different sites—are the best part of the experience.

For years, dating to my freshman year in college, the ACC Tournament was a can't-miss event for me. Even back then, I loved the first day. Until 1990 it was always played in Greensboro, and I remember paying fifty cents to park the first time I went and tingling as I walked inside the building.

Sadly, I no longer feel that way about the ACC Tournament. When I first went in the 1970s, the league had seven teams. Georgia Tech was added in 1980, and Florida State joined twelve years later. Nine was a slightly awkward number because it created an 8-9 game on Thursday night, but Friday was still a great day.

Now the league has fifteen teams, it takes five days to play the tournament, and it was actually played in *Brooklyn* for a couple of years. The ACC Tournament in Brooklyn is like Yankee Stadium being moved to Greensboro. As with most of the never-ending realignments in college athletics, the ACC, a conference built by basketball, sold its soul to the devil in the name of football. So, no thanks.

But I still enjoy the mid-major tournaments, especially the ones—like the Big South—where everyone knows only one team's name is going up on Selection Sunday, and if the regular-season champion wins the tournament, chances are no one will get an NIT bid.

I was on the Campbell campus by about 10:30 in the morning, which made life very easy. Stan Cole, who has been the sports information director at Campbell for almost thirty years, had sent me both a parking pass and a credential. It's amazing how the really good SIDs have no problem handling simple requests like parking and a credential. (I hope someone at Duke is reading this.)

I paused for several minutes to gaze at the handsome camel statue that sits directly in front of the Pope Center. Cole later told me the camel is *the* photo stop on campus tours. I could certainly understand that.

The opening quarterfinal game matched No. 7 Presbyterian against No. 2 Radford. The seedings were a little misleading, because once you got past Campbell and Radford the next six teams had finished within a game of one another. Winthrop and Gardner-Webb, seeded No. 3 and No. 4, had tied with 10-6 conference records, and High Point, Charleston Southern, Presbyterian, and Hampton had all finished 9-7.

There weren't more than two hundred people in the building when the first game began, which isn't uncommon when the home team isn't playing in the smaller leagues. Radford had brought its band and cheerleaders; Presbyterian had not. The Pope Center seats 3,095, and it would be packed for the seven o'clock game between Campbell and Hampton. But for the afternoon doubleheader, there were plenty of seats available.

Given how tight the final standings had been during the regular season, it was hardly a surprise that the quarterfinal games were close. Presbyterian led 31–27 at the half, and the game was tight until the last two minutes, when Radford's two best players, Ed Polite Jr. and Carlik Jones, made key buckets to allow Radford to escape with an 87–76 win. Polite, who normally played inside, stepped outside to make a couple of baskets, and Jones, who had been the hero a year earlier in the championship game against Liberty—hitting a buzzer-beating three to win the game—got inside the Blue Hose defense when the game was on the line.

"That's the advantage of being old," Presbyterian coach Dustin Kerns said when it was over. "There's very little these Radford kids haven't seen. They aren't going to panic in a tight situation. I thought we gave them everything we had, and when they had to, they made plays."

Presbyterian would go on to win two games in the CIT to finish with twenty wins. That success would earn Kerns the chance to move up in the mid-major ranks. He was hired in late March at Appalachian State. If there's a profile for coaches in a league like the Big South, Kerns fit it pretty closely: He was forty, and Presbyterian was his first head coaching job. He'd gone from eleven wins to twenty wins, and that was what got Appalachian State's attention.

The oldest coach in the conference was Charleston Southern's Barclay Radebaugh, who was fifty-three and had been at the school for fourteen years.

It was Radebaugh's team that pulled off the first upset of the tournament, beating Winthrop in the second game of the afternoon doubleheader. Radebaugh did something very few coaches are willing to do: he completely changed the way his team had played all season.

"We didn't press on one possession today," he said after his team's 77–63 win over Winthrop. "Before today, there wasn't a possession all season where we didn't press. That's what we do. But I knew from having played them, we couldn't press them. We had to make them play half-court offense and this was the only way to do it. It's to the kids' credit that they adapted so well and so quickly."

Radebaugh's team got 63 points—Winthrop's total—from three players, all underclassmen: junior Christian Keeling had 25 points; freshman point guard Dontrell Shuler had 22, and sophomore Phlandrous Fleming Jr. had 16.

Winthrop's leading scorer, Nych Smith, had a terrible shooting day, going 5-for-20 from the field. The only reason the game stayed close was senior point guard Bjorn Broman, who didn't want his college career to end. Every time it seemed Winthrop was done, Broman would make a shot. He scored 18 points—reaching 1,000 for his career—shooting 6-of-11 from the floor, five of the makes from outside the three-point line.

"He just didn't want to let us lose," Coach Pat Kelsey said after the game. "That's just who he is."

Almost every college basketball player closes his career in a game his team loses. Only the teams that win the national championship, the NIT, the CIT, or the CBI are guaranteed to finish the season with a win. Occasionally, a team that doesn't qualify for a conference tournament might win a finale, but even then, they're left with the bitter feeling of not getting a chance to play postseason at all.

Seniors always see the end coming. "You go through so many 'lasts,'" Broman said. "Last opening practice, last opening game, last home game, last conference tournament, and you're always hoping that the last game will come in the NCAA Tournament."

He smiled. "Not meant to be for us. I know this is the way most guys go out, but it's still very bittersweet. I feel good about my career here. I played in an NCAA Tournament [as a sophomore]; I got to play with my brother. I can honestly say I walk away with no regrets." He paused. "I just regret that it's over. I would have liked a couple more chances to play with these guys."

Broman's older brother, Anders, had played at South Dakota State for two years and then transferred to Winthrop, where the two had been the starting backcourt for two years, including 2016–17 when the Eagles won the conference title, played in the NCAA Tournament, and finished 26-7.

Now the end of his career had arrived—Broman had no more "lasts" left. There's nothing more real than a senior dealing with the finality of his last game.

"I'm not ready to give up basketball," Broman said. "It's been such an important part of my life for so long, I just can't envision walking away from it."

Playing overseas? Coaching? "I'd be happy with either one," Broman said.

He went to take his last shower as a college basketball player.

There were two people I absolutely had to talk to while I was in Buies Creek. One was Chris Clemons, the little Campbell guard who was the leading scorer in the country.

The other was Winthrop coach Pat Kelsey.

Kelsey was a very good coach, in his seventh season at Winthrop. Even with the disappointing loss to Charleston Southern, his team would finish 18-12—their sixth straight season with at least eighteen wins. There would be no CIT or CBI for the Eagles. "Our goal is the NCAA or the NIT," Kelsey said. "If we aren't good enough to make one or the other, we start getting ready for next season."

Basketball wasn't the reason that I wanted to talk to Kelsey. He was, I knew, a protégé of the late Skip Prosser, one of the best people I'd known in sports. Prosser had coached Loyola of Maryland for one season, Xavier for seven, and Wake Forest for six. His teams had made eight NCAA Tournaments and, in 2004, lost to St. Joseph's in the sweet sixteen in one of the best NCAA Tournament games I'd ever seen.

Prosser was not your typical college basketball coach. His favorite quote came from Ralph Waldo Emerson: "Our chief want in life is someone who will make us do what we can."

He quoted great writers often; he even quoted from one of my books on at least one occasion. I know this because I was standing outside the Wake Forest locker room on the first day of the 2007 ACC Tournament talking to Prosser about his eleventh-seeded team's 114–112 double-overtime upset of sixth-seeded Georgia Tech.

"Come in here, I want to show you something," Prosser said, taking me by the arm.

We walked into the Deacons' rapidly emptying locker room, and

Prosser walked to the whiteboard, where he had written the matchups and keys for his team prior to the game. He turned the board around and said, "This is the last thing I said to them before the game."

On the board were the words "The hardest thing in life is not rising to fight the battle. It's rising with no battle to fight."

I recognized the words right away. They weren't mine. Joel Davis, who had been Army's offensive captain in 1995, had quoted them to his teammates prior to Army's game that season at Air Force. He'd heard them from Anthony Noto, who had been his coach at the Army prep school.

"I told them the worst thing about losing today wouldn't be losing," Prosser said. "It would be waking up tomorrow morning with no battle to fight."

Anthony Noto would have been flattered. I certainly was.

On the afternoon of July 26, 2007—four months after Prosser had shown me what he'd written on the whiteboard inside the Greensboro Coliseum—I was on the phone with Lee Patterson, who had worked in public relations for the PGA Tour and is now in charge of PR for a number of PGA Tour events. I have no idea what we were talking about, but suddenly I heard Lee gasp.

"What's wrong?" I asked.

For a moment he didn't answer. Then he said, "I just got an email this second that Skip Prosser died." His voice was breaking.

"What?!!!"

Prosser was fifty-six. He'd gone for a prelunch run in brutal summer heat, gone into his office afterward, and collapsed. It was a stunning, shocking loss for everyone in basketball—for everyone who knew him. Every ACC coach showed up for the funeral.

Winthrop coach Pat Kelsey had played for Prosser at Xavier and then coached under him there and at Wake Forest. He had stayed at Wake Forest to work for Prosser's successor, Dino Gaudio, for two years and then returned to Xavier, where he worked for Chris Mack for three seasons.

In the spring of 2012, Kelsey had gotten the Winthrop job, succeeding Randy Peele. Two days after an impressive victory at Ohio

University, Kelsey—like everyone else—heard the news about the horrific massacre of twenty-six people, twenty of them young children, at Sandy Hook Elementary School in Newtown, Connecticut.

"I couldn't get it out of my mind," he said. "My daughters [Ruthie and Caroline] were five and four, just a little younger than the kids who were murdered. I had no idea what to do—or if there was anything to be done, except to mourn and grieve for those families.

"What happened at Ohio State wasn't planned. I was literally about to stand up and leave the room, and then I sat back down and just started talking."

Winthrop traveled back to Ohio on December 18 to play Ohio State—which was ranked fourth in the country at the time. The Eagles played well, before losing 75–65. Kelsey went to the interview room and answered all the usual postgame questions that coaches get asked. And then, as he stood to leave, he sat back down again.

"I'm a believer that faith matters," Kelsey said to me as we talked. "I honestly think there was some kind of divine intervention at that moment. The whole thing was completely unplanned." He shook his head. "I'm not as eloquent as I was that night. That's not me. I'm always politically correct. Something took hold of me at that moment."

After sitting back down, Kelsey abandoned any talk about basketball.

"The last thing I want to say is I'm really, really lucky because I'm gonna get on an eight-hour bus ride and I'm gonna arrive in Rock Hill, South Carolina, and I'm gonna walk into my house and I'm gonna walk upstairs, and walk into two pink rooms, okay, with a five-year-old and a four-year-old laying in that pink room with a bunch of teddy bears laying in that room.

"And I'm gonna give them the biggest hug and the biggest kiss I've ever given them. And there's twenty families in Newton, Connecticut, that are walking into a pink room with a bunch of teddy bears with nobody laying in those beds. And it's tragic.

"And I don't know what needs to be done. And I'm not smart enough to know what needs to be done. Okay? I know this country's got issues. Is it a gun issue? Is it a mental health issue? Or is it a society that's lost the fact, the understanding, that decent human values are important?

"And our leaders. I didn't vote for President Obama. But you know what? He's my president. He's my leader now. And I need him to step up. Mr. Boehner, the Speaker of the House, he's a Xavier guy, he's a Cincinnati guy. Okay, he needs to step up.

"Parents, teachers, rabbis, priests, coaches—everybody needs to step up. This has to be a time for change. And I know this microphone's powerful right now because we're playing the fourth-best team in the country. I'm not going to have a microphone like this the rest of the year, maybe the rest of my life.

"And I'm going to be an agent of change with the thirteen young men I get to coach and the two little girls that I get [to] raise. But hopefully, things start changing because it's really, really disappointing."

Kelsey was emotional, but hardly ranting. When he got home at 6:15 the next morning, he kept his word and went straight to see his girls to give them a huge hug and a kiss.

Naturally, the reaction from the right was less than positive.

"Oh, I got blasted by the right wing," he said. "It was hardly a surprise, I knew it was coming. But some of it was really serious, really angry. It didn't change the way I felt, though. I've never regretted a word I said."

He also heard from one of the Newtown families, Steve and Rebecca Kowalski. Their seven-year-old son, Chase, had been one of the victims.

They became friends, and Kelsey invited them to come to a game the next season. That night, all thirteen Winthrop players wore the names of the victims on the back of their uniforms. Some wore two names—thirteen players, twenty children who had been victims.

The Kowalskis had started a kids' triathlon in Newtown to honor Chase, who had just finished his first triathlon shortly before he was killed. In 2016, Kelsey and his wife, Lisa, started a triathlon in South Carolina. By then, they had a third child—a son named Johnny.

"When Steve and Rebecca came to the house and Johnny came running down the steps, they both froze," Kelsey said. "I wondered if they would notice. Johnny looks just like Chase. They noticed. It made them cry, of course, but I also think it gave them a moment to remember just how sweet and adorable their son had been."

I had wondered after his team's season had just ended with a thud if Kelsey would feel much like talking. Now he was starting to choke up a little. I understood. I was choking up myself.

"All I know," he said finally, "is we still haven't fixed the problem. Every time I hear about another shooting all I can think is 'Again? Really, again?' It has to stop. It just has to."

By the time the Hampton-Campbell game tipped off at just after seven o'clock, the empty building I had walked into at ten that morning was packed. The fans had come to see Campbell, but beyond that, they'd come to see Chris Clemons.

Clemons was one of those college hoops hidden gems who rarely got noticed. He'd gotten some notoriety when he'd scored 45 points in an early-season loss to Georgetown. He *was* the leading scorer in the country—averaging 30.1 points per game. Perhaps he'd have gotten more attention if he had been seen in the same shopping mall with Zion Williamson.

To be fair, Clemons had been overlooked by college basketball's big-time coaches coming out of high school for the simple reason that he was short—five feet nine—and, as much as coaches are supposed to understand that there are short players who can be stars, they tend to cross anyone under six feet off their list fairly quickly.

Clemons was short—but not little. He was a rock-solid 180 pounds and also had a forty-four-inch vertical leap. He was an excellent rebounder—averaging 5.1 rebounds a game from a guard spot.

"To judge him on just being five-nine is to not see the kind of player he is," Campbell coach Kevin McGeehan said. "He rebounds as well as any guard in the country, and no one posts him up because he's so strong. He's also as coachable a kid as you'll ever meet. He's never late for anything, he works like crazy, and he's a good student: he'll graduate in four years with a 3.0 GPA."

McGeehan had come to Campbell in 2013 at the age of thirty-six after working for ten years under Richmond coach Chris Mooney—one year at Air Force, nine at Richmond. During his second summer on the job, Pete Thomas, one of his assistant coaches, had recommended he take a look at a little guard out of Raleigh while he was at an AAU tournament in Myrtle Beach.

"I'll never forget it," McGeehan said. "It was the first day of summer recruiting and he was playing in a morning game. I watched him for two minutes, texted Pete, and said, 'This is the guy we have to have.'"

That was the beginning of an ardent courtship by McGeehan and his staff. If Clemons was playing and it was a day coaches were allowed on the road, they were there. "We really did put all our eggs in one basket," McGeehan said. "There was a definite gamble there.

"To be honest, I was nervous all summer he was going to have a game where he made nine threes, dunked the ball three times, and blocked three or four shots. Then the big guys would all go, 'Whoa, what about this kid?' Luckily for us, it never happened."

When McGeehan sat down with Clemons, he told him bluntly that if he came to Campbell he'd graduate as the school's leading scorer and would turn Campbell into a winner.

"I remember him telling me all the things that were going to happen if I came," Clemons said. "I didn't really believe it all at the time, but just about all of it has come true."

Growing up in Raleigh, Clemons had been an ACC fan in general and a North Carolina fan in specific. "You grow up where I grew up, you dream of playing in the ACC," he said. "By the time I was a junior, I knew it wasn't going to happen. I consider myself blessed to have gotten a Division 1 scholarship. It's all worked out pretty well."

Other schools at Campbell's level recruited him as a senior, but Campbell had been first and the most aggressive. Right from the start, he was a star, averaging 18.5 points per game as a freshman and being voted the Big South's freshman of the year.

And as McGeehan had predicted, the Camels got better, going from 12-18 to 19-18 to 18-16 and finally to 19-11, the top seed going into the conference tournament. During his senior season, Clemons had gone past the 3,000-point mark for his career and went into the tournament with 3,126 points—sixth on the all-time NCAA points list.

"He's not just a scorer," Presbyterian's Kerns had said earlier in the day. "He's got that feel for the game special players have. He just kind of *explodes* on you. I find myself looking around a lot and saying, 'How'd he do that?'"

That kind of summed up Clemons's college career: How'd he do that?

In addition to being a great player, Clemons was an incredibly likable kid. He was so soft-spoken that I had to lean forward to hear him while he was talking, and he punctuated most sentences with the word "man."

He was modest, but also understood that a lot of people looked up to him—if not literally, certainly figuratively.

"I like spending time with kids after games, man," he said. "I'll go back on the court and sign as many autographs or take as many pictures as they want. I think maybe they relate to me because they can almost look me in the eye." He laughed. "I'm kind of like a superhero to them. I put on my uniform and all of a sudden I have these powers."

His powers were evident that night against Hampton, a solid, well-coached team that was in its first season in the Big South. Hampton had been a power in the MEAC for years, reaching the NCAA Tournament six times dating to 2001, when it had stunned second-seeded Iowa State in the first round.

The decision to move to the Big South had been controversial, in part because Hampton was viewed as an HBCU power and because many—if not most—of its alumni believed its place was in an HBCU league.

But the Big South seemed to have more potential: the league was ranked much higher in the NCAA's NET rankings, and the possibility of postseason was more likely there. In fact, four Big South teams would play in postseason in 2019: one each in the NCAA, NIT, CIT, and CBI. Hampton, after finishing in that four-way tie for fifth in the conference, would reach the CIT semifinals.

Campbell's basketball history was very different. It had been to the NCAA Tournament only once—in 1992—and had never played in the NIT. But it had been the site of one of the first national basketball camps in the country and had hosted as guest speakers—among others—John Wooden, Dean Smith, and Lefty Driesell. Yes, John Wooden. *That* John Wooden.

The camp had been the brainchild of Fred McCall, who coached at Campbell from 1953 to 1969. It would last one week, and the cost would be $25 per camper. He enlisted his friend Bones McKinney—then the coach at Wake Forest—to help him and to bring some statewide notoriety to the camp.

It worked. By the time Wooden first showed up in 1966, there were two thousand campers. Among those who came to the camp through the years to take part in clinics and to speak to the campers were Pete Maravich, Michael Jordan, Christian Laettner, and Bobby Hurley.

They all came to Buies Creek. Talk about a legacy.

Now, though, the Camels were trying to make a different kind of history. "The good news is, we know we're going to play in either the NIT or the NCAA no matter what," Clemons said. He smiled. "But we all know the goal is the NCAA."

It wouldn't be easy even if the road to the NCAAs in the Big South led through Buies Creek. The Camels jumped to a quick 21–11 lead, but Hampton came right back to tie the game at 21. The Pirates had a pretty good guard of their own in Jermaine Marrow. He would score 22 points and do a pretty good job of chasing Clemons all over the court.

Campbell led 43–37 at the break, but Hampton started the second half on a 16–4 run and you could hear the crowd getting nervous. They had come to see the first step in a coronation, not an early March upset. Clemons sensed the same thing. On the Camels' next possession, knowing his team had to have a basket to slow Hampton down, he took the ball on the left wing, spun away from Marrow, and found six-six Ben Stanley coming to meet him. He went up, twisted in the air to create space, and laid the ball in as Stanley hammered him to the floor.

He bounced right up, smiled at Stanley, and made the free throw.

The play reminded me of something Griff Aldrich had said to me about Clemons earlier in the season. "What makes him so hard to guard is he hits tough shots all the time," he said. "The first time we played him, first play of the game, Jaylon Wilson, my best defender, is draped all over him. He hits a three practically falling out-of-bounds. A minute later, there's a whistle and he says to Jaylon, 'So, is it going to be like this all night?' Not cocky or anything but just sort of 'Okay, let's go.' We clamped down on him big-time—held him to thirty-nine."

Hampton clamped down and held him to 34, even on a night when his three-point shooting was off: 3-of-13. The problem for the Pirates was that they couldn't keep Clemons off the foul line, because he's so good at creating contact with his quickness and leaping ability. He made 17-of-19 free throws, hit the shot that finally gave Campbell the lead for good at 68–67, and left the crowd howling with glee before it was over.

Clemons is an 87.3 percent free-throw shooter. But it wasn't always that way. As a sophomore he shot 82 percent, still very good but not as good as he thought he should be. He studied tape and found that most of his misses were going a little bit long and a little bit left. So he moved to the right corner of the free-throw line and stepped back four inches from the stripe. It felt good and he shot better.

"Except he's not really an eighty-seven percent shooter," McGhee said. "He's more like a hundred percent when a game is on the line."

The final was 86–77, and you could almost feel the crowd breathe a collective sigh of relief.

The building gradually emptied during the final game of the day, Gardner-Webb's 75–69 victory over High Point. As I walked off the floor after the Campbell game, I bumped into G. G. Smith, son of Tubby and his top assistant coach.

"Good luck," I said as we shook hands briefly.

G.G. shook his head. "We're going to need it. These guys are probably the best team in the league right now."

I didn't pay much attention to the comment at the time. That's what coaches say just before they face an opponent—any opponent. Lefty Driesell once said of Dean Smith: "He's the only man in history who's won more than eight hundred games and been the underdog in every one of them."

That's what coaches do. Their next opponent is always a Lew Alcindor–led UCLA team.

Twenty-four hours later, I took G.G.'s comment far more seriously after Gardner-Webb ended Campbell's NCAA dreams with a 79–74 victory. The Runnin' Bulldogs held Clemons to 23 points—7 under his average—largely by taking the lane away from him and daring him to shoot threes. If he'd had a decent night shooting from behind the line, the Fightin' Camels (as they like to be called) would have survived. But he was 3-of-14, and Gardner-Webb advanced to the final—which would be played at Radford on Sunday after Radford got past Charleston Southern.

The Highlanders started three seniors; Charleston Southern three freshmen—again, being old helped.

Campbell's loss meant that Radford would host Gardner-Webb in the final. The Dedmon Center at Radford is 222 miles away from the Pope Center—which is also called Gore Arena by the locals in Buies Creek—meaning both teams had to take an almost four-hour bus ride on Saturday to play on Sunday afternoon.

That was what ESPN wanted. And as everyone knows, what ESPN wants, ESPN gets—especially during Champ Week.

THE MADNESS
COMES QUICKLY

On the same night that the Big South played its quarterfinal round in Buies Creek, the Patriot League played its quarterfinals at four different sites.

There was only one upset and it was a mild one: fifth-seeded Navy winning at fourth-seeded American, a disappointing finish for an AU team that had improved from 6-24 overall to 15-15 and from 3-13 in the conference to 9-9, jumping from tenth place to fourth place.

The top three seeds—Colgate, Bucknell, and Lehigh—all advanced.

Army's loss at Lehigh was one final twist of a painful knife that the Black Knights had been trying to fight off all winter. Once again they had a big lead, and once again they couldn't hold on. Army finished the first half on a 21–9 run and led 41–29 at the break. It was 44–29 when Tommy Funk opened the second half by hitting a three.

And then it was, once again, déjà vu all over again. It took Lehigh just under eight minutes to take the lead. Two Kyle Leufroy free throws with 11:50 to go put the Mountain Hawks up 48–47. They extended the lead to 60–53 (a 31–9 run for those of you scoring at home) on a Lance Tejada layup with 6:07 left.

Army was clearly dead. The run brought back bad memories from a year earlier in Stabler Arena, when the Black Knights had jumped to a quick 14–6 lead and then been buried by a 78–39 margin in the game's final thirty-four minutes. This wasn't quite that bad, but given what was at stake, this meltdown was worse.

Except Army didn't quit or roll over. Realizing that they couldn't buy a three (again), Funk and Fox kept punching the ball inside. The good news was the strategy worked; the bad news was the Black Knights went 1-of-2 at the foul line three straight times.

Still, they crept back, and when John Emezie got inside for a layup with fifty-seven seconds left—and made the free throw after being fouled—the lead was down to 70–68 and Army had life.

Jordan Cohen—who would lead Lehigh with 18 points—got inside to score, but Funk did the same, got fouled, and (finally) made both free throws. It was 72–70 with sixteen ticks left. Army fouled Jeameril Wilson four seconds later and he made only 1-of-2, leaving the Black Knights with a chance to tie.

By then, Allen had been going offense-defense every chance he got, and he put Matt Wilson and Jordan Fox back in the game. Unfortunately, Army needed a three and it had gone 5-of-26 on the night, so getting the ball inside to Wilson wouldn't do much good unless one of the Mountain Hawks was foolish enough to foul while Wilson was making a shot from the low post.

Instead, the ball swung to Fox. Even though he had struggled with his shot for much of the season and was 1-of-5 for the night, Fox was still about as good an option from outside as the Black Knights had.

But his shot rimmed out with two seconds left, and all Funk could do was foul Leufroy when he grabbed the rebound. His two free throws sealed the 75–70 final verdict.

For Army, it was a crushing end to a season that had been full of hope for a long time. Allen vividly remembered Mike Krzyzewski's postgame comment after the game at Duke: "Keep playing like that and you'll have a great season."

They had played like that—at times. After the comeback win at Lafayette in late January, they'd been 6-2 in conference play, and there was no reason to believe they couldn't win three tournament games in March.

"When I looked at the conference at that moment, I didn't see anyone we couldn't beat," Allen said. "We had leads deep into the second half against Bucknell twice and Lehigh twice. We *beat* Colgate once. It wasn't as if we weren't good enough to compete with them."

But when it mattered, they weren't good enough to beat them. Close doesn't count in basketball. "We are close," Allen said. "But that's not the goal."

The season ending on a Fox miss was, in many ways, a summation of what had gone wrong. Fox was the team's best shooter, but his shot got lost somewhere during the course of the winter. Allen had no theories on what happened.

"He never stopped working, always spent extra time in the gym, had a great attitude," he said. "I can't find anything about the kid to complain about, except we all wish—him more than anyone, I'm sure—he'd been able to make a few more shots."

Fox would graduate, and so would John Emezie. Everyone else would return for the 2019–20 season, most notably Tommy Funk and Matt Wilson—who would both be seniors.

"If you look ahead, Colgate's gotta be the favorite to win the league next year," Allen said. "They have almost everyone back from what became, without question, the best team last season.

"But I look at us and I say this: we start with the best center in the league and the best point guard. Funk's already our career leader in assists with another year to go. He's that good. We need some other guys to improve during the summer and fall to be as good as I think we can be.

"But we *are* close."

Of course, at Army, improving during the summer is never that simple. Cadets don't go on summer vacation, they go on summer assignments. Getting from close to there would never be easy—history proved that.

The first official NCAA bids went out on Sunday, March 10. The big conferences—the TV leagues, as I like to call them—were finishing their regular seasons that weekend. Selection Sunday was a week away.

There were three championship games on that Sunday: the Missouri Valley, the Atlantic Sun, and the Big South. The latter two were held at home sites: Gardner-Webb, having stunned Campbell in the semifinals, traveled to Radford for the Big South title game. Liberty, the No. 2 seed in the Atlantic Sun, played in Nashville against top-seeded Lipscomb.

Both road teams won.

Gardner-Webb, living up to G. G. Smith's prediction to me on Thursday in Buies Creek, beat Radford 72–65 to reach the Dance for the first time in school history. As I watched the Gardner-Webb kids celebrate, it occurred to me that for the players in the one-bid leagues, most of their dancing takes place before the Dance starts.

Gardner-Webb had made history of a different kind twelve years earlier, history that is only whispered about in basketball circles.

In 2007, the Runnin' Bulldogs had been invited to take part in one of the many early-season tournaments that now exist. Four power schools had been invited to play: Memphis (which would play in March in the national championship game), Connecticut, Oklahoma, and Kentucky.

The four power schools would play two home games against non–power schools and then move on to New York for the semifinals. Except Gardner-Webb messed up the script by walking into Rupp Arena and easily beating Kentucky, 84–68. That sent the Bulldogs to New York and Kentucky's players and coaches into hiding.

It also made the people running the tournament and ESPN extremely unhappy. They wanted Gardner-Webb in New York about as much as Mike Krzyzewski would be wanted at a North Carolina pep rally.

This sort of thing couldn't be allowed to happen again. And so, from that day forward, preseason tournaments have announced "semifinalists," meaning that the power schools playing in the tournament will come to the big city site regardless of the outcome of the games they play at home. The other four schools are sent to play one another at a campus site so they get the four exempt games they're promised for participating.

It's an absolutely shameful way to put on an alleged "tournament," and it takes away a good deal of the thrill for little guys when they pull an upset. But no one really cares: the tournament organizers get their money in ticket sales; the corporate sponsors get the name teams in the "semifinals"; and the TV network doesn't have to deal with the likes of Gardner-Webb.

Now, though, Gardner-Webb was in the finals of an actual tournament. Beating Radford would put them into the NCAA Tournament for the first time in school history—although it's likely that if CBS/ TBS had their way, the eleventh-place finisher in the ACC might somehow be granted the Atlantic Sun's automatic bid.

As they had done in the semifinals against Campbell, the Bulldogs played airtight defense, made the shots they needed to make down the stretch, and walked away with a resounding victory. For their efforts, they were rewarded a week later with a sixteenth seed and a first-round game against Virginia.

Radford, which had gone 22-11, went nowhere. Campbell had the league's NIT bid by virtue of being the top seed in the tournament, and there was little interest among the players or coaches in playing in the CIT or the CBI. It is very difficult for a team that has experienced the NCAA Tournament a year earlier to cope with the idea of playing in one of the pay-to-play tournaments.

The Atlantic Sun championship game matched the top two seeds: No. 1 Lipscomb and No. 2 Liberty, which had left the Big South a year earlier to join the Atlantic Sun. Just as Gardner-Webb had done, the Flames walked into a hostile arena and pulled off the upset. Allen Arena has a listed capacity of five thousand, and the announced attendance that day was 5,607. Apparently the fire marshals either took the day off or were given courtside seats.

For Liberty coach Ritchie McKay, the victory was proof that he had made the right decision in returning to Liberty after a successful run as Tony Bennett's top assistant at Virginia. He had been Liberty's coach, then left to work for Bennett for eight years, before being asked to come back to Liberty.

The Flames would be given a surprisingly high seed—No. 12—in the NCAA Tournament and would take advantage of the opportunity by upsetting Mississippi State in the first round. The only teams from one-bid conferences seeded higher than Liberty were Buffalo (a No. 6) and Wofford (a No. 7). Those schools came out of conferences that probably deserved a second bid, and most who understand basketball believed each was underseeded. All three of those teams—Liberty, Buffalo, and Wofford—won their first-round games.

The first team to officially stamp a ticket for Selection Sunday was Bradley—which beat Northern Iowa, 57–54, in the Missouri Valley championship game.

Bradley was the fifth seed and Northern Iowa was the sixth. Each had upset higher-seeded teams twice to get to the final, the real surprises coming on Saturday when they had beaten Loyola Chicago and Drake, who had tied for first place and were the top two seeds.

Drake had been picked ninth in the conference's preseason poll and had shocked everyone by going 12-6 and 23-8 in the regular season.

The Bulldogs had gone 17-17 the previous season, but they were picked near the bottom of the conference because most of their key players had graduated and because Coach Niko Medved had left after one season to take the job at Colorado State.

Darian DeVries, who had been an assistant at Creighton for eighteen seasons, was hired to take his place and got his team to buy into the notion that no one believed in them but them. The old chip-on-the-shoulder trick. It worked. Loyola had won the tiebreaker for first place and the top seed because it had beaten Drake twice.

Both teams saw their NCAA hopes go up in smoke on a warm, rainy afternoon in the shadow of the Arch.

For Drake, the loss meant they wouldn't be in either the NCAAs *or* the NIT after their wonderful season. Instead, they had to settle for the CIT, where they were sent on the road and lost at Southern Utah. Clearly they were unable to get past the two-point semifinal loss in St. Louis.

The semifinal loss might have been tougher on Loyola. After all the ups and downs of the Season After, the Ramblers had come together to win the regular season again.

"I think we honestly believed we were going back [to the NCAAs] after the way we finished the regular season," Porter Moser said. "Losing to Bradley was devastating, it really was. But it's basketball, it happens. I couldn't have been prouder of the way our kids handled everything. The culture they created made coming to practice every day a joy.

"I think the best example might have been Clayton Custer. As much as he struggled with his shot, no one could have played harder. I had a coach send me a note saying he had shown his players tape of Custer to show them what it meant to play all out.

"It was tough sometimes because so much attention got focused on our losses. But you know what? That's what you want. It means you're relevant, that your program matters not just locally, but nationally. This team continued what the Final Four team started."

Loyola went on to play in the NIT but, in spite of being the regular-season champion of a league that had won at least one NCAA Tournament game *ten years in a row* and had produced two Final Four teams (Wichita State in 2013 and Loyola), it was seeded *seventh* in their eight-team bracket and sent to play at Creighton—Moser's alma mater.

It's rough to play in the NIT a year after being in the NCAAs; it's even rougher after going to the Final Four.

The Bradley–Northern Iowa championship game was a perfect example of why conference tournaments are a good thing—even if they are a money grab in the bigger conferences. Both schools had peaked at the right time, and Bradley squeaked out a dramatic 57–54 victory. Bradley had once been a national power, playing in the national championship game in 1950 and 1954.

It had fallen on hard times in recent years, and the trip to the NCAAs would be its first since 2006 and only its second bid in twenty-three seasons.

Three tickets had officially been punched. There was a long week ahead before all sixty-eight bids were decided.

March 12, 2019, Catonsville, Maryland

It takes eight days to play the America East Tournament—largely because of television but also because of travel. Since it is a home-site event, two first-round winners have to travel to semifinal sites, and then one semifinal winner has to travel to the site of the championship game.

For the second straight season, Hartford and UMBC were playing in the tournament semifinals.

UMBC's miraculous comeback win over New Hampshire had allowed the Retrievers to finish 11-5 in conference play, one game better than the Hawks. If the teams had tied, Hartford would have had the tiebreaker since it had swept the two regular-season games.

The America East is the only conference in college basketball that reseeds after the quarterfinals. In a normal bracket, Hartford—as the fourth seed—would have been playing top-seeded Vermont, and UMBC—the third seed—would have been playing seventh-seeded Binghamton, which had stunned Stony Brook, the second seed, in the quarterfinals the previous Saturday.

After UMBC had beaten Albany in the opening game of the tournament, I had assumed that would be my last UMBC telecast of the season. The Retrievers would play their semifinal game at Stony

Brook, and even if they were to win, the championship game was on ESPN and the four letters would bring in "their own people." To me that meant two guys whose knowledge of the two teams would consist of whatever notes their researchers handed them and some pregame conversation with the two coaches.

Sour grapes? You bet.

But then, when Binghamton upset Stony Brook, I got a bonus game. And because of the reseeding, the opponent was Hartford.

One of the nice things about doing the games at UMBC was that I'd gotten to know all the America East coaches. I liked them all and, watching their teams play, was reminded that there are a lot of very good college basketball coaches not named Mike Krzyzewski, Roy Williams, Tony Bennett, or Tom Izzo.

John Gallagher certainly fell into that category. Hartford is not an easy job by any stretch. The only team in Connecticut that 99 percent of the basketball fans care about is UConn. Hartford has played Division 1 basketball since 1994. It has never reached the NCAA Tournament or the NIT.

Gallagher is about as pure Philadelphia hoops as they come. He grew up there, played for Cardinal O'Hara in the revered Philly Catholic League, and then spent four years at St. Joseph's under Phil Martelli. He was an assistant at La Salle and then at Lafayette—under Fran O'Hanlon, another born-and-bred Philly guy—then went to Hartford for two seasons, before going back to Philly to work at Penn.

When Steve Donahue—you guessed it, a Philly guy—offered him a job as his top assistant at Boston College in 2010, Gallagher took it. But two weeks later, he was offered the Hartford job and, at thirty-three, became a Division 1 head coach.

He'd kept Hartford on solid ground for most of his tenure. Twice, the Hawks had gone to the CIT—their first D-1 postseason appearances ever. Gallagher is about as upbeat as anyone I've ever met. He's one of those guys who, if he was told he'd won the lottery and then got a call an hour later saying, "Gee, sorry, someone misread the number, you didn't win," would respond, "How great is it that I got to be a multimillionaire for an hour?"

You tell someone who knows him a story about Gallagher's relentlessly upbeat nature, and the response will usually be two words: "That's Gal."

Gallagher had figured out that Hartford wasn't likely to become Vermont, which was the dominant team of the America East. But he believed he could piece together a very good team every two or three years and make a serious run at the league title. A year earlier, the Hawks had won a school-record nineteen games, finished third in the conference, and gone to the CIT. They had also been the only team to beat Vermont in the regular season.

With everybody back from that team, Gallagher thought the Hawks had their best chance to make it to the NCAAs. He had five senior starters, and the first two players off the bench were also seniors.

Hartford wasn't deep. Gallagher's starters usually played at least thirty-five minutes in a close game unless foul trouble limited them.

On paper, UMBC should have preferred a semifinal matchup with Binghamton—which in any other league would have been the case. But Ryan Odom was happy to play Hartford, if only because he wouldn't have any trouble getting his players emotionally ready to play a team it had already lost to twice.

Dean Smith often liked to say that beating a good team three times in a season was a difficult task. He usually said that before North Carolina was about to play a team it had already beaten twice. Of course, in 1981, when the Tar Heels played a Final Four game against a Virginia team that had beaten them twice, Smith insisted that the Cavaliers had a psychological advantage because they knew how to beat his team.

He wasn't wrong about the difficulty of beating a team three times—especially when the teams were evenly matched. Odom felt his team had let the game at Hartford get away in the final seconds, but had simply been outplayed when Hartford came to play in the REC. That game had been the Retrievers' only loss at home during the conference season.

When I walked into the REC about two hours before tipoff, I saw Joe Sherburne with a mop in his hands, clearing some wet spots off the floor so he could do some pregame shooting. Two thoughts occurred to me: one, Sherburne really did do everything for the Retrievers except (maybe) sell popcorn; and two, if the star of a big-time team found a wet spot on the floor before a game, he'd have half a dozen managers out there wiping it up for him. Or, in the case of Zion Williamson, closer to a dozen.

For twenty-five minutes, UMBC wiped the floor cleanly with the

Hawks. The Retrievers could do no wrong, the Hawks no right. After ten minutes, it was 28–9. UMBC was making everything it tossed in the direction of the basket; Hartford not only couldn't make a shot, it couldn't get a rebound. Every possession was one-and-done. At halftime, it was 37–19.

Before the start of the second half, as usual, Gary Stein, doing play-by-play, turned the microphone over to Paul Mittermeier, our sideline reporter. This was standard: interview Ryan Odom going off the court at halftime, talk to the visiting coach before the start of the second half. Sometimes the visiting coach was on camera, sometimes Paul just reported what he'd said.

There are some coaches who are down eighteen at the half of a win-or-go-home game in March and want nothing to do with any sort of halftime interview. Personally, I don't blame them.

But Gallagher was perfectly willing to talk to Paul. By the time he was finished I almost believed his team was going to rally. "They were great," he said of UMBC. "We were a lot less than great, and a lot less than as good as we can be. I absolutely believe we're going to rally, and I think we're going to win this game."

Gal was being Gal: down eighteen on the road, season on the line? Hey, we've got 'em right where we want 'em.

With 15:16 left in the game, UMBC freshman guard R. J. Eytle-Rock hit a three to make it 50–24. I remember wondering at that point if Gal still thought his team was going to come back and win.

He did. And, amazingly, they just about pulled it off.

It was one of those games where the trailing team finally makes a couple of shots and starts to suddenly feel confident, and the team in front starts trying to run out the clock. It had happened to New Hampshire ten days earlier in the same building. The difference was that UNH was a bad team playing on the road. UMBC was a good team playing at home, but nerves can affect good teams too.

"I think we kept thinking there wasn't enough time for them to catch up," Odom said later. "I caught myself looking at the clock a lot. We stopped running our offense the way we had been running it earlier. It was no longer 'have a good shot, take it'; instead it became 'run the clock, then take a shot.' That doesn't usually work."

It started with a Travis Weatherington three-pointer just eight seconds after Eytle-Rock's basket. When J. R. Lynch got through the

UMBC defense for a layup to make it 56–46 with 6:24 still to go, you could almost feel the tension oozing off the Retrievers every time they had the ball.

Another three, this one by Jason Dunne, cut the margin to 63–62 with 1:47 left. The lead was 64–63 when Sherburne hit a three with the shot clock way down and forty ticks left in regulation. That made it 67–63. It looked as if UMBC had survived the furious rally.

But it hadn't. Lynch again got inside for a layup and it was 67–65. UMBC ran its inbounds play perfectly and got the ball into the hands of Sherburne—a 90 percent free-throw shooter. This was exactly what Odom's team had failed to do with the lead late in the game back in January in Hartford.

Now Sherburne went to the line for a one-and-one. There were twenty-two seconds left. Two free throws would all but seal the game. Except Sherburne missed the front end. Down came Lynch on the attack again. This time K. J. Jackson fouled him as his spinning layup went in. When he made the free throw, Hartford *led*, 68–67.

In a stretch of exactly fifteen minutes, they had outscored UMBC 44–17. It was as stunning a rally as I'd ever witnessed.

Of course, the game wasn't close to over. Jackson drove to the basket, missed, but was fouled with three seconds to go. Two free throws and Hartford would need a miracle to win the game. But he missed the first. Now, if he failed to make the second, UMBC would need an offensive rebound to have any chance to stay alive. Jackson made the second.

Overtime. Naturally.

The first overtime was back-and-forth, neither team leading by more than a bucket. Lynch—who would finish with 22 points—made two free throws to give Hartford a 76–74 lead with sixteen seconds to go. Jackson missed at the other end, but Brandon Horvath got the rebound, was fouled, and made both free throws to tie the game again.

Offensive rebounding saved UMBC in this game: the Retrievers had fifteen of them, many in the crucial final minutes as the exhausted Hawks—every starter played at least forty-one minutes—just didn't have the legs or quickness to keep the better-rested, deeper Retrievers off the boards.

Overtime number two: this time UMBC jumped to a quick 80–76 lead, and Hartford rallied yet again, a Lynch three tying the game one more time at 84. Each team had a 1-for-2 trip to the line, and then Horvath converted another offensive rebound into two free throws.

By now, Lynch and John Carroll had fouled out for Hartford. Without Lynch on the floor, Hartford had trouble finding a shot. Finally, D. J. Mitchell, who had come in for him, had to shoot. Jackson got a hand on it and then got to the ball first and was fouled. His two free throws made it 89–85 with twenty-four seconds left. Dunne missed a three and Eytle-Rock rebounded and was fouled. He made 1-of-2 and—finally—it was over, 90–85.

The crowd of 3,042—largest of the season—was being led in cheers by, of all people, Odom, who grabbed the microphone to demand everyone spell out U-M-B-C. As always, at this time of year, I kept my eyes on the losers, knowing how brokenhearted they had to be.

I was happy for UMBC; I felt awful for Hartford. It was one of the most remarkable comebacks I'd ever seen, and in the end the Hartford kids had nothing to show for it.

"Except they got to walk off at the end of their careers with their heads held high," Gallagher said later. "Coaches say all the time, 'I'm proud of my guys.' Well, I couldn't be more proud of this group. They gave me everything a coach could possibly ask for."

It was one of those games where everyone leaves the building exhausted and exhilarated. Very few people around the country would even notice the score or know how that score had come about.

But for those who were there, it was a night to be remembered and savored for a long, long time.

THANKS FOR
THE MEMORIES

March 13, 2019, Brooklyn, New York

The only drawback for me to the amazing double-overtime game I had witnessed at UMBC was that I got on the road to drive to Brooklyn about forty-five minutes later than I had planned. All I can say is, it was worth it.

I was headed north for day one of the Atlantic 10 Tournament, which was being held in the Barclays Center—home of the Brooklyn Nets and semi-home of my beloved New York Islanders.

The Islanders had foolishly moved to Brooklyn when they couldn't get the town of Hempstead to commit millions of dollars to a renovation of the venerable Nassau Coliseum and had realized about fifteen minutes after arriving that the building wasn't designed for hockey and that a large chunk of their fan base wasn't going to make the trek to downtown Brooklyn to see them play.

Both sides—landlord and tenant—had agreed that the marriage wasn't working, and the Islanders were now supposed to move to a new building next to the Belmont racetrack in 2021. In the meantime, they were splitting their schedule between the Barclays Center and the Coliseum—which had finally been renovated, but too late.

I had known when I started the research on this book that I wanted to go to day one of at least one major tournament, if only because there are few more depressing places to be for players and coaches than playing in a mostly empty building with little hope of anything good coming of the last week of your season.

Yes, there was the example of Connecticut playing on day one of the

Big East Tournament in 2011, but that was a clear outlier. The Huskies had shown how good they could be in November when they'd beaten both Michigan State and Kentucky to win the Maui Invitational. They had struggled during the conference season, going 9-9, which landed them as a tenth seed in the bloated sixteen-team Big East.

But they peaked at the right time, and Kemba Walker came into his own at the right time: they won five games in five days to win the Big East title, went into the NCAAs as a No. 3 seed, and ended up winning the tournament.

That was once-in-a-lifetime, cue-the-syrupy-Disney-music stuff.

In 2019, the ACC had fifteen teams, and the Big Ten, the SEC, and the Atlantic 10 all had fourteen teams. That meant the bottom-feeding teams needed two wins just to reach the quarterfinals. For the most part, the teams playing on day one of the tournament would be long gone before the top four seeds even thought about playing a game.

But it was better than not playing at all, which is why these day ones—with the eleventh seed playing the fourteenth seed and the twelfth seed playing the thirteenth seed—existed. Or, in the case of the ACC, there were three games, the tenth seed being dragged kicking and screaming into day one.

I had decided to go to the Atlantic 10's day one for a simple reason: the conference asked me to do the games on television.

The A-10, which started as the Eastern Eight and then became the A-10 after its first expansion and decided to remain there even as it grew (much like the fourteen-team Big Ten, or in the opposite vein the ten-team Big 12 remaining the Big 12), had been around since 1976.

It had a unique TV package: two days of the tournament would be televised by NBC Sports Network; one day would be on CBS Sports Network, and the championship game would be on CBS. All would bring their own "talent" to work the games.

But day one was a TV orphan. The conference decided to produce the games themselves and asked me if I'd do the color. Absolutely.

The first game matched twelfth-seeded Massachusetts and thirteenth-seeded George Washington in the opener. The two teams had tied for twelfth place with 4-14 conference records, but GW had the tiebreaker. Richmond, the eleventh seed, would play Fordham, the fourteenth seed, in the second game.

Not surprisingly, three of the four coaches playing on opening day had been rumored to be in trouble during the season.

Richmond's Chris Mooney was by far the most established of the four. He was in his fourteenth season at Richmond; the other three had been at their schools a *combined* nine seasons.

Mooney had been successful for long stretches at Richmond—reaching the sweet sixteen for the second time in school history in 2011, reaching the tournament on a second occasion, and twice reaching the NIT quarterfinals. He'd won at least nineteen games on seven occasions, no small feat at Richmond, including 26-9 the year the Spiders had played into the second week of the NCAAs.

But after going 22-13 in 2017, Richmond had dropped to 12-20 the next year and came into the A-10 Tournament with a nearly identical 12-19 record a year later. Most mid-majors will have ups and downs. The best of them tend to be senior-laden when they succeed, and the drop-off the next season is almost inevitable.

But a couple of down seasons weren't Mooney's biggest problem. VCU was. The Rams, who had won the A-10 regular-season title, were about to go the NCAAs for the eighth time in nine seasons, including the Final Four run in 2011—which had completely overshadowed Richmond's trip to the sweet sixteen. While getting to the sweet sixteen is nice, it isn't the Final Four. Heck, it isn't even trademarked—only because the states of Illinois and Kentucky beat the NCAA to it by trademarking the sweet sixteen of their high school tournaments.

Three weeks prior to the start of the A-10 Tournament, a billboard had appeared on I-95 as one drove through Richmond with the words "We Want Our Program Back #Fire Mooney," emblazoned in white letters (except for "#Fire," which was in red) against a blue background.

It had been taken out by about two dozen angry fans and alumni, who apparently couldn't stand VCU's success at a time when Richmond was struggling.

"Actually, I think the billboard helped me," Mooney said to me the day before the tournament started. "Look, there are always going to be fans who get upset when things aren't going well. I'm upset too. But I think the billboard kind of galvanized a lot of our fans who realize we've had some very good moments and we have a chance to be very good again next year."

Richmond was starting four sophomores and a freshman in a non-one-and-done league where the best teams were often the most experienced. The Spiders had struggled in preconference, losing games at home to Longwood, Hampton (by twenty), and Oral Roberts. The only saving grace was a win over Wake Forest, which may have been a perennial ACC Tournament day one participant but was still in the ACC.

They'd started 2-7 in conference play before winning four out of five, including a win at La Salle three days after the billboard appeared. But losing their last four conference games had bumped them back to day one.

Mooney, however, was safe. He had two more years left on his contract and lots of hope for the near future.

There had also been rumors about Fordham coach Jeff Neubauer, who was in his fourth season on a job that had become a coach-killer when the school had decided to drop out of the Patriot League and join the Atlantic 10. The Rams had been very competitive in the Patriot League, going to the NCAAs in 1992. But they were way over their head—especially financially—in the A-10.

Nick Macarchuk had been the coach when the school transitioned to the A-10 in 1996. His eight-season record at that moment was 133-112, including the NCAA trip and an NIT bid. His last four seasons, coaching in the A-10, his record was 28-80, including 10-54 in conference play.

That began a procession of good coaches with solid résumés who came to Fordham and failed: Bob Hill, Dereck Whittenburg, and Tom Pecora had all had success in other places. Whittenburg miraculously finished 9-7 in the A-10 in 2005 but dropped to last place two seasons later and was fired. Pecora was never better than 4-14 in the league before being fired in 2015.

Enter Neubauer. He had been an assistant to John Beilein at West Virginia and then had coached ten seasons at Eastern Kentucky, twice reaching the NCAAs and winning twenty or more games five times. His Fordham experience had been similar to his recent predecessor's: a good start, 17-14, 8-10 his first year and then a descent into the A-10 basement that Fordham had owned without a mortgage for most of twenty-three years.

"Sometimes you can't see progress," he said to me. "We've had some moments this season where we've shown that we can be very good. I hope we have a couple more left in us this week."

The coach who had almost no chance to survive was GW's Maurice Joseph, which was a shame because he was as nice a man as you could hope to meet and had been thrown into an impossible situation three seasons earlier.

GW was a school that had reached the sweet sixteen once—in 1993 under Mike Jarvis—and had some very good moments since then under Tom Penders, Karl Hobbs, and Mike Lonergan.

Lonergan had won a Division 3 national championship at Catholic, had coached under Gary Williams at Maryland, and then had been successful at Vermont, succeeding Tom Brennan—no easy task.

He'd been thrilled to come back to the DC area in 2011, and by 2014 he had GW in the tournament. He was an intense, tireless recruiter who tended to believe that most of the world was out to get him: officials, high school coaches, and, eventually, Patrick Nero—the athletic director who had hired him.

He and Nero got into what can only be described as an ugly pissing match. Many of the details are locked away because Lonergan sued the school after being fired in September 2016 and agreed, as part of the settlement he eventually received (reportedly for $1 million), not to speak publicly about what had gone on.

Suffice to say, Lonergan told anyone who would listen that Nero was interfering with his team and that, while he "wasn't bothered at all" by Nero being gay, he told anyone who would listen that Nero was gay. The battle reached the president's office and then was leaked to the *Washington Post*.

Lonergan was buried by a story filled with anonymous quotes accusing him of verbally abusing players—many of those quotes coming from players who had left the program. Why they were allowed to hide behind anonymity while attacking a coach they no longer played for, I never understood.

Lonergan was fired soon after the story appeared, and Joseph was named to succeed him. At the time, Joseph was the number three assistant on the staff, the youngest and least-experienced coach on the bench.

But the players expressed their support for him, and he was given the job on an interim basis, a tag he lived with for an entire season.

GW still had some very solid players in the program and managed to go 20-15 in Joseph's first season, but trying to recruit in the midst of all the bad publicity the school had received, and with an interim tag hanging around Joseph's neck, was almost impossible.

GW finally dropped the interim label at the end of the season, but an entire recruiting cycle had been lost. The record dropped to 15-18 a year later and 2018–19 had been a disaster literally from day one—when the Colonials had jumped to a 22–0 lead at home on opening night against Stony Brook, only to lose the game in overtime.

Tom Izzo, who Joseph had played for at Michigan State for two seasons, would have had trouble surviving under the circumstances handed to Joseph. He was thirty-one when he got the job and had probably figured he was at least five years away from his first shot at being a head coach.

He'd remained remarkably upbeat throughout the season, even as the rumors swirled that GW was already looking for a new coach. "Nothing I can do about any of that," he said. "All I can do is try to win every game we can possibly win."

His opponent in the opener, Matt McCall, was the only coach involved in day one who didn't need to worry about his job. McCall was only in his second season at UMass, but it hadn't been an easy ride.

He'd been hired after Pat Kelsey had pulled out less than an hour before the press conference in which he was supposed to be introduced as the new coach and decided to stay at Winthrop.

McCall had replaced Will Wade at Chattanooga when Wade left to take the VCU job and had gone 29-6 his first season, earning an NCAA bid. The next year hadn't been as good but was still solid: 19-12. He took over a UMass program that had great history—but none of it recent.

Julius Erving and Rick Pitino had been teammates in the late sixties and early seventies, one a great player, the other a great future coach. In 1996, John Calipari had coached the Minutemen, led by Marcus Camby, to the Final Four. Unfortunately, Camby had an agent during the season, and the Final Four banner had been ordered taken down by the NCAA after it finished its investigation. Of course, by then both Calipari and Camby were in the NBA.

UMass had one very good player, Luwane Pipkins. During McCall's first season, Pipkins had averaged more than 21 points per game. His numbers had dropped, in part because of injury and in part because of attitude during the season. He'd made it pretty clear that he planned to graduate in June and use his final year of eligibility to play someplace else as a graduate transfer.

He'd unofficially made that official on the day of his Senior Night game when he had posted "last night in this uniform at home" on Snapchat, with a photo of his UMass uniform.

McCall had decided not to bring him to Brooklyn. "He's told his teammates he doesn't plan to be part of the program in the future," McCall said. "We'll go with the guys who want to be here." Publicly, the school announced that Pipkins was injured. It was easier that way.

I ran into the six officials who would be working that day having breakfast in the hotel in the morning.

I like officials, especially basketball referees. I think their job is as difficult as any in sports, because the game is so fast and almost every call is split-second. At the college level, only a handful make enough money during the season to give up their real jobs.

I've traveled with officials on occasion, dined with them, and almost always make a point of trying to talk to them before a game. They tend to know a lot, and most are good storytellers.

I've met very few who aren't devoted to their job. It is instructive, I think, that when they talk about coaches they almost always say, "I like working for him" or "It's tough to work for them." They tend to take the approach that they are there to make the game as fair as possible for both teams. And the best ones approach every game as if it is the most important one they'll work all season—even when it's not. On this day, they all knew the loser of whichever game they worked would be hanging up their uniforms for the last time this season.

Dwayne Gladden was the most experienced of the refs who were in Brooklyn that day. He was a retired Air Force officer who had worked the last eleven NCAA Tournaments—and would make it twelve the following week.

A year earlier, I'd asked Gladden how many NCAAs he'd worked, because when I'm doing a game on television I like to give people an idea how experienced an officiating crew is, and working NCAAs certainly gives one a good idea.

"This will be my eleventh," he said.

"I like your confidence," I answered.

"If you don't believe in what you're doing on this job," he said, "you better find something else to do."

We all sipped coffee and talked about the things basketball fans talk about in March: who might make the Final Four; which bubble teams would get in and which ones wouldn't; how nerve-racking Sunday would be for each of them waiting to hear if *they* were in or out of the tournament.

I suspected Dwayne Gladden wouldn't be terribly nervous.

Not surprisingly, the atmosphere inside Barclays Center on a cold but sunny Wednesday morning was quiet. The attendance for the doubleheader would be announced at 4,720—in a building that seats 17,772 for basketball—although it looked to me as if the crowd came in segments: fans of UMass and GW arriving for game one; fans of Richmond and Fordham showing up in time for game two.

Those who did see both games saw two hard-fought, intense contests. That's the way March basketball tends to be. As I watch games like these, I'm reminded of Anthony Noto's words all those years ago: "The hardest thing in life isn't waking up to face the battle, it's waking up with no battle to face."

All four teams wanted the chance to face another battle the next day.

For most of the game, it looked like UMass would be one of those teams. The Minutemen came out hot and had an early 25–11 lead but cooled in the final ten minutes of the half, allowing the Colonials to close the gap to 30–29 at halftime.

Often, in largely empty buildings in games being played by second-tier teams (to be kind), the shooting is bad. This was along those lines, with the exception of UMass guard Keon Clergeot and GW's Maceo Jack and Terry Nolan Jr.

Clergeot, a six-one sophomore, was averaging just over 7 points a game. But he had a career day, making 5-of-10 shots from outside the three-point line—the rest of his teammates combined to shoot 3-of-18 from distance—and finishing the game with 25 points. Outside of Clergeot, the other four UMass starters combined to shoot 6-of-36.

The difference in the game proved to be Nolan, whom Joseph had moved to the bench, hoping he could provide an offensive spark off the bench. He did exactly that, with 20 points—6 of them coming in overtime.

The game reached overtime because UMass, after leading almost the entire afternoon, could never deliver a knockout punch. GW led *twice* in regulation, each time by a point and for less than a minute total.

After Tre Wood's layup with 2:03 to go gave UMass what would turn out to be its last lead of the game at 56–54, Justin Williams tied it at 56 with a layup of his own. Then—fittingly—neither team was able to score again, regulation ending with Clergeot missing a three that would have won the game.

Nolan opened the overtime scoring with a three to give GW a 59–56 lead—its largest margin of the game. A Sy Chatman drive tied the game one final time, this time at 63; the Minutemen being the ones who had to rally in the extra period. But Nolan believed he could get to the basket whenever he touched the ball, and he did it again, making it 65–63 with twenty-seven seconds left.

Carl Pierre was fouled with eleven seconds left, but made only 1-of-2. If there was one stat that killed UMass, it was free-throw shooting. The Minutemen were 10-of-22 compared to GW's 24-of-36. Shoot under 50 percent from the foul line, and you are likely to lose most of the time.

Down one, UMass had to foul, and Justin Mazzulla made both with nine seconds to go for a 67–64 lead.

Joseph then made a decision many coaches are loath to make: rather than hope his defense would be able to deny an open three-point shot, he ordered his players to foul Wood with seven seconds left before he could get the ball into position to take a three.

Many coaches are unwilling to make this move because they're afraid if the shooter makes one, misses the second intentionally, and his teammates tip back an offensive rebound, the game can be lost on a buzzer-beating three. That's a far less likely scenario than someone making a three in the open floor, but if it happens, a coach will be second-guessed. If someone makes a three, the coach is rarely second-guessed.

Few coaches like to be second-guessed.

Maybe Joseph figured he had nothing to lose at that moment. His fate had already been decided.

Wood missed the first free throw. Even if he missed the second, UMass would need a back-tap to shoot a three to tie. He missed, and Nolan, appropriately, grabbed the rebound and was fouled. His free throw with three seconds left clinched a 68–64 victory.

For UMass, it was a merciful ending to a season that had gone over the cliff early and crashed late when Pipkins announced his intention to leave. For Joseph and his players, it was a nice consolation prize in what had been a long, cold winter.

A day later, GW would lose a very competitive game to George Mason, 61–57, ending their season with a 9-24 record. The Colonials played the entire season without leading rebounder Arnaldo Toro and played their final game without leading scorer D. J. Williams—who had been injured in the UMass game.

But 9-24 was 9-24, and athletic director Tanya Vogel—who had replaced Patrick Nero when Nero resigned fifteen months after Mike Lonergan's firing—didn't wait long to pull the trigger. The day after the Mason game, she announced that Joseph had been fired.

ADs always seem to think they can soften the blow when they fire someone with empty words. Vogel went on about Joseph's integrity, the fact that he'd met his wife while at GW, and that he would "always be part of the GW family."

I suspect Joseph didn't feel very much a part of the GW family on the ides of March. Et tu, Tanya?

Game two of day one was almost eerily identical to game one. Fordham couldn't find the Brooklyn Bridge with a telescope to start the game: Richmond led 4–0 at the first TV time-out. The Spiders lead grew to 18–8, but by halftime it was 23–18; a pitcher's duel in shorts.

Richmond got the lead back to 36–30 before an 8–0 Fordham run gave the Rams a 38–36 lead. Fordham's two best players were a pair of freshman guards, Nick Honor and Jalen Cobb. If the Rams had hope for the future, it started with those two.

Fordham rallied from six down once again late, Anthony Portley, a St. Peter's transfer, hitting two free throws to make it 50–50 with six seconds left.

Mooney opted not to call time, hoping to catch Fordham's defense in scramble mode. The ploy worked: Jacob Gilyard found Nathan

Cayo cutting to the basket, and his layup with 0.02 seconds left gave Richmond a 52–50 victory.

Everyone on the Spiders' side breathed a sigh of relief: a loss to Fordham before most of the league had even reached Brooklyn would have been embarrassing.

In spite of rumors to the contrary, Neubauer would live to coach a fifth season in the Bronx. The school had brought in an advisory panel, led by Dave Odom—father of Ryan—to discuss the basketball program's future during the season, and that sort of thing often leads to a new coach. In this case, though, most of the recommendations were about the commitment—most of it financial—that Fordham needed to make to be competitive in the Atlantic 10.

Like GW, Richmond lost the next day, but it also did so with honor: losing 61–58 to a St. Louis team that would go on to win the tournament and steal an NCAA bid. It was possible—even likely—that if top-seeded VCU had won the tournament, the A-10 might have been a one-bid league for the first time since 2005 and for only the second time since 1990. But VCU lost in the quarterfinals to Rhode Island, and when St. Louis beat St. Bonaventure in the championship game, it joined the Rams on the board on Selection Sunday.

I walked out of the Barclays Center at the end of day one having enjoyed the afternoon. Both games had been highly competitive, and while the quality of play hadn't been top-drawer, the win-or-die nature of the games, even among teams almost certainly going nowhere the following week, was intriguing for me to watch and feel.

All the big-time tournaments were underway by then, with the top teams jockeying for seeding in the tournament—nothing more.

I was headed south for a game on Saturday that would end in celebration and heartbreak. It would be, I knew, my kind of day.

THE ROAD TO DAYTON ...
LEADS THROUGH NORFOLK

March 16, 2019, Norfolk, Virginia

I had attended basketball games involving Mid-Eastern Athletic Conference (MEAC) teams for a long time—most of them at Howard.

But I'd never been to the MEAC Tournament, in large part because it is always held in the week leading up to Selection Sunday, and most years I'd been at the ACC Tournament that week.

This, though, was my chance to make it to the MEAC. The championship game was Saturday afternoon at the Scope in Norfolk, and I was back on the familiar path to Norfolk—I-95 to I-295 to I-64—early on Saturday morning. As I've said, when I'm going to a building I've never been to before, I leave extra time to get lost—even with Google Maps, which is pretty good, but less than perfect.

It definitely felt like spring as I pulled into the parking lot across the street from the Scope. The building opened in 1971 and was the first professional home to Julius Erving, who played for the Virginia Squires for two seasons before the cash-strapped ABA team sent him to the team then known as the New York Nets.

The building can seat up to eleven thousand for basketball, but with the curtains pulled across the upper deck, the capacity for the MEAC Tournament was closer to six thousand. The attendance for the championship game would be 3,688.

The MEAC was launched in 1971 as a Division 2 basketball conference. It was dominated in the early years by North Carolina A&T, which won sixteen of the first nineteen titles. The tournament has always been played in big-time places, starting with Duke's Cameron

Indoor Stadium in 1972 for two seasons. Later it was played for one year in the Palestra. It has frequently been played in the Greensboro Coliseum and has also gone to Raleigh's PNC Arena (North Carolina State's home court) and, recently, to the Scope. It has been there for the last seven seasons.

There was one problem with playing in the Scope: hockey. The building is the home of the ECHL's Norfolk Admirals, and there is ice underneath the court. When the weather warms, the ice begins to melt, which can lead to condensation on the basketball court.

On Friday, the high temperature in Norfolk had been eighty, and wet spots on the court had been an issue throughout the semifinals. That was why, an hour before tipoff of the title game between Norfolk State and North Carolina Central, the three officials—led by my friend Dwayne Gladden—were on the court, walking it carefully, searching for any wet spots they could find.

Whether because of the court or not, Norfolk State had lost a key player the night before in its 75–69 win over Howard. Derrik Jamerson, who led the nation in three-point shooting percentage at 51.2 percent, had rolled an ankle during the game, and his status for the final was questionable.

Gladden—who would be listed in the final box score as "Dwayne Golden"—and fellow refs Haywood Bostic and Lionel Butler covered every inch of the court, pointing to any wet spots they found so that members of the arena's maintenance crew could dry them before the game started.

I was standing watching the refs do their work with Kevin Nickelberry, Howard's coach. "The court was brutal last night," he said. "For everyone. I thought it was dangerous, but there wasn't much to be done. It's a little cooler today [the high would be about seventy], so I hope it won't be as much of a problem." The Bison's dreams of an NCAA bid—and, in all likelihood, Nickelberry's hopes of keeping his job—had gone a-glimmering the night before in the loss to Norfolk State.

"We knew we were good enough to beat that team," Nickelberry said, shaking his head. "We should have beaten them at home, we *did* beat them at their place, and we had them on the ropes last night. We just couldn't get the shots to go down when they had to go down."

Howard had cut a thirteen-point deficit to two with more than three minutes to play, but could never get even. The Bison had been invited to play in the CBI. Nickelberry was hoping a couple of wins there might grant him a stay of job execution.

"Look at the progress we made this year," Nickelberry said. "We were 10-6 in the league, had the player of the year, won seventeen games, and everyone's back next year."

That was all true. Athletic director Kery Davis wasn't quite as convinced. He had insisted to me that the incident after the Norfolk State game in January wouldn't be a factor in his decision on Nickelberry's future.

"Wins will be a factor," he said. "We were better, sure, but how much better? Go down to Coastal Carolina [in the CIT] and win, then win a couple more after that and let's talk."

There was an edge in his voice that told me Nickelberry's best chance to survive—a MEAC Tournament title—had already passed.

Norfolk State had been the clear-cut best team in the league all season. The Spartans had gone 14-2, the second loss coming to Howard after they had clinched first place. NCCU had finished tied for third with Howard at 10-6, but had upset second-seeded North Carolina A&T in the semis.

Both had young coaches with impressive résumés. Robert Jones wasn't yet forty but was in his sixth season at Norfolk State. Jones had succeeded Anthony Evans, who had taken the school to its first trip ever to the NCAAs in 2012—and a stunning first-round upset of second-seeded Missouri—and followed that up with the school's first NIT bid the next year.

Those two seasons had gotten him the job at Florida International, one of those schools that tended to be coach-killers, because it was over its head playing in Conference USA. Five losing seasons later, Evans was out of a job.

Jones hadn't yet reached the heights Evans had gone to, but the regular-season title meant his team would do no worse than play in the NIT. "That's not the goal of this group," he'd said.

LeVelle Moton was already something of a coaching icon at NCCU, even at the age of forty-four. He'd been a star player at the school in the 1990s. His nickname in those days was "Poetry-N-Moton." He'd then played overseas—in Indonesia and Israel—and had coached high school for four seasons before becoming an assistant coach at his alma mater in 2007.

Two seasons later, the Eagles made the transition from Division 2 to Division 1. When the MEAC had transitioned from D-2 to D-1 in 1988–89, NCCU had dropped out to remain in D-2. That decision had paid off when it won the D-2 national title in 1989.

It had returned to full-fledged status in D-1 in time for the 2010–11 season, and Moton had built a MEAC power. The Eagles had won at least twenty-two games in four seasons out of five (including a 28-6 record in 2014) and had won the conference tournament and gone to the NCAAs in 2014, 2017, and 2018. They'd gone 16-0 in conference play in 2015, only to lose in the conference tournament and end up in the NIT. This would be their fourth championship game appearance in six years.

Each school had one big-time NBA star it could point to as a graduate: Norfolk State grad Bob Dandridge had come into the league as a Milwaukee Bucks rookie alongside the player then known as Lew Alcindor, and had played on a championship team with the Bucks in 1971 and then on another with the Washington Bullets in 1978. Interestingly, neither team had won an NBA title since then.

Dandridge was a fine player who scored 15,530 points in a thirteen-year career, but he couldn't match North Carolina Central alum Sam Jones.

The Boston Celtics had the No. 8 pick (last one of the first round) in the 1957 NBA draft, and Red Auerbach had no idea who to take. There were no scouts in those days—coaches like Auerbach did the best they could to see college players when they had the chance.

As he often did, Auerbach called around to college coaches he knew asking for recommendations. One of them, Wake Forest's Bones McKinney—who had played for Auerbach on the Washington Caps right after World War II—told him about a kid named Sam Jones from NCCU he'd seen play a few times. "Great shooter—I mean great," McKinney said.

Without ever seeing him play, Auerbach used the pick on Jones, who played twelve NBA seasons and was on ten championship teams. He was Mr. Outside to Bill Russell's Mr. Inside. Jones was voted into the Hall of Fame in 1983 and was named one of the NBA's fifty greatest players on the league's fiftieth anniversary in 1996.

NBA history was not at stake in the Scope as the teams took the court. Jamerson would try to play on his ankle but would limp through eleven minutes without scoring.

"You hate for anyone to get injured, especially this time of year," Moton would say after the game. "But it's awfully hard for everyone to stay healthy in March."

Jamerson's absence didn't seem to matter much in the first half. The Spartans finished on an 8–0 run and led 32–22 at the break.

Moton is, for the most part, soft-spoken, someone as likely to quote Shakespeare as Bob Knight. But he got after his team at halftime for not being aggressive enough—especially on the offensive end of the floor.

"We had to start taking some chances," he said. "We had to get some baskets in transition. Settling for a half-court game wasn't working for us. That much was clear."

After Norfolk State's Alex Long started the second half with a jumper to make it 34–22, NCCU took complete control of the game. In the next 11:30, the Eagles outscored the Spartans 25–6. Unable to make a three (3-of-21), they attacked the basket, frequently in transition. The Spartans, who had shot a solid 48 percent in the first half, couldn't find the hoop. They made only four field goals in the second half and scored a total of fifteen points.

"You shoot eighteen percent for a half, that's going to get you beat most of the time," Robert Jones said sadly when it was over. "I saw a lot of tension in the huddle once they got going in the second half. Finally, when we got down 47–40, I just said, 'Fellas, if we're going to go down, let's go down fighting.' At least we did that."

They did—clamping down on defense and holding NCCU to a total of three points in the game's last eight minutes. In fact, the Eagles didn't score at all in the game's last four minutes, and the Spartans had a golden opportunity to rally and win the game.

They couldn't get it done. In fact, after Steven Whitley had hit a short jumper in the lane to make it 50–44 with 3:53 to go, Norfolk State didn't make another field goal—missing their final seven shots. They had chances until the very end because they shut NCCU down, but the game ended on a missed three by Mastadi Pitt, after Jones had called time-out with eight seconds left to set up a final shot that would have sent the game into overtime.

As soon as Pitt's shot hit the rim and bounced away, the Eagles and their fans celebrated. This sort of court-storming made sense, unlike so many of the regular-season made-for-TV court-stormings. NCCU was going dancing for the third time in four years.

"That's a tough locker room right now," Jones said, even while the Eagles were still on court, cutting down nets and posing for photos. "You spend all year to get to a championship game like this, to fall just short is tough to take. We got six straight stops at the end and couldn't get the ball in the basket."

He said he had reminded his players that the season wasn't over, that they would have another game to play—in the NIT—in a few days.

As Jones walked down the hall after his press conference, I asked him about the difficulty of getting his players to bounce back from a loss like this, go on the road (as I knew Norfolk State would be told to do by the NIT committee), and play in a tournament they didn't really want to play in.

Jones stopped and forced a weary smile. "That's a very good question," he said. "But it's my job to come up with an answer the next few days. It's not something I've thought about—or wanted to think about. Now I've got to think about it."

Jones apparently came up with the answer. Norfolk State traveled to Tuscaloosa and stunned Alabama, a No. 1 seed, in its first-round NIT game. That was a credit to Jones—and to his players.

The MVP of the tournament was Raasean Davis, who had scored 8 points in the championship game. But he'd pulled down 14 rebounds and had been the main reason NCCU outrebounded Norfolk State, 41–29. That was no small feat.

Moton and his players said all the right things about the win—how they had rallied; how tough Norfolk State had been right to the end; how proud they were to win the tournament again.

Moton and I sat alone in the interview room for a few minutes after he and his players had finished. I asked him if he thought there was any chance his team wouldn't be sent to Dayton. He laughed.

"Two years ago, we won twenty-five games, finished 13-3 in the league, and won the tournament. They sent us to Dayton. Last year, they sent us to Dayton. Trust me, they'll send us to Dayton."

He smiled. "I'm not complaining. I love Dayton this time of year."

34

AND THEN THERE WERE SIXTY-EIGHT: SELECTION SUNDAY

March 17, 2019

Most basketball fans, especially younger ones, just assume that Selection Sunday was invented at about the same time 130 years ago that James Naismith put up the first peach basket in Springfield, Massachusetts.

That's not exactly true.

In fact, the unveiling of the NCAA Tournament bracket wasn't done on television until 1982, after CBS had outbid NBC for the rights to the tournament, paying what was then an astonishing $16 million a year for three years after NBC had paid a total of $18.8 million on its last two-year contract. The increase—about 70 percent—was, at the time, the largest in the history of a rights fee for a sports entity.

NBC had started televising the Final Four in 1968. It had moved the championship game to Monday night in 1973, and its three-man broadcast team of Dick Enberg, Al McGuire, and Billy Packer had become synonymous with the college game.

CBS was able to lure Packer away from NBC, but it needed a way to let college basketball fans know that, even though NBC continued to televise regular-season games, it was now the March home of college basketball.

Enter Len DeLuca. Diminutive and balding, DeLuca had the job of promoting CBS's new role in college basketball. It was DeLuca who began labeling every game CBS televised as part of the "Road to the Final Four." And it was DeLuca who came up with the idea of a television show on the Sunday before the tournament began to announce the field.

Until then, college coaches sat by their phones on Sunday waiting to find out if they were in the field and, if so, where they were going and whom they were playing. The news of the field and the brackets would become public in dribs and drabs during the day on Sunday.

And so "Selection Sunday," later trademarked (of course) by the NCAA, came into being in 1982. Nowadays, even though the show has been through numerous format changes, the day is a national holiday for anyone who follows college hoops.

By 1985, the field had expanded to sixty-four teams. The money CBS paid the NCAA continued to grow and grow. In 1999, the network signed a deal that would pay the NCAA an astounding $546 million a year for eleven years.

The sixty-four-team field was pretty close to a perfect number. There were thirty conferences with automatic bids, allowing for thirty-four at-large bids. There were no byes; everyone played in the first round.

Then, in 2000, the Mountain West became eligible for an automatic bid, pushing the number to thirty-one. By then, because of the huge dollars being paid by CBS, every bid was worth several hundred thousand dollars—specifically $222,206—for every team in the field and an additional $222,206 for every win (called "units")—and the basketball committee was loath to take an at-large bid away from a power conference.

Thus they "expanded" the field to sixty-five teams, sending two automatic-bid teams to Dayton to play what was euphemistically called an "opening round" game. It was, in truth a play-in game. The winner didn't even receive a "unit" for the victory. It was as if it never happened—at least financially.

The play-in game was an embarrassment. The two teams sent to Dayton might as well have worn red *P*s (for play-in) on their foreheads. Inevitably, one of the two teams sent to play-in came from the two HBCU conferences. The committee would never send both HBCU champions to Dayton because that would have been seen—probably correctly—as blatant racism: send the black guys to Dayton and see which one gets let in the back door to play a No. 1 seed a couple of days later.

In the nineteen seasons since the first play-in game was staged, there has been only one year in which one of the HBCU teams didn't get sent to Dayton: the first year, 2001, when Northwestern State and Winthrop played for the right to advance to the field of sixty-four. Since then, one team or another from the HBCUs has been in Dayton, except in 2019, when both conference champions were sent there.

When the tournament was expanded to sixty-eight teams in 2011—after the NCAA seriously considered going to ninety-six teams, which would have been a disaster—Dayton was labeled "The First Four." That was the year the current twelve-year contract with CBS and TNT came online, increasing each unit to a value of $280,367. Since eight teams were now being sent to Dayton, including some from power conferences, the committee generously began crediting a unit to each of the four Dayton winners.

To get to sixty-eight teams, the tournament added three at-large teams, bringing the total to thirty-seven. Instead of playing one game in Dayton, it would play four—two on Tuesday and two on Wednesday. There would be two games between potential No. 16 seeds and two involving the last four at-large teams added to the field. The term "First Four," which the NCAA trademarked about five minutes (or less) after announcing it, actually makes no sense if it is supposed to be some kind of spinoff of the Final Four.

The Final Four means the last four *teams* playing. The First Four is the first four *games* being played. It sounds good, and with television hyping it at every turn, it quickly took root. Heck, I even use it.

Selection Sunday has always been one of my favorite days of the year, trailing only Christmas, Thanksgiving, and the opening night of hockey season. I sit down at some point and write down the thirty-seven teams I think should get at-large berths and the thirty-seven I expect to get at-large berths. The two lists are always quite different: the tournament committee will almost always give benefit of the doubt to power schools; I will almost always give benefit of the doubt to the smaller ones.

I do this without ever looking at the predictions made by the so-called bracketologists. To me, they're like weathermen: they change their predictions hourly, which means sooner or later they'll get it right. Their brackets have nothing to do with what's right or wrong but with what they expect the committee to do based on all its various criteria.

When they miss on one—or two—it's only because the committee ignores the numbers to put someone in the field they want playing for one reason or another.

The best example in 2019 was St. John's, which had finished 8-10 in a down Big East and clearly belonged in the NIT. The Red Storm got a bid. Why? It was a New York team with a Hall of Fame player (Chris Mullin) coaching. That's a better TV draw than, say, UNC Greensboro or Toledo.

The Big East would end up with four bids and would win *one* NCAA Tournament game—Villanova beating St. Mary's before losing in the second round, 87–61, to Purdue.

For years now, I've gone into the *Washington Post* on Selection Sunday to write a semi-prediction column on each of the four brackets. I don't pick game by game, just point out some that may have upset potential. Mostly I question a lot of the committee's decisions.

It's a fun evening, but not as much fun as it was years ago. Then, most of the staff would be in the office, and we'd sit around, eat pizza, and argue before and after the brackets and then decide who was going where. Now most of the people I grew up at the *Post* with are gone: Ken Denlinger, Dave Kindred, Tony Kornheiser, Michael Wilbon; I even miss George Solomon—a little.

Now when I walk in, most of the people sitting at the various desks could be one of my children. At least it feels that way. I know Matt Rennie, the deputy sports editor, who edits my copy that night, and David Larimer, the college editor. That's usually about it. When I shout something about the committee screwing someone just like they screwed Drexel in 2012 or Monmouth in 2016, I get blank looks.

Or a "shut up and keep writing" wave or look from Rennie or Larimer.

That said, the pizza's still pretty good.

There had been two games played that afternoon that would decide bids: the Atlantic 10 final between fifth-seeded St. Bonaventure and sixth-seeded St. Louis. The only team clearly worthy of an at-large bid from the A-10 was VCU, so only the winner was going. This was known as a "bid-stealer" game. Since neither the Bonnies nor the Billikens would have made the field as an at-large, their presence had to knock someone out. St. Louis won and made the field as a No. 13 seed.

Already, Oregon had stolen a bid by beating second-seeded Arizona

State and then top-seeded Washington to win the Pac-12 Tournament. There had been speculation that the Pac-12 was so down, it might receive only one bid—the automatic. But when Washington didn't win the tournament, it had to receive an at-large, and Arizona State won just enough to get invited to Dayton. The fact that the committee chairman was from the Pac-12—Stanford athletic director Bernard Muir—probably didn't hurt ASU's cause.

The second game with a bid at stake was played in the John J. Lee Amphitheater at Yale between Harvard and Yale for the Ivy League title. The John J. Lee was almost packed, a crowd of 2,572 in a building that seats 2,700. For the second straight season, Tommy Amaker's Harvard team had to play a road game for the Ivy championship, even though it was the No. 1 seed.

The Crimson had beaten Yale twice during the regular season, which had given them the top seed after both finished 10-4 in the conference, but this was one of those games that would have caused Dean Smith to remind people how hard it is to beat a good team three times in a season.

And Yale *was* good. Harvard had done an excellent job in the regular-season meetings of keeping Miye Oni, who had succeeded Seth Towns as the Ivy League player of the year, under control.

But Oni brought help with him this time, most notably senior guard Alex Copeland, who poured in 25 points—11 over his average—and sophomore guard Azar Swain, who came off the bench to go 4-of-5 from three-point range (his teammates combined to go 1-of-6 from three) and scored 15 points.

Harvard got an otherworldly game from Bryce Aiken, who shot 11-of-21 from the field and 12-of-12 from the free-throw line to finish with 38 points. But he simply didn't get enough help. Center Chris Lewis was held to 2 points, Justin Bassey had only 6, and Christian Juzang was scoreless. The only other Crimson player in double figures was freshman Noah Kirkwood, who scored 19.

Harvard actually led 52–45 early in the second half after a Kirkwood dunk, but Yale—which shot *60 percent* for the game—simply stopped missing after that. The Bulldogs went on a 28–7 run to lead 73–59 with six minutes left and never looked back. The final was 97–85.

"The better team won that day," Amaker said. "We just couldn't guard them when we had to. All credit to them."

It was the second straight year that Harvard would have to settle for playing in the NIT, and they would—of course—have to play on the road: at Georgetown. That meant Amaker would be facing the school whose former coach—John Thompson the elder—had been his boyhood hero. Amaker loved the idea.

Thompson's last game as a coach had been in 1999, a midseason loss to Seton Hall, coached then by one Harold Tommy Amaker. Thompson often referred to Amaker as "the motherf—— who was the last coach to beat my ass."

Patrick Ewing, who had been Thompson's greatest player and had led the Hoyas to three Final Fours in four years between 1982 and 1985, was now the coach. But Thompson was still an omnipresent figure at Georgetown.

"I know he'll be there," Amaker said, laughing. "He'll be pulling for Ewing, but my mom will be there pulling for me."

There were few surprises when the brackets came out on Sunday evening. For me, the only thing the committee did that I didn't expect was give Belmont an at-large bid, sending the Bruins to Dayton to play Temple on Tuesday night.

I thought the Bruins were worthy of a bid—they'd lost to a Murray State team led by Ja Morant in the Ohio Valley final. Morant would be the No. 2 pick in the NBA draft in June. Or, as I joked on draft night, "number one pick among mortals," behind Zion Williamson, who I'm assuming is already in the Hall of Fame as I write this.

Belmont was the committee's token non–power at-large selection. Nevada got an at-large after losing the Mountain West championship game to Utah State, but it had been ranked in the top ten most of the season. Buffalo was a No. 6 seed after winning the MAC Tournament, but none of the league's other good teams had any chance to get an at-large. The same was true in the Southern Conference, where a 29-4 Wofford team received a No. 7 seed, while UNC Greensboro and Furman were left out.

If you believed the committee, UNC Greensboro would have gotten in if not for bid-stealers Oregon and St. Louis. UNC Greensboro, Alabama, Indiana, and TCU were listed as the "first four out," and each was given a top seed in the NIT.

Those who got into the NIT after winning regular-season titles in one-bid leagues, but failing to win their conference tournaments, were treated about as well as their one-bid brethren who were in the Big Dance.

Lipscomb was a fifth seed for the NIT; Harvard was a sixth seed; Wright State was a seventh seed; Loyola Chicago was also a seventh seed; and Norfolk State was an eight. That meant all had to go on the road to play their first-round games. Lipscomb, Harvard, and Norfolk State all won. Lipscomb ended up making it to Madison Square Garden before losing to Texas in the championship game. Harvard won at Georgetown, in a game played in McDonough Gym, the three-thousand-seat on-campus building that had been the team's home until it moved to an NBA arena in 1982. Since the Capital One Arena in downtown DC was occupied that night by the NHL's Washington Capitals, the game was played at McDonough.

It definitely made for a better atmosphere than a two-thirds-empty NBA arena would have provided. The Crimson won 71–68, and when it was over, Thompson the elder put a massive arm around Amaker and said: "Now you're the motherf—— who was the last coach to beat my ass, *and* you beat my son."

Thompson has two sons: John III and Ron. He thinks of Ewing as his third son. He should. Without him he probably wouldn't be in the Hall of Fame.

Norfolk State's win might have been the most surprising—playing on the road against a team that had just missed an at-large bid—three days after the crushing defeat to NCCU.

"I don't want this team's defining moment to be one game," Robert Jones had said after the loss in Norfolk. "We've won twenty-one games. We deserve a better ending than this."

Their ending came at Colorado a few nights later, but the win over Alabama allowed the Spartans to walk away from the season with one very important happy memory. A win over an SEC team on the road—not a bad legacy.

Even before the brackets went up, I knew where I was going, regardless of who went where: Dayton.

The first night would match sixteenth-seeded Fairleigh Dickinson with sixteenth-seeded Prairie View. That would be followed by eleventh-seeded Temple playing eleventh-seeded Belmont. I knew Fran

Dunphy was one loss from the end of his career. What I wouldn't learn until later was that Belmont coach Rick Byrd had already made the same decision.

Wednesday's games would match sixteenth-seeded North Carolina Central and sixteenth-seeded North Dakota State, the surprise winner as the fifth seed of the Summit League Tournament. The finale would be eleventh-seeded Arizona State against eleventh-seeded St. John's.

The winner of that game would go to Tulsa to play Buffalo. That meant an ASU victory would match former Buffalo coach Bobby Hurley against Nate Oats—the man he'd hired from the high school ranks to be his top assistant at Buffalo.

Sunday afternoon, shortly before the brackets went up, Danny Hurley, whose first UConn team was going nowhere after a 16-17 season, had called Oats.

"I guarantee they're going to try to set the bracket up so you play Bob," he'd told Oats.

"You think so?" Oats asked.

"Just wait and see," the younger Hurley brother had answered.

Shortly after six o'clock the draw went up, and there it was: Buffalo against the Arizona State–St. John's winner.

Danny, Oats thought, *knows his stuff.*

BACK TO THE
BEGINNING

March 19, 2019, Dayton, Ohio

I have a warm spot in my heart for Dayton, especially for the University of Dayton.

The first basketball coach I ever met was Don (Mick) Donoher. The only sport my father ever really cared about was basketball. Being a graduate of CCNY during the school's glory days, he had always maintained an interest in the college game.

Each year, he would take me to the NIT a couple of times. This was a big deal to me—time with my dad, but also *great* seats because he often worked with a man named Fred Podesta, who played a major role in putting together the Garden's college basketball schedule every year.

That meant I went from my normal seats in section 406 at the very top of the building to the second or third row, a few yards from the court. There were no Spike Lee seats in those days, so this was about as good as it got.

On the second night of quarterfinals in 1968, we went to see a doubleheader involving two New York–area teams: Fordham played the opener against Dayton, and then St. Peter's played Notre Dame. I was an ardent fan of all the New York–area teams: Columbia and Army first, but St. John's, Fordham, St. Peter's, and Seton Hall not far behind. I often listened to games on the student radio stations: WKCR at Columbia; WFUV at Fordham; WSOU at Seton Hall.

Yeah, I was that crazy.

Fordham-Dayton was tight all night. Johnny Bach, Fordham's coach—who later was an assistant coach on the Michael Jordan Bulls teams—was leaving after eighteen seasons to coach at Penn State, so I was fully aware that his next loss would be his last as the Rams' coach.

A few seats down from my dad and me sat a group of women, rooting for Dayton with at least as much enthusiasm as I was showing for Fordham. "I'm betting those are the wives of the Dayton coaches," my dad said at one point.

The game ended with Frank McLaughlin, who would go on to be Fordham's athletic director, missing a ten-foot jumper at the buzzer. Dayton won, 61–60.

In between games, as I sat quietly mourning the Fordham loss, one of the women who had been seated nearby walked over, introduced herself to my dad and me, and said to me, "You're quite a fan, aren't you?"

She introduced herself: Sonia Donoher, wife of Dayton coach Don Donoher. She was apparently impressed with my knowledge of hoops and said to me, "I'm sorry your team lost—for you—but not *really* sorry." We all laughed. "Now that Fordham is out, do you think you might root for us on Thursday night?"

I told her I couldn't honestly commit to that because if St. Peter's won, I'd have to pull for the Peacocks. But if Notre Dame won, heck, sure, I'd happily root for Dayton. She thought that was fair. Notre Dame won and I jumped on the Dayton bandwagon.

The Flyers beat Notre Dame—in overtime—in the semis and then played Jo Jo White and Kansas in the championship game. By now I was all in. Dayton won. As the awards were being handed out, Mrs. Donoher asked if I'd like to walk down to the locker room with her and meet her husband and the players.

Are you kidding?

Mick Donoher could not have been nicer, and he walked me around the locker room so I could get autographs from all the players. A week later an autographed photo of Donnie May, the team's star who would be drafted that spring by my (then) beloved Knicks, showed up.

Years passed. I continued to follow the fortunes of Dayton as I grew up and then through college. In 1981, now covering college hoops for the *Washington Post,* I was killing time on press row waiting for the start of the first Final Four game in Philadelphia's Spectrum, when I spotted Coach Donoher (as I have always called him) a few rows up in the stands talking to several other coaches.

Timidly, I approached, introduced myself, and told him that, even though I knew he wouldn't remember it, I would never forget how kind he and his wife had been to me at the 1968 NIT.

He broke into a warm smile and said, "So it is you! My son lives in Annapolis and reads the *Post* all the time. Sonia and I have been wondering if the wonderful young college basketball writer might be the little Johnny Feinstein we met all those years ago. She said she was *sure* it was you because she just knew you'd end up doing something in basketball."

I can't tell you how thrilling that was for me.

In 1985–86, when I was researching *A Season on the Brink,* I drove to Dayton from Bloomington on several occasions to have dinner with the Donohers—both for enjoyment and also for research purposes. Mick had been friends with Knight for years and had been one of his assistants with the Olympic team two years earlier.

The University of Dayton Arena—known to everyone as the UD Arena—is one of college basketball's great venues. It opened in 1969 and seats 13,409. Most Dayton games sell out or come close to it. The city is a genuine college hoops hotbed, which is why the NCAA actually did a smart thing when it put the play-in game in Dayton beginning in 2001. Even with two teams playing that few people knew anything about, attendance was always respectable—between seven and ten thousand. Once the First Four came into existence in 2011, the two doubleheaders have almost always been sellouts or near sellouts.

To get to the floor of the UD Arena, one walks down a steep ramp. I can remember walking up that ramp in 1981 after St. Joseph's had shocked top-ranked DePaul in a second-round NCAA Tournament game, winning the game at the buzzer on a Bryan Warrick pass to a wide-open John Smith in transition for a 50–49 win.

Mark Aguirre, DePaul's star, walked out of the locker room before it was open to the media, still in his game sweats, headphones on, pushing past everyone to head up the ramp. Several of us turned to follow him. Joey Meyer, who was then his father Ray's top assistant, grabbed my arm as I started to follow Aguirre.

"Be careful," Joey said. "No telling what he might do right now."

Aguirre walked out of the building and began crossing the bridge over the Dayton River that led back to DePaul's hotel. Halfway across the bridge, he stopped, turned, took the headphones off, and said, "The game is the game. We lost the game."

He put the headphones back on and continued his walk. I went back to the arena, almost fell racing down the ramp, and got to my seat—I now had to write an extra story because of the upset—just in time for tipoff of the Indiana-Maryland game, which was the reason I was in Dayton—to cover Maryland.

The Terrapins burst to a quick lead, Ernest Graham burying what would have been a three-point shot if the line existed, to make it 8–0. The Maryland fans were going nuts. I looked at Bob Knight, wondering if he would call time-out; get up and scream at someone; kick a chair. He did none of the above; just sat, hand on chin, and watched. Something told me he knew something the rest of us didn't.

I turned to my colleague Dave Kindred, who had known Knight since he first arrived at Indiana in 1971, and said, "I think Maryland's in trouble."

Kindred knew Knight a lot better than I did. "I think you're right," he said.

We were both right. Indiana won 99–64. Thirty-eight years later, I can still see Isaiah Thomas slicing through the Maryland defense like a knife through melted butter.

"If that team doesn't win the national championship, I don't know anything about basketball," Lefty Driesell said when the carnage was finally over.

Lefty knows his hoops. Indiana won the title and was never seriously challenged, even in the championship game against a North Carolina team that included James Worthy and Sam Perkins.

Thirty-eight years after I first walked down the ramp at the UD Arena, I walked down it again prior to the start of the opening game of the First Four. The ramp seemed a lot steeper than in 1981—especially when I walked back up several times during the two days.

Wheeling into the parking lot, I had smiled when I noticed the sign for the Donoher Center, an expansion of the building that housed training facilities for the school's athletic teams.

Game one each night of the First Four matches sixteenth seeds. The second game always matches at-large teams from schools that are likely to draw a bigger TV audience. No shock there.

Prairie View had won the automatic bid in the Southwestern Athletic Conference, the farther west of the two HBCU conferences. Fairleigh Dickinson had won the NEC title, winning the championship game on the road at St. Francis (Pennsylvania), which had won the regular-season title.

Fairleigh Dickinson was making its sixth NCAA Tournament appearance; Prairie View its second. Neither had ever won a game.

The building wasn't full when the game began, but there were plenty of people already there. Prairie View came out hot—especially from outside—and jumped to leads of 19–6 and 23–11. They hit eight threes by halftime, but Fairleigh Dickinson senior Darnell Edge kept his team in the game almost single-handedly, scoring 18 points and not allowing Prairie View to pull away.

"We were lucky to only be down seven [41–34] at halftime," FDU coach Greg Herenda said. "If not for Darnell, we might have gotten blown out completely."

Edge was a senior who had gone from a nonstarter averaging 4.4 points as a freshman to a first-team All-NEC player averaging 19 points per game as a senior. He was a lot like his coach: overlooked in high school, but someone who kept working and improving.

Herenda had been fifty-two when he got his first Division 1 coaching chance in 2013 after being a D-1 assistant and then a junior college and Division 2 head coach. He'd taken UMass Lowell to the D-2 NCAA Tournament four times in five years (just prior to the school transitioning to D-1) before the Fairleigh Dickinson opportunity came along.

Herenda was a character. He hosted a radio show in New Jersey during the season and was about as outgoing as any coach I knew. He was almost manic on the bench, but it was clear his players were paying attention, especially as the game got tighter.

I'd been impressed during the first half by both bands. But when I took a walk at halftime, I noticed that the conductor for the FDU band was wearing a shirt that said, "Dayton Band."

When I asked him why, he said, "Because we're Dayton's band. Fairleigh Dickinson didn't send a band, so we're representing them."

It turned out that Fairleigh Dickinson didn't *have* a band to send. So the NCAA had outfitted the Dayton kids with FDU gear, they'd learned the fight song, and—voilà!—there they were cheering on and playing for their Knights.

I asked some of the kids what they knew about Fairleigh Dickinson.

"Absolutely nothing," said one.

"It's near New York," said another.

That was accurate: Teaneck is located about six miles from the George Washington Bridge. Depending on the time of day, it could take ten minutes or two hours to get to the bridge.

"Isn't it in New York?" one kid asked.

"No, New Jersey," another corrected.

What the heck, I figured, they were doing a good job playing for their team-for-a-night.

Their team played much better in the second half. Prairie View, which had made 8-of-12 three-point shots in the first half, stayed just as hot early. Devonte Patterson opened the scoring with a three; Gary Blackston hit another one thirty seconds later, making it 47–34. It was still 50–38 right after the first TV time-out of the half. (For the record, the NCAA insists these are "media time-outs." I have never once asked for a time-out in forty years as a media member. They are called for the purpose of injecting TV commercials into the game. They are TV time-outs. Period.)

At that point, FDU sophomore Jahlil Jenkins, the team's second-leading scorer, more or less took over the game. Jenkins, who averaged 13.5 points per game, had scored just 2 in the first half. He made a jumper. Then he made another one. He cut the lead to 56–50 with an old-fashioned three-point play with 10:39 left. Then he hit a three and the lead was down to 59–57.

The Dayton/FDU band members were going wild. By now, the building was close to full—the attendance would be 11,784. A Mike Holloway Jr. jump shot with 6:47 left gave FDU its first lead since 6–5. The Panthers weren't done. A dunk by Patterson in transition gave Prairie View a 66–63 lead, but FDU then went on a 12–0 run, capped by Jenkins making a pair of free throws to make it 75–66 with 1:32 left. Herenda had become a complete dervish on the bench, hugging everyone in sight as his team sealed the win.

The final was 82–76. Edge finished with 33 points; Jenkins with 22. Herenda and his players dashed across court to where the band was playing the FDU fight song and danced to the music—led by Herenda. It wasn't exactly a pretty sight, but it was certainly a joyous one.

Eleven months earlier, Herenda had been taking a walk at the Final Four with his son Trey when he felt so weak he couldn't walk any farther. Trey got him to an emergency room and he was admitted to intensive care—where he stayed for eight days. It turned out he had two blood clots that caused him to run a dangerously high fever. After he got out of intensive care, he was in the hospital for another week.

A New Jersey guy through and through, Herenda told his wife, "I don't want to die in Texas."

He didn't. But it was a long road back. He couldn't coach at 100 percent when practice began in September, and his players noticed. Before an early-season game, he felt so weak during the national anthem that assistant coach Darius Stokes literally had to hold him up to keep him from falling down.

But he got better—and so did his team. That led to a night in Dayton where the term "going dancing" literally became true.

With four teams playing on the same night, the narrow hallway leading from the locker room area to the arena floor was jammed between games.

Herenda was leaning against a wall talking to me about what the win meant to him and to the school, when Fran Dunphy walked out of the Temple locker room. Spotting Herenda, he turned, walked over to him, and wrapped him in a hug.

"I'm so proud of you," he said. "What a win."

"Typical Dunph," Herenda said after Dunphy walked away. "He's coaching to keep his career alive, but he still has time to think about what this means to me."

The game two matchup was Temple and Belmont—the Bruins being the lone at-large team from what are normally thought of as one-bid conferences. Rick Byrd had coached at Belmont for thirty-three years, taking over in 1986 when the school was still competing at the NAIA level. His team had made the NAIA playoffs nine times in ten years, gone to three Final Fours, and won a national championship in 1989.

They'd transitioned to Division 1 beginning in 1996, and since becoming eligible for the tournament in 2001, they'd made the NCAA field eight times. But they hadn't won a game, the closest call coming in 2008 when they'd had Duke down late, only to lose 71–70.

"It's been the one monkey on my back," Byrd would admit later that night.

I'd gotten to know Byrd doing a number of his games on TV and had only one complaint about him when we talked: I wanted to talk basketball, he wanted to talk golf. Byrd was a golf addict, a very good player with a handicap that usually hovered between one and four. Most game nights, he wore a golf sweater on the bench.

I had finished up in the Fairleigh Dickinson locker room and started down the hall when I heard someone calling my name. It was Byrd, who had walked out of his locker room to check the pregame clock.

"I thought about you on Sunday night," he said as we shook hands. "When the brackets went up and I saw we were in, I was thrilled. Then I realized we were going to have to fly here on Monday and we had just about no time to prepare for Temple. We had to start getting ready almost the minute we saw we were playing here."

"So where did I come in?" I asked.

He laughed. "I know how much you like Rory [McIlroy], and I had taped the last round of the Players Championship. I'd taped it to watch that night and I knew he'd won, and I was looking forward to going home and relaxing and seeing how he did it. But I had no time. I still haven't watched it."

Byrd and his coaches had done a good job preparing. Temple's best player was shooting guard Shizz Alston Jr., and there was a hand in his face almost every time he touched the ball. He ended up with 21 points but did so on 8-of-22 shooting from the field, including 4-of-14 from three. Belmont led the entire first half and took a 37–31 lead into the break.

Temple started the second half hot and built a 52–47 lead eight minutes in, but the Bruins came right back, retook the lead at 53–52 on a Kevin McClain fast-break layup, and never looked back.

Just as Belmont did an excellent job on Alston Jr., Temple did a very good job on Belmont's leading scorer, six-foot-eight-inch senior Dylan Windler. In forty minutes, Windler took only seven shots—and made two—but he was still a force on the boards with 14 rebounds. Windler had developed into a player NBA scouts were looking at very hard and would end up being a first-round draft pick—taken by Cleveland in June with the twenty-sixth pick.

With Windler shut down, the scoring was left to McClain, who finished with 29 points, and freshman center Nick Muszynski, who scored 16, most from the low post. At six-eleven and 230 pounds, Muszynski was a throwback, a kid who played with his back to the basket a lot and could score from anywhere in the paint. He'd taken a total of eighteen threes all season and rarely wandered to the perimeter.

Belmont gradually pulled away, leading by as many as twelve. Temple never quit. Dunphy used all his time-outs hoping to set up his defense for a couple of quick steals that might make the final minute nerve-racking. The Owls just weren't good enough.

Byrd and Dunphy hugged when it was over, and Dunphy walked off the court head down, no final look around, no waving to the Temple fans.

Dunphy said all the right things in his press conference; credited Byrd and the Belmont players and talked about how proud he was of his team for winning twenty-three games and getting back to the NCAA Tournament. He had known for almost a year this night was coming. As disappointing as the loss was, the fact that it had come in the tournament softened things a little.

After he came off the podium and began walking down the ramp to the locker room, I asked him how he was doing.

"I'm just so disappointed about Phil," he said. "I'm still in shock that they did that."

He was talking about his close friend Phil Martelli, who had been fired by St. Joseph's earlier that day. Dunphy had called Martelli as soon as he heard the news.

"Why didn't you call me?" he asked.

"You have a game tonight," Martelli said. "I didn't want to bother you."

Typical Martelli. Typical Dunphy.

Philadelphia reporters approached. Did Dunphy think that Aaron McKie, his already-anointed successor, would be able to keep the program at a high level?

"Aaron will be great, really great," Dunphy said. "He's ready for this. I've got absolute confidence in him."

That confidence was well placed. After all, McKie had learned from the best.

When the Philly guys finished, Dunphy continued down the ramp to talk to his players as their coach one last time.

He looked a little sad and a little tired, as if the adrenaline had gone out of him at the final buzzer. I checked the time. It was midnight.

36

MIDNIGHT FOR CINDERELLA...
AND FOR ME

Forty-five minutes later, the Belmont players and coaches boarded a bus to go straight to the airport. A plane chartered by the NCAA waited there to take them to Orlando, where they would play sixth-seeded Maryland in an East Regional game in the tournament's first round on Thursday.

Fairleigh Dickinson's plane had left a couple of hours earlier, headed for Salt Lake City and a first-round West Regional matchup with top-seeded Gonzaga.

Nowadays, NCAA tournament games take forever because there are now ten TV (not media) time-outs that last about three minutes each and a halftime that lasts twenty-two minutes. The clock says twenty minutes, but it isn't started until the sideline reporter finishes listening to one of the coaches spout a few meaningless clichés. There are also what were once thirty-second time-outs that now last a full minute, the better to sneak in a few more commercials.

That's why it was midnight when Fran Dunphy walked down the ramp to his locker room and closing in on 1 a.m. by the time Belmont left the building. The Bruins wouldn't arrive in Orlando until about five in the morning and would then play Maryland about thirty-one hours later.

That's the conundrum that is Dayton. Fairleigh Dickinson and Belmont had just won NCAA Tournament games for the first time in school history, and it meant a lot to everyone involved. Without Dayton, the chances that a sixteenth seed is going to win a game are close to zero: UMBC had become the only No. 16 seed to take down a No. 1 seed a year earlier. After the 2019 tournament No. 16 seeds were 1-139 playing against No. 1 seeds.

The eleventh seeds that advanced did have a chance, playing against a sixth seed in the first round. But their chances were taken down several notches by spending two days preparing to play in Dayton; flying there; playing a late-night game; flying to another site; and then playing again a day later. The sixth seed flew to the first-round site two days early, practiced there, and was well rested when the ball went up.

That didn't mean teams coming out of Dayton couldn't win. The very first year of the First Four, eleventh-seeded VCU had won in Dayton, beaten sixth-seeded Georgetown in the first round, and gone all the way to the Final Four. In fact, in nine seasons, at-large teams advancing from Dayton are a more-than-respectable 8-10 in first-round games. In addition to VCU, three others have reached the sweet sixteen. Those numbers prove one of two things: a lot of teams sent to Dayton were underseeded; or playing in Dayton isn't as big a disadvantage as one might think. Both are probably true.

The second night was much like the first. During dinner—fajitas, one of my favorites—I sat with Mike LoPresti, who had been a *USA Today* columnist for years and now worked for NCAA.com. LoPresti, who lives in Indiana, had covered the First Four every year since its inception.

"They serve pasta on Tuesday, Mexican on Wednesday, every year," he said. Then he added: "You know you've covered an event too long when you know what the food's going to be before you arrive."

North Carolina Central hadn't been to Dayton as often as LoPresti, but it had been sent to play in the UD Arena three years in a row. "We know where the locker rooms are," Raasean Davis joked.

North Dakota State hadn't been to Dayton in the past. Like North Carolina Central, it had transitioned from Division 2 to Division 1 recently (NDSU eligible for the NCAAs in 2009; NCCU in 2010) and had almost instantly had success. The Bison had reached the tournament in 2009, the first team since 1972 to do so in their first year of eligibility. They'd gone back in 2014 and pulled a first-round upset, beating Oklahoma.

That upset had led to Coach Saul Phillips getting the job at Ohio University. There's an old saying among coaches: "Don't run away from happiness." Ohio was in a more prestigious conference (MAC vs. Summit), and Phillips was offered a good deal more money. Five years later, even though he'd won twenty-plus games in years two and three, he was fired after back-to-back 14-17 seasons.

David Richman had succeeded Phillips. He had lived in North Dakota his entire life, growing up in Wahpeton, a town of about eight thousand, before matriculating at North Dakota State. He'd graduated in 2002 and been an assistant coach at the school and was the top assistant when Phillips left. He was in his fifth season as coach, and this was his second NCAA Tournament trip.

I spent most of the first half trying to figure out what the green writing on the T-shirt Richman was wearing said. He was wearing a normal coach's blue blazer, but instead of a shirt and tie or some kind of fashionable turtleneck, he was wearing a dark T-shirt with bright green lettering on it.

When in doubt, go talk to the locals. So, at halftime I found members of the North Dakota State media contingent and asked.

I was told the words on the T-shirt were "Landon's Light," and Richman was wearing it to honor an eleven-year-old named Landon Solberg, who had been fighting brain cancer since 2017. Landon's story and the cause taken up by Richman and others to raise money for his medical treatment had become a big deal in North Dakota. Richman had even brought Landon to a postgame press conference the previous season to put his plight in the spotlight.

Of course, almost no one outside the state had any idea about Landon's story or about the efforts Richman and others had made on his behalf. If Richman had been a big-name coach, the national TV announcers would have been drooling about his efforts.

It reminded me of something Jim Valvano had said to me once about Bob Knight. Valvano was—to put it mildly—skeptical when I told him I was going to spend a season with Knight. He didn't like Knight, thought he was a bully and a bad person. I defended Knight—whom I liked—by saying, among other things, that Knight did a lot of work for various charities and had used his platform as Indiana's coach to raise money for Landon Turner when his former player was paralyzed from the waist down in a car accident in the summer of 1981.

Valvano nodded. "A lot of coaches do a lot of good things for charity," he'd said. "They just don't have the national media praising them to the skies for it all the time."

Richman was clearly an example of the kind of coach Valvano had been talking about. Sadly, Solberg died in September, two years after he had been diagnosed.

North Dakota State finished the first half on a 6–0 run to lead 40–34 and extended the margin to 49–36 early in the second. But NCCU was a tough-minded, veteran team that wasn't going to fold in the face of a deficit. It had already proven that in the MEAC championship game. Led by Davis, who would finish his final college game with 20 points and 16 rebounds, and Zacarry Douglas—also a senior, who added 14 and 8—they roared back to take a 66–61 lead.

Tyson Ward, the Bison's leading scorer, tied the game at 70 with two free throws with 2:32 to play. Then came what was, in the minds of Moton and his players, the most important play of the game. Douglas missed a shot inside, got his rebound, and went back up. NDSU's Rocky Kreuser blocked the shot, but it looked like there was a lot of contact.

The officials no-called it.

Ward—who finished with 23 points—was fouled a few seconds later and made 1-of-2 to give NDSU the lead—for good as it turned out. Davis got fouled on the next possession but critically missed the front end of a one-and-one. Ward, taking advantage of what looked like a tiring NCCU team, got to the basket for a layup to make it 73–70 with 1:06 to go. Larry McKnight Jr. missed a jumper. Ward hit a jump shot in the lane and it was 75–70.

That was the game; the final was 78–74.

As usual, in a tight game, there were all sorts of moments to point to as critical, but the no-call on Douglas irked Moton. "See if they get that call on Friday night," he said, referring to the fact that NDSU would be playing Duke next.

Ward had been superb down the stretch, getting inside for layups and short jumpers. Davis's missed one-and-one had hurt. But it might have been an unnoticed part of the stat sheet that provided the answer to how the Bison pulled the game out: depth.

NCCU's five starters played 184 of a possible 200 minutes; scored all 74 of the team's points, and grabbed 35 of 38 rebounds. It wasn't as if NDSU's bench players lit up the world, but they played 53 minutes, had 17 points, and grabbed 7 rebounds. More important perhaps, the minutes they played allowed the starters to be just a little fresher in the closing minutes. In the last 5:11, NDSU outscored NCCU 17–8.

The NCCU locker room was almost dead silent. Three seniors had started, and there were six on the roster. All of them and the juniors had been through this for three straight seasons.

"It hurts, a lot," Moton said as he walked to the locker room. "I really wanted the chance to play Duke. It would have meant a lot to those kids and to our school to have that chance."

Duke and NCCU are five miles apart in Durham, but separated by light-years in the college hoops universe.

"I tell our kids in games like this you have to assume you're going to be ten points down because of the whistle [the referees]. You hope that's not the case, but I tell 'em they have to play through it and not worry about it. But when a couple key calls go against you late, there isn't time to make up for it."

North Dakota State would take the NCAA charter to Columbia, South Carolina, and would lose to Duke on Friday night, 85–62. All Moton could do was sit at home and wish his team had been given the chance to play that night. It probably wouldn't have gotten much help from the whistle, but that would have been better than not getting any calls at all.

The last game of the First Four was between Arizona State and St. John's. The winner, as Danny Hurley had predicted, would take the postmidnight charter to Tulsa to play Buffalo on Friday. The younger Hurley was in the UD Arena with his teenage son sitting behind his brother's bench.

One thing that was impossible to miss covering the First Four was the difference in media guides between the schools from multi-bid conferences and those from one-bid conferences. Nowhere was this more evident than when hefting the St. John's media guide—208 laminated pages with the words "We Are New York's Team" on the back cover and the postseason media guide, which didn't number the pages but was at least as heavy as the regular-season guide. I worried about getting a hernia as I walked them down the ramp.

I have always had a warm spot in my heart for St. John's. The first time I'd seen college basketball games in person had been on the final day of the 1965 NIT. I'd first watched Army that day—with Bob Knight on the bench as an assistant coach—beat NYU in the consolation game and then saw St. John's beat Villanova, 55–51, in the championship game. Ken McIntyre scored 18 points and was the MVP. It was the great Joe Lapchick's final game. I can tell you the score and McIntyre's numbers without looking them up.

Chris Mullin had come back to coach St. John's four years earlier—thirty years after he had led St. John's to the 1985 Final Four—with no coaching experience at all. But he probably ranked only behind Hall of Fame coach Lou Carnesecca as a St. John's legend. Mullin had been the star of that 1985 team that had made the school's first and last appearance in the Final Four. He had played for Knight on the 1984 Olympic team while in college and then on the Dream Team in 1992.

His first three teams had finished with losing records—not easy to do when you're a big-time team that can buy wins with guarantee games during the preconference season. This team, built largely on transfers, had managed to go 20-13 in the regular season. But it had lost four of its last five games, including an embarrassing 86–54 loss to Marquette in Madison Square Garden in the Big East Tournament.

If ever a team was worthy of an NIT bid, it was St. John's. But the basketball committee wanted "New York City's Team," and Mullin in the tournament. So, there they were.

I first covered the NCAA tournament as a college junior in 1976. I've seen a lot of games in person since then. I'm not sure I've ever seen a worse game than St. John's–Arizona State. ASU was merely not good; St. John's was awful. The Sun Devils should have won the game by at least twenty. They went from an early 8–8 tie to a 33–15 lead with 5:57 left in the half. Then they got careless and let the Red Storm cut the margin to 38–25 at the break.

Bobby Hurley was so frustrated with what he was seeing that he got himself teed up in the final minute of the half and walked off the court barking at the officials. He wasn't really that upset with them; he was upset with his team. With good reason.

In the second half, the Sun Devils would build the lead—to sixteen on several occasions—and then let the Red Storm creep back into the game. It never really got close, the lead never went below seven, and the game ended (mercifully) with Arizona State an 84–75 winner.

I was never so happy to see a game end.

The two teams combined to shoot 13-of-43 from three-point range. They committed 40 fouls. One stat stood out: Arizona State turned the ball over 21 times. You can't win a basketball game turning the ball over 21 times. Except it won—easily. Shamorie Ponds, the sometimes spectacular, sometimes hard-to-watch St. John's star, scored 25 points on 8-of-20 shooting. The rest of his teammates combined to shoot 14-of-49.

Ponds had already decided to turn pro with a year of eligibility remaining. He had been told constantly that the NBA was panting for him. He went undrafted.

After the game I couldn't resist telling Hurley that the game reminded me of the classic 1992 Duke-Kentucky NCAA Tournament game he had played in, generally regarded as the best college basketball game ever played.

"What?" he said, looking at me like I was crazy.

"Two baskets, court was ninety-four feet, rims were ten feet high, five players on each side," I said. "After that, not so much."

He laughed—relieved to get out of Dayton with another game to play, less than thrilled at the thought of who he'd be playing next: Buffalo.

"Tough enough to have to play Nate [Oats]," he said. "But that's not the worst part. The worst part is they're a really good team."

Hurley knew from whence he spoke. Buffalo beat his ASU team, 94–71, and it could have been worse. Oats pulled his team back in the game's final minutes.

"I didn't want to embarrass Bobby," Oats said later. "But honestly, there was only so much I could do."

On the night of the national championship game, St. John's announced that Mullin had decided not to return for a fifth season. Maybe, I thought, he just didn't want to watch his team play again. One of the coaches athletic director Mike Cragg contacted about the job was Hurley—which made sense since Cragg, who worked at Duke for thirty years, had known Hurley since his undergraduate days.

Hurley said no thanks. Maybe he didn't want to watch St. John's play either.

March 21, Columbus, Ohio

I was on the road early the next morning for the seventy-two-mile trip from Dayton to Columbus. The NCAA—always looking out for me—had done me a favor by selecting Columbus as one of the eight first–second round sites.

The first round of the tournament would begin Thursday at a little after noon. There would be sixteen games Thursday, sixteen more on Friday. All eight teams assigned to Columbus would practice Thursday. I wanted to be at the practices. I needed a *Washington Post* column, and I wanted a chance to talk to the Colgate players and Coach Matt Langel. The Raiders were a fifteenth-seed and would play second-seeded Tennessee in the second game on Friday afternoon.

Thursday and Friday, are, in my mind, what separate the NCAA Tournament from other sporting events. The chances that one will see Colgate play Tennessee to the final minute in football are pretty close to zero. College basketball is the one big-time sport where David beating Goliath is rarely a surprise.

"This is the kind of game that makes this tournament special," Tennessee coach Rick Barnes said after his team survived, 77–70. "You can't tell those kids in the Colgate locker room they weren't good enough today. They scared the heck out of us."

The bright lights appeared too bright for Colgate when they fell behind 9–0 right away and trailed by sixteen late in the first half. But the Raiders came back to actually lead, 52–50, on a Tucker Richardson three with 11:37 left. The game stayed close until the end: a jumper by Jordan Burns, the kid Langel saw in a Vegas summer league game no other coach bothered to watch, cut the Tennessee margin to 67–64 with 2:02 left.

But with Nationwide Arena about to explode at the notion of a huge upset, Admiral Schofield, who would go on to be the forty-second player taken in the NBA draft, hit back-to-back threes and Tennessee hung on to win.

Later that night, Iona, which—as Steve Masiello had all but predicted in November—had won both the MAAC regular-season and tournament titles, gave top-seeded North Carolina a scare.

The Gaels actually led 38–33 at halftime. I had already written twice for the *Post* that day, writing first on a kid playing for Iowa named Luka Garza, who had scored 20 points in Iowa's upset of Cincinnati. Garza was a DC kid and had played at Maret for Chuck Driesell—son of Lefty.

The Lefthander had pleaded with Duke coach Mike Krzyzewski and Maryland coach Mark Turgeon to recruit him, but both had decided against it. Garza had played AAU ball with Iowa coach Fran McCaffery's son, so McCaffery had seen a good deal of him and offered him a scholarship. The column was a natural for me, since it gave me an excuse to call Lefty.

Seeing my number come up and—as usual—knowing why I was calling, Lefty picked up and said, "I told you he could play, Faahnsteen." Then he—with some help from Chuck—more or less wrote the column for me.

My second column was for Sunday and was on Barnes and his rebirth at Tennessee after being fired at Texas, having only taken the Longhorns to a Final Four and sixteen NCAA berths in seventeen years.

So I was more or less babysitting Iona-Carolina in case a UMBC-Virginia game broke out. It did—for a half. The Tar Heels, after a thorough tongue-lashing at halftime from Roy Williams, came out in the second half and quickly took control, winning 88–73. The writer part of me was relieved not to have to scramble to write again after midnight. The hoops fan part of me was hoping Iona could do the impossible.

Meanwhile, in Columbia, South Carolina, Gardner-Webb was trying to put Tony Bennett and the Cavaliers through déjà vu all over again.

The Runnin' Bulldogs jumped to a fourteen-point first-half lead, and I was getting texts asking for Ryan Odom's cell phone number just in case it happened all over again. My friends in the media weren't the only ones thinking that way.

Two weeks later, at the Final Four, I asked Tony Bennett what he was thinking when the score was 28–14. By then, he could laugh and tell the truth, the whole truth, and nothing but the truth.

"I was thinking, 'We can't go through this again,'" he said. "It was just unthinkable to even have to contemplate going through that all over again. Just impossible."

The lead was down to 36–30 by halftime, but there still had to be some nervous Cavalier stomachs at that juncture. After all, the UMBC game had been 21–21 at the break. This time, though, Virginia came out looking like a No. 1 seed. It began with a 14–2 run to take a 44–38 lead and stretched that to 27–8 and a 57–44 lead a few minutes later. From there, the Cavaliers were able to cruise to a 71–56 victory. But it certainly hadn't been easy. As Barnes had said, teams from one-bid conferences being able to challenge—and occasionally beat—the big-time, big-money teams is what makes the NCAA tournament worth all the commercials and trademarks and screaming about so-called student-athletes.

The No. 1 seeds returned to normalcy, going 4-0. One year after the UMBC first-round stunner and Buffalo's shockingly easy win over Arizona, the first weekend went largely to chalk.

The lowest seed to advance out of the first round was UC Irvine, a No. 13 seed, which shocked fourth-seeded Kansas State in the South Regional. The Wildcats had reached the elite eight a year earlier before losing to Loyola Chicago.

Three No. 12 seeds won: Murray State, clearly underseeded as a No. 12, blasted Marquette, 83–64, and Liberty beat Mississippi State. The third No. 12 seed was hardly an upset to sing about: Power Five school Oregon beating Power Five school Wisconsin.

Buffalo, from a one-bid conference, did crush Arizona State, but the Bulls were a sixth seed, and Wofford—a seventh seed—cruised past Seton Hall. Both those teams were probably underseeded.

"I had honestly hoped with our schedule and winning the MAC regular season and the tournament that we'd get a five, maybe a four," Nate Oats said. "But you know how it goes. Texas Tech wasn't exactly an easy number three to play in the second round."

The Red Raiders easily beat Buffalo and ended up coming within seconds of the national title.

Wofford had to play Kentucky in the second round and stayed in the game all the way, before finally losing 62–56.

There were other close calls: Auburn, which would end up in the Final Four, was the only No. 5 seed to advance, squeaking past New Mexico State—another underseeded team—78–77.

Of the four teams that came out of Dayton, Belmont had the best chance to advance: losing 79–77 to Maryland after leading for much of the afternoon. The difference in rest seemed to make a difference down the stretch. Arizona State, North Dakota State, and Fairleigh Dickinson were all beaten soundly, but the latter two had experienced their moment of glory in Dayton.

By the end of the first weekend, fourteen of the top sixteen seeds had reached the sweet sixteen. The only teams who were top four seeds in a region to lose were fourth-seeded Kansas, which lost in the second round to Auburn in the Midwest Region, and fourth-seeded Kansas State, which had lost in the first round to UC Irvine. Oregon then beat the Anteaters in a rare 12-13 second-round game in the South region to reach the sweet sixteen.

The closest thing to a stunning upset came in the second round when ninth-seeded UCF came within an inch or two of knocking Duke out of the tournament. The Knights were coached by Johnny Dawkins, who had been Mike Krzyzewski's first and, arguably, most important recruit at Duke when he signed to play for Krzyzewski in 1982.

"If Johnny doesn't make that decision, I might have been long gone after another year or two," Krzyzewski had said to me a few years back. "That recruiting class ['82] was the most important in my life because those guys [Dawkins, Mark Alarie, Jay Bilas, David Henderson, Weldon Williams, Bill Jackman] believed in me before there was any reason to believe in me. Johnny was the star of the group."

Dawkins had played ten years in the NBA and been a Krzyzewski assistant before getting the Stanford job and then the UCF job. His son Aubrey had grown up—more or less—at Cameron Indoor Stadium. It was Aubrey who had a tip-in attempt at the buzzer that *just* rolled off the rim, allowing Duke to escape, 77–76.

What was clear after that game was just how beatable Duke was heading into the sweet sixteen.

There were no Cinderellas left. The last two weeks of the tournament would be about big-money TV teams—which, naturally, made the TV people happy.

Me, not so much. Midnight had struck on my joyride down the back roads of college hoops. I'd enjoyed just about every single minute.

EPILOGUE

For me, the last two weeks of the NCAA tournament were a return to the big time, whether I liked it or not.

None of the teams, players, or coaches I had followed throughout the fall and winter were still playing. I missed the intimacy of the gyms I'd been in and the up-close access I'd had to players and coaches.

The Final Four, in Minneapolis, was my fortieth, and although I enjoyed spending time with old friends like Hoops Weiss and his wife Joan and Bob Ryan and his wife Elaine, I couldn't find the old feelings I'd had for the games—even though Virginia's two wins were classics.

I was happy for Tony Bennett because I like and respect him greatly and because he had handled the UMBC upset a year earlier with so much grace. Ryan Odom had sent him a text a few days after the game thanking him for being so gracious about the way his team had played, and Bennett had responded right away with a text again complimenting Odom and his team on what they'd accomplished.

"Couldn't have been kinder about it all," Ryan told me. "Class act."

When the final buzzer sounded in UVA's overtime win over Texas Tech, I noticed Bennett sitting on the little stool the NCAA gives head coaches to sit on during the games so they can be on floor level and not on the bench—which is below the floor in the football stadiums where the Final Four is now contested.

As the confetti flew and his players rushed to celebrate, Bennett sat unmoving for several seconds, eyes closed. I knew he was saying a prayer of thanks and—knowing him—it wasn't for the victory but for the opportunity. That's who he is.

After Bennett finished with his press conference, I took a quick break from writing my column to go and congratulate him.

As we shook hands he said, "It's really an amazing story, isn't it?"

He was talking about the journey from UMBC to having to endure "One Shining Moment" on the awards podium a few minutes earlier.

"Tony," I said, "the way you won those last three games [all last-second escapes] almost makes me believe in God."

He looked at me very seriously and said, "You should believe in God, John."

I smiled and said, "I'm working on it."

If as good a man as Tony Bennett thinks I should believe in God, it's worth considering.

In Division 3, "March Madness" begins in February with conference tournaments, leading to the NCAA Tournament, which starts the first week in March and, in 2019, concluded the day before D-1's Selection Sunday.

Remarkably, Jim Calhoun's University of St. Joseph team almost made it to March.

The Blue Jays had to win their season finale against Regis just to qualify for the Great Northeast Athletic Conference (GNAC) Tournament. Only eight of the eleven teams got to play, and St. Joseph's victory on the last day of the regular season earned it the No. 7 seed.

That had been Calhoun's unspoken goal all season: make the conference tournament in the school's first year playing men's basketball.

Of course, St. Joseph's had to play on the road in the tournament, and it almost stunned the D-3 world by getting to the championship game—and almost winning. It won at second-seeded Suffolk and then at St. Joseph's (Maine), meaning it got to play the championship game at top-seeded Albertus Magnus. The Blue Jays had a real chance to win all afternoon, before finally succumbing, 81–77. As disappointed as Calhoun was with the final outcome, he had to be thrilled with the season: a 16-13 overall record and coming within a few points of making the D-3 tournament.

He enjoyed the experience so much that he decided to come back, at seventy-seven, for a second season.

Coaches—especially great coaches—coach.

Six weeks later, on the night of the national championship game, St. John's athletic director Mike Cragg, who had flown home from Minneapolis that afternoon, got a phone call. It was from Chris Mullin, his basketball coach.

After thinking long and hard about his future, Mullin had decided he didn't want to be a college basketball coach anymore. Four difficult years—climaxed by an embarrassing loss in Dayton—had convinced him this wasn't the life he wanted to lead.

Cragg wasn't shocked. There had been rumors all season that Mullin might step down. Like any smart athletic director, he had a list of potential candidates in his pocket if he needed a new coach.

One of the names on that list was Porter Moser. He certainly fit the profile Cragg was looking for: he wasn't very young, but at fifty he had plenty of good years left in coaching. Just as important, he had a good deal of experience as a coach, having run programs at Central Arkansas, Illinois State, and Loyola. He had also learned from one of basketball's great minds when he'd been at St. Louis working for Rick Majerus.

The Final Four run and Moser's ability to handle all that came with it—both during the run to San Antonio and a year later in the aftermath—were proof that Moser could handle the pressures of the New York media and the Big East. He had the kind of outgoing personality that would aid him greatly in dealing with the inevitable ups and downs of rebuilding in the New York crucible.

The fact that he was a devout Catholic, coaching at a Catholic school, was a bonus—not a necessity by any means, but it wouldn't hurt.

Moser was certainly tempted when Cragg called. If there was one thing about the Loyola job that bothered him, it was coaching in a one-bid conference. He knew that if his team hadn't won the conference tournament in 2018, the basketball committee know-nothings wouldn't have known enough to give his team an at-large bid. A year later, when the Ramblers won the regular-season conference title but not the tournament, they had no shot at an at-large bid.

"The simple fact is the NET [the NCAA's new computerized system for ranking teams] is geared to help the power conference schools," he said. "It's never going to be easy to get an at-large bid for us."

St. John's was at the opposite end of the spectrum—as the just-concluded season had proven. The Red Storm had finished 8-10 in the Big East, been blown out by thirty-two in their conference tournament, and still got an at-large bid. The Big East would always be a multi-bid league.

Plus, Moser would make a lot more money at St. John's than Loyola could possibly pay him.

Moser flew to New York to meet with Cragg and St. John's officials a week after Mullin had resigned. He liked Cragg instantly and was a little blown away by the money on the table: $16 million for eight years—more than double what he was making at Loyola, even after receiving a substantial boost in the wake of the Final Four run. He would be in a multi-bid league, playing a conference tournament in Madison Square Garden. Clearly, the big time in every way.

He told Cragg he would give him an answer by the next afternoon and flew home on Tuesday morning. On the plane, he started writing a farewell letter to "Rambler Nation."

"It's been an amazing eight years," he began. His final words were "It's now time for a new journey."

"When I finished, I felt terrible," he said.

So he drafted a second letter, this one announcing that he was staying at Loyola.

"I felt so much better finishing the second letter, I knew that was the way to go," he said. "It just felt right.

"Look, we have a twenty-million-dollar practice facility that my office is a sky-walk away from. I sit at my desk and look out at Lake Michigan. We've changed the campus at Loyola and the way people feel about Loyola basketball. After we lost in the NIT, I sat on the podium with Clayton [Custer] and Marques [Townes] on my right and Cameron Krutwig on my left. Someone asked Cameron about what it was going to be like going forward without Clayton and Marques. He said, 'We'll miss them a lot. We'll have different guys next year, but we'll have the same expectations.'

"I got chills when he said that because that's exactly how I want our players to feel. No drop in expectations."

—

While Moser was deciding to stay put, Nate Oats knew it was time to move. And yet, he was almost hoping to be talked out of it.

Within forty-eight hours of Buffalo's loss to Texas Tech, Oats's agent had been contacted by two schools: Alabama and UCLA. Once upon a time, a choice like that would have been a no-brainer: UCLA *was* college basketball. Now, though, it was definitely a question mark job, because the expectations were still Wooden-like but the school was a long, long way from being part of the national elite.

So was Alabama. The school has never been to a Final Four, and the number one winter sport there is preparing for football spring practice. But that can be a plus, especially for a new coach trying to build a program. Plus, Alabama would almost certainly pay much better: UCLA is notorious for underpaying coaches because it thinks coaches should consider being offered the job a privilege.

As soon as his plane landed in Buffalo on the day after the Texas Tech game, Oats saw a message from Alabama athletic director Greg Byrne. As he walked to his car, he saw an Alabama bumper sticker on the car next to his.

"A sign," he said, laughing.

Oats knew that Alabama would offer him a lot more money than he was making at Buffalo: about $840,000 a year. That made him the highest-paid coach in the MAC. It would have made him the lowest-paid coach in the SEC. But he still wasn't certain he wanted to leave.

"It had only been six years since I was making eighty-five thousand a year as a high school coach and math teacher," he said. "So what I was making at Buffalo felt like plenty. We had just renovated our house and we were happy where we were.

"I called Brad Stevens and Mark Few to ask them what they thought. I was really kind of hoping they'd talk me out of it."

They didn't. Stevens told him how awkward he'd felt after getting a huge raise at Butler following the two Final Four seasons. He knew he was making far more than anyone else working at the school, and it wasn't a comfortable feeling.

Few's concerns were different. Oats asked if he thought he could build a program at Buffalo comparable to Gonzaga's. Few's honest answer was that it was unlikely.

"He pointed out that Gonzaga had built a new arena within five years of his becoming head coach," Oats said. "He also reminded me that Gonzaga didn't have football, so all the school's resources were pointed first at basketball. Buffalo plays FBS football. I was having trouble just getting a practice facility we didn't have to share with everyone else at the school.

"I realized they were both making sense."

Byrne's offer was for blow-away money: just under $2.5 million a year for five years. In addition, Alabama would pay the $750,000 buyout in Oats's Buffalo contract. It was too good a deal with too much potential to say no.

"Even though I knew I was making a lot more money when I signed the contract, it really didn't hit me until I got my first paycheck," Oats said with a laugh. "We get paid monthly, so the first check I got was for more money—*after* taxes—than I was making in a year when I was still at Romulus."

Oats never made the trip to UCLA. Three days after coaching his last game at Buffalo, he was introduced as the new coach at Alabama.

Two months later, when John Beilein surprised the basketball world by leaving Michigan to coach the Cleveland Cavaliers, I asked Oats if there was any part of him that wished Beilein had left sooner because he almost certainly would have had a shot at the Michigan job.

"Honestly, no," he said. "I think Tuscaloosa is a great place to raise kids, and the weather's a lot warmer than Buffalo or Ann Arbor. I never had a 'dream' job, to be honest. I grew up in Wisconsin and was a Badger fan, but they never played a style I'd be comfortable coaching. Michigan's a great job, no doubt, but it was never my goal to coach there. I'm very happy right now being exactly where I am."

Ryan Odom could have changed jobs too but opted to stay for a fourth season at UMBC. Odom's name had been tossed around for the Wake Forest job—but Danny Manning survived to coach another year. His name was also in the mix at Virginia Tech when it became apparent that Buzz Williams was going to leave to go home to Texas and coach at Texas A&M. In fact, several hours before the national semifinals began, a rumor spread on Twitter that Tech had hired Odom.

At the behest of my *Washington Post* colleague Gene Wang—who said he'd been told it was true by two sources he trusted—I called Odom. "They've never even contacted me," he said, laughing. "I'll bet this is some Virginia Tech person trying to somehow take attention away from Virginia playing in the Final Four."

As it turned out, Odom's guess was correct.

He probably could have had the George Washington job, but on the day before he was supposed to drive to downtown DC to interview, he was sent a memorandum of understanding (MOI) by the headhunting firm GW had hired. That was strange—sending out an MOI before a job interview—and when Odom read it, he knew the job wasn't right for him.

The money he was being offered was almost the same as what he was making at UMBC and—more important—the basketball budget was also about the same. In short, he was being asked to compete in the Atlantic 10 on an America East budget. That wasn't going to work. He called GW athletic director Tanya Vogel, thanked her for her interest, and told her he didn't think this would work out.

Within days, GW hired Jamion Christian, who'd had success at Mount St. Mary's and had spent one year at Siena. Christian is all enthusiasm and up-tempo play and should be a good hire for the school. Maurice Joseph landed on his feet—getting hired by Greg Herenda at Fairleigh Dickinson. Prediction: Joseph will be a head coach again in the not-too-distant future and, given a level playing field, will do very well.

Kevin Nickelberry was fired at Howard soon after the Bison lost in the CBI to Coastal Carolina to finish the season at 17-17. He wasn't close to shocked. A month later, Will Wade hired him as an assistant coach at LSU. Once, when Nickelberry was an assistant at Clemson and Wade was a grad assistant, Wade had answered to Nickelberry. Now it would be the other way around—and Nickelberry was more than happy to be in that position.

If any coach walked away from his season with high hopes for next year, it was Tommy Amaker. After Harvard stunned Georgetown in the first round of the NIT, it traveled to North Carolina State and lost, 78–77. A win over a Big East school and a last-second loss to an ACC school that had been in the hunt until Selection Sunday for an NCAA bid had to be encouraging.

Beyond that, every key player would be returning, and Amaker expected Seth Towns to be back and healthy for his senior year. "If we stay healthy and all goes well, we should have a chance to do something special," Amaker said.

There was one more bonus: the Ivy League Tournament would be played in Lavietes Pavilion in 2020. If the Crimson could get to a third straight championship game, they wouldn't be playing on the road.

Justin Wright-Foreman's dream of playing in the NCAA Tournament before he graduated died in Charleston on the final night of the CAA Tournament. It wasn't for lack of effort on Wright-Foreman's part. In the semifinals, he had single-handedly saved the Pride from defeat, scoring 42 points in an 82–74 overtime win over Delaware. The next night, even though he had played forty-four minutes against Delaware, Wright-Foreman played all forty minutes and scored 29 points.

Unfortunately for the Pride, the game I had seen in Boston proved to be a harbinger. Hofstra was a tired team; Northeastern was better rested and playing better basketball. The Huskies led 42–26 at halftime. The Pride didn't quit, fighting back to tie the game at 54 with 9:13 left. But redshirt senior Vasa Pusica, who would be voted MVP of the tournament, made arguably the biggest basket of his career when he hit a three on Northeastern's next possession to give the Huskies the lead back at 57–54.

No doubt drained by the energy it took to come back and tie, the Pride had nothing left. Pusica's basket started a 17–6 run, and that was the game. It was Bill Coen's second NCAA trip as Northeastern's coach. Four years earlier, his team had the last shot with a chance to win the game against Notre Dame.

That game was in Pittsburgh, and afterward I asked Notre Dame coach Mike Brey what he was thinking watching helplessly during those final seconds, hoping his players could get a stop.

He smiled. "I thought, 'Rehobeth's nice this time of year.'" Brey has a house there. The Irish ended up falling just short of the Final Four. Brey didn't get to Rehobeth until April.

This time, Northeastern got a thirteenth seed, but the committee did the Huskies no favors, sending them to Salt Lake City to play Kansas. Northeastern was overmatched, losing 87–53.

No one did Hofstra any favors either. Even though the Pride had finished 27-7, it was sent on the road for a first-round NIT game against NC State. This time, Wright-Foreman played thirty-nine minutes and scored 29 points. In his last three college games he played 123 of a possible 125 minutes. He scored exactly 100 points in those three games. Hofstra stayed with the Wolfpack to the finish before losing, 84–78.

It was a disappointing ending to what had been a great season. But Joe Mihalich's belief that another year in college would benefit Wright-Foreman turned out to be correct. On the night of the NBA draft, the Utah Jazz took him with the fifty-third pick. He had come a long way from being overlooked by most of D-1 while at Construction High School.

Old Dominion's season had a better ending than Hofstra's, if only because it came in the NCAAs. The Monarchs finally got through the Conference USA tournament, but it wasn't easy. They escaped Louisiana Tech 57–56 in the first round and UAB 61–59 in the semis. Then, facing Western Kentucky, the team that had been their nemesis in the past, ODU came up with one of its best performances of the season and won, 62–56.

Jones's "coughing-towel" came in handy in the final seconds as he buried his head in it to try to hide tears. It was the first time ODU had reached the tournament since 2011 and Jones's first trip since he'd taken American to back-to-back bids in 2008 and 2009.

"We won a lot of really tough games," Jones said later. "I think that's what I was most proud of with this group. They never blinked all season."

The word on Jones's cancer was good. His doctors decided to skip his March chemo shot in order to give him a break from the side effects and to see if the cancer would stay in remission. As of the summer, it remained, as Jones put it, "under control."

Old Dominion was a fourteenth seed (low for a team with its résumé) and drew Purdue in the first round, a Purdue team that would come within one second of beating Virginia in the elite eight. Predictably, the final score was 61–48. Against a team with Purdue's size and experience, the Monarchs' inability to score consistently proved fatal.

Even so, ODU finished 26-9 and would have an NCAA banner to hang in the Ted come November. Jones's tears—after all he'd been through on and off the court—made absolute sense.

—

One coach I was hoping to see at the Final Four didn't make the trip: Mark Few.

"I'm still sulking," Few said to me when I talked to him on the phone that week. "I haven't missed a Final Four in almost thirty years, but I can't face it right now. I feel like we should be playing."

Gonzaga had come achingly close to playing—losing a down-to-the-wire West Regional final to Texas Tech. Few was unhappy with some of the officiating, which made the loss tougher to take.

"Part of the game, I get that," he said with a sigh. "I honestly thought this group was good enough to take that last step."

It was worth remembering that it was Gonzaga who brought Duke down from its supposedly unbeatable pedestal on Maui in November. The 'Zags lost three games in the regular season: to Tennessee on a neutral court, at North Carolina, and to St. Mary's in a stunning upset in the WCC championship game. They took a 30-3 record into the NCAAs and were the No. 1 seed in the west.

They breezed to the regional final—easily beating Fairleigh Dickinson and then beating Baylor and Florida State by double-digit margins. But Texas Tech might have been the best defensive team in the country at that point in the season. The Raiders held the 'Zags, averaging 87.4 points per game, to 69. In the end, that was the difference.

"Coming up just short of the Final Four reminded me how hard it is to get there," Few said. "I'm really happy that the year we made it [2017] we did the week right. We brought back all of our former players to make them feel part of it. We enjoyed what we had accomplished and we went out and played really well—even coming up just short against [North] Carolina.

"All we can do is keep knocking on the door as often as possible. We've built a program I know people respect. About the only time I get upset is when someone calls us a mid-major. We're way beyond that."

Gonzaga's not a mid-major anymore. It's a power school that plays in a conference that is solid, but not a power conference. It is the envy of most who play college basketball. That's why, when Nate Oats and Porter Moser were making decisions last spring about whether to leave hugely successful mid-majors, one of the questions they asked was: "Can we become the next Gonzaga?"

The answer's probably no. There's only one Gonzaga.

—

And so, my joyride through a college hoops season following players, coaches, and teams that only rarely show up in the national spotlight ended in Minneapolis, at a Final Four involving three schools that had never won a national championship: Virginia, Auburn, and Texas Tech.

The outlier was Michigan State, which won the title in 1979 when Jud Heathcote was the coach and Magic Johnson was the star, and again in 2000 when Tom Izzo was the coach. The trip to Minneapolis was Izzo's eighth appearance in a Final Four.

It was the Spartans who knocked off Duke, beating the Blue Devils 68–67 in the East Regional final. Later, after Michigan State had lost to Texas Tech in the national semifinals, Izzo would say to me: "We were tougher than Duke. Texas Tech was tougher than we were."

Duke, with all its one-and-done talent, wasn't tough enough when it had to be. The Blue Devils had been lucky to survive against UCF and then in the sweet sixteen against Virginia Tech. Apparently, their players thought they were destined to win as long as they showed up in time for tipoff.

Mike Krzyzewski knew better. He is an ardent believer in the basketball gods, and deep down he knew his team didn't have the toughness it needed to win the national title. Talent? Absolutely. But toughness, the ability to get a stop on defense when it absolutely had to have one? Not so much.

I watched the Duke kids—and they *were* kids—heads down, tears of shock in their eyes, after the final buzzer on the last day of March and felt badly for them. But, being honest, not *that* badly. Three freshmen—Zion Williamson, R. J. Barrett, and Cam Reddish—would be declaring for the draft in about fifteen minutes. They were at Duke because the rules required them to go to college somewhere. They should have been allowed to turn pro coming out of high school. It would be better for them and better for basketball.

After winning the championship, four of Virginia's players would also turn pro with eligibility left. That's the way of the big-time college basketball world nowadays: when the chance comes to turn pro and make big money, you take it. I don't blame any of them. They're training to play basketball. When the time comes that they can get paid (over the table) to play, why should they hang around in college? To go to another fraternity mixer? Or to listen to some overpaid administrator call them "student-athletes"?

I didn't get to go everywhere I wanted to go during the 2018–19 season. I didn't get to pursue every good story, but I went to a lot of places I'd never been, met a lot of people, reacquainted myself with many others, and enjoyed it all. There's no doubt in my mind I could do another book on another season with an entirely different cast of characters and find just as many compelling stories.

When I think back to my season on the back roads of college basketball, warm memories flood back: the ovation for Fran Dunphy that wouldn't stop; Martin Luther King Day in Burr Gym; Hartford's miraculous near comeback at UMBC; time spent with old friends Jim Phelan and Lefty Driesell; the mettle of a bunch of future Army officers going nose to nose with a bunch of future NBA players in Cameron; the toughness and smarts of a Camel named Chris Clemons.

There's more—lots more, as I hope this book makes clear. In the end, though, I always seem to come back to the sign in the Palestra. "To win the game is great . . . to play the game is greater . . . but to love the game is the greatest of all."

I never played the game very well, so I didn't win anything above the junior high school level or three-on-three games in Riverside Park. But I have loved the game for almost as long as I can remember.

This book—this journey—was my chance to revisit the love I felt for basketball as a kid listening to games on college radio stations; sneaking into seats near the court at Madison Square Garden; riding the subway to Columbia to watch the Jim McMillian–Heyward Dotson teams play.

I can honestly say it was a season of pure joy for me. And yes, Christine, there is a Farmville, Virginia.

ACKNOWLEDGMENTS

The Back Roads to March is my forty-second book—twenty-nine of them nonfiction. If I have been consistent in one area throughout the thirty-three years that I've been writing books, it is the extreme length of my acknowledgments.

And yet, I always manage to leave someone out.

This book's no different because there are so many people to thank. I just hope I remember everyone this time.

I start, as usual, with the people who made it possible for me to write the book. They are, in no particular order: Tommy Amaker; Jim Calhoun; Fran Dunphy; Ashley Howard; Phil Martelli; Jay Wright; Zach Spiker; John Giannini; Steve Donahue; Jeff Jones; Tony Shaver; Ryan Odom; John Gallagher; Jimmy Allen; Nate Oats; Fran O'Hanlon; Mike Brennan; Nathan Davis; Tubby Smith; Griff Aldrich; Lefty and Joyce Driesell; Bill Herrion; Jim and Dottie Phelan; Porter Moser; Kevin Nickelberry; Maurice Joseph; Greg Paulus; Matt McCall; Chris Mooney; Mike Rhoades; Dave Paulsen; Ed DeChellis; Tommy Dempsey; Pat Kelsey; Richard Barron; Will Brown; Joe Mihalich; Bill Coen; Tim Cluess; Tony Bennett; Tom Izzo; Mark Few; Mike Krzyzewski; Pat Skerry; Mike Brey; Martin Ingelsby; Jeff Neubauer; Dustin Kerns; Glenn Braica; Ron Ganulin; the inimitable Nate Dixon—and Matt Henry, who rescued me when I showed up for a TV game without a tie. Also: Seth Towns; Tommy Funk and Jordan Fox; Justin Wright-Foreman; Joe Sherburne and Arkel Lamar; Clayton

Custer; Chris Clemons; Bjorn Broman; and college basketball's only second-year law student, Paul Rowley.

As you can imagine, given how much travel I did and how many games I went to, I was aided immeasurably by countless sports information directors. They include Drew Dickerson at the Atlantic 10; Steve Levy at UMBC; Chris Kowalcyk at VCU; Larry Dougherty and Karen Angell at Temple; Dan Lobacz at La Salle; Jason Vida at Richmond; Matt Tedino at Army; Nick Guerrero at American; Derek Bryant at Howard; Brian Sereno and Justin Moore at George Washington; Kris Sears at William and Mary; Rob Knox at Towson; Mike Sheridan at Villanova; the great Marie Wozniak at St. Joseph's; Rob DeVita at St. Francis (Brooklyn); Grant Gardner at Old Dominion; Betsy Devine at Northeastern; Mike Mahoney at Penn; Justin Kischefsky at Navy; John Sinnett at Massachusetts; Ryan Eigenbrode at Loyola (Baltimore); Bill Behrns at Loyola (Chicago); Chris Cook at Longwood; Scott Morse; Phil LaBella and Brian Ludrof at Lafayette; Steven Gorchov at Hofstra; Brian Dennison at Akron; Brian Wolff at Buffalo; Mark LaFrance and Zach Bolno at George Mason; Roy Allen at FGCU; Doug Hauschild at Dayton (who should be in all caps for the help he gave me during the "First Four"); Stan Cole at Campbell—who should also be in caps for making the Big South Tournament such a pleasure for me; Jon Terry at Bucknell; Mex Carey at Michigan State and his boss, Matt Larson, or as Izzo always calls him, "your fellow Duke guy." I don't think he means it as a compliment.

I realize many of these people no longer carry SID titles, but to me they will always be SIDs—which I think of as a compliment. Special thanks to Boo Corrigan for allowing me to be a regular part of Army football and basketball.

There are lots of other basketball folks who may not have played a major role in this book but whom I always look to for advice and guidance. Among them: Jay Bilas, Bobby and Danny Hurley, Bobby Dwyer, Tom Konchalski (still the only honest man in the gym), Gerry Brown, Mike Cragg, Gary Williams, Terry Holland, Jim Boeheim, Mike Brey, Fran McCaffery, and Roy Williams.

My friends list is always long, which is proof of how lucky I am: Keith and Barbie Drum; Jackson Diehl and Jean Halperin; Lexie Verdon and Steve Barr; David and Linda Maraniss; Bob Woodward and his wife, Elsa Walsh; Sally Jenkins; Marty Weil; Mark Maske;

Kathy Orton; and my editors at the *Post:* Matt Vita, Matt Rennie, and David Larimer.

More friends: Doug and Beth Doughty, Terry and Patti Hanson, Bob DeStefano, Wes Seeley, Andy Dolich, David Teel, Gary Cohen, Beth Shumway-Brown, Beth Sherry-Downes, Pete Van Poppel, Omar Nelson, Chet Gladchuk, Mike Werteen, Phil Hoffmann, Joe Speed, Andrew Thompson, Gordon Austin, Eddie Tapscott, Chris Knoche, Tim Kelly, Dick Hall, Anthony and Kristen Noto, Jim Cantelupe, Bob Sutton, Rich DeMarco, Joe Beckerle, Dean Darling, Bob Zurfluh, Vivian Thompson-Goldstein, Mike and David Sanders, Tony and Karril Kornheiser, Mike Wilbon, Tim Maloney, General Steve Sachs, Pete (GB) Alfano, Nancy Denlinger, Holland and Jill Mickle, Tom Stathakes, Joe Riley, Mike Purkey, Bob Edwards, Tom and Jane Goldman, Mike Gastineau, Joanie Weiss, Bob and Elaine Ryan, Jerry Tarde, Mike O'Malley, Sam Weinman, Ryan Herrington, Larry Dorman, Marsha Edwards, Jay Edwards, Chris Edwards and John Cutcher, Len and Gwyn Edwards-Dieterle, Bill Leahey, Neil Oxman, Paul Goydos, Steve Flesch, Billy Andrade, Erik Compton, Gary Crandall, Drew Miceli, Brian Henninger, and Tom Watson. It is impossible to put into words how much his wife, Hilary, will be missed.

In some cases, it has been years since I've had any regular contact with these people, but they remain very much in my mind and my heart. Governor Harry Hughes passed away early in 2019. Knowing him, as I did for thirty-seven years, was an honor.

I miss seeing a number of my former colleagues at Golf Channel on a regular basis but am happy they have remained friends: Todd Lewis, Frank Nobilo, Brandel Chamblee, David Duval, Rich Lerner, Kristi Setaro, Andrew Bradley, Mark Rolfing, John Feyko, Notah Begay, Gary Williams, Jay Coffin, and the MVP, Courtney Holt.

Others: David Fay, Mike Davis, Mike Butz, Frank and Jayme Bussey. Marty Caffey, Henry Hughes and Sid Wilson, Doug Milne, Colin Murray, John Bush, James Cramer, Dave Lancer, and Guy Scheipers. Denise Taylor—now and always. Joe Steranka, Julius Mason, and Pete Bevacqua. Also: Mark Russell, Laura Russell, and future Democrat Alex Russell. Steve Rintoul, Slugger White, Jon Brendle, Stephen Cox, Robbie Ware, Dillard Pruitt, and John Paramour.

I've enjoyed most of the people I have worked with in one form or another for the past seven years at CBS Sports Radio: they include my old team of Andrew Bogusch, Max Herman, and Peter Bellotti. Anthony Pierno and Billy Giacalone still put up with me on a regular basis, and I'm grateful for bosses like Mark Chernoff and David Mayurnik.

I would be remiss if I didn't include David Stern, who was largely responsible for Lefty Driesell *finally* getting into the Hall of Fame. Also: Tim Frank, Brian McIntyre, Seth and Brad Greenberg, Brad Stevens, Dave and Lynne Odom, Larry Shyatt, Tom Brennan, Jim and Liz Larrañaga, Mack McCarthy, Pat Flannery, Ralph Willard, Emmett Davis, Billy Lange, and Bob Huggins.

Doctors—the list is much too long: Eddie McDevitt, Dean and Ann Taylor, Bob Arciero, Gus Mazzocca, Murray Lieberman, Steve Boyce (who, thankfully, I haven't seen since he cut my chest open ten years ago), and Joe Vassallo. The more I see of them as friends, the less I see of them as docs, the better.

The swimming knuckleheads, who will stage a major reunion later this year: Jason Crist, Jeff Roddin, Clay F. Britt, Wally Dicks, Mike Fell, Mark Pugliese, Paul Doremus, Danny Pick, Erik (Dr. Post) Osbourne, John Craig, Doug Chestnut, Mary Dowling, Tom Denes, A. J. Block, and Peter Lawler.

None of us have recovered yet from Margot Pettijohn's death. She held more world records in Masters swimming than the rest of us combined and was *always* the first one there after a race to say something encouraging—even when you swam badly. She is very much missed by us all.

The China Doll/Shanghai Village/City Lights gang: Aubre Jones, Murray Lieberman, Jack Kvancz, Stanley Copeland, Harry Huang, Geoff Kaplan, Jeff Gemunder, Lou Flashenberg, Mark Hughes. In absentia but always welcome: Pete Dowling, Bob Campbell, Joe McKeown, Morgan Wootten—who is coming any day now—and Ric McPherson. It will always be Red and Zang's table no matter where it may be located.

The Rio Gang: Tate Armstrong, Terry Chili, Mark Alarie, and Clay Buckley. Terry's politics are completely hopeless, but I love him anyway.

The Feinstein Advisory Board: Dave Kindred, Keith Drum, and Frank Mastrandrea. I miss Bill Brill terribly, but doubt I could have lived with him after the 2016 election. Special mention here to Frank and Susan Sullivan—great friends. Frank was a wonderful basketball coach; he is a much better person. I am so thankful he's a friend of mine.

Esther Newberg has been my agent for thirty-four years and forty-one books, which proves—contrary to popular belief—that she is one of the world's more patient humans. John Delaney has been her legal eyes and ears for much of that time, and Alex Heimann and Estie Bukowitz are more proof that Esther's absolutely brilliant when it comes to hiring assistants. I should know—I married one of them.

And, again, thanks to all the folks I work with at Doubleday: Jason Kaufman, Bill Thomas, Carolyn Williams, Nora Reichard, John Pitts, and Michael Goldsmith.

My family: sister Margaret and her boys, Ethan and Ben. Brother Bobby and his wife Jennifer and their boys, Matthew and Brian.

And last but never least: Christine, Danny, Brigid, and Jane. They are my rocks, and God knows I need them every single day.

INDEX

QUARTERBACK
Inside the Most Important Position in Professional Sports

Quarterback dives deep into the most coveted and hallowed position in the National Football League. John Feinstein builds his profile around Alex Smith, Andrew Luck, Joe Flacco, Ryan Fitzpatrick, and Doug Williams. With incredible inside access, we get the full quarterback experience: being drafted number one overall, pushing through grueling injuries, winning Super Bowls, being named a starter on multiple teams, being the first African American QB to lead a franchise to a title. Feinstein explores the controversies of a league embroiled in questions of substance abuse and racism, TV revenue, corporate greed, and the value placed on player health. This is Feinstein's most fascinating behind-the-scenes book.

Sports

THE FIRST MAJOR
The Inside Story of the 2016 Ryder Cup

The rivalry between the U.S. and European teams was at an all-time high even before the 2016 Ryder Cup. The Americans had lost an astounding six out of the last seven matches. With the U.S. team out for revenge and the Europeans determined to keep the Cup out of American hands, the showdown took place in Hazeltine, Minnesota, and became one of the most raucous and heated face-offs in the Cup's history. John Feinstein provides an inside view of the dramatic stories as they unfolded, including the assembly of veteran Phil Mickelson's superb team, the intense match between European superstar Rory McIlroy and American Patrick Reed that almost came to blows, and the return of Tiger Woods.

Sports

THE LEGENDS CLUB
Dean Smith, Mike Krzyzewski, Jim Valvano, and an Epic College Basketball Rivalry

On March 18, 1980, the Duke basketball program announced the hiring of Mike Krzyzewski, the man who would restore glory to the team. Nine days later, Jim Valvano was hired by North Carolina State to be their new head coach. The two new coaches had a similar goal: to unseat North Carolina's Dean Smith as the king of college basketball. And just like that, the most sensational competitive decade in history was about to unfold. *The Legends Club* captures an era in American sport, documenting a decade of absolutely incredible matchups. Feinstein pulls back the curtain on the recruiting wars, the intensely personal competition that wasn't always friendly, the enormous pressure and national stakes, and the battle for the very soul of college basketball.

Sports

WHERE NOBODY KNOWS YOUR NAME
Life in the Minor Leagues of Baseball

Minor league baseball is quintessentially American, but looming above it all is always the real deal: Major League Baseball. *Where Nobody Knows Your Name* explores the trials and travails of the inhabitants of Triple-A, focusing on nine men—including players, managers, and umpires—living on the cusp of the dream. The book tells the stories of former World Series hero Scott Podsednik, giving it one more shot; Durham Bulls manager Charlie Montoyo, shepherding generations across the line; and designated hitter Jon Lindsey, a lifelong minor leaguer waiting for his day to come.

Sports

ANCHOR BOOKS
Available wherever books are sold.
www.anchorbooks.com

Finished 3-23